IN
PURSUIT
OF
GIANTS

IN
PURSUIT
OF
GIANTS

*One Man's Global Search
for the Last of the
Great Fish*

Matt Rigney

VIKING

VIKING
Published by the Penguin Group
Penguin Group (USA) Inc., 375 Hudson Street,
New York, New York 10014, U.S.A.
Penguin Group (Canada), 90 Eglinton Avenue East,
Suite 700, Toronto, Ontario, Canada M4P 2Y3
(a division of Pearson Penguin Canada Inc.)
Penguin Books Ltd, 80 Strand, London WC2R 0RL, England
Penguin Ireland, 25 St. Stephen's Green, Dublin 2, Ireland
(a division of Penguin Books Ltd)
Penguin Books Australia Ltd, 250 Camberwell Road, Camberwell,
Victoria 3124, Australia (a division of Pearson Australia Group Pty Ltd)
Penguin Books India Pvt Ltd, 11 Community Centre,
Panchsheel Park, New Delhi–110 017, India
Penguin Group (NZ), 67 Apollo Drive, Rosedale, Auckland 0632,
New Zealand (a division of Pearson New Zealand Ltd)
Penguin Books (South Africa) (Pty) Ltd, 24 Sturdee Avenue,
Rosebank, Johannesburg 2196, South Africa

Penguin Books Ltd, Registered Offices: 80 Strand, London WC2R 0RL, England

First published in 2012 by Viking Penguin, a member of Penguin Group (USA) Inc.

1 3 5 7 9 10 8 6 4 2

Page 337 constitutes a continuation of this copyright page.

LIBRARY OF CONGRESS CATALOGING-IN-PUBLICATION DATA
Rigney, Matt.
In pursuit of giants : one man's global search for the last of the great fish / Matt Rigney.
p. cm.
Includes bibliographical references and index.
ISBN 978-0-670-02335-6
1. Marine fishes—Conservation. 2. Marine fishes—Ecology. 3. Rare fishes—Conservation.
4. Fish populations—Research. 5. Endangered species—Research. 6. Wildlife
conservation. 7. Fishing—History. 8. Fisheries—History. I. Title.
QL620.R54 2012
597'.48—dc23
2012003442

Printed in the United States of America
Set in Adobe Garamond Pro

~For my DAUGHTER first~

and for her generation, who will inherit this world,

&

FOR THE FISH

without which I never would have

DREAMT OF THE SEA

Yours was I born, and ye,
The sea-wind and the sea,
Made all my soul in me
A song for ever . . .

—Algernon Charles Swinburne,
"Ex-Voto"

CONTENTS

IN
PURSUIT
OF
GIANTS

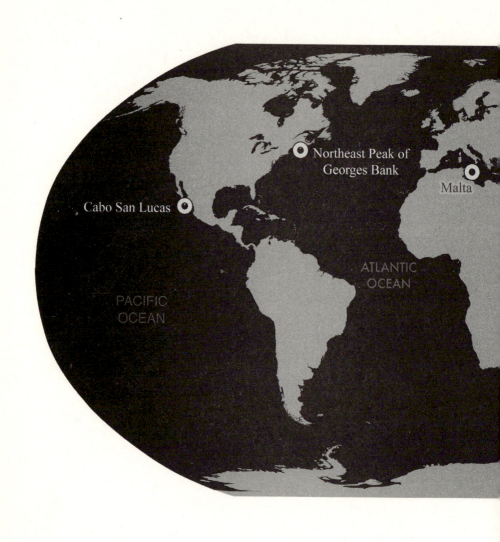

Cabo San Lucas

Northeast Peak of
Georges Bank

Malta

PACIFIC
OCEAN

ATLANTIC
OCEAN

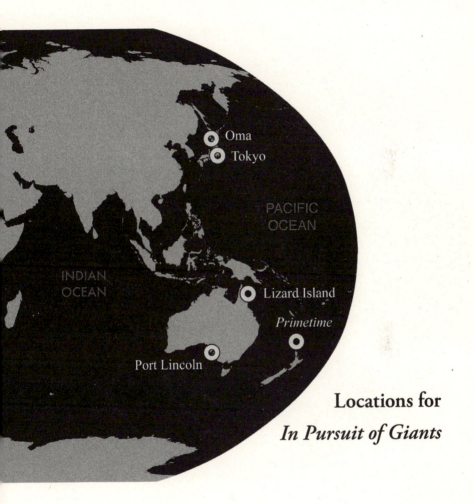

Oma

Tokyo

PACIFIC
OCEAN

INDIAN
OCEAN

Lizard Island

Primetime

Port Lincoln

Locations for

In Pursuit of Giants

Prologue

A book must be the ax for the frozen sea within us.

—Franz Kafka, letter to Oskar Pollak

The largest, fastest fish ever to have roamed the oceans during the time we have walked on land is remembered only by the force that made it. That fish's life, its battles, its procreation, its fantastic speed, and its vaulting jumps clear of the medium that sustained it were observed, as all of creation is observed, by God's vigil over Nature, a Nature that includes us. But we are not the only creatures of consequence within the scope of heaven's view. God rejoiced in the vitality of that animal as God rejoices in our own laughter, in the blinking code of fireflies across summer fields, in the silent nocturnal migrations of Leviathan in the deep.

What fish was it—a black marlin? A giant bluefin tuna? And how beautiful did it look as it broke the surface, its colors—iridescent blue and yellow, glinting silver and shimmering black—alive and vibrant in the diamond light a thousand miles from shore? Did it live before humans built the first boat? Was it before the time of villages? How much did it weigh, how long was it, and how fast?

Great fish—that group possessed of great strength and speed, and excluding sharks and rays—remain, for the majority of us, both beyond our experience and beyond our comprehension. They fall into a few select families: the billfish, composed of blue and black marlin, sailfish, and striped marlin; the tunas, including yellowfin, bigeye, and the giant bluefin; and the broadbill swordfish, the sole member of the family Xiphiidae. Each of these animals is an offshore apex predator, will attain speeds through the water in excess of forty-five miles per hour (with some reaching as high as seventy miles per hour), and will naturally attain weights in excess of three hundred pounds. The largest of these great fish can exceed fifteen feet in length and tip the scales at more than two thousand pounds, and although fish of this size and larger have been caught on commercial gear, none this big has ever been landed with rod and reel according to the stringent standards of the International Game Fish Association (IGFA), the rule-making body of international sportfishing. There have been rumors of marlin approaching three thousand pounds and lengths of twenty-five feet, but no fish of this size has ever been caught or otherwise verified.

Our collective knowledge of the few species of great fish has grown in the past fifty years, but there remains much we do not know. We are uncertain about their migrations and where and when they spawn, and in most cases we can only estimate the full potential of their growth, longevity, and power. We have only recently come to understand how seriously their numbers have been depleted and the risk that some of them face of becoming effectively extinct—not merely within the span of a human life but within the next few decades.

But they remain, in large part, as they have always been. They look the same now as they did a hundred thousand years ago—the same span of time in which our species has gone from not existing to an estimated three hundred million of us at the time of Christ, to 1.6 billion in 1900, to four times that number as of the year 2000, and most recently having crossed, in 2011, the threshold of seven billion human beings spread across the globe. Much of that explosive growth has occurred within the past one hundred years, and today we are adding a billion people every thirteen years. Also in that brief hundred years of the twentieth century, we went from wooden-wheeled horse-drawn carts to the internal combustion engine, jet-powered flight, splitting the atom, kicking moondust, and tinkering with the very building blocks of life.

Is it not also within our power to exterminate the great fish and other forms of oceanic life, to irreparably harm and change the oceans? A single modern purse-seine fishing vessel can capture three thousand adult bluefin tuna in one encirclement of its net. If their average weight were four hundred pounds, that catch would weigh in excess of six hundred tons (1.2 million pounds). The largest of these nets can haul in more than three thousand tons (six million pounds). If a fish aggregation device (FAD)* is used, the nets catch all age ranges and varieties of fish as well as many unintended victims (called bycatch). These include turtles, seabirds, whales, sharks, rays, and dolphins.† There are thousands of purse seiners working the oceans of the world and thousands of longliners, which lay up to seventy-five miles of line with hooks set mere yards apart. Longliners lay enough line every year to circle the globe 550 times, and all varieties of industrial gear kill a total of sixteen *billion* pounds of wasted sea life annually. Bottom trawling is no better. Boats towing huge nets and dredges over the bottom to harvest species like cod, scallops, flounder, and haddock destroy bottom habitat over an area the equivalent of *twice* the United States—six million square miles—every year on the coastal shelves of the world's oceans. In 2011, the world's fishing fleets baited more than 1.5 billion hooks. How many fish will each hook catch? How many *are* there to catch?

During the short period of time it has taken our species and its technology to explode across the face of the Earth, the great fish—like all fish—have remained virtually unchanged. Read the historical texts, look at images from a hundred or a thousand years ago: Our dress is different, our societies, our technology, our understanding of the world and our place in it—all are different. But the fish are the same. From the time we roamed the edges of the ice sheets of prehistory until today, the great fish have been with us, but always living apart in a world defined by a single dividing line: the surface of the water. We share the world with the creatures of the land and sky, but we have not lived in the oceans for millions of years, and we are as separate from their inhabitants today as whales are from the land-walking creatures they once were.

Our lack of understanding of that world has already affected the oceans, which scientists in the 1960s predicted could produce 500 million metric tons of food per year without depletion. The fact that they were

---

*A floating object intentionally set to attract fish.

†Videos of bycatch from longlines and other devices are readily available on YouTube. For video of bycatch in FADs, see "Helicoper Pilot Blows Whistle on Tuna Industry," http://www.youtube.com/watch?v=6JlKwoUtMk4&feature=player_embedded.

wrong—the fact that the fishing industry overbuilt and fishermen over-fished and governments responsible for "managing the resource" did nothing but manage its destruction based on that optimistic prediction—cost us the oceans we could have had in the latter half of the twentieth century. Instead we were faced with diminishing and exhausted seas, and except for those of us who lived near the water or worked on it every day, few were likely to notice that diminishment. We looked out over the water and reasoned that because most of the life there exists below the surface, out of sight, the ocean remained at the same mythical levels of abundance. But those of us who searched our memories could look back and realize that baitfish had disappeared from the estuaries in early summer; that the schools of bluefish were smaller; that cod and pollock and mackerel were harder and harder to find. Only when we began to put these facts together did we suspect what had been lost.

But what were we to do about it? What is any one of us to do in the face of changes of this magnitude—changes taking place not in a single region or among a small population but moving like tidal waves across nations and continents, through oceans?

The one thing we cannot do is sit and simply watch these changes happen.

The complex causes for why there are fewer fish in the sea may seem beyond our understanding, if we are not marine scientists—or we may tell ourselves they are ultimately the purview of government, of fishermen, or of industry. But this assertion is no longer an acceptable position for anyone who cares about the sea. We are where we find ourselves today because human beings have always believed that the oceans are inexhaustible, that we can continue to harvest life from them without any real impact. While this may have been true for most of human history, we have grown too numerous and our technologies have become far too powerful to sustain such beliefs. Most important, we have not developed the social will, the economic and ethical principles, and the necessary international cooperation to commit ourselves to confronting the true gravity of the situation facing the world's oceans.

For centuries—with the greatest negative effect being felt within the past fifty years—the priority of governments, not just in the United States but across the globe, has been to maximize the yield of fisheries. The priorities of fishermen have been to provide for their families, stay employed in an environment of increasingly intense competition, and, if the opportunity presented itself, make a lot of money. The priority for industry has been to make as much money as possible by harvesting the most fish and the most desirable varieties of fish, and to remain ahead of the competition.

These factors, operating in an environment where conservation and intelligent resource management took a backseat, and in which effective international cooperation was all but nonexistent, drove the adoption of new technologies to land ever bigger catches. Scientists estimate that the waters where I have spent most of my life fishing—the nearshore region of southern Maine, near Kennebunkport—have lost 97 to 99 percent of the weight of *all* finfish and bivalve mollusks compared with what existed there 150 years ago.

There are no arguments or conditional factors—whether jobs or mouths to feed—that can make these facts acceptable, because the short-term benefits in no way compensate for the long-term costs. Those costs are not just environmental; they include catastrophic losses to communities that can no longer sustain themselves with livelihoods that rely on the sea. These include jobs from sportfishing, nature tours, recreational diving—and commercial fisheries. More important than even these, however, is the vast damage to entire ecosystems, the loss of sea-bottom habitat and estuaries, species diversity, balance, and population. Also incalculable are the costs we will continue to pay into the future for what has already been done—losses to our quality of life and our ability to encounter wilderness, as well as the costs of what will happen economically and socially if, as some scientists predict, all commercially viable species of wild fish are exhausted within the next forty years.

The boom-and-bust cycle of fisheries is the result of a lack of knowledge, yes, but it is also very much the result of bad fisheries management, apathy and ignorance on the part of the public, cowardice on the part of decision makers and fishermen who knew better, and greed on the part of the people who saw that they could profit in the short term and didn't give a damn about the rest.

If our lack of understanding about the limits of the world's oceans continues—if the ineptitude of management and the failure of international cooperation persists—we will lose what little is left in the next few decades.

The time to act is now.

〜〜〜〜

I came to this project by chance. In the spring of 2007, I picked up the April edition of *National Geographic* magazine, the cover of which featured a photograph of a juvenile swordfish, dead, hanging in a gill net, under the title "Saving the Sea's Bounty." The series of articles inside examined the annihilation of bluefin tuna in the Mediterranean; the destruction of the Grand Banks cod fishery off Canada and the impact of that event on coastal Newfoundland communities; and New Zealand's success in establishing marine reserves, as well as the profusion of life that resulted from allowing sections of the ocean to heal. Reading these three articles raised in me a sense of alarm, outrage, despair, and, finally, hope.

I had been aware of the damage being done to the seas. I knew that fertilizer runoff had created a dead zone off the Mississippi Delta in the Gulf of Mexico, that the Chesapeake Bay had been degraded, that the population of bluefin tuna was shrinking. But the more I read, the more it became clear to me that the situation was critical and that it had to be solved soon.

I came to love the ocean as a boy, growing up in Guilford, Connecticut, whose beaches and estuaries look out upon Long Island Sound. I caught snapper blues, blue crabs, eels, and bunker in the estuary river that ran a mile from my family's house. I listened to stories about my great-grandfather, Big Pomp, a Danish immigrant who came to this country in 1908 and married an Irish girl just off the *Lusitania*. Between the two of them they had fifty cents to their name, and from that they built a family and a successful dairy business in Hartford, and eventually, in 1933, they bought a small beach house at a place called Point O' Woods, in Old Lyme, Connecticut, twenty miles east of Guilford in the direction of Rhode Island.

The legend of this man—his stinking Limburger cheese rotting in the fridge, his gravelly voice and stormy moods, his alcoholism, his generosity and toughness, his slablike hands, his fishing prowess—was recorded in photos and in family lore, making him into something of our own God-father. But what I recall most from when I was a boy, and what my uncles and aunts remembered, was that this man could fish. He *never* came back empty. Three hundred fifty pounds of beer-drinking, Old World love and hardness rowing a dinghy out to a leaky wooden boat to dangle hermit crabs for blackfish was, they tell me, a sight to behold. My parents brought me to Point O' Woods as a child in Pomp's last days, and I remember sit-ting on his lap. They took me back there when I was eight years old, after Pomp had died, and gave me a fishing rod and a worm, and I passed the hours angling for cunners on the jetty below the yellow house on the cliff.

What I saw, looking down into the water at those fish, as the seaweed on the pylons undulated in the waves, has never stopped fascinating me: alien life forms that breathe water, whose entire world has almost nothing in common with mine, whose experience of life constitutes such a radical departure from what I understand that I realized I had to know something of what they live.

In 1981, when I was fourteen, my parents bought a summer house on Goose Rocks Beach, in southern Maine. From then on I spent part of almost every summer on that beach, exploring its estuaries and shallow bays and outlying islands. My brothers and I would fish in the brightly colored field of lobster buoys three-quarters of a mile out at the entrance of the bay. We would row out there and drop our diamond jigs over the side, and, as night and cold fogs set in, we would feel as if we were on the edge of something—the edge of risk, the edge of possibility. Just past the entrance to the bay, the bottom dropped and the real ocean—the open ocean, the North Atlantic—began. You could see it in the heave of waves. You could smell it in the cold, damp, heartless air that blew in from the darkening sea. Fishing there, I would stare out beyond the wave tops as far as I could see, sensing the power, the distance, the utter forsakenness of the open ocean. And while it frightened me, I felt, even then, the need for it. I wanted to see the things I had read about—whales, huge sharks, codfish, bluefin tuna, the wind tearing the tops off twenty-foot waves. I wanted to feel the power of storms, to see if they would intimidate me or make me feel more alive. A mackerel on the line would bring me back from my reveries.

Pulling it into the boat, I would hold the fish briefly in my hands, gazing at its blue and green zigzags, marveling at the perfect beauty of its design, knowing it was part of that ocean I feared but had also come to love.

In 1984 my father bought a small, used seventeen-foot fiberglass boat, a McKee. A precursor to the Boston Whaler, the McKee has a flat bottom and a tri-hull design up front—three small bows instead of the single bow of the classic V-hull. The boat is extremely stable but takes a severe beating in any kind of chop over half a foot. It is an excellent flat-water fishing boat, and its center-console design allows movement all around the steering station, especially up front, where there is a raised deck platform, the best fishing spot on the boat. In the ensuing years, my brothers and I learned how to water-ski off that boat, began fishing more, and learned by trial and error where the rocks in the bay were.

In 1986 I went off to college in Lewiston, Maine, but I returned every summer to Kennebunkport, where my brothers and I ran our own house-painting business. After quitting at the end of the day, one of us would row out to get the boat while the others cleaned brushes and packed drop cloths, and then we would converge on the McKee as it pulled up to the beach and throw the skis in. If the tide was right we'd take off to the back estuary for a few hours of waterskiing. Occasionally my brother John and I would go fishing, but the striped bass had not come back yet, and bluefish were rare. We contented ourselves with pollock and mackerel.

By the late 1990s I was returning alone every year in late August to Goose Rocks Beach to fish. After Labor Day, there was no one at the house and barely anyone on the beach, which allowed me to see a different Maine. I spent every day on the water from dawn until nightfall, heading up the coast, fishing every bay and cove, every rock pile and outcropping within five miles of shore. Except for lobstermen, I was the only boat out there. I trolled, jigged, chummed and chunked, live-lined; used clams, sandworms, dead bait, fake bait, surface plugs, sinking lures. After what had been many years of inconsistent and meager results, I started catching fish—bluefish by the dozen, and striped bass. I explored the small, wind- and wave-swept islands, little more than a few hundred square feet in size, where I would anchor the boat and walk up onto the rock piles to find dead and wounded gulls, the carcasses of seals, lobster traps and fishing nets, the complete skeletons of bluefish. I would sit for hours on those small outcroppings, watching the birds and the unceasing waves, letting the wind cleanse me. I learned something in those hours about the power of solitude, about what you see when you sit quietly and observe Nature. You cannot watch the Atlantic in the early fall for long hours in the dying sunlight, alone on a pile of stones used as a way station for seabirds, and not come away knowing that you are but a whisper in eternity.

Every year after that, I made a point of taking at least a week, and sometimes as much as two weeks, alone at the house in late August and the first part of September. I had rediscovered what I had been looking for, that thing I could return to again and again, regardless of any and all other circumstances—what I had known as a boy fishing out on the jetty under my great-grandfather's house and with friends on the estuary river in Guilford: I had rediscovered peace.

After reading those *National Geographic* articles in April 2007, I realized that the peace I had come to feel in the presence of the ocean was an illusion. I had imagined the ocean as pristine, as eternal and unchanging, as something that transcended the moment or any of the particular circumstances of my life. I now realized that it was in fact highly vulnerable to the impact of human beings. I realized that if I really cared about the ocean, I had to move beyond the romance it inspired and understand its reality in the twenty-first century.

From research I did through the summer and fall of 2007, it became clear that all the relevant parties—conservationists, scientists, lobbyists, commercial fishers, and sportfishermen—were saying different, and often contradictory, things. Fishermen didn't think much of science or of policymakers who used science to establish fisheries law and whose findings, it was widely held, were illegitimate, because they had never "done an honest day's work in their lives or spent enough actual time on the water." Conservationists didn't think much of fishermen, whom they saw as fishing down the oceans for their own profit and doing so in the face of accurate, hard science. And on and on. The more I read, the more important it became for me to figure out for myself what had happened and why, and to tell the story of the decline of the oceans—and particularly of the great fish—in terms everyone could understand.

My search took me around the world—to government lobbyists and conservation organizations in Washington, D.C.; to Catalina Island, California, the birthplace of offshore sportfishing; to the world's most prestigious catch-and-release sportfishing tournament, in Cabo San Lucas, Mexico. I went to the fogbound coast of Nova Scotia to fish with some of the last harpoon swordfishers a hundred miles out at sea. I traveled to Tokyo's Tsukiji fish market, which processes 10 percent of the world's fresh catch per day, and to the Mediterranean, where a conspiracy of stupidity and greed threatens to wipe out the northern bluefin tuna. I talked with some of the premier marine scientists in the world—men and women desperately pushing to expand our frontiers of knowledge about the sea before it's too late. And I had the rare opportunity to fish in some of the wildest and most remote places on the planet—off the Great Barrier Reef in Australia, angling for thousand-pound black marlin, and two hundred miles north of New Zealand, where I witnessed firsthand the courage of the broadbill swordfish. I delved into the history of sport and commercial fishing to find out how it all began, and how in the course of the past fifty years we have fished down some of the most abundant stocks of wildlife this planet has ever known.

As much as anything, I went on a personal pilgrimage to encounter the great fish. I wanted to know what these creatures are like, what we stand to lose. I wanted to know what my daughter will not know when she grows up, should things continue as they are. I went to find and experience firsthand the creatures that Nature took millions of years to engineer, creatures that have captivated the imagination of humankind since we first developed the capacity for imagining—the capacity for myths and dreams, for legends and for notions of the divine.

I went in pursuit of giants, in the hope that they might show us a new way of thinking about the oceans. I went so that those giants and their kin might not migrate into the void forever.

This book is the story of that journey.

BOOK 1

DISCOVERY

In the Kingdom of Sapphire Waters

Cabo San Lucas, Mexico

"Our worst enemies here are not the ignorant and simple, however cruel; our worst enemies are the intelligent and the corrupt."

—Graham Greene, *The Human Factor*

1

The dorado is a fish that God has played a joke upon. Its stunning neon colors shimmer like iridescent glass jewelry, but its body is shaped like a Chinese machete, squared off at the front end and tapered toward the tail. It has a tall, vertical forehead, a small, bunched face, and an overshot lower jaw. Its mouth looks both disappointed and perturbed, and its eyes have the fervent, maniacal stare of the deranged.

It is not often that you first hear a fish before you see it. I hear this one as a hot sizzle tearing through the water behind me and turn to see a rooster tail spurting up from the clear, sapphire-blue Sea of Cortez. Before I can identify it, the dorado has smacked the big orange-and-black jet-head lure Ernesto put out, rigged with two cruel, offset double J-hooks. Upon feeling the bite of the hooks, the fish flips eight feet into the air in a head-over-tail somersault and then tears away.

The dorado* is a surprisingly strong fish, given its small tail, which looks like two long feathers arranged in a V. But the fish swims with its entire flat machete body, so it is not just the power of the tail that pulls against you. This one weighs perhaps thirty pounds, and yet it strips line

---

*Dorado is also sometimes called a "dolphin fish" (not to be confused with the dolphin family of mammals) and is commonly known as mahi mahi.

off my reel, which is set with the drag at about twenty-five pounds, as though the reel were in free spool.

Twenty minutes later the dorado is next to the boat, ten feet down, looking like a four-foot-long blazing yellow neon sign with electric purple dots scattered across its back, sprays of what looks like bright green dye, and a royal blue dorsal blade running from its forehead down most of its back. I bring the fish up closer and see that the first hook is lodged in its jaw, and the second one sunk into the underside of its skull. In an instant Ernesto brings out a gaff, sinks it into the fish's backbone, and pulls it aboard.

"Wait—" I protest, far too late.

"But it is finished," he says, showing me the wound in the fish's head.

It is my mistake. I had no plans to eat the fish or to kill it, and I neglected to look closely at the jet-head rig before Ernesto put it out, and then I did not inform him what I wanted to do with any fish we hooked.

"No double hook," I tell him, pointing to the gash. "We can't release this fish now."

"I feed my family with it," he insists. His eyes, a mixture of bloodshot red and the jaundiced yellow of an autumn leaf, are watery with age. He is a toothless sixty-four-year-old man, tan as toffee but spry as a twelve-year-old boy around the boat, given to cackling laughter that follows comments I can rarely discern. His English is not good, and I speak almost no Spanish, but I enjoy his company.

"You will not sell this to a restaurant, right?" I ask.

"No," he assures me, his face serious. "I feed my family."

He has a large family—eight children and a brood of grandchildren and great-grandchildren—but the fish is likely worth more to him as merchandise than as food.

I nod and tell him, "No more double hooks. Only circle hooks.* Catch and release."

Ernesto agrees and drops the dorado in the fish box, where I watch its colors fade and its mouth silently gasp for water that will never come. He

---

*Traditional J-shaped hooks easily injure fish. The circle hook's curved shape is designed to lodge in the corner of the jaw, making injury less likely.

resets the lines with fresh one-pound caballitos—goggle-eyes, or bigeye shad—while I take a knife and sever the dorado's spine behind the head. Instantly the fish blanches gray-white and is dead.

It is nearly noon, and the sun high above beats me about the head until I retreat to the shade under the flybridge. The air itself burns a dry, luminous gold, with the water flashing needlelike shards of white light. This is our second day fishing aboard the *Adriana*. Yesterday we left the marina just after dawn, swinging around the curled tip of Cabo San Lucas, heading west into twelve-knot winds and four-foot seas, with the air smelling of cool ocean. We trolled for eight hours, halfway to Migriño and out ten miles, and had no hits nor saw any fish, although one of the other boats reported a small yellowfin tuna caught early that morning. This was a surprise, not because yellowfin are unusual around Cabo but because a group of large purse seiners had been taking entire schools of them off the coast for a week.

In the thirty-six hours I had been in Mexico, I had heard numerous complaints about the seiners, a topic of particular concern because Cabo is built on sportfishing and is considered among the top five places on the planet to fish. On a boat here you can expect to see anything. More striped marlin are caught here on rod and reel than anywhere in the world—an estimated thirty thousand per year—as well as yellowfin tuna, yellowtail, roosterfish, grouper, sea bass, and the rare swordfish. On the first day, we encountered three enormous Pacific gray whales thirty feet from the *Adriana*. Orcas are not uncommon and will surf the curling transom wave ten feet behind the boat if they are in the mood. Given that they can be over twenty feet long, can weigh six tons, and have the teeth of tyrannosaurs, this can be a thrilling and unsettling sight. The diving is excellent, and humpback whales, rays, dolphins, and other creatures abound.

Cabo lies at the intersection of the Pacific Ocean and the narrow Sea of Cortez, which runs up the gap between mainland Mexico and the long stiletto heel of the Baja Peninsula. Thirty years ago, Cabo was little more than a dusty cul-de-sac at the end of a vast, lonely web of dirt roads running eight hundred miles south from Tijuana. Its perpetual sunshine and proximity to major population centers in the United States began to attract huge numbers of tourists, who now fuel the economy and the massive development of resort hotels along the coast. Sportfishing brings in more than $400 million annually and contributes a total yearly economic impact of more than $1 billion to the Los Cabos region, an area slightly larger than Greater Los Angeles, with a permanent population of 180,000 and growing fast. But without sportfishing, the region would revert to the scrub-brush desert it used to be. The hotels arrayed like hulking clay bird-houses along the cliffs would bake in the unforgiving sun while wind-blown dust and sand accumulated in their deserted hallways, and lizards skittered up their flaking, abandoned walls.

For this reason, and despite its booming economy, Cabo San Lucas is fragile, its ecosystem under threat not only from the purse seiners but also from longliners. Cabo is under threat the same way so many other places around the world are—from the competing interests of humankind, where natural resources (in this case fish) are the meaty bone fought over in the dust.

We begin trolling again and head northeast up the curving coastline in the direction of Gorda Banks. Ernesto tends the lines faithfully and expertly, and his clowning provides for welcome entertainment. Enrique, the captain, is lively today as well. With his neatly trimmed white hair and small, clipped mustache he resembles a don, and during the doldrum hours of trolling he will occasionally interrupt the songs he sings to himself in Spanish to ask, scanning the horizon, *"Pesca, pesca?"* "Where are the fish?"

Seated next to him on the flybridge, I notice the duct-tape-and-baling-wire condition of the boat. Its bridge faring is secured with multiple wraps of fishing line and hooks, padded against the vibration of the engine and the banging of each wave by yellow carbon invoice sheets and wads of Kleenex stuffed between the Plexiglas and the frame. The *Adriana* must be more than thirty years old, perhaps as old as forty, but in a climate so relentlessly sunny, even workhorse charter boats like this one can have remarkable longevity.

Time slips by and I try to mentally plumb the depths below me, down through the diminishing azure light into darkness, calling the fish, willing them up to us. To the nonfisher, it is these periods of waiting that try patience, but if fishing is to be enjoyed, the doldrums must be accepted as part of the experience. They offer opportunities to ruminate on many subjects, learn from all you observe, and hone your fishing skill, preparing everything properly and leaving nothing to chance. And while you might even stumble upon new insights into both fishing and life during these periods of waiting, the truth is that any fisherman's real goal is to land fish. Some will eat that fish, others want only to catch it and let it go, and still others fish out of a naturalist's spiritual need to encounter the wild, to see and experience what would otherwise be beyond their reach. I go for this reason. The experience of seeing the ocean's great fish has made staying close to shore a betrayal of a part of me that is stronger and better, truer and freer, than any other part.

The first great fish I saw was a bluefin tuna, spotted off the coast of southern Maine in late August 2006. In gray, windy seas, my brothers and I chased schools of Atlantic bluefish, which normally hit anything thrown at them. But these didn't; their behavior was erratic, as though they were fleeing. Then, looking to port from the steering station, I saw why when, out of the gray chaos of the ocean's surface, a tuna leaped into the air. It wasn't even a large one—only about forty or fifty pounds—but it seemed to hover there above the waves, its huge eye meeting mine, and I thought to myself, *My God, that's a bluefin*. Here was a fish I had long heard about but had never seen, a fish of legendary speed and gigantic size, once abundant in the Gulf of Maine but now so rare that to my knowledge they were found only far offshore. And yet here one was, within sight of land. The encounter was at best a fraction of a second, but something in me suddenly and explosively awakened at the sight of that fish, and my soul took a snapshot of it. In the eye of that fish I saw something secret about the ocean, something old and elemental, something utterly and fiercely wild.

Most people have no conception of the "great" fish of the sea—the ocean giants that grow to hundreds of pounds, sometimes as large as a ton, possess tremendous speed and power, and are capable of ranging across entire oceans. When I tell them that an adult swordfish can swim as fast as a cheetah can run, would fill a living room wall to wall, and could take a man's head off with one slash of its broadsword, they stare at me. When I describe how a giant bluefin tuna weighing six hundred pounds will hit a ten-pound bait at fifty miles an hour and how, upon feeling the bite of the hook, that fish is capable of burning off four or five hundred yards of line against resistance that would leave an Olympic sprinter on the ground puking at a fraction of that distance, they begin to suspect either that I'm exaggerating or that here is a realm of the natural world that challenges their vocabulary, their entire language of experience.

But that's exactly what I came to know as I began to encounter these creatures. I came to know that if the fish I hooked was among the great offshore species and had reached maturity, it would fight me with every wild sinew in its body. It would show me more nobility and dignity, more pure bravery and heart, during the course of its struggle with me than I was likely to be asked to demonstrate in my entire lifetime. The fact that I might eventually subdue it would be a testament to the technical capabilities of our species, but that would be all. I realized that if I were a true fisherman, I wouldn't allow myself the delusion that I was superior to the fish, or that by catching it my stature was somehow improved or my worth increased. The fish would be better than me every time, because all it would ever have was itself.

And this, ultimately, is why I fish—to be reminded that their lives, however brief, however solitary or hard, are pure. I fish to be reminded that as wild things from the deep, they are part of the ageless sea and the ageless force that created it. I fish to be reminded that this is what we ourselves are also born to: not waves at sea, not thousand-fathom deeps, but wildness.

~~~~~

It is late morning when we come upon Gorda Banks. Los Cabos is one of those unusual places in the world where only half a mile from shore you can find yourself in a thousand feet of water, and at twice that distance the depths can drop to three thousand feet. Gorda Banks lies twenty-eight miles northeast of Cabo San Lucas, and in contrast to the surrounding depths, the two seamounts that constitute the banks rise to within a few dozen meters of the surface, even though they're ten miles from shore. These upward spikes in the ocean floor force currents to the surface, where nutrients and other life-forms bask in the sun and multiply, drawing humpback whales, sharks, marlin, seabirds, and sardines to feed there.

As the *Adriana* approaches the vicinity of the banks, we begin to see leaping eagle rays, and then a giant black manta heaving itself upward twice in succession, doing a triple rotation each time to dislodge parasites. In a halo of cigarette smoke, Ernesto adjusts the drag on one of the reels while keeping a keen squint on the water. At the wheel, Enrique looks over his shoulder, gauging the swimming motion of the baits behind us, then adjusts his speed.

"You fish many marlin?" Ernesto asks me in heavily accented English.

"No. First time."

"Oh, then we get you one for sure. Ernesto, he is very good."

"How long have you been fishing?" I ask.

"*Treinta años.* Thirty years."

Then from the flybridge we hear Enrique say, "Whale shark." He is leaning with his elbow over the rail, staring down into the water.

Ernesto and I move to the port gunwale, and five feet off the side, ten feet deep at most, moving in the opposite direction, I glimpse a broad, brown field punctuated with white dots the size of soccer balls moving to stern.

"Can you stop the boat?" I ask Enrique. "I have a mask and snorkel and would like to look."

Enrique looks at me and shrugs, puts the throttle in neutral, and tells Ernesto to pull in the lines. After stripping off my clothes, I throw myself over the side. The mask slips up my face; I sputter and adjust, stuff the snorkel in my mouth, start to swim, and put my head under. Through the water I hear my own involuntary gasp of *"Oh my God!"* in the mouthpiece.

Thirty feet long, as big as a school bus, the whale shark is the largest thing I have ever seen underwater, and my awe is mingled with momentary, primitive, base-of-the-brain fear. But then I look at what is only yards in front of me—brown skin with the soft appearance of suede, the white splotches running forward over the striated flanks of what is actually a gargantuan plankton eater. Up ahead, its dorsal fin rises like a tall, thick sail, its stiff pectorals extending like aircraft wings, and all around it, as though it were a moving reef, are schools of fish—black-and-white sergeant majors dashing forward in a shivering mass, a three-foot-long remora, thin and serpentine, beating a hasty advance to a better anchorage up front, and a swift squadron of small, oval, cobalt-and-black surgeonfish arcing over the whale shark's back and out of sight. All of this set against a sunlit prism field of supermarine blue and the massive head of the whale shark, murky in the distance. Ahead to my left, a three-foot-long clear corkscrew jelly hangs suspended and twinkling in space, floating like a glass mobile. Each if its small, round segments is lit and pulsing from within with fine, shimmering, electric rainbow filaments, arrayed like the vertical ribs of a lantern. I learn later that this is a salp—not a single creature but a colony of individuals—and that it can reach dozens of feet long.

Then I notice that below me, sweeping slowly back and forth mere feet away, bigger than a four-by-eight sheet of plywood, is the whale shark's tail. Suddenly I am seized by a wild urge. *Grab it,* I think to myself. *You have to grab it. Now—*

Rushing forward to catch up to it, I am overtaken by an insane thrill as I reach forward with my right hand to take hold of the top of the whale shark's tail. I am gently thrown from side to side as this twenty-ton animal tows me through the sea. The texture of its skin—like the pebbly, vulcanized rubber of a car tire, and just as hard—is a surprise. On the right side of its tail are three curved striations—nicks from a boat propeller, white with scarring.

If a whale shark can look over its shoulder, this one does, as though curious to see what has suddenly fastened onto it, hitching a ride. Slowly it bends downward, angling into the darker, murkier blue. I long to follow it, but by now my lungs are out of air, so I return to the surface and burst through, laughing.

Back on the boat, both Enrique and Ernesto regard me with amusement: I have proven myself a stereotypically crazy American. But I also sense they share the joy of the moment, and the rarity of it, with me. I try to describe what I saw but quickly realize I lack the language to express any of it adequately. Changing into a dry pair of shorts, I cannot help but feel I have just been blessed by the ocean, given a sign that this search I'm on is not utterly futile; that as a nonscientist and a non–commercial fisherman I will somehow not be met with skepticism and resistance, or denied at every turn.

Ernesto resets the lines, and we are fishing again. There are perhaps a dozen other boats in the area, scattered over ten square miles of flat water, outriggers spread high, giving them the appearance of skimming water bugs. These vessels are all from Cabo, most of them carrying anglers who have come a few days before the start of the International Game Fish Association (IGFA) Offshore World Championship to polish up on their caballito casting. The local style here is to cast the small one-pound goggle-eyes from a trolling rod with a stiff-armed heaving action, as though you were throwing a heavy shovelful of wet dirt. It takes sure thumb pressure on the reel as it spins out: Too much and the bait will drop short, too little and the reel will overspin, leaving you with a bird's nest on the spool and a lost fish.

The tournament is one of several reasons I have come to Cabo. There are other, more famous tournaments I might have chosen—big-money contests like Bisbee's Black & Blue or the Hawaiian International—but I've opted for the IGFA because it represents the fullest development of the ethics of the sport. It is the true fisherman's tournament, emphasizing angling prowess and conservation through the number and species of fish caught and let go, as opposed to simply the biggest fish caught and killed.

I have also traveled here in hopes of encountering a marlin, perhaps the best known of all the great sportfish. There are several varieties of marlin, which constitute the bulk of the group called billfish, the "bill" referring to the elongated upper jaw, which grows into a long, round, pointed spike. In the case of the broadbill swordfish, however, the bill is a true broadsword—hard, heavy, flat, made of bone, sharp at the edges, broad at the base and tapering to a point like the weapon of a medieval knight. It is a lethal tool used for defense and attack. In the case of the other billfish, the spike is used similarly to the swordfish's sword, to stun, skewer, dent, snag, slash, impale, rip, and otherwise maim luckless prey.

Marlin are the darlings of offshore fishermen because they jump so beautifully and powerfully. Depending on their mood and condition, their skin will flash lavender or copper, rubbed silver or a blazing hyacinth blue. Blue and black marlin are by far the largest, growing to more than a thousand pounds and over twelve feet long, with a pronounced hump behind the head. These giants have the stamina and strength to battle an angler for half a day or more. The largest marlin ever caught on rod and reel, according to the rules of the IGFA, was a black marlin landed off Cabo

Blanco, Peru, in 1953, that weighed 1,560 pounds, had a girth of six feet nine inches, and measured fourteen feet six inches long. Larger blue and black marlin, caught with commercial gear and on rod and reel (although not in accordance with IGFA rules), have weighed well over a ton, with some surpassing 2,500 pounds. Tales are told of marlin over twenty feet long and weighing three thousand pounds, spotted by knowledgeable, experienced anglers.

If blue and black marlin are the superheavyweights, then the middle-weight class belongs to the striped marlin, a graceful fish with electric-blue vertical bars against a background of coppery bronze along its flanks. Striped marlin can reach 500 pounds but are more commonly half that. Around Cabo San Lucas, the striped marlin are on the small side, between 100 and 200 pounds, about five to seven feet long, with some reaching 250 or 300 pounds. Striped marlin will congregate and feed in groups and even among other fish, but this kind of feeding aggregation is all but unheard of in blues and blacks.

The lightweight group of billfish includes the sailfish, the white marlin, and the various spearfish. Sailfish are distinctive because of their large dorsal sail, which they can flip up and down like a pleated fan and which ripples and twirls with the movement of the fish like the dress of a tango dancer. The fish use the sail to communicate as they feed in groups. Sail-fish also have slim, elongated fins on their throats that trail elegantly behind them in the water like the ends of a bolo tie. A sailfish in full rega-lia coming at a baitfish under the water, sail up and waving, fins flared, pennants trailing, must look like a beautiful, dark angel of death decked out in rippling silk, concealing a lethal rapier. They are among the fastest of all fish, capable of burst speeds close to seventy miles an hour. One second they will be moving stately and grand as a parade float, and then suddenly all their frills will collapse tight against their bodies, and with a rapid serpentine vibration they rocket away. All of the lightweight billfish are slender, and the sailfish is no exception, topping out in the vicinity of two hundred pounds but growing as long as eleven feet.

But if there is a true acrobat among the billfish it is the white marlin, which tail-walks, skims like a stone, and flips and spins out of the water with remarkable agility and lightness. White marlin are found only in the

Atlantic, and if you are fishing off Hatteras or the Chesapeake on one of that region's hot and humid summer days and go out an easy forty or fifty miles into the Gulf Stream, you might encounter one in the form of a smallish marlin with little bolos at the throat but no sail, silvered like an antique mercury mirror with a dark topside like a black marlin's. You should feel smiled upon, because white marlin sightings are rare.

Even rarer are the spearfish, which look as if they were prehistoric ancestors of the marlin. Either that, you think, or what you're looking at is the result of an unholy union between a marlin and a wahoo. There are four types of spearfish: the longbill, shortbill, roundscale (or hatchet marlin), and Mediterranean. They are all small, usually in the 70-to-150 pound range, and measure up to eight feet. The one feature common to all the spearfish except the roundscale is a long razorback dorsal fin. You'll need a knowledge of the placement of anal vents to distinguish a roundscale from a white marlin, as both have dorsals rounded at the top. The longbill and the roundscale are found only in the Atlantic. Identification of the shortbill and the Mediterranean is easier, since each has a stubby bill, barely longer than its bottom jaw, making it look bashful and inadequate. The shortbill is found mostly in the Indian and Pacific oceans, while the Mediterranean spearfish lives anywhere within the confines of the Strait of Gibraltar.

The third reason I have come to Cabo is to look into a controversy that seems to be affecting every region in the world where there are remaining fish stocks of any size: the battle among commercial interests, government, conservation groups, and sportfishing enthusiasts. The alliances and positions of the players change depending on the relevant issue and the locale, but in Baja the sportfishers (generally) and the conservationists are united against the commercial interests and the government. Here in Cabo, the most recent battle is over a regulation called Shark Norma 029, which was passed in 2007 by the Mexican government, ostensibly to protect sharks and rays by limiting the number of shark-fishing permits, the argument being that the regulations would bring Mexican fisheries management into compliance with international standards. While that was true on paper, the new rules also threw open the doors to a number of evils that, up until then, had supposedly been contained.

Shark Norma allows the violation of a 1997 law called the Ley de Pesca, which set aside the entire Sea of Cortez and established a fifty-mile conservation zone along the Pacific coast to protect sportfish species, sharks, sea turtles, and marine mammals. Norma allows damaging commercial longline and driftnet gear* into these protected areas—as many as 243 medium longline vessels (mostly old, converted shrimpers) fishing a maximum of 10,185 miles of line, with an estimated 218,000 hooks. Add this to the number of existing permitted vessels and there will be thousands more miles of line and more than 1.5 million hooks being fished commercially in the Sea of Cortez on any given day. The daily impact of even a single medium longliner is the equivalent of 250 sportfishing yachts fishing twenty-four hours a day.

Consider, too, that the majority of what is being caught on longlines is not typical "target" species like shark, but accidental bycatch species like marlin, dorado, sailfish, swordfish, sea turtles, whales, and other animals. A 1999 report conducted by the Instituto Nacional de la Pesca (INP), Mexico's national fisheries institute, found that bycatch accounted for 60 to 80 percent of a longliner's take around Baja. Two longliners from Magdalena Bay killed 11,743 striped marlin—77.5 percent of their total catch—over a nine-month period. The same report found that smaller, traditional panga longliners, fishing with shark permits out of Manzanillo, killed mostly sailfish (80 percent of their catch) and sold 150 to 200 tons of it every month.

Norma permits fishermen to accidentally catch these species, but when you look at how much of their catch is made up of such fish, you realize that the bycatch species are actually the targets. Norma is, in effect, a gaping loophole that allows commercial harvesting of billfish and other species under the guise of shark fishing.

---

*Driftnets are walls of vertical netting that hang in the water and can extend many miles. They catch fish by entangling the gills and body of the animal; they are called "walls of death" because they kill indiscriminately. If a driftnet is lost at sea, it eventually sinks to the bottom, encumbered with the deadweight of its victims. When the carcasses decompose and are eaten by bottom life, the driftnet floats to the surface to begin killing again. It is a lethal gear outlawed in many countries, but there are many still used in Mexico.

The fact is, a number of Mexican commercial fleets—especially shrimp fishermen—reported their worst season in history in 2003, catching only seven tons of shrimp per boat in six months. (Notice that the longliners slated to fish under Shark Norma are retooled shrimpers.) Shark Norma sanctions short-term profit at the long-term expense of fish populations, sustainable industries (primarily sportfishing, but indirectly tourism, diving, and other types of sustainable fishing), and possibly even whole ecosystems.

The region has already seen a steady decline in top-tier predators like sharks, billfish, dorado, and grouper, and a simultaneous increase in creatures lower in the food chain, like squid and sardines. This is the classic pattern of overfishing: Take away the top layer of the food chain and populations lower down increase. Unrestricted commercial fishing will then turn its sights on new areas (like those opened through Shark Norma) or it will target species at lower levels, taking them as well. What you end up with is a sea full of jellyfish—literally—because the ocean's diversity has been eradicated. Ecosystems thrown out of balance are more susceptible to disease, fluctuations in water temperature and quality, loss of habitat, and invasion by competing species. Overharvesting thus destroys the very mechanisms that would allow species and ecosystems to sustain themselves at healthy levels. In contrast, fishing intelligently means fishing within the limits of what various species can tolerate. The sea is neither endlessly fertile nor endlessly giving.

～～～～～

Sitting in the fighting chair on the *Adriana*, I eat a simple lunch of two bean burritos, bought this morning from a woman selling them from her pickup truck on the street beside the boat docks. Five hundred yards in the distance, one of the other boats is fighting a marlin. I watch, admiring the beauty of the fish as it bounds across, leaping and splashing and shaking all its sinewy length. In a short ten minutes, they have it at the transom and instantly let it go, hardly laying hands on it except to grasp the tip of the bill.

I marvel at this place, the Sea of Cortez. It is hard to imagine how remote and untouched it was as recently as thirty years ago, even after having been familiar for more than five hundred years to Europeans—specifically Spaniards, pirates, and priests—to say nothing of the indigenous Indians who lived here for hundreds of generations before. While that sort of exposure usually spelled doom for any point of contact in the New World, both Baja and the Cortez were spared, remaining all but unspoiled for those five centuries. The ancestors of the native peoples, having migrated over the land bridge connecting Russia and Alaska, lived a nomadic existence here in a landscape of calm, crystal-blue waters, pale hills, and barren, charred peaks—a vast, empty silence interrupted only by the sound of wind and the soft hush of breakers on the rocks.

In Cabo now, this kind of peace is impossible to find. But away from Cabo, up the coast, looking from the water at the stark shore, a very old part of the human soul stirs in the presence of wilderness and says "yes" to the rhythm of life without clocks or machinery—a world of quiet punctuated by the dull shush of waves, the muted cries of birds spilling in multitudes off cliffs in the distance. And after they are gone, silence reclaiming the still mountains, and the gold atmospheric fog of this place streaming down from the sun.

I do not see the marlin hit. Ernesto clambers down from the flybridge as the reel goes off like a hundred-yard zipper being ripped open, and I am up and heading for the rod when I see, about a hundred feet behind us, a slender, dark, glistening striped marlin leap out of the water. It jumps three times, beating its blue tail in the air and down into the water again, out for a fourth time, then takes off diagonally a distance of a hundred yards. I'm on the rod, line peeling off as the marlin makes its run, while Ernesto works to get the fighting belt* around my waist. I get the rod butt into the gimbal, hand on the reel crank, and pull back on the rod, applying pressure on the line. The marlin keeps running, leaps again, then turns and dives. I crank and crank, reeling in the slack the fish has given up. The marlin comes out skipping sideways across the water, throwing off sheets, and dives again. The fish whacks the leader with its bill, shaking its head,

---

*The belt has a hard, thick plastic shield that sits on your lower abdomen, with a gimbaled socket for the butt of the rod.

the rod vibrating and tugging in my hands, and then the marlin peels off again. Only minutes into the fight and my face is already lined with rivulets of sweat. Ernesto smiles his toothless smile. "He no come easy, eh? He make you work."

As I continue to gain and lose line, Enrique stops the boat, keeping the stern pointed in line with the fish, which enables me to fight from a standing position. I lift and reel, lift and reel, and after fifteen minutes I spot a flash of blue stripes under the water twenty feet back to my left. The fish is tired now—I can feel it—so I increase the drag on the reel and lift the rod steadily, reeling as I lower, then lift again. Slowly the fish comes up diagonally from under the reflective surface of the water, and it is magnificent—almost six feet long and lit from within. Its pectoral fins and tail, its dorsal fin and the stripes along its sides, all glow a bright pastel violet. The marlin planes under the water, slowly beating its tail back and forth in long sweeps, holding down ten feet. Gently I ease it up and see the hook, slotted nicely in the crook of its upper jaw. I guide the fish parallel to the starboard rail until Ernesto can lean over and grab it by the bill. Enrique drops lightly onto the deck from the flybridge and is at Ernesto's side in an instant. They struggle briefly, then together lift the fish over the side and lay it across the top of the transom.

I had not expected this. Because it is my first marlin, they want to take a photograph, and while I appreciate the thought, I would rather not have had the fish hauled out of the water to endure this additional stress. Enrique pulls the hook as I quickly grab my camera and hand it to Ernesto. I take hold of the marlin's bill from Enrique and am amazed to find it has a heavily burred surface, like a piece of wood badly in need of sanding. The fish's eyes are quite large, the circumference of a small orange, and its head is surprisingly birdlike, with the same broad spread of skull between the eyes, the long, thin face and triangular jaw extending into the slender spike.

After clicking off a few frames, Ernesto asks if I want some video taken as well.

"No," I tell him. "Let's get it back in."

Together he and Enrique slide the marlin off the transom and into the water. I watch it glide into the depths, its body still, the fish perhaps surprised to find itself returned to its element. I can't help smiling: I've just laid eyes on a marlin from only a foot away, touched its bill, looked for a moment into its eye. Until now the thought of ever experiencing something like this seemed a remote dream. My sense of awe at the strange beauty of the sea was enlivened one particular day on Cape Cod when, as a boy, I found a large, heavy silver surf spoon washed up in a patch of seaweed and wondered what kind of fish would go after a lure that large. The dream was infinitely deepened when I saw the film version of Hemingway's *The Old Man and the Sea;* I remember wondering, when that impossible, titanic marlin emerged from the ocean as though erupting from the unconscious, if it was real, if a fish of such size and beauty could actually exist in the world. I could not have been more than nine or ten at the time, but I remember the love of the old man for the fish, and his struggle to kill it so that he could sell it and be able to eat. It was the paradox of his situation that saddened me as much as the fact that the fish would die if the old man succeeded. And then, after spending all his aged strength fighting the fish over three days and nights—a fish to which he was now strangely bonded— it was taken from him by sharks. The final image of the marlin's massive white backbone and tail, stripped of flesh and all that remained of its beauty, lying in the wash of waves on the beach, broke my heart.

The marlin I just caught was an infant by comparison with that great fish, only 120 pounds and about four years old, but it is not size that matters here. What matters is that that fish, and the whale shark, and this whole day, are proof that the wonders of the sea are not only real but tangible. Through the shivering line I felt a vibrant creature whose existence confirmed our companionship in the greater mystery. To release that animal was to acknowledge its sanctity, to appreciate its solidity and reality, and the profound truth that we humans are not abandoned to solitude and aloneness in the world. It is easy to think of ourselves as existing on a higher, separate plane from all other life on this planet, but this is not true, and we are no more the authors of our abilities or the architects of our psyches than the bee can take credit for having invented honey or the hive mind. Handicapped by an assumed superiority, we risk remaining blind to the special brilliance of beings whose lives we define only by their utility to us. The price of this attitude is disconnection, a deep separateness from Nature that allows us to do to other creatures and to entire species—and ultimately to ourselves—things that are unforgivable.

To continue in these ways guarantees there will be a reckoning, and it will not come in the form of a single judgment day. It will come over time, in the impoverished lives of our children, who will experience Nature not as abundance for their table, or as a personal means of connecting with the divine, but as a fundamental barrenness, a wreckage of former beauty with only rare, fleeting glimpses of what once was. In truth, this reckoning has already begun. We live in a world where Nature is diminished, and we persist in viewing what remains as normal or simply as pretty backdrop. We see it through thin conceptions of beauty and usefulness, and we accept its reduced state as something we cannot change. Worst of all, we operate without an understanding of ecosystems as our life-support systems, requiring balance and health to sustain themselves and us—an equilibrium that depends on *our* intelligent self-control.

Back on the flybridge, Enrique points the *Adriana* southwest to begin our trip back to Cabo San Lucas. Ernesto resets the lines, and we are trolling again. Halfway home, I see another sleek bill emerge five feet behind the center bait. The marlin slashes at the fish four times, thrusting its entire head out of the water, then drops back, circles, and rushes again at the caballito. I am too slow on the reel, too clumsy in my touch to let the bait drop back subtly enough to make the marlin think it's killed it. But the marlin does not strike me as being hungry, and it merely plays with the bait, practicing its swordplay until it's had its fun and disappears.

We are about five miles from port when Ernesto brings out three triangular flags and runs them up the starboard outrigger line. One is a yellow flag showing a dorado, the second is a blue flag with the image of a marlin, and the third is a red flag with perpendicular lines denoting the release of the marlin. With the fishing over for the day, I sit back in the fighting chair, watching the coast roll by, admiring the flags, and admit to myself that it is indeed good to be on a boat coming back into port with flags flying.

2

Iam staying at the Finisterra, one of the area's early hotels, now grown into a resort, located about a half-mile from the marina. It's the sort of place where the house staff wipes dust off the leaves of the landscaped bushes with wet sponges. On the cliff behind the Finisterra, there is a restaurant, the Blue Marlin, and above this, accessible by stairs through the restaurant, is a bar, Mirador de Ballenas. I am halfway through the Blue Marlin, on my way to the bar, when I stop. There on the back wall is the largest stuffed fish I have ever seen. I cross the empty dining room to look at it.

No matter how many photos you have seen of dead marlin strung up at the dock, or films of marlin jumping and splashing around, or paintings immortalizing huge marlin exploding out of waves, wide-mouthed and slashing after little panicked skipjacks, none of them compares to being physically close to an animal of this size, even if it is dead and stuffed. The fish hanging on the back wall of the Blue Marlin restaurant is thirteen feet three inches long and measures twenty-seven inches tall from its belly to its backbone. It is a foot and a half thick at the thickest point, and its girth is six feet four inches. The sickle blade of that marlin's tail is four feet eight inches from point to point. Its bill is an order of magnitude larger than what I held in my hand earlier in the day on that small, 120-pound striped marlin aboard the *Adriana*.

Standing in the restaurant looking at that big fish, I understand one thing clearly that I have not understood before: all the subtler nuances of the word *oceanic*. All those associations having to do with the true scale of planetary waters: the dark-blue weightless firmament; the black void so profound it swallows as a morsel the infinity of the drowning man's soul; the vast, wave-strewn wastes of the old, gray-bearded man-face of the sea. To the giant marlin, that monumental and unfathomable wilderness is home, a place that in its totality is yet beyond the reach of human technology. And it makes me wonder, *What did that fish see with its fist-size eyes in the murky, dull thunder of the Pacific? In the bright, clear sapphire kingdom of the Cabo San Lucas deeps?*

The small photo next to the mount shows two men—captain and

angler—and the huge fish, strung up by the tail. It was caught in 1979 on eighty-pound test line* and took four hours to land. It weighed 1,110 pounds.

There have been marlin half again as big. On his excellent Web site, BigMarineFish.com, Jim Chambers provides photographs of a seventeen-foot Pacific blue marlin caught off Kona, Hawaii, in 1984 that weighed 1,656 pounds and a blue marlin known as "Choy's Monster," also caught off Kona, fourteen years earlier, by multiple members of a holiday sport-fishing charter, that weighed 1,805 pounds. Chambers also cites a huge Pacific blue marlin caught by a commercial fisherman off Okinawa, Japan, that exceeded the capacity of the one-metric-ton scale at the dock. (A metric ton is 1,000 kilograms, or 2,205 pounds, and is also called a "tonne.")

George Reiger, one of the twentieth century's great sportfishing editors, discusses, in a commemorative edition of Zane Grey's writings on sport-fishing, a marlin caught near Tahiti in 1966 that was so large it had to be cut up to be weighed. The total of the pieces was 2,400 pounds.

In *Big Fish and Blue Water* (1970), Peter Goadby includes a photograph of two marlin spikes side by side, the smaller one from a Pacific blue marlin that weighed 1,852 pounds. It's as thick as the business end of a baseball bat. The spike next to it is fully one-third longer and twice as thick and looks like a picket-fence post. It came off a fish estimated at 2,500 pounds, caught commercially off Moorea, near Tahiti.

In *Tales of Tahitian Waters* (1928), Zane Grey himself writes about the first thousand-pound marlin ever caught. He brought it ashore, its body mutilated by sharks, and it still weighed 1,040 pounds after having lost an estimated two hundred pounds of flesh and blood. It was fourteen feet two inches long, six feet nine inches in girth. Grey was one of the first hard-core sportfishermen, who early in the last century fished some of the most remote waters on the planet and saw some of the best offshore fishing

---

*Fishing line is rated according to tensile strength, i.e., the number of pounds pulling against the line that will cause it to break. This has nothing to do with the weight of the fish, but rather with the weight at which the line parts under a load. (Think of a rubber band breaking as it's pulled apart.) Through careful use of the reel's drag (its braking system) and even his or her hands, a skilled angler can use a very light (low-weight) line against a large fish and subdue it. Many fishing lines have a certain amount of stretch to them, which adds an element of forgiveness. The more line out from the reel, the more stretch there is.

grounds that ever existed, decades before they were discovered by sport and commercial fishermen. Standing on that Tahitian beach at the end of the day, sunburned, exhausted, agog at his mangled grander strung up from the cross-trees, Grey thought to himself, "I could not help but remember the giant marlin Captain had lost in 1928, which we estimated at twenty-two or twenty-three feet, or the twenty-foot one I had raised at Tautira, or the twenty-eight foot one the natives had seen repeatedly alongside their canoes."

So what about tales of the ones that cannot be caught? The ones who heave their hoary heads out of the sea and speak disdainful telepathic utterances into your brain from their great distance before they roar away? Chambers features a photograph of one estimated at close to three thousand pounds, steaming casually toward the horizon. This is the very fish that Black Bart Miller, famed captain from Hawaii, had near the transom of his boat in July 1986 but simply could not bring in. For six hours that bright Hawaiian afternoon, this queen among fish fought against Black Bart's shrewd boating skill and the amateur angler who struggled on the rod in the presence of one of Nature's giants. Black Bart had been at the helm for over thirty years by that time, and he'd presided over the capture of some enormous fish—sixteen-hundred-pounders, seventeen feet long— but as the light faded and the fish finally broke the line and sank from view, Black Bart knew he'd just seen the largest fish he would ever see in his life.

"I watched her for six hours," he told me. "I know exactly how long she was. She was twenty-five feet."

There are fish out there—or perhaps there were—that cannot be caught by the lone angler sitting in a chair, and perhaps this is best.

3

I am up before dawn the next morning, walking to the car in the dim, bruised light on my way to the marina for the start of the IGFA tournament. At the Administración Portuaria Integral (API) dock, I see an impressive display of boat handling as nearly seventy different local charter captains maneuver their craft in and out of slips in a narrow dogleg of the marina where they pick up their teams. There is much good-humored shouting back and forth, and not once do the rails of the craft touch. With their teams aboard, each boat has to verify that its passengers are in possession of their fishing licenses, which the harbormaster checks at the marina mouth. The boats then make their way outside the marina entrance to the waiting fleet of pangas, each with two or three men standing shirtless or in stained tees and shorts. These are the baitmen, who have fished the day before or during the night and sell live goggle-eyes or halfbeaks or whatever else is running for a dollar each. The tournament boats are limited to ten live baits for the day.

The IGFA runs an observer boat for the press and the families and friends of the anglers. The vessel does service most days on coastal tours or inshore fishing charters, and has an enclosed first deck and an open upper deck. I move up top to get in position for the spectacle as the boat heads out through the harbor into Medano Bay. The sportfishing boats have spread themselves out across ten or eleven acres of the bay, while the observation boat slides up along Land's End—the slim ridge extending into the sea from Cabo—and for the first time I get a close look at the spires and cut-through of "the Arch" at this famous terminus. Land's End is composed of beautiful, rough sculptured forms, honeycombed and aged, bearing a similarity to Gaudí's famous La Sagrada Família cathedral in Barcelona. Its edges plunge straight down into the abyss.

With the sun lifting out of the sea like a dripping maraschino cherry, the signal is given and seventy sport boats take off en masse, leaving long, frothing wakes. They fan out in all directions—some directly offshore, others hooking to starboard up the coast on the Pacific side, others heading east in the direction of Gorda Banks and beyond. They are allowed to go out nearly fifty miles, as far as Punta Lobos on the Pacific side and just shy of Los Frailes in the Cortez. The noise of the fishing boats fades as they grow smaller speeding away from us, and then we turn back to the marina.

At 10:00 A.M., I go to meet Minerva Saenz de Smith, probably the best-known and most vocal member of Cabo's business community when it comes to the Shark Norma law. She has been instrumental in gathering support among sportfishers, scientists, and conservationists against the law and has led the Cabo sportfishing sector in promoting the use of circle hooks and the release of all billfish, and in encouraging local restaurants to stop serving marlin. She owns Minerva's Baja Tackle and runs five charter boats, all between thirty-one and forty feet.

I figure Minerva to be in her early fifties; she's pretty and plump, with long, dark hair and a strong, high, cordial voice. She was eighteen when she first came to Cabo in the fall of 1976. Early one morning she walked out of camp, up over the rise of dunes, and there before her eyes, broad Medano Beach stretched away up the coast with not a soul on it. She walked across that sunny, windblown solitude, waded into the water up to her waist, and found it so clear she could see her toes. In a matter of minutes she was surrounded by schools of baby black-and-white-striped roosterfish, small jacks, and other tropical fish. She believed she had found paradise. *I'm going to stay here,* she said to herself.

She describes Cabo at that time as remote from the rest of the world. "There were only eight hundred people here when I came. This coffee shop used to be a tiny wooden building where they sold potatoes and onions and canned food. There was a man who went up and down the street selling avocados and tomatoes from a box. Because there was no refrigeration, every little house along the streets had salted, butterflied marlin drying on the clotheslines. It would dry like jerky in the sun."

Minerva describes how fishing has changed since then. "When we first started, we had one boat and we fished 320 days a year. Now I have four boats working and I bet you it's been three years since I've caught a fish over four hundred pounds. And we used to catch them *all the time.* What's really shocking is swordfish. We used to get swordfish in the same abundance as marlin. Three years ago, I counted all the swordfish that were caught in Cabo: eleven. *In the whole year.* We don't go out and specifically target them. But *eleven* in the whole year, for the entire Cabo fleet! There used to be a time when you could catch three and four in a single day all within a short distance from port."

When I ask Minerva about the Shark Norma law, she explains that it was initiated by commercial fishing interests from Ensenada, Sinaloa, and Sonora, who pushed the government fisheries agency, CONAPESCA (Comisión Nacional de Acuacultura y Pesca, or National Commission of Aquaculture and Fishing), to write it. "They came up with this wolf-in-sheep's-clothing language about protection of sharks and rays, and meanwhile the whole thing is not really about sharks; it's about letting the longliners come within the protected zone to fish. When you look at what the longliners are catching, it's billfish. There's no regulation, no enforcement, and the companies are selling hundreds of tons of marlin every month, because that's their real target. Your average person doesn't know the truth about it. If you ask anyone, 'Do you want to protect manta rays?' every person will say yes, because the law is advertised as being about protecting sharks and rays. But in truth the law is a manipulation to give the commercial interests free access to the protected zones."

"But why should CONAPESCA favor commercial fishing when sport-fishing is such a powerful economic engine for Los Cabos?" I ask.

"Two reasons," she says. "First, the economic contributions *and sustain-ability* of catch-and-release sportfishing have never carried as much weight in government as they should, and second, the commercial sector has lob-byists. Sportfishing tends to be small-scale, independently owned, not cor-porate. We don't have lobbyists in Mexico City. They do and always have. Their profits are far greater, their damage far more, and the benefits accrue to fewer people."

I look at Minerva and see a combination of fatigue and anger, sadness and stubbornness, in her eyes.

"I used to have old film footage of turtles in the Baja," she says to me. "I'm not talking nestlings hatching. I'm talking full-grown turtles, so many that they look like a black cloud coming onto the beach. And I have pictures of my father-in-law catching totoaba in the sixties—beautiful two-hundred-pound, five-foot-long fish that used to make migrations in huge schools up into the northern Cortez. The schools are gone. My husband has never caught a totoaba. How must that feel?"

Remembering the case of the striped bass in New England, I say to her, "But I can tell you how it feels to see them come back. The striped bass were gone from New England for years, and I never caught one until the early nineties. I was anchored a hundred feet outside the mouth of an estu-ary as the tide flowed out, and I saw this silver thing shoot a hundred feet underwater and smash my lure. I thought it was a bluefish. I brought it up and could not believe what I had in my hands: a striped bass about twenty inches long."

"Yes," she says. "And that is why you have to fight for it. For that day."

⌁⌁⌁⌁⌁

Guillermo Alvarez is a Mexican scientist from La Paz who works for the Mexican Billfish Foundation* and is a veteran of the fish-resource wars in Greater Los Cabos and the Sea of Cortez. I talk with Alvarez on the phone at his house in La Paz, where he says, "The thing you must understand is that Shark Norma is a backlash by the commercial interests against the original Ley de Pesca, the Mexican fisheries law that set aside the Sea of Cortez and the fifty-mile protection zone. In order to create the protection zone, forty-eight commercial longline licenses, which had permitted longlining in the areas now under protection, were canceled. The law says certain fish are to be reserved for sportfishing, and this is for good economic and ecological reasons. Economically, they are the foundation of very robust sportfishing and tourism industries worth billions. Ecologically, these species are critical to maintaining the balance of the ecosystems in these areas.

"But the real issue with Norma is not the big commercial boats," he continues. "The problem is the pangas, the small boats. With or without Shark Norma permits, they are wiping out the protected species. The small panga fishermen are called *ribereños*. It means traditional fishers, or artisanal fishermen, as you say in English."

I take a moment to let all this sink in, then ask, "If they're just local guys fishing in small boats, why is this a problem? Aren't they entitled to eat?"

"The law allows for subsistence fishing, yes, but once you are taking more fish than you and your family can use and you are selling those fish, you are fishing commercially. These fishermen are poor, and they stay poor; the fishing does not help them. But they are a threat because they go after the last fish, because of their numbers and how much damage they are doing."

---

*La Fundación para la Conservación de los Picudos.

"The pangas are essentially a commercial fleet," I observe.

"Yes—a huge commercial fleet fishing illegally in full view. Sadly, it is done everywhere. In Todos Santos, La Paz, Cabo San Lucas, San José del Cabo, they do it in secret, but farther south in Mazatlán and Puerto Vallarta, Acapulco, they do it openly. A small panga can still put out many kilometers of line. People do not realize it, but there are lots of fish killed in Cabo San Lucas every day—a lot by pangas, and some by the sportfishing fleet acting as commercial boats. Marlin and dorado are sold if they are taken by a sportfishing boat and the angler gives the fish to the crew."

"Come on," I say. "That's not commercial fishing. That's a gift, a tip."

"Don't be naive," he answers. "What is the difference between a dorado caught illegally from a panga and sold versus the same dorado caught by a gringo angler, given to the crew, and the crew sells it for their own profit? And they do this day in and day out? And especially when the crew sets it up like this?"

I think of Ernesto and how quick he was with the gaff on my first dorado.

Guillermo says, "My point in illustrating this to you is to show that, even within the sportfishing community, there are those who do not respect the law or the spirit of the law, which is to conserve the resource. The disregard for the law is far worse with the commercial longliners and the *ribereños,* and that must not be overlooked. Sportfishing and commercial fishing must not be equated in terms of impact. But in Cabo alone, the sportfishers are responsible for hundreds of metric tons per year of illegal dorado and marlin taken. There is an expression in Spanish— '*El buen juez por su casa empieza,*' or 'The good judge starts at his own home.'"

"So how much are we talking about, in total, for the commercial guys—the big longliners and the *ribereños*?" I ask.

"I am hesitant to quote numbers, because it is so poorly tracked. But the commercial fleets, including the *ribereños,* must be killing ten to twenty times as many marlin and dorado as the sportfishers. At an absolute minimum—it is probably more. You must bear in mind that any solution to these problems must involve both the commercial fishers and the *ribere-ños* and the tourist sector. If all of these are not part of the solution, the destruction will continue. They must be provided with sustainable alternatives for their livelihoods, and they must understand what their own stake is in maintaining the health of the various fisheries."

Then Guillermo changes the subject and adds, as though in a final plea, "The last thing you must understand is that the waters off Los Cabos and in the Sea of Cortez are a central base for striped marlin. They do not move very far from Baja and generally stay within the waters of Los Cabos and the Sea of Cortez. The waters offshore of this area are unlike any in the world. They are among the richest and most diverse on the planet, not just for striped marlin. They must be protected because they are special, and already so much has been lost."

4

The tournament boats begin returning to the API dock later that afternoon, first in a trickle, then in a rush. Cruising between the sportfishers are the enormous shapes of sea lions, whose heavy black heads lift above the water, blowing, as they watch for dorado carcasses. The fishing teams offload and report their figures to the tournament officials, and some, who have come back with dorado they hope will win the day's prize, weigh them and stand on a small platform for pictures with the blotchy, drooling fish and a pretty brunette Corona beer girl. The Italian team from San Benedetto del Tronto are all smiles, with seven marlin tagged and released. Beyond the weigh station there are dozens of umbrella tables and several bars serving free beer and food courtesy of Corona. Van Halen thumps from the speakers as the sun beats mercilessly down.

I order a beer and get into a conversation with the team from Fremantle, Australia, all four of whom are longtime offshore anglers. One of them has fished twenty-eight straight Blue Marlin Classics in Perth. The team captain tells me they've spent about $10,000 each to get here.

"Now multiply that, or something close to it, by every angler you see here," he tells me. "And throw in their wives and girlfriends and family members, too. There's a lot of money flowing because of this tourney, something like $14 million* into Cabo in less than a week."

The captain, like a lot of these fishermen, is aware of the controversy over Shark Norma. "Fifty thousand† marlin caught and released each year by sportfishers, and they pass a law that jeopardizes marlin!" He drinks from his beer and asks me, the disbelief and bewilderment clear in his voice, "Can you imagine this place without marlin?"

By early evening the majority of the sportfishers have moved over to the Finisterra for some R&R before they descend on Cabo to ingest large quantities of seafood and hit the clubs. The sultry offshore wind blows across the hotel's broad beach and the palapas and over the glowing pools. Nearby, fishermen and their female companions float in the luminous turquoise water by the bar. I take a seat at a table next to the largest of the hotel's palapas, talking with two Brazilians from the Cabo Frio team.

"If you were to come to Brazil, you must visit Cabo Frio," says Ricardo. "We have very good fishing for bigeye tuna. Over 100 kilos—220 pounds. My two best are 128 and 148 kilos. You should also meet Flavio. Flavio is the best fisherman on the Rio team and can tell you everything you want to know about fishing in Rio."

Ricardo reaches Flavio on his cell phone as another round of beers arrives, and within five minutes Flavio himself appears out of the darkness: six foot six, with a shock of white hair and massive proportions. He is the mirror image of James Coburn as he appeared in the film *Affliction*—same large teeth, enormous head and hands, and towering stature, but younger and with better hair. His voice is one of those strange permutations of Nature, wherein the acoustics of larynx and chest cavity produce a basso profundo foghorn so naturally loud and penetrating you feel it in your torso.

"So we are talking fish!" he booms, shaking my hand and sitting next to me. He listens as I give him the quick summary of my conversation with his teammates.

---

*The actual figure is between $3 million and $4 million during the tournament, which typically runs over a week's time.

† This is a reasonable estimate for the entire Los Cabos region.

He nods and says in a thoughtful, slow, grumbling voice, "In my time the blue runner has disappeared from Rio—we think because of the purse seiners and longliners—and now they hit the bottom fish. They use two boats for the trawl, and they put a huge net between them. The net size is too small, so of course they kill everything. None of the young fish can escape. South of Brazil they have better enforcement of rules, but in Brazil we are separate states, and each state makes its own rules. The problem is not simply fisheries but politics. Three years ago the politicians sold fishing rights to the Koreans, and they are now fishing for shrimp in Brazilian waters. For every kilo of shrimp they take, they kill many pounds of bycatch. It is very sad."

Flavio's phone suddenly goes off to a tune being sung by one of the Disney chipmunks, and holding it in front of his face like a walkie-talkie he says in Italian, "*Sì siamo fuori dalla piscina. Stiamo per prendere un taxi. Arriviamo fra due o tre minuti, va bene? Sì mangeremo.*"

Then he turns to me and says, "Come, eat with us. We go."

The white shuttle van we crowd into holds fifteen grown men, stuffed on seats and floors like luggage: two of the Italian crews, several Brazilians, and a smattering of others. There is much debate about the location of the restaurant, and we trace a looping course through Cabo until we finally disembark in front of what looks like a cafeteria. Linoleum floors, televisions mounted on the wall, cheap beer-sign mirrors, and long tables and chairs like those you'd see in a school. The menus are stiff plasticized sheets picturing various fish dishes arranged as decorative platters and pinwheels. Flavio, switching between Portuguese, Italian, and Spanish, consults with the various teams and then submits orders. Bottled beers arrive on ice in galvanized buckets, followed by half a dozen bottles of wine.

In the swarm of languages, I pick out some I understand and begin conversing with the Italian opposite me. Sandro is a sportfishing guide, IGFA rep, and record holder from Naples.

"I am very lucky," he tells me. "I have managed to make a living as a guide and have succeeded in getting a sponsor. They have given me a boat, which is of course a fantastic gift. We go after tuna and other species in the Mediterranean."

"By all accounts the bluefin in the Med have been badly overfished. Have you seen this?" I ask.

"Yes. There are less of them, and they are smaller. I know of only one location where they still catch them the traditional way—in the shore cages, the *tonnara*—and that is on the island of Favignana. But they catch very few, and they are also small. In freshwater we catch *trota*—trout—and they are beautiful. One in particular we call 'macrostigmata' because it is marked with bloodred patches on its flesh. Of course, being Italy, everything is religious. Whoever named it was reminded of the stigmata of Christ."

The food arrives—enormous platters with battered jumbo shrimp, lobster tails, scallops, and whole fried sea bass, the flesh of which has been cut in a crisscross pattern.

"Like this," Flavio says to me, and he reaches over and starts taking random handfuls of food and piling them high on his plate. "Just take it. Take what you want. There is plenty of food and if not, we order more. If you have never had this"—and here he indicates the whole sea bass—"you just do like this," and he seizes whole chunks with his fingers, picking them off like grapes and popping them in his mouth, smiling and chewing, and booming, "It is delicious!"

Then, with a sudden percussive blast, he roars something down the table in his slurring, lazy Italian. He does it with an expansive, embracing joviality, and everyone laughs as shouts and rebuttals fly back and forth.

Moments later, the discussion at the far end of the table suddenly turns vigorous. One of the Romans is disgusted at the thought of the seven marlin supposedly caught by the first-place team from San Benedetto.

"Seven marlin—this is impossible!"

Someone says, "Did they not have an observer on board?"

"Of course they did not have an observer. How could they have had an observer and rightfully claim seven marlin?"

"But the second-place team caught six marlin."

"This, too, is impossible!"

"Because you did not catch them?"

Everyone laughs.

Flavio leans over and says, "These guys . . . It is not winning that matters, not for most of them. It is the fishing. We come to fish. I come to fish. I come to learn, always learning. That is how it stays interesting," he says, and pours me more wine.

5

Another of my contacts among scientists and conservationists doing work in the Sea of Cortez is Vince Radice. Radice runs a sportfishing charter outside of Guaymas, a town midway up the Sea of Cortez on the mainland side. Several years ago, he noticed the increasing volume of illegal panga fishing in the area and started documenting it. He began interviewing the *ribereños* catching the dorado and the restaurateurs who served it. He also began secretly filming the illegal offloading of dorado at the docks.

"I'll send you links to the videos I've posted on YouTube* and you can see for yourself," Vince tells me when I reach him. "But here's the short version of what I've found: The local fishermen—the very guys fishing illegally—have seen the number of dorado decline 90 to 95 percent. In Sonora thirteen, fourteen years ago, there were no panga longliners fishing for dorado. Then we had some transient fishermen come up from Chiapas to fish for shark with steel leaders and longlines. They would shoot sea lions and bait their hooks with them and catch a lot of sharks, and soon the Sonorans were following suit. The shark fishery went to hell, and then sardine, shrimp, and sierra and corvina fishing, which have basically stabilized at very low levels with no growth. As far as fisheries go, it's the Wild West down here. Take the shrimp fishery. When the season opens up, the small pangas get the first ten days or so for themselves before they let the big boats go out. Now there are probably three thousand pangas registered to go shrimping, but probably eight thousand or so actually go out after shrimp. A decade ago an effort was made to impose a simple decal registration system for the boats, like in the States. But these guys would just take someone else's registration number and paint it on their pangas and they

---

* "Part 1 Oro de Cortez," http://www.youtube.com/watch?v=4vN_g2-JU_E. "Part 2," http://www.youtube.com/watch?v=ZXp0U8yXsoY&feature=related. "Part 3," http://www.youtube.com/watch?v=0__kyyAXSUU&feature=related.

were good to go. So they've moved through the various fisheries, depleting them, and now they're hammering dorado, among other things."

"Does anyone know how much dorado is caught?"

Vince says, "There was a report done in 2006 by CIBNOR* that was commissioned by the states of Sinaloa and Sonora and by CONAPESCA. Juana López, the lead CIBNOR scientist on the study, told me that about 950 metric tons of dorado are caught illegally per year in the state of Sonora alone. I've hounded them but they've never released the report to the general public. The other thing the study found was that bycatch of sea turtles from this illegal dorado fishing amounted to one turtle for every five dorado caught. These are loggerheads, olive ridleys, greens, and hawksbills—all endangered species. The fishermen hog-tie their flippers and leave them alive in caves on islands outside of Guaymas or in the Cortez until they can find buyers on the black market. I wanted to see how easy it was to buy one, so I worked through a friend of mine who had a contact. We went and met this guy and he led us to a storage room in his house. He opened the door, and there was a *golfina*, an olive ridley, lying there on the floor next to all the usual crap you'd see in a shed. The turtle weighed thirty-six kilos, and we paid 1,750 pesos for it, about 120 bucks. We tried to free it, but it was too exhausted and died the next day. There are thousands caught and killed this way every year."

"So where do the dorado go?" I ask him.

"My best estimate is that about 60 percent of it goes to the States. They offload the fish day and night, load it into semis, and run it up to the border, then across into the southwestern states and California. I followed and filmed one of these runs all the way up to the border at Nogales. They sell it in the States as mahi mahi, or they label the boxes as something different—yellowtail or whatever. But it's still dorado. What people need to know is that for every pound of Mexican dorado served at a U.S. restaurant, there are a few pounds of dead sea turtle attached to it."

I ask the question that has been puzzling me ever since I left Cabo: "So why isn't any of this enforced?"

---

* Centro de Investigaciones Biológicas del Noroeste, or the Northwest Center for Biological Research.

Vince says, "A few years ago, when I started all this, I wondered, is it that CONAPESCA lacks the resources, are they incompetent, or are they corrupt? I started out thinking it was lack of funds, so I got together with some locals and we raised money and paid for gas, a boat, and wages for a few inspectors' time. We started patrolling and in the first week alone busted two shrimpers carrying four tonnes of dorado. I thought, *Shit, we're in business!* But over time, as the program progressed, we realized that CONAPESCA itself is compromised in its ability and in its interest in enforcing the law. Some of it is lack of will, but some of it is politics and corruption, bribes and kickbacks. The current guy in charge of enforcement is Ramón Corral, who has quickly earned a nickname: El Asesino del Mar de Cortés—the Murderer of the Sea of Cortez.

"The bottom line is that Shark Norma doesn't matter, and the permits don't matter, and the Ley de Pesca doesn't matter. None of it matters because there is no enforcement whatsoever, and there is no will to enforce. The reality is a lot of people think dorado should be fished, that it should be commercialized, so they just break the law and send in the kickbacks, or they do it and get caught and get a court-ordered injunction permitting them an exclusion, and that's how it goes. Most of the local inspectors are honest; it's the bigwigs who keep the cash. The other thing to realize about this entire trade is that the small-scale fisherman, out there in his little panga with no life jacket, no radio, no GPS, an old crappy motor, rusted hooks—this guy who risks his life every day, he doesn't get shit. Because it's illegal, he has to move his catch through so-called phantom cooperatives—*las cooperativas fantasmas*—groups that pay for a permit from CONAPESCA to buy and sell fish. In a lot of cases these *cooperativas* don't even own any boats and are fronts for the people who control the trade, which are called the fish mafia.

"The Mexican government made the Ley de Pesca law for solid economic and ecological reasons. The problem is, without enforcement, none of it means anything. It's a free-for-all, and you have a lot of fish getting killed. They're fishing for dorado now because all the other stuff they used to fish for—sharks, totoaba, tuna, shrimp, manta rays, callo de hacha scallops, and myriad other species—have all been overfished. If it keeps going the way it is, there will be very little left in the Sea of Cortez. It's as simple as that. And the *ribereños* will be as poor as ever."

6

Before dawn the following day, I make my way through the quiet streets of Cabo to the marina, through the strange waiting quality of the atmosphere hanging in the stillness of things, the blank windows of the buildings and the streetlights casting their dim beams over the empty sidewalks. One of the many pleasures of being up before dawn on your way to a daylong offshore charter is that you get to feel this everlasting sentinel presence over the world.

I see the charters in their slips behind the Bahia Hotel and hear the throaty diesels of the sportfishers, the gnash of transmission gears shifting. Other sounds and smells greet me as I approach the dock: the scuff of rubber-soled sneakers on pavement, muffled Spanish conversation, laughter, the acrid smell of diesel exhaust, and the fading, warm fragrance of the night. I look for Oscar with his clipboard.

"Another day of fishing, *señor*?" he asks.

"Good morning, Oscar. Is Ernesto with me?"

"He worked well for you, yes? Customers like him."

"He's a good companion and he knows what he's doing."

I sign in and walk down the gangway to the floating dock below, where I find the *Adriana* in her berth.

"*Buenos días, capitán,*" I say to Enrique, who is already seated on the flybridge smoking a cigarette. He smiles and gives me a nod. "Ernesto, *cómo estás, amigo?*"

"I am fine!" he says, smiling as he drops two trolling rods into their holders. "We get more marlin today!" he says hopefully.

Enrique maneuvers the boat out of its slip and across the marina to the dockmaster, who verifies our license, and we move on to the baitmen in their pangas, from whom we buy half a dozen baits. It is a new fish today, palometa, with the curved forehead of the jack family and long, tapered dorsal and ventral fins that flare off like thin ribbons, giving it the appearance of an oblong, flattened, hand-size version of *Sputnik*.

Twenty minutes later we have crossed Medano Bay with Land's End shrinking behind us in the distance. The sun cuts like an acetylene torch from under the horizon into the thin blue metal of the sky. We head northeast toward Gorda Banks as marlin leap and shiver out of the sea three hundred yards to starboard. They shoot out at forty-five-degree angles into the golden air, gleaming long and fast like Exocet missiles, but after fifteen feet they fall back into the sea as though their engines had died. Ernesto puts out the trolling spread and in short order we get a good, hard hit on the middle bait. I'm hot on the rod, but there is nothing on the other end, and I reel it in to find only the head of the palometa, nipped off behind the gills.

"I think it is our yellow friend," I say.

"*Sí*. Dorado," says Ernesto.

We lay the spread out again and wait. Within minutes one of the other lines suddenly pays out at a steady pace, and I bring in a small female dorado. She lacks the blunt forehead of the males, and her undersize mouth, low on her face, is more proportionate to her head. She is a prettier fish, certainly, and lacks the male's appearance of demonic possession. We unhook her and watch her flit into the darkness, then set our lines out again as we resume our northeasterly heading. The humidity thickens over the next hour as we approach the banks, and the sky is floating a high skim of clouds that begins clearing toward midmorning.

In the vicinity of Palmilla, Enrique slows the boat and turns toward shore and an approaching motorized panga. As it comes up alongside us, there are quick exchanges in Spanish, and Enrique asks if I want to buy live sardines.

"For marlin?" I ask, surprised that they will take such a small bait.

"Yes, why not?" he assures me.

We buy two netfuls—about seventy-five—for $10.

The panga pilot tells us that large schools of sardines gathered near the beach before dawn this morning but have moved offshore now. It is a good sign.

We part ways with the panga and within half an hour have joined the tournament fleet—sixty-three boats spread over about six square miles. All the tourney craft are local charters, but there are a number of the bigger, privately owned sportfishers, too—forty, sixty, eighty feet long, some built for hard-core fishing and others with too much gold trim and glitz to be taken entirely seriously. But together the fleet is a lovely sight, dozens of boats trolling in myriad trajectories across the lightly choppy sea, outriggers spread high and trailing graceful tendrils of monofilament that shine in the sun like spider silk. I watch as a pale butter-yellow sportfisher in the fifty-foot range starts backing up on a fish. The boat is 200 yards away and perpendicular to our stern, and in a gorgeous tableau we witness the whole drama of the angler bent and reeling in the chair, spray flying up over him from the chop bashing into the transom, and the faint growl of the engines coming to us over the water. Then a slashing silver movement out of the corner of my eye, 150 yards to the right, and there's the fish, coming toward us at an oblique angle, a beautiful striped marlin ripping out of the water, dorsal fin flattened against its back making it look like a slender, needle-nose greyhound, bounding in lovely slow motion as it skims across the waves, shaking its mane of water, and then down, and then up again. It leaps and shakes and dives a total of seventeen times, in and out of the waves in its glory, bill and head thrust forward, sides tarnished silver in the light, its blue bars humming and its topside rich with that aged bronze color. By the end of it I am brimming with an awesome joy, as satisfied and topped up full as a human can feel before the splendor of Nature.

Now we are seeing lots of marlin, bronze tails and dorsal fins slicing through the waves. They appear anywhere from twenty to a hundred feet away, tantalizingly close, and I check to make sure Ernesto has one of the rods rigged for throwing with a live sardine nipped through the nose with a circle hook.

"You want me to throw, or you?" he asks.

"You show me first, then I'll do it."

The next marlin we see rises off the aft port quarter.

"There," I say, pointing.

Ernesto gauges the distance and heaves the sardine. It is a very good cast, especially considering how light the single sardine is, and it lands five feet in front of the marlin. Ernesto disengages the gear on the reel and waits for the hit. When it does not come, he grunts his disapproval and reels the sardine back in, checks it, and is about to throw again when he sees the marlin is gone. Instantly another one is up on the starboard rail and he jumps to my side of the boat and heaves. Another good shot and we wait a minute for the marlin to hit, but it, too, turns and swims off in the other direction.

The marlin are everywhere now, fins bending through the surface chop as they chase whatever bait is in the water, six and eight fish at a time, their coppery heads and slender rapier bills lifting briefly above the water, jutting between the waves. I am throwing on one rod, Ernesto on the other. My first attempt dies ten feet out—too much thumb pressure on the spool. The second one goes farther but still falls well shy of the thirty-foot shot I need to put it in front of the fish. It'd be much easier with a one- or two-pound caballito, but because the sardine weighs only a few ounces, distance is significantly cut.

Ernesto and I both watch the spectacle. Ernesto exclaims in Spanish to Enrique, and Enrique shouts back, laughing. This is a lot of marlin, even for these guys who are out here every day. We watch the surface, planning our next throw to the fins as they appear, and then the incredible happens: The surface of the water over an area the size of the entire infield of a baseball diamond begins to shiver with life as the top of a giant baitball of sardines breaks the surface fifty feet away. The congregation of these finger-size fish is enormous, and for a moment the water itself seems to swirl circularly in a white, roiling gyre. Then, as though part of a choreographed ballet, thirteen bronze marlin heads emerge, randomly spaced around the periphery, heading in clockwise and counterclockwise directions. They rise up as one, hold, and then gracefully recede.

This is why they're not biting: What are two live sardines compared with hundreds of thousands?

For the next two hours we spot and throw and fail, spot again and throw and wait, laughing and howling in frustration as nothing happens and the marlin dance by under our noses. None hit, and as noon approaches they disappear entirely, and we go back to trolling.

Ernesto assumes a position on the flybridge at a better height for scanning, and I hold my station on the back deck, watching the baits behind the boat. I gaze down at the sardines spinning in the live well and wonder if they have any notion of where they are. Then, as we roll with a wave, one lucky fish is borne up with the slosh and washed back into the sea, and freedom. Alone, either it will sneak by on stealth until it can find a school or it will be easy picking for any one of many predators. This is the fate of baitfish—short lives and sudden death. The great wheel spins rapidly for them, in most cases less than two years. But it is terrible to be alone and so small in the ocean, and I take pity on the lone ranger and free four or five more to give him courage and company. After all, it is better to die fighting with your comrades than to die alone.

In a second, empty well nearby, I find another sardine, used during the marlin frenzy earlier. It lies on its side near the bottom of the trough, with fresh seawater washing over it intermittently from the overflow of the live well pump. I watch it for a moment and see that it is weak from its trials and will not live. I pick it up and notice the clean hole in its nose from the circle hook, and that its scales are rubbed off along its sides. Quickly I whack it against the transom and hold it in my hand as the last quivers of life leave it, and I'm struck by the wave of sadness I feel as it dies. This morning in the darkness before sunrise this creature swam with the multitudes against the shore at Palmilla, and then the hand of fate intervened in the form of a net, and it was sold in the harsh midmorning glare and has endured everything that has happened to it since, merely for my pleasure.

Herein lies the conundrum of this pastime: How does the value of the pleasure I derive from fishing square with the realities of the hook for the creatures that feel its bite?

To be human in the world means that we, by the very act of our living, impose our will upon others, which can destroy, kill, wound, displace, and in a thousand other ways subjugate the innocent life-forms of this planet. If we are to accept that all life is precious because it is life, then we must also acknowledge the truth that living exacts a cost that others pay. The act of living, if you are a human being, is an act sustained through the exercise of power, whether you exercise it directly when you crush the wasp that is about to sting your child, or indirectly through your support of the farmer who uses chemical pesticides to grow the ear of corn you buy.

The relevant questions here concern necessity, scale, and impact. Is recreational fishing necessary? Would it be more permissible for me to prick the hook through the nose of the sardine if I were starving and needed it to catch a bigger fish? Does the fact that fishing feeds not my body but my soul diminish or increase its necessity? And at what point does greed become a factor?

Greed is inextricable from scale. If I take one sardine from an enormous bait ball, it can hardly be considered greed, but what if I were to take the entire bait ball? Do the lives of half a million sardines change the equation, or is it changed only when we consider that the marlin would consequently be left hungry? To what degree do the concerns of marlin matter?

The real difficulty of the question relates to impact, which has two aspects: cruelty and balance. To weigh cruelty, especially in fishing, you must ask yourself: Do fish feel pain? Or fear? Do they suffer? For a sardine, is a hook through the nose the equivalent of a knitting needle shoved into the sinuses, or in truth is it little more than the prick of an ear piercing, or is it nothing at all? Rather than pain or fear in the terms we know them, do they feel only pressure and urgency? Do they have the neurological complexity to feel pain and to suffer, and how do these considerations bear on the fact that using them as bait is likely to result in death?

Where pain in fish is concerned, science is only recently beginning to look closely at the location and prevalence of nociceptors—nerve endings that send pain signals—in various locations on fishes' bodies. Scientists are also looking at the brains of fish and have found considerable variation across species, suggesting that some fish may be disposed to have more complex pain experiences. The cognitive capacity of a fish will influence how the pain is experienced. While some fish have limited cognition skills, others are capable of more sophisticated responses. These tend to be fish that are higher on the food chain and live in more complex environments, including reefs, and the ones that tend to have more sophisticated social interactions (not schooling, but defending territory, etc.). Fish have shown themselves to be capable of various types of cognition—for example, creating spatial representations of their terrain. Some are even capable of interspecies cooperative hunting behavior, as in the case of groupers and moray eels. The grouper will approach the den of moray eel in a reef and vigorously shake its head, at which point the moray will emerge and follow the grouper. The grouper seeks out the eel's assistance in pursuing prey in a section of the reef it cannot enter because of its size. In about half the cases, the eel gets the prey; in the other half, the grouper gets it.

Fish at the top of the food chain have among the most sophisticated brains of all fishes because of the complexity of hunting and pursuing prey. In many fish, there are large numbers of nociceptors around the head, eyes, mouth, and face, followed by certain parts of the body, like the fins. It is very unlikely that the bony face and mouth portions of a tuna, for example, have many nociceptors; it is more likely to be sensitive in the mouth, around the eyes, and along the flanks.

It is important to be careful about how we talk about pain in fish, because it is easy to associate our own experiences with pain—which often include the psychological experience of suffering in the form of foreboding, fear, anxiety, etc.—with the pain that fish experience. Much still needs to be understood, but it is clear that some level of pain can be felt by certain species.

Another point to consider in weighing the impact of our actions in fishing is the perspective that our intervention does little more than Nature does when left to its own devices: The marlin still get fed, and the circle of life remains complete, and the role played by the sardine is merely hastened to its conclusion by the intervention of the person in the boat. This was Hemingway's view, but Hemingway did not live in the world we live in, where ecological balance is a genuine concern. In that light you must ask yourself whether what you are doing will contribute meaningfully to the creation of imbalance. What is the health of the population of sardines in the Sea of Cortez, and will my killing one, or a dozen, have an impact on the balance of Nature?

In the case of sardines, it won't. But what if I am one of a hundred thousand anglers, each taking a dozen sardines? Given the great fecundity of sardines, even those 1.2 million are unlikely to matter. But what if it's not a sardine I take, but a fish whose reproduction is slow and whose breeding population is at only 5 or 10 percent of what the best science believes is enough to sustain the species? And what if that breeding population represents, say, only twenty thousand fish left in the world? Do you take one?

Some of these questions cannot be answered for lack of knowledge, for lack of science, or for reasons of practicality. Some are not within the power of those of us who are nonscientists to stay constantly informed about. But it seems that impact is the key element in judging the appropriateness of one's actions, and you owe it to yourself to know the repercussions of what you're doing. If you're keeping a fish you've caught, you should be aware of what science and conservation have to say about the health of that species. An angler, if he or she is worth anything, takes great care and limits his or her impact as much as possible, going so far as to abstain from fishing for species (like bluefin tuna) when doing so has the potential to contribute to the further imbalance of an already precarious state. This should apply to commercial and sportfishers alike, and it seems like the least we can do to tread lightly on the sea.

7

By now I understand that the problem with the conservation of marine resources around Baja and the Cortez is clearly rooted in corruption, lack of enforcement, and widespread illegal fishing, mostly by intensive, small-scale fishing operations but also by significant large-ship illegal longlining and the suspect sportfishing catches. A fourth element comes into play that adds to the challenges Mexico faces in preserving the Sea of Cortez.

Dr. Wallace "J." Nichols is a research associate at the California Academy of Sciences and a cofounder of Ocean Revolution, a program that engages new leaders in conservation and ecological activism. J. has been involved in the Baja Peninsula for over twenty years, specializing in sea turtle research, during which time he has developed relationships with commercial and sportfishermen, poachers, *ribereños,* environmental enforcement officers, politicians, and community members in the coastal towns rimming Baja and the Sea of Cortez. The element he adds to the overall picture is the drug trade.

"The quickest, safest way to traffic drugs is over water," J. explains by phone from the States. "Given its geography, the Sea of Cortez is a perfect narco-trafficking route. It brings you pretty much to the doorstep of your biggest customer. So when you start pulling the strings of all these conservation problems in Mexico, the web starts to unravel and you see that some of those strings are connected to the narco industry. Some fishermen and some corrupt officials are involved in both illegal fishing and the drug trade, and one infects the other. One way drug money gets laundered is through funding coastal development, smoothing the way or bypassing altogether the process of environmental review. You'll get these hotels going up along the coast where the rumor in town is that it's drug money paying for the construction.

"The other way the drug trade infects the communities," he continues, "is through the fishermen. Drug runners aren't just born; they get there through a series of steps. A fisherman who is good at moving illegal lobster or abalone or sea turtles might be approached to run something a little more illegal, a little more dangerous, but for more money. A lot of times the actual drugs are used as payment, so you get fishermen becoming addicts and selling the drugs cheaply at the local level, which increases the prevalence of addiction in the community. On top of that, you get families and small businesses having to pay protection money to the narco-traffickers. So you can imagine how difficult it is to talk to a community of fishermen about the economic and environmental value of setting up a protected area nearby when 70 percent of the audience are drug addicted and tied into the very systems that undermine protection. It's so pervasive in some areas, it's hard to imagine environmental resource solutions that don't somehow have to work around or accommodate the traffickers. Some communities are able to largely resist the threat of being involved in the trade. Punta Abreojos, on the Pacific coast of Baja, is one. These places tend to have good fisheries, women involved in leadership, good baseball teams, strong families, a high regard for education—all of which help the community stay resistant."

After making the connections to what I'd already learned about the situation, I ask, "What about higher up? What kind of influence does the narco trade have there?"

"Higher up you have the desk officer working for the government who wants to put some enforcement on the water to make sure an area is safe for, say, vaquita* at the northern end of the Cortez. It also turns out your vaquita area is one of the most intensive drug-trafficking areas in the world. You have people in the United States willing to fund millions of dollars' worth of conservation efforts to make sure vaquita don't go extinct, and you have that Mexican desk officer saying, 'How do I work with the funders to save these animals and also make sure my real boss, the narco industry, is not inconvenienced?'

"One of the hardest things I've found," J. offers, "regardless of the drug influence, is that among the poor who have very little to lose, conservation offers almost nothing in real gains. Not because conservation won't work but because their expectation in life, generally, is that if you build something and it works well, someone else will take it, whether it be the government or an outside force or some authority that's more powerful than you."

"I suppose that's one of the legacies of corruption," I suggest.

"Yes, and when it's as pervasive as it is in Mexico, it's as though the whole system is brilliantly designed to ensure the destruction of natural resources. Corruption flows through all the cracks of the system and undermines conservation solutions. And yet," he adds, offering a ray of hope, "it is not impossible. Conservation efforts in Mexico have contributed to an uptick in the number of sea turtles we're starting to see on the beaches of Baja. Given the reproductive capacity of some of these species, like marlin and dorado, if you can control the trade, you can bring the fish back. People go to the Cortez today and are amazed. It is still a magical place, and you can spend a week there and it will be the best week of your life. But you will not be aware that what you are looking at, as incredible as it is, is an illusion of untouched wilderness. It is barren of life compared to what was there only thirty years ago."

"*Can* it be brought back?" I ask, encouraged by the data on turtles.

As a veteran of these struggles, J. is understandably slow in answering, but finally he acknowledges, "Yes, it can be, but it will take political will.

---

*Vaquita is a rare species of porpoise found only in the northern Sea of Cortez. Only a few hundred individuals are thought to survive. Dozens die each year as bycatch in gill nets.

It will take real leadership to enforce the law. Basically, it will take a lot of courage."

There are indeed signs of hope for Baja and the Sea of Cortez. Vince Radice told me about a long-standing American law, the Lacey Act, that if enforced could stop the importation of illegal dorado, marlin, and other species into the United States. The Lacey Act outlaws the international and interstate trafficking of illegally obtained wildlife, plants, and fish. It specifically states that "it is unlawful for any person . . . to import, export, transport, sell, receive, acquire, or purchase in interstate or foreign commerce . . . any fish or wildlife taken, possessed, transported, or sold in violation of any law or regulation of any State *or in violation of any foreign law*" (emphasis mine).

The Lacey Act falls under the jurisdiction of the U.S. Department of Commerce and the National Oceanic and Atmospheric Administration (NOAA). NOAA typically will not enforce the foreign clause of the Lacey Act without the request of the nation in which the violations are occurring, but if Mexico did make such a request or if NOAA determined it was appropriate to enforce the act for other reasons (such as the involvement of a protected species or the existence of a detriment to the environment), the market for dorado and marlin from the Sea of Cortez would evaporate overnight. In a positive move in this direction, Mexican senator Luis Coppola proposed a regulation on October 13, 2009, that would make it illegal to sell any of the incidental bycatch.* This would remove any doubt about whether it is illegal to sell dorado in Mexico, and the Lacey Act could be enforced.

Progress is also being made on the conservation front. For a number of years, sportfishers themselves have increasingly taken on the role of de facto informants of illegal activity. On July 27, 2006, a Mexican naval cruiser, tipped off by recreational sportfishers, intercepted the *Salada I*, a trawler working with two pangas setting longlines for dorado in the southern Sea of Cortez. The Guaymas-based *Salada I* had permits only for squid

---

* This regulation is still under consideration in the Mexican legislature.

but had seven metric tons of dorado in its hold. The captain and five crew members were prosecuted.

In June 2007, sportfishing boats of the Pisces fleet from Cabo San Lucas alerted the Mexican navy to the activities of an eighty-foot converted shrimp vessel, *Jesus Omar "El Concho,"* from Mazatlán, fishing fifteen miles off Bahia Chileno. The vessel was fishing with a forged shark permit and carrying close to two miles of drift gill nets. It was found to have three sharks and three marlin in the hold. Later that month, the seventy-foot *Tele,* out of Puerto Peñasco, Sonora, was seized. It was fishing drift gill nets of greater than one thousand meters, in violation of the law. In the hold were eighty-eight sharks, forty-three marlin, and an estimated twenty giant manta rays.

In early September 2008, two boats seized in Magdalena Bay were found to be carrying fourteen metric tons of dorado and several tons of sharks. The boats were owned by Henry Collard, the king of Mexican longlining and president of the Mexican commercial fishing union.* According to Seawatch, the U.S.-based Billfish Foundation, and *El Sudcaliforniano* newspaper in La Paz, Collard howled at CONAPESCA enforcement agents that he was "a personal friend of Ramón Corral, and you can't do this to me!" Senior officials in Mexico City called the CONAPESCA agents, forcing them to withdraw, and the bust was made by inspectors from FONMAR,† the Fund for the Protection of Marine Resources, established in 2004 by the Billfish Foundation and its Mexican partners. FONMAR is funded by sportfishing licenses paid by anglers anywhere in the state of Baja California Sur and, along with the Center for Marine Protection, in La Paz, works to improve fisheries science and enforcement in Baja and the Sea of Cortez. FONMAR's concept is sound and still holds promise, but recent criticism of high administrative costs and ineffective or inappropriate use of its funds has marred its reputation and blunted its impact.

Perhaps most encouraging of all, however, is a development that began in the summer of 2009, in which Mexican communities began taking

---

*Cámara Nacional de la Industria Pesquera.
† Fondo para la Protección de los Recursos Marinos.

matters into their own hands. On June 1, a group of lifelong fishermen from Loreto officially formed a union to protect their waters, especially the Loreto Marine Park, where over a dozen years of pillaging by hookah divers and *pistolero* (speargun) fishermen had removed an estimated 90 percent of fish from one of the world's most magnificent reefs. A month later, a similar group was formed in La Paz, and within weeks these two organizations had busted dozens of illegal fishing boats. Both formal and informal local fishermen's watch groups—*pescadores vigilantes*—have begun to crop up all over the Sea of Cortez and report illegal fishing activity to the authorities, then hold them accountable by publicizing the outcomes of lawsuits and arrests. As of November 2011, there are *pescadores vigilantes* groups from Todos Santos on the Pacific coast, all the way around the tip of Baja to Loreto.

8

At the IGFA closing ceremonies the final night of the tournament, I sit at a table far back from the main stage erected near the pools and palapas of the Finisterra. In the cool, windy evening air I watch as the championship trophy goes to the team from Islamorada, Florida, who won by a hair on the last day with one marlin released and a twenty-five-pound dorado brought in for the weight score. Speeches are made and other awards given, including one to Minerva, who is recognized for her substantial contribution to sportfish conservation in Los Cabos.

After dinner, I leave the ceremonies and walk across the broad, flat expanse of coarse sand behind the Finisterra to the ocean. The size of the berm and the long, steep slope of the beach speak to the power of the tides and currents here and to the depth of the waters that have broken upon this place for an eternity. I head southeast toward the hunched shoulder of the first of the formations at Land's End, and looking up, I realize I have seen this beach profile and this particular rock formation before: It is the same shot framed in Zane Grey's *Tales of Fishing Virgin Seas,* Plate XCII, "The Beach at Cape San Lucas," taken eighty-four years earlier.

Fading sunlight falls on the formation, which remains untouched since humans first walked here. I am aware that in the eighty-four years since

Zane Grey passed through on his white schooner and fished these virgin seas, human beings have shorn this paradise of the one thing that made it unique in all the world: its special, and lonely, wilderness. Cabo and the Sea of Cortez are not completely lost—not yet—but they are already too perfect an example of how much the grinding mill of human industry churns ceaselessly through the oceans of the world, spewing its oily bone-and-pulp slurry of sea life, in a process largely ungoverned, unregulated, unenforced, unrecorded, and beyond the purview of most people. I understand in new ways the battle that the likes of Minerva find themselves struggling with every day. Cabo is still remarkable, but less so, and the trouble I see growing in the shadows at Land's End is a disturbance that will not be easily quelled.

Scientists estimate that in the next ten to twenty years, the fate of the Sea of Cortez—and of all the oceans—will be decided. Will we be able to preserve them in some semblance of their natural state, or will we have altered them permanently, for all time?

Have we already?

The Harpooner's Last Stand

The Northeast Peak of Georges Bank

Was he the only fisherman left in the world
using the old ways, who believed his work was prayer,
who caught only enough, since the sea had to live,
because it was life?

—Derek Walcott

1

It is nine in the morning and we are a hundred miles at sea, directly
south of the southernmost tip of Nova Scotia, 225 miles due east of the
elbow of Cape Cod. After a breakfast of eggs, bacon, potatoes, bread slath-
ered with margarine, tea, and instant coffee, we layer ourselves against the
chill and come up topside. The wind in our faces is heavy with moisture
but there is as yet no fog, and the sky overhead has the appearance of dirty
gray wool. I am fishing with the crew of the harpoon boat *Brittany &*
Brothers, out of Cape Sable Island, Nova Scotia. The harpoon stand, suspended like an aluminum drawbridge, runs eighteen feet out from the bow
and plunges down into the troughs, then swings up fifteen or twenty feet
in the air as we climb the next wave. The swells are between six and eight
feet, the wind moderate at twelve knots. I take a spot on the foredeck,
leaning against the welded ladder running up the spotting tower. As the
whole ship rocks, the tower swings violently back and forth like the bar on
a metronome. Fifteen feet up the tower is the steering station, and fifteen
feet above that is the high spotting post. Saul Newell, the captain, is up
there getting his ass kicked. Dwaine d'Eon, the harpooner, and Saul's
father, Gabby Newell, are in the steering station. We are looking for the
crescent-shaped fins of the broadbill swordfish.

If there is one fish among all the great pelagics* possessed of an aura of myth, it is the broadbill. In weight broadbills tend to run smaller† than the great marlin, but in pure strength and raw, sustained power, they have absolutely no equal among the bony fishes. They will dive and hunt at depths of greater than three thousand feet, slashing through darting masses of squid and serpentine lancet fish, then turning back into the carnage to devour their bisected victims. Afterward they will rise over half a mile to the surface to bask in the comparatively warm water and dim sunlight of this lonely sweep of the North Atlantic. And it is then that the swordfish reveals itself: two dark, rounded fins above the steel-gray waves.

The broadbill is armed with a long, heavy bone sword, sharp on the edges, tapered to a point, and up to one-third its body length. It uses this weapon for hunting and for defense against its chief predator, the mako shark. Swordfish are among the fastest of fish, but it is their dauntless power, their abyssal solitude, and their warrior heart that makes them unique. Tales of marlin or tuna attacking boats are all but unheard of, but accounts from historians, early explorers, and the old dory harpooners repeatedly cite instances of swordfish running their swords clean through the thin lapstrake shells of wooden skiffs and the thick oak hulls of colonial sailing ships. Of all the great pelagics, only the swordfish has the brio, the pugnacity, the courage, and the brawling disposition to earn the nickname given to it: the gladiator.

We are bucking these seas over an area called the Northeast Peak of Georges Bank, six hundred feet above a gravel-and-rock sea bottom of gentle hills and flats, dotted (where it has not been scraped lifeless by draggers) with bright-pink, orange, and red fan corals and populated with skates, cod, haddock, scallops, and other bottom species. A few miles behind us lies the edge of a thirty-mile-wide U-shaped trough known as the Northeast Channel of the Gulf of Maine. We are headed over the peak to the edge of the continent itself.

I imagine that we are sailing toward cliffs like those at the edge of the

---

*The word *pelagic* means having to do with the open ocean, the offshore realm.
† The world record for a swordfish caught on rod and reel is 1,182 pounds, caught off Iquique, Chile, on May 7, 1953, by Louis Marron. I have spoken with commercial and sportfishermen who claim to have seen swordfish in the 1,500-to-2,000-pound range.

Grand Canyon, and this is not far from the truth. The edge of the continental shelf is fissured with steep canyons that cut back into the plateaus of the banks and plunge three thousand feet in the space of a quarter-mile. We are headed for a specific area that our navigation software reveals to be an enormous plunging amphitheater, its steep walls and slopes falling into frigid, yawning blackness. For the next week we will occupy a twenty-mile-by-twenty-mile box over this chasm, spending most of our time scanning the waves.

It might seem like a strategy unlikely to pay off. But overhead, Saul calls out in the wind, "Swordfish, two o'clock. You see him, Dwaine?"

"Yuh. I got him." The metal gate in the steering station rattles open, and Dwaine drops down the ladder.

Gabby throttles back the engine and the boat slows. The fins are visible now, two rounded crescents about eighty feet ahead of us. The fish disappears in the swell, then appears again as the wave passes. Dwaine unties the harpoon from where it's lashed at the end of the stand and swings it around to his right side.

"Where is it?" he yells, leaning forward and scanning.

"Right in front of you, fifty feet, starboard side," I shout.

It looks like a small fish, the fins maybe two, three feet apart. We keep coming on it, so slow it feels as if the swells are pushing us back. Twenty feet now, and Dwaine poises. Ten feet, and now for the first time in my life I am seeing a broadbill swordfish tip to tail. It is not as small as it seemed from a distance: its dorsal and tail fins are four to five feet apart, with the sword extending another three feet forward. Its topside is a luminous, unforgettable lavender. It has a strange, wide caudal keel like two stiff squid wings just forward of its tail, and all the way up front a strange, birdlike head and that prodigious sword.

I hardly get a look before Dwaine's over it and leaning to plant the harpoon. In that instant the fish senses him and bends in an arc—not even quickly; it just bends, and the harpoon misses. Then, with a sudden, massive pump of its tail, the swordfish turns, dives, and is gone. Dwaine lets out a roar of frustration.

"Aw, hell! He was right there, for God's sake!" He hasn't shot a harpoon in three years and he's rusty. He lashes the harpoon back on the stand, muttering to himself.

Dwaine's about six feet tall and burly, with biceps that have pumped their fair share of iron. His face has a heavy, rounded jaw with a thick mustache and goatee. His slightly hound-dog eyes give him a relaxed, easygoing expression, which matches perfectly his deep voice and patient cadences, all the consonants softened by his gentle Acadian accent. Dwaine is from Pubnico, one of the French Acadian bastions in southern Nova Scotia. He is thirty years old and has been fishing since he was eighteen. He has fished longliners, bottom draggers, slime eels, and more, and in the winter he fishes lobster.

He finishes fastening the harpoon and walks back from the stand, holding the rails on either side. Giving me a look of pure bafflement, he gazes back at the water and shakes his head, then climbs back up the tower.

Many fishermen would rather not harpoon. The demands it places on accuracy and nerves simply make for too much pressure. The day before we left the wharf, Saul took me over to West Pubnico to meet Franklyn d'Entremont, one of Nova Scotia's legendary harpooners. We sat in his living room watching a documentary of harpoon swordfishing that featured Franklyn sticking swordfish on his last day at sea, in 2006. In the footage, he looked as calm as if he were planting a flag in a golf hole from a boom truck. Franklyn fished for over forty-five years, and his best showing was 60 swordfish harpooned in a single day. Given a typical nine-hour day, that works out to be a swordfish about every nine minutes. His best percentage over a longer period was 93 percent: 107 swords spotted, 100 struck.

"Oh, I don't know why guys get excited," he said in his soft francophone patois. "You keep your eyes on the dorsal and drop the pole right onto it. The weight of the pole drives the dart in. Around that dorsal there's so much heavy cordage, that dart will never come out. Of course, a lot of guys make the mistake of looking at the whole fish. They start thinking, *Oh, God, that's a big fish,* and their heart starts goin' and their knees get shaky and suddenly they can't shoot. And the worst thing you can do is look at that eye. For God's sake, don't look at the eye! It'll mesmerize you. You've never seen anythin' like it. It's got a big eye, that fish. If that swordfish looks up at you, you might as well just wave at it, because if it sees you, it's gone."

He left the room and returned with a harpoon mock-up he uses to give demonstrations to schoolkids. The pole section was about four feet long (on an actual harpoon it would be closer to twelve feet long) and made of hollow aluminum with a tapered brass fitting on the end, into which was screwed a foot-and-a-half-long, quarter-inch-thick steel rod. The harpoon dart has a notch that fits onto the tip of this rod. The dart itself looks like an arrowhead on one end and half a bow tie on the other, with a hole through the middle where the harpoon line attaches. The bow-tie end of the dart is slightly canted so that when it penetrates the fish, the tension on the line forces the broad bow-tie end sideways, anchoring the dart in the fish.

Once the dart anchors in the fish, it detaches from the rod and the fish runs with the harpoon line trailing it. About fifty feet back on the line is a fifteen-pound weight; this is thrown over once the fish takes off. The purpose of the weight is deception: The fish, feeling the downward pull, perceives the weight to be its tormentor and chases it into the depths. Trailing behind the weight is the remainder of the harpoon rig: six hundred feet of half-inch nylon line that ends in a series of beach-ball-size floats and finally a tall wooden pole on a buoy. This is the high-flier, with an aluminum radar reflector on top. The boat's radar pings off the reflector so the fish can be located an hour or two after it's been stuck. The weight, the floats, and the line drag on the fish, tiring and finally killing it.

"Now you see a lot of guys using stainless steel darts," Franklyn said, "but they're too hard, too sharp. You can drive them through bone. The better dart is the New Bedford dart, made of bronze. The bronze is soft. It'll give a little and won't tear the hell outta the fish."

"How did you start harpooning?" I asked.

"Oh, I always knew I would. I went to sea when I was twelve. As boys we'd stick a nail or a straightened hook on the end of a piece of wooden lath and we'd practice for hours, day after day, hittin' small targets. That was life. We lived off the sea. No one was rich, but everyone lived. In the spring the glass eels would come in and then the small fish—the sand lance and capelin. They would come and then the herring and pollock and cod would follow. And then it would be time to go swordfishin'."

Those days were not that long ago: Franklyn was in the prime of his years at sea when I was a boy myself. I thought of all those years he had spent out in the North Atlantic, and then I posed a question that I hesitated to ask.

"What did you think about when you were over a swordfish about to harpoon it?"

Franklyn paused, then said, "I would think to myself, *Look what the supreme power did. Look at what it made.*"

Out on the foredeck of the *Brittany & Brothers,* I scan the water for fins, with that image of Franklyn in my mind: out on the stand with the harpoon raised by his right ear, suspended in that moment throughout his four and a half decades on the water. The sentiment he shared is one that should underlie all such acts: respect and awe for the strange miracles of creation, along with gratitude for what killing that single animal means: bread on the table, a roof over one's head, clothes for one's children. Looking back through the tide of industrialization that swept through fisheries in the last half of the twentieth century—which included the development of improved diesel engines, powerful winches and hydraulic systems, fish-finding sonar, and gigantic steel ships containing entire processing factories—it seems inevitable that even this ultimate fact of Nature's supremacy would be overturned by the dark magic of our technical cunning, and our even darker ignorance. We are a species that shoots first and asks questions later, if we ask them at all. We use new tools without first considering what effects they might have, and whether those effects are ultimately to our benefit, much less the benefit or detriment of other creatures.

In his decades on the water, Franklyn no doubt took thousands of swordfish, but there is a saying among harpooners: "One man. One fish. One arrow." It is this ethic that makes them proud and persistent in the practice of their craft despite its difficulty and its slim margin for profit. Harpooning is as clean, "green," and sustainable a fishery as you can get. The only waste occurs in those instances when the swordfish is mortally wounded but is not successfully brought aboard, because it has either pulled off the dart or fallen to a predator. Occasionally an undersize fish is taken—one below 110 pounds, roughly the weight at which they can breed—but these instances are rare.

I look out over the endless expanse around us, where half a dozen other harpoon vessels are spread out, low clouds cruising fast overhead, wave crests rolling and shivering in the wind. I try but fail to imagine all that

Franklyn and his forebears must have seen in their years out here. A hundred years ago, along the coastal communities of the Nova Scotia peninsula and Cape Breton, to the north, all the way down past Cape Sable and Yarmouth, down the coast of Maine to Cape Cod, Martha's Vineyard, and Block Island, and as far south as Long Island, swordfish were abundant in the summer months and could occasionally be harpooned or netted within sight of land. Just over a hundred years ago, ten miles offshore of the very location where I grew up spending summers on the coast of Maine were the best swordfish-hunting grounds in New England. You could sail out five or ten miles and be in the midst of dozens of swordfish, with an average weight of three hundred pounds or better.

A number of factors conspired to change that. In the 1950s, Canadian subsidies modernized the small, coastal wooden ship fleets, enabling more and more men to fish all the way to the continental shelf, where swordfish concentrate. In 1956, Japan started longlining for tuna in the North Atlantic, followed by the Norwegians targeting porbeagle shark. Word soon spread that these crews were catching a lot of swordfish in addition to their intended targets. By 1963 hundreds of Canadian boats had converted to longlining, using lines that ran anywhere from ten to thirty miles long, with fifteen hundred to five thousand hooks in a single set. In the 1962–63 season, swordfish landings more than tripled from the previous year (1961–62), from 2,092 metric tons to 7,482 metric tons. From that point on, the Canadian landings began falling, and they have never returned to the same level, despite increases in effort* and major improvements in technology and gear. Today the swordfish allocation† for the entire Canadian fishery in the North Atlantic is 1,400 metric tons. The harpooners get only 10 percent of that figure, or 140 metric tons. When measured in the context of total swordfish allocation for all participating countries in the Atlantic, the harpooners are granted a paltry 1 percent of the total.

When you go from harpooning to longlining, you go from a selective, sustainable method of fishing to a nonselective, unsustainable one. Despite

---

    * Fishing "effort" is the amount of fishing taking place over time, usually described in terms of gear type and duration of time in which the gear is in use.

    † Allocations of stock are determined by the International Commission for the Conservation of Atlantic Tunas, or ICCAT.

real efforts to mitigate the problem of longline bycatch, the fact remains that you can't prevent a wide range of species from being killed, including leatherback sea turtles, the largest on the planet and an endangered species; three-ton pilot whales, also called blackfish; and thousands of bluefin tuna, a species so heavily overfished it is on the brink of commercial extinction in the western North Atlantic and the Mediterranean. In addition to these creatures, however, the largest percentage of bycatch is made up of slowly reproducing pelagic sharks—primarily the porbeagle, blue, and mako.

The other way longlining does harm is by killing across all age groups of the stock being targeted. The early longliners caught far greater tonnages of swordfish than they had with harpooning, but a significant amount of that increased catch was made up of juveniles—swordfish that had not even reached breeding maturity.* They were hauling aboard fish as small as five pounds—fish so young their swords were still soft, and instead of a dorsal fin they retained the long razorback of their earlier morphology.

In a short fifty-year period, overfishing with longlines, gill nets, purse seines, and other industrial gear—not only by the Canadians but by fleets from the United States and every other nation that fished these waters—has transformed the western North Atlantic coastal and continental-shelf ecosystems so that they no longer bear any resemblance to their natural historical state. Scripps Institution of Oceanography scientist Jeremy Jackson refers to "the persistent myth of the oceans as wilderness"—a stunning phrase to contemplate, especially when one reads his work and realizes that Jackson is talking about the fact that truly wild oceans have not existed for several centuries, and that the true, natural state of estuaries, coastal communities, offshore continental shelves, and open-ocean ecosystems before human impact is beyond our ability to imagine. We simply do not know a world in which there is an abundance of large whales and fish, turtles, sharks, groundfish, mollusks, and other creatures, because the ecosystems we live with are so degraded. Jackson writes that in the Caribbean at the time of Columbus, "even the smallest estimate for green turtles exceeds the highest recorded wildebeest abundances in the Serengeti," and that "cod

---

*Swordfish reach maturity at four to five years of age. For the average female, this corresponds to a weight of about 125 pounds; for the male, about 90 pounds.

remains constitute 80–90% of the bone mass in middens [bone piles] in Maine dating from 500 to 2,500 years ago. Vertebrae in middens suggest that cod commonly reached 1½ to 2 m [4.9 to 6.5 feet] in length, a size in accord with early European illustrations of drying cod the size of fishermen." In general, Jackson says, "we are more aware of the mass extinction of large vertebrates [like woolly mammoths] at the end of the Pleistocene [the last ice age, ten thousand years ago] than [we are aware of] what happened in coastal seas only a century ago."

When longlining began off Canada in the 1960s, you were more likely to catch sharks than anything else, and there were many reports of two hundred, three hundred, and sometimes upwards of a thousand sharks caught on a single longline set. The sharks were being clear-cut like forests, and the impact of the same gear on swordfish was quickly evident. In 1959, the average swordfish weighed 260 pounds dressed (head, tail, fins, and guts removed). Three years later, in 1962, the average weight was 180 pounds. By 1970 it was down to 88 pounds.

We continue scanning through midmorning, the waves holding in the eight-foot range and the wind strong enough to make your eyes water. I scan in patterns, gazing out a few hundred yards then slowly back to the boat and out again, looking for that subtle anomaly: a line, a curve, a ripple on the water. Hours pass as the sun floats silver and cool in a monochrome sky.

Then, around eleven o'clock, Saul calls out again from the tower: "Swordfish! Port side, two hundred yards!"

Dwaine comes down the ladder and heads out on the stand, but Gabby doesn't slow the boat, keeping it on its heading. I have the lowest sight line on the boat, scanning horizontally over the surface, and I don't pick up the fins until Gabby has gotten all the way upwind, turned, and started to come downwind onto the fish, the sun throwing our shadow behind us. At 120 feet I see it—two little brown skegs sticking up as though it were an overturned surfboard. We rock and lurch and slide toward it, and I can only imagine how hard a shot this will be with the bow lifting and falling. Eighty feet and Dwaine crouches slightly and leans into a hard wave that rolls under him, throwing him and the stand a good fifteen feet in the air and then down. Fifty feet and the fish turns across our bow, moving to port. Gabby compensates on the wheel. At thirty feet he cuts the throttle, and as the noise of the diesel fades away, so do the wind and the sound of the waves. Everything slows, and I see small details: the blur of the wind on the silvery liquid skin of the rising waves; the swinging fall of the stand down and to the right; Dwaine leaning forward at the waist, the twisting fabric of his camouflaged deer-hunting jacket, work boots flexing up on tiptoe, hands gripping the shaft and butt end of the harpoon.

The fish is perpendicular to us now, fins just cutting the surface, its body a gorgeous smear of wild lavender beneath the clear water. I see a soft, glass glimmer, the subtle shine of something like a crystal orb up front: It's the eye.

Dwaine finally breaks the silence with a wild yell, the water in front of him exploding as though he had thrown a hand grenade, and then his cry changes, run through with a note of anguish: His second shot has missed.

2

In the steering station midway up the tower, I take a seat with Gabby, Saul's seventy-four-year-old father, who is in the midst of spewing forth a wave of foul-mouthed invective so full of bitter derision I feel like a choirboy. Gabby is old school—*original* old school, leather-strop-across-your-ass, you-speak-when-spoken-to, the-last-time-I-ate-was-last-week-and-it-was-a-cod-head old school. He is the kind of guy who grew up eating the occasional seal or gull, who either made, raised, or earned by the work of his own hands everything he had—every beam and clapboard of his house, every stitch of clothing, and every morsel of food. Gabby is an iron man from the age of wooden ships. He smokes four packs of unfiltered cigarettes a day, sleeps a total of four hours in every twenty-four, and has a liver hardened by forty-five years of drinking rum—"the darker the better."

Between his accent, the cigarette in his mouth, his lack of teeth, and his habit of turning his face away as he talks, I'm lucky if I understand half of what he says to me. He sums up that morning's two misses thus: "That ain't no way to make a *fuckin'* livin'!"

While Dwaine stands alone, searching his soul for answers on the deck below us, Gabby says, "This ain't no Carnival cruise, for fucksake."

After he's done describing the new asshole he will fit on Dwaine if he misses again, Gabby turns briefly in my direction and says, "So, young feller, you're writin' a book? I say why bother. These days, nobody fuckin' reads. They're all caught up in their *fuckin'* computers. You ask me, chances are it won't change a *goddamn* thing." Taking a deep, final haul off his cigarette, he flicks the butt into the wind, which instantly snatches it away to stern. "Ah, Jeezus," he says quietly to himself, "I don't know why I keep comin' out here. Get beat up all day, chilled to the bone, looking for a needle in a *goddamn* haystack. I'm too old for this *shit*."

I am not entirely persuaded by Gabby's bitterness. There's a look in his eye that tells me part of it is an act intended for our shared amusement, a way of passing the time. Every time he swears, he jerks his head slightly, putting a hard shove behind the word, and as often as he drops a verbal bomb, he also gives a dry little chuckle and I catch fleeting glimpses of a smile. As we sit together on the narrow bench, scanning the waves, he suddenly announces, "This is it for me, you know. Last trip."

"Seriously?" I ask.

"Yep. I'm sick of this. Spend six, seven days out here, and for what? For this kind of punishment? I don't think so." He shakes his head. "No, sir. I've had enough. If it was like before, when you could come out all summer, I might keep it up. But this is crap. They keep it so *goddamn* tight, you're hardly out before they're calling you back in. And for chrissake, you can't harpoon in this kind of weather! How the hell you supposed to see anything?"

The "they" he refers to is the Canadian Department of Fisheries and Oceans (DFO). It's the agency responsible for regulating fishing in Canada and which in 1995 set the controversial 10 percent allotment for the harpooners.

As the boat lurches hard to port, Gabby groans, his old bones grinding. He turns the wheel into the next wave and we ride up and over it, coming down hard into the trough with big blooms of white water bursting from the bow. Gabby holds the wheel with his knees and leans forward to light another cigarette, cupping it close to his face. The wind's so strong it blows the flame sideways and out. He tries twice more, with the same result.

"Son of a *bitch*!" he shouts, and puts his hands down. He looks out over

the waves a moment, muttering his own private thoughts, then leans forward and tries again. I catch a glimpse of Gabby's sallow cheek, rough with
coarse gray stubble, and his neck, deeply creased like walrus hide. This
time the flame catches and he draws hard, brightening the end of the
smoke and sending out a bluish cloud.

He and the cigarettes have a fond affection for one another. He must
light and suck down about eight an hour, and it doesn't take long to figure
out that Gabby's secret to longevity is not your yogurt-and-yoga variety but
the too-stubborn-to-die mentality, augmented by the belief that a steady
diet of bile and various poisons will destroy any of the prevailing modern
causes of death.

It is getting on toward noon when down below I hear the sweet music
of Dwaine's possible redemption.

"Swordfish!" he yells, pointing ahead slightly to starboard.

He runs out on the stand, his hands flying as he unties the harpoon,
and calls up, "You see him, Gab?"

"No, for fucksake, I don't see him!"

Saul's deep, calm voice comes down from the top of the tower. "'Bout
sixty feet ahead there, Dad, little to starboard . . . "

Gabby finds it, mutters, "There he is, the little *fucker*," and starts turning the wheel to put the boat on it.

Slowly, Dwaine swings the harpoon around to his right side, keeping
the butt at waist level like a pole-vaulter, left arm crossing his body to
steady the shaft out front. The stand corkscrews forward through space.

We're all pulling for Dwaine. I climb down the ladder to watch the
action up close from the foredeck. From forty feet it looks again like a
small fish, only it grows a foot for every ten feet we close on it. Swordfish
are completely unlike marlin, which have a vertically flat body form;
instead they are as thick and round as trees, right through the caudal keel.

Dwaine, it would appear, has put himself in a Zen frame of mind;
everything about his body says "relaxed." The fish is now oblique to the
boat, pointed away at about eleven o'clock. The dark vertical of its tail is
visible, tip just clearing the surface, with the stiff, dark pectoral fins down
about five feet. Its shining metallic-silver undersides and the uniform
bright, young-plum purple of its back shimmer in the teal-green Atlantic.

Dwaine holds, letting us come up on it, and then, as he feels the stand start to kick up and away to the left, he leans and stiffly plants the harpoon. It's a solid shot—so solid, in fact, that Dwaine never lets go of the butt end of the shaft. Feeling the hit, he yells and leans his whole body into the pole, shoving hard and quickly twice to drive the dart home.

"Throw the weight!" he yells.

I hustle down the starboard side by the wheelhouse and yank the rope that releases the fifteen-pound chunk of rusting steel over the side. The swordfish turns away right as we slide past and glides directly under me. I'm amazed to see it swimming casually—stunned, probably—with the bright harpoon line trailing from dead center in the base of the dorsal. Dwaine has hit the bull's-eye on a fish of about 175 pounds, seven feet long and sleek as a torpedo.

In a flash, Dwaine's off the stand, across the foredeck, and down the wooden ladder to the main deck below. He pulls the first coil of half-inch rope out of a wooden tub and casts it over the side as if he were throwing a net. Then he tosses out a second coil and moves quickly to the back of the boat, where he heaves the big floats and then the buoy with the high-flier and the radar deflector on top. He accomplishes all this in less than thirty seconds, and in eight-foot seas.

"Boy, that feels good to have hit that fish," Dwaine says. "Now all's we got to do is wait and come back in an hour or two. In the meantime, I'm goin' to have a bite."

When Dwaine returns on deck, I go in for a peanut butter sandwich and another cup of coffee, sweetened with evaporated milk, in the area at the front of the boat called the "cud," short for cuddy. The cud is a triangular space under the foredeck, extending about eight feet back from the bow. Two sets of bunks lined with old foam rubber and sleeping bags are stacked one over the other against the hull walls to either side of the bow. In the middle of this space is a triangular dining table, the lower bunks serving as benches. On the wall at the back of the cud, opposite the bow, are a propane cookstove and overhead cupboards holding dry stores.

The cud is where the strange, gyroscopic magnetism of wave motion gathers, along with festering vapors of propane, diesel, cigarette smoke, and farts. The cud is where, even if you are not prone to seasickness, you are most likely to feel green. And, if you are prone to it, the cud must be avoided at all costs.

The cud leads up a three-step ladder to the wheelhouse itself, no deeper than four feet and running the entire width of the boat. Here is where the radar, depth finder, logbook, engine controls, main wheel, and navigation electronics are located. There is no shower on the boat, nor is there a head (the maritime term for toilet). Instead, for "solids," you have two options: avoid crapping for a week or shit in a well-used, crusted five-gallon bucket. For "liquids," you can be a gentleman and use the bucket or you can go off the stern directly into the Atlantic. If you are a bit stiff in the hoofs, like Gabby, you hold the doorframe of the wheelhouse and urinate right onto the deck, anticipating that each day there'll be enough spray or even a wave or two to wash away the stench.

Bolted directly to the outside wall of the wheelhouse on the back deck is a hydraulic winch. This device, and the other hydraulic winch (the Hydro-Slave) affixed to the starboard gunwale, are used to haul heavy traplines for lobster, which Saul sets in the winter. When he is not sword-fishing or lobstering, Saul bottom-fishes using these same winches on trawl line* for halibut. A block and tackle, run through with heavy line, is anchored off a steel cable attached to a girded section on the back of the high spotting post. The block and tackle is used to hoist swordfish aboard the boat.

In the center of the expansive back deck is a single large, insulated fiberglass hold, about four feet high and ten-by-ten across, and three smaller insulated plastic pens, each about four-by-four-by-four. All of these are filled with fresh ice. The swordfish, after being dressed, will be packed and covered in ice in the main hold and two of the smaller ones. The last pen contains our cold stores, water, and other supplies.

---

*The terms "trawl" and "trawling" have different meanings depending on where they are used. In Nova Scotia, both refer to the use of longlines laid on the ocean floor. In other locales, "trawling" and "trawl" refer to the use of large nets dragged through the water (midwater trawl) or on the bottom (bottom trawl or dragging). Bottom dragging is enormously destructive: It effectively bulldozes the sea bottom. Bottom longlining, like other types of longlining, has a bycatch problem.

Toward the transom on the port side stands the welded aluminum rack for the high-fliers and floats, and then the transom itself, which is a three-foot-high welded metal gate, sheathed in aluminum diamond plate, running the entire width of the vessel. Depending on the operation, the transom gate can be raised, like it is now, or it can be down, with the entire back of the boat open to the Atlantic. An open transom is one of the reasons winter lobstering in Nova Scotia is so dangerous: Men go over nearly every year when they are dragged off by a turn of the line around the ankle as one of the heavy traps runs off the deck or when they lose their footing in heavy seas and slide off into the frigid water. Not all make it back.

After drinking the last of my coffee, I take up my place at the base of the tower ladder again, Dwaine having resumed his seat next to Gabby in the steering station. Eight harpoon boats are visible within our 360-degree view, each with some form of tower and stand, with high-fliers, neon floats, and colorful buoys on racks to stern. The small, dark figures of men are visible as thick silhouettes, bundled as most of them are in insulated coveralls. The boats are all in the forty-to-sixty-foot range, not including the stand off the bow, and they vary in beam from eighteen to twenty-five feet. They are all of a type of craft known as a Novi boat: short, pug-nosed bow, broad beam, deep keel heavy-breasted toward the front, tapering to stern, with a widening, squared-off back end. They are not fast, but they are very stable in the chaotic seas encountered on these comparatively shallow offshore banks. They are a design created by the necessities and conditions of the North Atlantic.

At nearly 5:00 P.M., with the smear of the sun hanging thirty degrees above our starboard quarter, Gabby spots a sword. Dwaine gets in position, and the fish, which had been heading toward us, starts arcing away to the right in a long, swooping pass. Gabby holds steady on the throttle and spins the wheel, swinging Dwaine hard to starboard as though he were on the end of a crane. He comes fast onto the fish, and in the last twenty feet Gabby eases off the speed of the turn, giving Dwaine a chance to time it and putting him dime-on to the fish. Dwaine sights, holds, and at just the right moment jams the harpoon in, forward of the dorsal and down on the flank. He yells as a brownish-red blood cloud blooms out from the head. The swordfish rolls over partway, pumping its tail and shooting under the boat.

After Dwaine and I put out the second set of gear, Gabby resumes the search, and within twenty minutes we spot the first high-flier. Saul climbs down from the high post as Gabby pulls the boat out of gear coming onto the buoy. Dwaine and Saul make their way to the back deck, and while Dwaine hooks the high-flier with a short gaff, Saul unties the block and tackle from where it's anchored at the Hydro-Slave. With the high-flier and floats aboard, he takes the main line, plants his feet wide, and starts hauling the line barehanded. Saul is a block of a man, with heavy shoulders and chest, stocky legs, faded blue tattoos on his forearms (one shows a tall ship under sail and the other a crude semblance of his name), and wide, thick, stone-hard hands. He moves with a ponderous, lurking power. He's about the same height as his father but must outweigh him by a hundred pounds. Saul hauls the line with a steady, even, side-to-side pivoting of his torso. The power comes less from his arms than from that rotating motion of his shoulders.

Earlier today, I watched one of the other harpoon boats hauling a swordfish on board, using a hydraulic block to pull the fish up from six hundred feet below the surface. I ask Saul why he doesn't do the same.

"Those hydraulics ain't got no sensitivity," he explains. "That winch'll keep pulling no matter if you're comin' up hard against the fish in a swell or gettin' all kinds of slack in a trough. If there's enough strain, it'll pull the dart out. This way, you feel a swell tightening the line, you just ease off. Same thing if that swordie ain't quite dead. Just gives you a little bit of touch."

For about five minutes he keeps hauling the line with the same steady motion until Dwaine says, "There he is, Saul," nodding at the sword spiking out of the sea sixty feet back. As Saul pulls, the body levels off on the surface, the sword, head, and part of the stiff right pectoral above the water, the mouth of the fish open. As it draws near, I can see that its skin has the glistening appearance of oiled bronze.

When the fish is alongside the rail, Dwaine takes the small homemade gaff and hooks it in the meat of the tail, then grabs the loop at the end of the hoist line running through the block and secures it around the tailfins.

"All set," he says, and Saul starts hauling down two-handed on his end of the line, the block squeaking. The swordfish lifts tailfirst out of the water until all but the last two feet of the sword has cleared the gunwale. Dwaine grabs hold of the body and pulls the fish into the boat, and then Saul eases up and lets it down gently onto the deck.

"Look at that," Saul says. "You buttoned him."

It's a textbook shot: Dwaine's thrust went clean through from the dorsal and out the front of the fish. The bronze dart sits flush against the swordfish's underside between the pectoral fins, in the exact position of a bow tie.

Dwaine undoes the wrap on the swordfish's tail while I marvel at its form—sleek, powerful, hydrodynamic—and at its size, which is easily over seven feet. I have never seen a swordfish except in photographs, and to see one now, albeit dead, is still a moving experience. For me swordfish have always been the most distant and enigmatic of the great fish—so deep, so solitary, as to be beyond any probable encounter.

And yet here I stand over one. I stare at its tapered face, those fantastic eyes, and that strange adaptation, the sword. The eyes are magnificent—clear glass globes the size of apples, irises like black plums. The sword, in particular, strikes me as a remarkably simple and rudimentary design, like the bony armor of a dinosaur and yet so brilliantly devised for its purpose. I kneel and reach to touch the sword, but Dwaine stops me: "Let me take that off first. If it ain't dead, he'll open you up." He places his boot on the sword, pinning it to the deck, and takes a carpenter's handsaw and saws down through the forward section of the face, cutting off not only the sword but the front three inches of the pointed bottom jaw. Dwaine explains, "You gotta take off both the sword and that point of the jaw there. I've known guys who've left that on and had the fish drive that right through their boot."

Dwaine now begins to dress the swordfish. He removes the pectoral fins, the dorsal, and the large anal fin angling down from the rear of the fish like a second, upside-down dorsal. With the knife he notches into the caudal keel, turns a right angle, cuts through the space between the last vertebra and the caudal peduncle (the tail joint), and removes the tail. With the handsaw he cuts down through the top half of the skull to the

top of the gill plates, then takes his knife and continues cutting behind
these, separating the gills, the gill plates, the bottom jaw, and the entire
head from the body. Now the blood flows, red as crimson ink, viscous as
oil. Dwaine fetches the deck hose and calls out to Saul to flick the pump
switch in the wheelhouse. He lays the hose by the body, cuts a donut hole
around the anus, and slices forward, opening the gut like a purse. He takes
the knife and makes a few cuts inside the throat cavity, leaving the large
collarbones (napes) intact where the gill plates shut against the body. "You
leave those on so the ice don't crush the meat," he says, then lays the knife
on the deck and sweeps his hands deep inside the fish, back and forth
along the sides of the abdominal cavity, separating the innards from the
viscera netting that holds them in place. Finally he grabs the mass of the
innards by one of the forward anchor points and pulls; they fall as a single,
sloppy mass onto the deck. With the knife he finds and separates the stom-
ach, slicing it open, and we examine the contents: It's full of half-digested
squid about the length of my hand, each of which has been cut in pieces
as perfectly as if it had been done with a butcher's knife.

Dwaine uses a stiff brush to clean out the rest of the viscera while I
examine the sword. The first thing I'm struck by is its heft. It's about three
feet long and must weigh almost three pounds. Where it's still wet, the
sword is smooth and slippery, its edges literally sharp; where dry, it has
the feel of superfine sandpaper, the kind you'd use for wet-sanding a car.
The top is dark, while the underside is light with faint hints of pink. The
butt of the sword, where Dwaine separated it from the head, is not solid
bone but rather a densely honeycombed bone matrix, bloody and oily,
with a hard, thick, ivory-yellow bone exterior.

I put the sword to the side and touch the broad, dark back of the fish.
The creature is as round, and has the same solidity, as a very large wheel of
cheddar cheese. It is all muscle, and as I contemplate the mass of this
animal—how much muscle there is compared with innards and pretty
much anything else—I am struck by the fact that there is no fat whatsoever, and that its flesh, even dead, is as firm as my thigh when tensed to its
maximum. It is yet another testament to the fact that wilderness forces a
level of efficiency and strength few of us can fathom.

I look up to see Dwaine standing over me, holding out with his bloody left hand the purple fist of the swordfish's heart. He takes the knife and carves off the bottom lobe, a chunk about the size of a large marshmallow, and offers it to me.

"It's tradition that every first-time swordfisherman is offered a piece of the heart. You don't have to; it's up to you, but I thought I'd offer it to ya."

I take the sticky chunk and pop it in my mouth. Its consistency is hard and rubbery, like kidney, and its taste is simple but strong: oily fish and metallic, high-iron blood. As I start to chew, Dwaine begins laughing. "Oh God, spit it out! Spit it out! I was only jokin'!"

It's too late. I've swallowed it. "You son of a bitch," I say, smiling a bloody smile.

Dwaine is incredulous and truly disgusted that I would eat raw heart, but to me it seems a reasonable initiation, and in keeping with the fact that the old Nova Scotia harpooners cherished pan-fried swordfish heart.

Dwaine finishes cleaning out the swordfish, heaves the offal overboard, and sprays the deck, pushing miscellaneous chunks of flesh and connective tissue, parts of organs, and ragged clots of blood out through the scuppers into the sea, where it is fought over by surprisingly few birds: half a dozen storm petrels and a handful of shearwaters.

Over the next hour we work to haul aboard and dress the second swordfish and pack the two loglike carcasses on ice in the hold. The entire time, I can feel that piece of swordfish heart spreading its warmth, its strength and power, through my body as though it were a fistful of sunlight.

3

Evening of the first day comes with a slow darkening of the cloud cover from gray to Prussian blue, the gap of sky at the horizon shifting from pink to hot orange until the sun passes by the crack like the molten eye of a god peering under the lid of the world. When it's gone, an indigo dark settles over us. The waves move black and spiked, their crests furred in white, barely visible, and the wind thrums the steel wires overhead.

The aroma of boiled potatoes, fried pork chops, and canned peas greets us from the cud entrance as we step into the wheelhouse. Gabby smokes at the wheel, his face illuminated by the small yellow binnacle light, the cool blue glow of the navigation screen, and the faint lime haze of the overhead radar. We sit on stools against the back wall and face forward, looking out dark windows. The diesel drums evenly beneath our feet. We will drift for a few hours, then make our way back to position, then drift again, repeating the pattern through the night. Watches are four hours each, but lacking any formal training, I am excused from this duty.

"This is the best part of the day, y'ask me," Dwaine says as Saul starts handing up plates of food. "You done your work and now all's you gotta do is fill your belly and have a yarn and get some sleep. It's not a bad way to live."

"So what'd you think of them swordfish out there today, Matty?" Saul asks. "They got a hell of a big wheel on the ass end, don't they?"

"I had no idea," I reply, then ask about something that has been puzzling me. "You normally see more sharks?"

"Used to. I was surprised we didn't see any today. Not a goddamn one."

"What kind would you normally see?"

"All sorts—porbeagle, whitetip, blue dog, tiger sharks. Dozens of 'em. But it's been how many years would you say now, Gab, since we seen any good numbers?"

"Hell if I know," Gabby says. "Ten or twelve at least. Used to see more sharks than swordfish. There was a *shitload* of sharks out here. But you can't longline like those bastards do and expect there to be anything left. You just can't fuckin' do it, but they do."

Dwaine spears a piece of pork chop and says, "I been on them longliners."

"What's it like?" I ask.

"You get bycatch, that's true. Some of it you let go and hope it lives. Depending on how you do it, some of it will. But it can get pretty bad, pretty messy." He pauses, and I sense his reluctance to talk about it. "I seen a lotta sharks come in. And tuna—the big bluefins. I seen them turtles, green ones and the big leatherbacks. Those things can get huge. We got one must've been nine hundred pounds."

Saul says, "I know one guy went longlinin' and they hauled up a porpoise. He said that thing cried like a baby. Just cried like a baby on deck until they killed it. They had to; it wasn't gonna make it. That did it for him. He said right there, 'Fuck this. I'm done. I ain't never doin' this again.' And he didn't. That was his first trip an' his last. Now the same guy's got a lotta longline quota for swordfish, but he won't fish it with longline. He uses the quota but he harpoons on it. It might take longer, but it's cleaner, and he figures it's better to sleep at night."

Indiscernible crackling speech comes over the radio. Saul reaches for the transmitter and holds a brief conversation with one of the men aboard another boat. He signs off, clips the transmitter back in its cradle, and dials down the squelch. "One of these fellas out here tells the story of a swordfish he stuck: went back a few hours later, tried to pull up on the line and couldn't. Could not budge the thing. Said it was like he was hooked to the bottom of the ocean. He leaves the line and goes out after more swords, then comes back an hour later. Still can't budge the damn thing. He has no idea what's going on. Goes out again and finally comes back three, four hours after he harpooned the fish, and he pulls on the line and he can haul it. That swordfish comes up nothing but bones and a head. Just a skeleton. He said it was picked as clean as if it'd been done by a bunch of ants."

"What was it?" I ask.

"What do you think?"

I puzzle this. "Couldn't have been a shark."

Saul laughs and finally tells me. "Giant squid. That's the only thing coulda done it. You know sharks; they're sloppy eaters. None of them toothed whales coulda done it either—they woulda torn it all to hell. Giant squid, though, they got that beak and they'll just pick it clean. He figures it come up from down deep and sucked onto that swordfish and refused to let go, that's why it was deadweight. Three hundred pounds of meat off that swordfish in a coupla hours—that musta been *some* fuckin' squid."

From the corner, from within a dim haze of smoke, Gabby says, "There's things down there that's scarier than your worst nightmares. There's things nobody's ever seen, things you can't imagine."

I ask Saul how common the big swords are, what's the average size of swordfish they normally harpoon.

"The real big ones, you ain't likely to see them this time of year. They come up later. Some guys say the real big fish don't hardly ever bask on the surface, so there's no telling if they're down there right now. The average we get is a hundred fifty to three hundred pounds. You'll get a few bigger 'n that—one or two four-hundred-pounders, and there's one big girl out here called Stumpy 'cause her sword's broke off, and she's eight hundred or better—but generally they'll be 'bout two hundred pounds. Course, in the last few years, we've actually been gettin' a few fish. I'd say it's the most fish we've seen in twenty-five years. For a long time it was a losin' proposition comin' out here. But the last three years, it's started to come back. Now, you'd think there'd be a hard lesson there, wouldn't you? Don't overfish the goddamn stock. But I guarantee it, if we don't stay on top of it, that lesson will be unlearned quick. Brown's Bank is a good example: There's more fish on my lawn than there are on Brown's. They dragged that to shit and left nothing. Absolutely nothing."

"Why do you think the swords have started to come back?"

"You ask me, it's 'cause you guys down south actually did somethin' to conserve the fish. The U.S. shut down a lot of square miles. The DFO hasn't done shit, not one single thing."

Saul is referring to the fact that in 2000, the National Marine Fisheries Service (NMFS) closed down more than 133,000 square miles of U.S. waters off the southeastern states and in the Gulf of Mexico to longlining. These areas included prime swordfish breeding grounds. This action was the result of a lawsuit brought against the U.S. secretary of commerce by the National Coalition for Marine Conservation (NCMC) in response to a fishery management plan for swordfish that failed to account for the longline bycatch of swordfish. The NMFS settled the case by using bycatch hot-spot data submitted by the NCMC, which in turn was used to define the closed areas. The closure of these U.S. grounds is part of a rebuilding plan for swordfish that is largely considered successful—the only example of a large pelagic species brought back from a very dire scenario.

Preceding this large-scale closure, conservationists and U.S. commercial longliners had battled fiercely throughout the nineties over what to do with the depleted stock. In 1998 the Natural Resources Defense Council and SeaWeb spearheaded the "Give Swordfish a Break" campaign to raise awareness of the issue and decrease demand for the fish. The longliners claimed (probably legitimately) that the boycott did not significantly decrease overall demand, except in high-end restaurants, but it did change who was supplying the swordfish: foreign fleets fishing under fewer restrictions, exceeding their legal quotas, violating gear regulations, and providing a lower-quality product.

While U.S. longliners rightly complained that other nations ought to be held accountable to the same degree they were, their arguments obscured some basic truths. Over a nine-year period, between 1987 and 1996, U.S. longlining effort had increased 70 percent, from 6.5 million hooks to more than 11 million annually. In that same period, U.S. longline catches actually fell 60 percent. In other words, their effort almost doubled but they caught only about one-quarter the amount of swordfish. This pattern of increasing effort and falling catches is a signal that a stock is in trouble. And this was just the U.S. boats; the statistics don't account for Canada, Japan, Spain, Taiwan, Portugal, or any other nations fishing in the North Atlantic during that time. Income from the U.S. fishery during those nine years fell from $35.6 million to $17.6 million and the number of U.S. longline boats began dropping from a high of nearly five hundred in 1992 to about seventy in 2009. American and other longliners had fished too hard with too many vessels and had ruined their own livelihoods.

In truth, no argument can counter the reality that longlining, by the United States or any other nation, is an indiscriminate means of killing and can be a devastating method of fishing. There are precautions that can and have been taken to minimize bycatch, especially among U.S. boats, but the practice has done enormous damage and in general results in unacceptable levels of bycatch. Nearly two of every three swordfish caught in the U.S. fishery in the mid-nineties had never reached sexual maturity. A conservative estimate indicates that 40 percent of the swordfish caught were discarded, dead, because they were below the ICCAT minimum-weight limit of fifty-five pounds. In 1996 alone, U.S. longliners threw forty thousand swordfish overboard, dead, because they were too small, and none of these figures include the millions of pounds of other species that were killed annually by North Atlantic longliners—species that included and still include the giant bluefin tuna, white marlin, blue marlin, and nearly two dozen species of overfished sharks.

During that entire time, the Canadian Department of Fisheries and Oceans did not close one square mile of territory. There is a reason for this: Swordfish are not known to spawn in their waters. Canada's quota, like everyone else's, was decreased by ICCAT, but this decrease still set the total quota above ICCAT's own scientists' recommendations for sustainable limits. The Canadian longliners did make certain gear adjustments, but whether these were voluntarily adopted or forced on them depends on whom you talk to.

One could rightly argue that all of this is old history. As of 2009, scientists estimated that the U.S. closures, combined with more stringent catch limits by ICCAT, had resulted in a recovery of the swordfish population in the North Atlantic to a minimally sustainable level in seven rather than the predicted ten years. The story of this successful swordfish recovery deserves to be told, and it should stand as an example of an effective fisheries management effort. The problem is, the threat remains. First of all, the swordfish stock is considered rebuilt according to the stock's current calculated biomass, but there is no sense of what the age distribution is among the population. A stock with a preponderance of juveniles, in which those juveniles will have to survive a range of threats before they arrive at adulthood, is not as robust as a population with a strong percentage of breeding adults. From this perspective, the nature of the "rebuilt" status of the North Atlantic stock remains in question. Furthermore, U.S. longliners continue to lobby to open the closed grounds under the guise of testing new bycatch-reduction gear or establishing population cross-sections, but both of these open the door to the possibility of more access. Not only that, but the legacy of longlining over the past fifty years is that it has changed the balance of species in the North Atlantic, massively reducing sharks, bluefin tuna, and other populations. The "success" of this swordfish recovery is belied by the point that Scripps scientist Jeremy Jackson makes in his papers exploring the degree to which we fail to understand what's been lost. What kind of ocean are we looking to rebuild with these efforts? Should we be thinking in broader terms, working from a real historical picture of what was? Or are we looking to "rebuild" swordfish populations according to a baseline that itself represents a significantly depleted state, when instead we should be interested in fostering a renaissance of the ocean in closer approximation of its full, sustainable potential for abundance? Certainly more could be done to support the reemergence of fully robust ocean ecosystems, and as regards Canada and other nations fishing the North Atlantic, the real problem of unobserved and unrecorded longlining continues to pose a threat. In Canada specifically, the DFO has failed to effectively regulate longlining's negative impacts on the ocean since it began nearly sixty years ago, and there continues to be no meaningful observer coverage, either human or video, aboard Canadian longline vessels. It is therefore impossible to determine how many juvenile and adult swordfish, leatherback turtles, giant bluefin tuna, sharks, and other species are being killed and discarded.

The lack of observer coverage matters because it is in this blind spot that longlining's damage continues. It may seem perplexing that swordfish would be discarded, until you look at why. The majority of the Canadian swordfish longline quota is owned by a few dozen individuals. Their main income from longlining comes not from swordfish but from bigeye and yellowfin tuna. To deal with this in the context of changing market prices for their catch, the Canadian longliners' strategy is to fish in the early part of the season for bigeye and yellowfin and discard everything else, including bluefin tuna, swordfish, and bycatch. In late June, the swordfish harpooners have their two-week season, harvesting their 10 percent of the Canadian swordfish quota. Meanwhile, the longliners continue fishing for yellowfin and bigeye all summer, discarding unwanted bycatch the entire time. When market conditions are favorable, they will keep swordfish or the occasional bluefin tuna. (They are allotted only so many per year.) From September through November, they will "target" swordfish until they fill their swordfish quota and the season closes. So, for their entire fishing season, from May through November, the longliners selectively keep the fish they want to apply against their quota and throw the rest overboard, leaving a trail of dead juvenile and large pelagic fish in their wake. The Nova Scotian term for this is "shacking."

The second destructive practice made possible by lack of observer coverage is what's called high-grading. This is when you catch a fish—say, a ninety-pound bluefin—in the morning. In the afternoon you catch one that weighs four hundred pounds. You can get a better price per pound for the bigger one, so you chuck the dead ninety-pounder overboard. In your logbook you record: "One bluefin tuna, four hundred pounds," and that's what you bring to the dock. Nowhere except in the memory of those onboard is it recorded that there was another bluefin tuna, or another hundred bluefin, dumped over the side.

As Saul explains all this to me in the dim light of the wheelhouse, Gabby, who has spent the majority of the time looking out the window by the wheel, blowing smoke into the night, flicks the glowing ember of his cigarette butt out into the darkness, stands up, and says, "Most of those DFO assholes have never even stepped on a *goddamn* boat. They actually think logbooks are true! You can put any *fucking* thing you want in there. It's that simple."

As Gabby lurches past us out into the doorway to urinate, Saul says, "You do get some right bastards in this business. Couple of years ago, after they'd dragged the shit outta these banks, a few boys went lookin' over the edge, down onto the slope, into the canyons. Normally that's a bitch of a place to fish, near impossible. But now they got GPS linked to the sonar, which is linked to the dragger gear. They can lower and raise the gear to cut in tight to almost any terrain. So they make a few drags on the slope and tear the shit outta their gear. They haul it up in tatters and what do they find in it but huge three- and four-foot coral trees. They've found a goddamn coral forest. So what do these boys do but rig a big chain between two boats and drag it right up that canyon. In one shot they cut down the whole thing. Turned out that coral forest was old—hundreds and hundreds of years. Now where do you suppose those assholes think the bottom fish spawn and hide out? They went back and dragged it again, and sure enough they got their fish, but how many generations of fish did they destroy that would have spawned there? You ask me, that oughta be illegal. It's criminal. It's plain fuckin' wrong."

One thing I've learned about Saul is that there is a subtle, immovable patience to him, a bedrock certainty that he knows bullshit when he smells it. He cannot abide lies and manipulation, especially when it comes to fishing and men's livelihoods. He is also a relentless fighter, a man who knows what's right and is willing to stand by it no matter what.

Prior to leaving for the harpooning trip, Saul took me down to the site of a protest at the head of the causeway that connects the mainland to Cape Sable Island. Camped out there for close to sixteen hours a day around a folding table under a tent, with a grill nearby and some handmade signs and pictures posted by the road, was a small band of local fishermen. They were protesting the fact that the DFO was allowing draggers from over forty miles away, down near Yarmouth, to come up and drag the waters off Cape Sable for scallops.

A scallop dredge is essentially a heavy steel square with teeth dragging a chain-link bag behind it. The rig is hauled behind a boat, and the weight and design of the dredge force it into the mud and sand of the bottom. The teeth rake through the sand, kicking up scallops and other debris into the bag. Dredges vary in size but can get quite large—up to sixteen tons.

The scallop dredge is yet another industrialized method of bulldozing the ocean floor.* What normally exists on the bottom off Cape Sable and other shallow shelf areas of the North Atlantic is a thin layer of soft sponges, seaweeds, small soft and hard corals, and whole gardens of creatures—crabs, sea cucumbers, fish fry, lobsters, and much more. This fragile layer is where the juveniles of dozens of species hide for safety and forage. After a dragger or a scallop dredge passes through, all that is left is a wasteland of sand, rock, or mud. Draggers claim that their gear is the equivalent of a garden tiller, turning the soil, but the resulting damage belies that argument. The protest at the causeway, of which Saul was one of the chief organizers, focused on the damage to the lobster fishery by the scallop dredges. The lobster fishery off Cape Sable is one of the best in Canada and is the backbone of a lot of the local fishermen's incomes. Lobsters hunker down in shallow holes they excavate, both for protection and to carve out their bit of territory. The Cape Sable lobstermen knew there was a problem when they started hauling up traps full of lobsters with holes punched in their shells, claws torn off, and so on. The lobstermen estimated that up to 15 percent of their catch showed this kind of damage after the scallop draggers passed through, making the lobsters unsalable.

Saul says, "Used to be, you pulled any of this monkey business with men's

---

*A preferred, sustainable method of harvesting scallops is to dive for them, hence the name "diver scallops."

livelihoods, you'd get a bullet through your head. Those of us who are left, we've kept our cool. Tried to do it legal, protested to the right authorities. Defended ourselves. The problem is, most of us don't have education. We're at the mercy of the wolves. The DFO gets workin' with a big company, and suddenly it has access to grounds that have been closed to the rest of us. They're able to do things we're prevented from doing. They have the money to pay for the lawyers and lobbyists to get exceptions to the rules. They have the money to make campaign contributions to the politicians or the DFO administrators who vote on this stuff. We're poor fishermen. We have none of that. You gotta look at which group is better for the politicians. We're a bunch of troublemakers out here on Cape Sable. We're independent, and we want to stay independent. We got a long history of protesting. Few years back, we closed the causeway for the whole winter, burned piles of tires, even burned a DFO boat because they was fuckin' with our lobster prices. A couple of years before that, a bunch of us took over the DFO offices in Barrington because they was getting rid of all the handliners. Now if you know handlining, you know there is no harm done by that method. Handlining is what the old cod and halibut fishermen did out on the Grand Banks and Georges for centuries. Handlining is one of the oldest methods of fishing there is. All it is is a man on a line with one or two hooks on it. Lowers the line down, waits for the fish to bite, pulls it back up. That's it. DFO was just going to cut them out, close all the licenses. They agreed to negotiate, we stopped our siege, and when we got to the bargaining table they fucked us. They closed the licenses anyway. Families went under. Men died because of that. The DFO said the handline fishery was 'overcapitalized.' Too many boats."

I pause, thinking this through. "That doesn't sound right," I say. "I doubt a fleet of handliners is equivalent in environmental impact to dragging for the same fish."

"Exactly. And do you think they cut the dragger fleet?"

"Let me guess."

"Right you are, ol' boy. They did not. You gotta ask yourself who's gonna make the bigger contribution to the reelection campaign: a bunch of independent fishermen using low-tech gear, makin' a living but not getting rich, or draggers running huge boats and operating as corporations?

The DFO, the fishing industry, they're in bed together. The corruption would make your head spin."

I am struck by how Saul is able to remain embroiled in these conflicts, walking the thin line of survival while trying to do the right thing, and through all of it somehow maintaining his sense of humor and generosity. He has welcomed me onto his vessel, tutored me in the finer points of swordfishing and fisheries regulations, shared with me the history of his community and his family. The story he tells of Cape Sable, where he has lived all his life and where his people go back over three hundred years, is a story familiar almost everywhere in the industrialized world. It is the story of the consolidation of the wealth of natural resources—in this case, fish—into the hands of a few through the vehicle of the corporation. In the case of fisheries, it's the story of what I think of as "the industrial fallacy"—the idea that the application of more powerful technologies as an answer to the problems of market competitiveness, increased population, decreased fish stocks, and the perpetual demand for profits is inevitable and without alternative, leads to better living, and can happen without real consequences to the natural world. As Paul Newlin of the Center for Environmental Civics writes: "It's a reflection of the human tendency to subscribe to the cornucopian, utopian fantasy that no matter how the environment reacts, [or] the resource declines and degrades, we will be able to conjure up a new technology, or substitute one resource for another, [in a process of] seemingly infinite replacement." Governments support the industrial fallacy in the belief that, especially in the case of the sea, natural resources cannot be diminished or, if they can be, that the trade-off in things like job creation, industry contracts, and political capital is worth the loss. These policies support short-term gain at the expense of long-term stability and profit for whole communities and societies, a practice that leads to the destruction of ecosystems and species. It may be, as one scientist commented to me, that the consolidation of fisheries into the hands of corporate commercial fleets is necessary to make viable the enterprise of going farther offshore to find fish. If this is the case, then the choice of consolidation for this reason, in the corporate-industrial format, represents the endgame of wiping out fish, especially when control of the resource is not governed by science but rather is negotiated between corporations and government, with science and conservation taking a backseat.

In many countries, the history of fish stock decline and fisheries management failures since the rise of industrial fishing follows a similar pattern: adoption of new technologies enabled more intensive fishing; more intensive fishing decreased stocks while increasing competition and the demand for greater fishing power; greater fishing power decimated stocks further; and in the meantime governments were subsidizing new shipbuilding to continue to increase fleet power. In many cases, this first phase of evolution to a corporate-industrial model of fishing happened by default. But the buy-in to the industrial fallacy happens when, against scientific evidence that fish stocks are being wiped out and against clear evidence that the gear is too powerful and damaging, governments and private enterprise choose merely to continue in the same vein. The boom-and-bust cycle of poor fisheries management costs the world economy $50 billion annually—more than $2 trillion since the 1960s. Consumers who prefer low-cost fish products certainly play a role, but the money saved at the fish counter is lost or paid elsewhere in the form of vanished jobs, collapsed fisheries, and all the ways healthy ecosystems supply "services" to us—for example, clean water, recreational opportunities, and more accessible, abundant, and stable stocks.

In the case of Canada's DFO, its adherence to the industrial fallacy would appear to have played out to disastrous effect, aided and abetted by fishermen and entrepreneurs willing to go the full industrial route, as well as by the DFO's own mismanagement, ineptitude, corruption, and poorly conceived "solutions" to the problem of diminishing returns. The collective result is the radical transformation in the past fifty years of Canada's offshore waters, at one time among the most fertile on the planet. Remember, it is the DFO that presided over the destruction of the Grand Banks cod. It is the DFO that has resisted holding the longline and dragger industries accountable for negative impacts to ecosystems and wildlife by not imposing meaningful observer or video coverage. The DFO, whose supposed mission is to support "healthy and productive aquatic ecosystems, sustainable fisheries and aquaculture," acts more as a facilitator of corporate-industrial ownership of the sea than it does as a steward of natural resources for the benefit of Canadians. A July 2009 study published in *Science* found that 60 percent of the assessed fish stocks on the Newfoundland-Labrador continental shelf, off eastern Canada, are collapsed. Fish stocks are defined as collapsed when the biomass of a stock (the weight of all the fish) is estimated to be less than 10 percent of the natural, unfished state of the stock. This is anything but confirmation of successful stewardship.

"How do you stay sane?" I finally ask Saul.

With his characteristic dry humor, he answers, "Who says we've stayed sane? Yer lookin' at the few survivors out here."

For the next hour or so, Saul tells me stories about life on Cape Sable, stories of uncles and neighbors who made an honest living when there were still plenty of fish, and then how it started to get complicated when the fish began to disappear. Saul and these thirty or forty boats out here are among the last to keep the tradition of swordfish harpooning alive in the Atlantic, not as a quaint anachronism but because, in the face of all that's happened in fishing, harpooning still makes sense—for the environment, for the spirits of the men who do it, for the future of the fish.

Which brings me back to my question: Given the way things are, how does he survive?

For a while he says nothing; then he answers: "There's only so much a man can take, isn't there? They keep puttin' the screws to us. But I ain't gonna quit. I'm gonna fight the bastards. There's nothin' else to do. Your back's to the wall, that's all you got."

4

The next morning we're on deck and scanning for fins by 8:30. The wind is harder today, the waves over eight feet, and I take up position with Saul in the high spotting post thirty feet above the deck. The view is spectacular but the ride is brutal. It's like being on a telephone pole on top of an elephant. It's a slow-motion carnival ride gone bad. The slow, forward bucking into the waves has a certain rhythmic predictability until Gabby turns the wheel and we run with the swells on the forward or aft quarter, or smack on the beam. Then the oscillations become erratic, and suddenly we're being thrown around. I'm trying to shoot video and stills, occasionally jotting notes, but when we take a hard, uneven series of slams, I lose a handhold, taking the square aluminum box frame hard in the ribs and almost dropping my gear into the sea.

As hard as the ride is, the high angle makes it worth the pain. I can see twenty feet down into the water, and the elevation gives a far greater sense of the sheer volume of space out here. It's as if the seascape has gone from two to three dimensions. Harpoon boats in the distance don't look flattened against the horizon but alive and plunging in a world textured with moving wave hills and rolling crests everywhere I look. Today I am starting to be able to spot fins and the murky forms of ocean life. We sight our first shark, a solitary blue dog rising like a shadow from the depths with lithe, sinuous motions. We see an ocean sunfish, also called a *Mola mola*—proof, if it was ever needed, that God occasionally goes on a bender. At ten feet long and maxing out at weights over five thousand pounds, the sunfish is the largest bony fish in the world, and yet it's shaped like something that died under a car tire. It is a giant head propelled by two vertical fins at the back and is called "moon fish" in several languages, "millstone" in Latin, and *Schwimmender Kopf*—the swimming head—in German. The *Mola mola* cannot be said to eat so much as suck on jellyfish. With its eyes and mouth frozen in an expression of brainless delight, it is a peaceful, sweet oddity of the offshore world.

I also notice a tight grouping of three pale-pink creatures that look like massive bottlenose dolphins. They are northern bottlenose whales, a rare variety of beaked whale of which only ten thousand are thought to exist. As they pass, I see that their flesh has a raw, abraded look. Around mid-morning, I point off in the distance about half a mile to a tight pod of dark shapes plunging in and out of the swells.

"Blackfish," Saul says. "Pilot whales."

A member of the dolphin family, they're the size of pickup trucks, with bulbous black heads.

I say to Saul, "Gab tells me this is his last trip."

Saul smiles at me. "Is that so?"

"Not true?"

"No, it's not true. He says it every time he comes out here. He looks forward to this all year. Keeps him alive. He loves to bitch, but he wouldn't have it any other way."

"I'd say he's got that part down."

"What, the bitchin'? Oh, he's the champ. He's the bitch king."

After a few hours, Saul climbs down to the steering station, leaving me alone at the top. At one point he yells up to me, "Matty! You see it? Whale comin' up ahead—"

A long smear darkens the water 150 feet ahead of us. Gabby slows the boat, and then suddenly the pointed prow of a finback whale breaks the surface, huge body glistening and sliding forward after it. It jets a cloud of breath into the air and slides under the waves, its massive fluke beating slow strokes, and its bomb-shaped body, long as a subway car, passes surprisingly quickly under our bow. The mist of its breath drifts to starboard in the breeze, shot through with rainbows. Minutes later, another finback comes up fifty feet to starboard, blows, arches, and dives almost vertically.

As we approach late morning, Dwaine sights and quickly harpoons a swordfish, he and Saul set out the gear, and we resume our search. Soon thereafter, the cloud cover thickens and begins to drop, and by noon we are swallowed by fog. The rolling sound of waves now seems to come from far away, and I hear the disembodied clicks and chirps of dolphins. Occasionally another boat, looking at first like a bruise deep in the cloud bank, grows in clarity and finally emerges with the aura of a ghost ship, trailing the sound of its engine and the waves off its bow. There are times when the fog blows by us in masses the size of buildings, whole walls and storm clouds roiling by. Other times it gathers in so close, the world becomes a narrow cone of clear air twenty feet around the boat, leaving our chances of spotting fins at nearly zero.

Hours pass. As my eyes keep up their pattern scan, out from the bow and back in a fan shape, a kind of autopilot kicks in, leaving my mind to wander. I know from the charts that our depth is roughly equivalent to the height of the Empire State Building, and I imagine what is happening below: whales the size of city buses cruise among darting pink concentrations of squid as mackerel schools swoop and turn like flocks of city pigeons. Swordfish—solitary purple missiles glinting silver—fly and turn, slaying ranks of prey unlike anything we know on land. I realize that whatever lives down there must remain unknown to me in its true scale. The ocean's real majesty is unknown to any of us—and will remain so, because it is a world we lack the full apparatus to perceive, a world we have yet to really explore, and because the full vibrancy of the ocean has been diminished. This is not to say that it cannot exist again, if not wholly then in some portion of its glory, but this will take enormous will and profound changes in how we live in relation to the natural world.

It is impossible to be out here, to know all I've learned from research and the testimony of scientists and fishermen, and not think about the morality in the destruction our species has wrought, and whether it matters. I find myself asking, "So why life?" Why pine barrens and boreal forests instead of lifeless rock and dirt? Why the blue whale and the beaded anemone, the conochilus rotifer and the broadbill swordfish, rather than vast, lifeless liquid enormities? Why all the ages of life that have passed before us rather than nothingness?

The pale blind eye of the sun materializes and disappears overhead, pulsing like a slow and distant heartbeat behind the veil of fog. I am reminded of C. S. Lewis, who wrote, "Nature never taught me that there exists a God of glory and of infinite majesty. . . . But Nature gave the word *glory* a meaning for me."

Nature is not God, nor is God Nature, but is not wilderness the song, the painting, the masterpiece that offers some answer to the question of why there is life? Does it not stand to reason that we should regard life—all life, animal, insect, and otherwise—as proof of some greater mystery of which we are a part? Does this not necessitate a deeper understanding of our role, and should we not be compelled by this highest wisdom to be wiser? To exemplify in our laws and as a matter of daily practice that a moral obligation exists to exercise precaution in our encounters with Nature? Shouldn't its ruin be avoided as a moral and spiritual imperative?

In the early afternoon, I climb down the tower to the main deck for lunch. Gabby is in a search pattern for the buoy. We've seen one other sword, but it dived before we were able to draw near.

"Won't get many swords today, it stays like this," Dwaine says.

Eventually Gabby locates the buoy and I help Dwaine haul in the high-flier and the line. Together he and Saul bring the swordfish over the gunwale onto the deck. I gaze closely at the fish, and while it is quite dead, its skin still reacts to changes in temperature. I place my right hand, fingers outspread, on its gill plate. When I remove it, my handprint, burnished silver against the bronze, remains as though seared upon its flesh. I ask Dwaine if he will guide me in dressing the fish. He hands me the sharpened knife and I remove the fins, make the notch behind the caudal keel, separate the tail, and then cut off the head. I open the belly, removing innards, and am stunned to find that the heart is still beating.

"Don't tell me this fish is alive," I say to Dwaine.

"No. It was dead when it came aboard. Sometimes the heart just keeps goin' for a bit."

I hold the beating heart in my hand, feeling its soft pulsations, then gently lay it on top of the ice hold. I watch, dumbfounded, as the heart propels itself forward like a soft, spade-shaped creature. It would be ghastly were it not also an overwhelming testament to this creature's life force.

As Dwaine begins to scrub the abdominal cavity with a stiff brush, I regard the swordfish's head, draining gore and blood across the deck. Possessing only the most rudimentary understanding of its biology, I begin a crude dissection and encounter a series of revelations. The gills are not at all like those of freshwater fish such as bass or even the more common saltwater fishes but rather are shaped like enormous commas, fitting in perfect symmetry behind the gill plate and curving in a long thin section forward to form the floor of the mouth. The bottom jaw is a lightweight V-shaped bone; the tapered gill sections attach here. The gills themselves are not frilled at the edges, as in many other fish, nor are they soft and fleshy; instead they're like a superfine and delicate coral mesh lacking any discernible veins or capillaries. Pressing between thumb and forefinger, I feel the mesh crush and watch the blood froth under my fingers. Each gill is actually a pair of gills, opening like a bread pocket hinged along the inner curve of the comma shape. The surface area and the blood saturation are incredibly dense—remarkable devices for extracting oxygen from water.

Delicately, using the tip of the knife, I remove one of the swordfish's eyes. The portion of the eye visible from the outside is roughly the size of a medium tomato, but removed from its socket the eye exceeds the size of a baseball. Gazing into its pupil is like looking into the front of a telephoto lens—clear and receding into black, optically distorted depths. Then I notice that the pupil has, near its bottom, a single copper divot. The pupil is rimmed ever so faintly with what looks like gold foil.

Surprisingly, the texture of the eyeball is not uniform. The front and the back are soft, while around its circumference is a sort of hard collar with the same feel as the molded plastic used in football shoulder pads. I wonder if this serves as a mechanism to support the eye shape at extreme depth.

Although I cannot see it, I know that the retina at the back of this eye is among the most sophisticated in the animal kingdom. At a thousand feet deep in clear seawater, there is only 0.003 percent of the light that's available at the surface, and yet the swordfish hunts in this nearly absolute night—and on rare occasions, to depths almost three times as great. One reason it's able to do so is because of the thick straps of extraocular muscle near the eye. Having sacrificed the ability to twitch, these muscles instead generate heat for the eyes and brain, which in deep, very cold water helps maintain the transmission speed of nerve signals. This adaptation gives the swordfish huge predatory sight advantages over its prey, which lack the same mechanisms.

Behind the eye I find the optic nerve, round and thick as a pencil, buried in deep waddings of pillowy yellow fat. I try but am unable to follow the nerve to the brain itself, where I hoped to locate the vision center, called the optic tectum, which is among the most highly developed of those of all fishes. What I do find, however, is striking: The swordfish's eyes are so large and outsize for its head that they protrude on either side like crystalline domes and nearly touch at the back, deep within the head, where they are separated by a section of cartilaginous tissue so thin it is translucent.

The visual acuity of swordfish is only one of their striking physiological adaptations. The other is speed. Considered among the fastest of all fish, their top speed has been calculated at seventy-eight miles per hour by propulsion dynamicists in China, who refer to the swordfish's ability to use "kidnapped airfoils" and "circulating horsepower" to achieve propulsion efficiencies that exceed 500 percent. In 2007, magnetic resonance image scans done by researchers in the Netherlands revealed a highly specialized organ at the front of the swordfish's head. Just above the root of the sword, the skull contains three oil-producing glands from which a system of dense, complex ducts extends through the tissue, dispersing at the skin via a network of minute holes. This area of skin corresponds with "a region of extreme dynamic pressure decrease." In other words, as the swordfish speeds through the water, the shape of its forehead creates a low-pressure area that sucks oil out of the glands, lubricating the head to minimize drag.

When I am through with my dissection, I take the hose and spray down the deck, then return the gills, fins, tail, and innards to the sea. The eyeball and heart I also give back, watching them sink away from the gunwale, aware that they are lifeless now, the heart no longer beating, the eye blind to the dimming sunlight of its world.

5

Not just hours but days begin to merge together. At one point, walking through the wheelhouse, I catch sight of myself in a small mirror hanging on the wall. Heavy stubble covers my jaw, and my face is a raw reddish brown, the result of days of windburn.

The boat climbs and falls, running in the chaos of ten-to-twelve-foot swells that look as though they will roll over the gunwales and clear the decks, but they never do. My eyes feel hollowed out, literally burned from their sockets after days aloft in the wind watching the ocean's rippling hide, and I begin to wonder whether I am seeing things that aren't there. I watch what appears to be a deep, streaking purple-blue object the size of a Volkswagen a hundred feet off the starboard rail, moving parallel to us but in the opposite direction. It's like the shadow of a plane, without definite shape, just a smudge, a traveling ripple of deep color in the water. I *feel* it move as I watch it, as though it were magnetic, as though it had an infinitesimal tug of gravity.

"Bluefin tuna," Saul says when I tell him.

The largest swordfish we haul aboard weighs more than three hundred pounds and emerges from the deep alive, though mortally wounded. It repeatedly whacks the side of the boat with its sword, bone smacking stone-hard fiberglass, and writhes its streaked bronze dinosaur body, round as a keg, with its remaining strength. It is one of the few times I've felt pure animal instinct utterly inhabit me. To see this creature living, to watch its body animated and out of the water, mere feet from me, rather than lying inert and dead on the deck, is an epiphany. Its diminished power, even now, alludes to a preternatural strength. And its attempt to wound the boat I recognize for what it is: courage. However its mind is constructed, whatever similar or alien consciousness resides therein, the ability to confront one's aggressor, to rise up rather than yield, is proof of nothing less.

It took Saul ten minutes to pull the swordfish up from six hundred feet. It and the ocean swells conspired against him, leaving him winded, and he says, struggling for breath, "I wadn't gonna let him have it. He wanted it, but I wadn't gonna let him have it." He and Dwaine are both smiling, glad that after almost twenty-four hours without a fish, they have landed one whose weight is the equivalent of two of the average size we've been catching.

Minutes later, as Dwaine clears the high-flier and the buoys from near the transom and then goes to fetch the knife, I step closer to the swordfish and realize it is still alive. I cannot bear the thought that it will suffer more, and from the lid of the ice hold I seize a rusted hatchet, placed there to sever line in case of emergency. I straddle the animal and kill it with four deep blows to the head. Part of me is sickened as I feel the hatchet plunge up to the handle through the fish's lightweight skull, as though it were balsawood. I am also horrified that this act of mercy is so savage, though I am merely hastening its end. It is inevitable that the fish will die, but there is no ending more absolute than the one I force it through, the shift from life to death, from being into oblivion. There is no way to be out here, to be part of this boat and its purpose, without also being involved in blood and death and the act of killing. If I did it every day—did it for a living—I can imagine that I would inevitably become detached from the reality of butchering and I might even get to the point that my shipmates have: able to walk by a mortally wounded animal and allow it to simply die. I don't believe they are cruel, for they have long recognized and accepted that they are hunters harvesting meat, and there is simply no way to do what they do without being executioners. But the taking of life should be acknowledged as such, and as such it should never be taken lightly.

And these men don't. Later that day, standing with Dwaine on deck, I ask him what he thinks about when he's coming onto a fish.

"I usually say a little prayer," he answers. "I say, 'Please, God, let me hit this one,' and if I hit it, I say, 'Thank you, God, for letting me hit that fish.' And when I take a fish aboard, I say, 'Thank you for the life of this fish.' "

The high post remains my station despite the increasingly unforgiving ride. Late one afternoon, with the ocean shimmering iridescent and the sun low in the sky, I watch a solitary dolphin gallop across the sea. From a quarter-mile away, it has heard our progress and comes leaping across the rolling blue hilltops, full of beauty and grace, to play and ride our bow wave.

Dwaine's accuracy, meanwhile, has been steadily improving, and I watch each of his strikes, admiring their athleticism and skill, their dance-like quality. The most magnificent shot occurs with a fish that must be close in weight to the three-hundred-pounder we landed. The boat and the fish approach each other stand-to-sword, and at the last moment the fish jukes left then quickly right, and Dwaine makes a skillful strike off to the side, in the area of the dorsal. The fish tips over from the impact, exposing its sharply delineated silver-purple side to me as it pumps its tail, but I am not convinced the hit is solid. When we go to retrieve the high-flier hours later, the dart comes up empty. I wish for more swordfish for my ship-mates, but I am pleased at this particular fish's escape. Through its cunning and speed it earned it, and it likely got away with only a torn dorsal fin.

We have been averaging two swords a day—low for what we could expect—and though we have sighted perhaps twice as many, there have been misses or instances in which the fish ran before Dwaine could take his shot. But Saul was right: With a few more days under my belt, I have begun to spot fins. I help dress some of the fish and otherwise try to make myself useful—coiling line, washing blood off the deck, keeping company on the watch. In the evening, all four of us occupy the narrow wheelhouse, trading stories, until it is joke time. A fisherman named Gunsmoke transmits through the night air from somewhere in the fleet.

"So, boys," he starts off. "Little Red Ridin' Hood got all dressed up ready to go to her grandma's house, and her mother tells her, 'You shouldn't go. The Big Bad Wolf might do bad things to ya.' And Little Red Ridin' Hood says, 'Oh yeah? Like what?' Her mother says, 'Well, he might wanna hie your little red dress up and your little red panties down and jig on your little red butt.' Red Ridin' Hood says to her, 'Aw, he wouldn't do that!' So she gets halfway to Grandma's house and the wolf jumps out on her and says, 'You know what I'm gonna do to you, don't ya?' She says, 'What?' He says, 'I'm gonna hie your little red dress up and your little red panties down and jig your little red ass.' She says, 'Oh, no, you ain't!' and she runs home and gets a gun. She comes back on her way to Grandma's and the wolf jumps out on her again. She says, '*Now* what're you gonna do?' and the wolf says, 'I'm gonna hie your little red dress up and your little red panties down and I'm gonna jig your little red ass.' She points that gun at him and says, 'Oh, no, you ain't. I'm gonna lay down right here and you're gonna eat me just like the book says.'"

Laughter from a dozen boats comes in waves through the handset, joining our own.

Gabby takes the first watch as Dwaine, then Saul, head below to sleep. I pull up a stool next to Gab. In the days I've been aboard, I've learned to understand him more clearly, but in the wheelhouse with the diesel going, it remains difficult. Sometime after midnight I head out the doorway to the deck to urinate over the side. Save for the faint running lights behind me, it is utterly black, cloud cover obscuring the stars. There are no other ships' lights. The wind, which hasn't left us for a week, troubles the waves heaving dimly past. With an abrupt unsettled feeling, I become acutely aware of how close death is: A slip of my boot on this wet deck and I would be over the side and lost. Then, at my feet, trailing in glowing streaks from the hull, I notice the bioluminescence—small creatures, lighting and fading away like sparks. I am overcome by the poignancy of this world, its shifting tides of joy and sadness, beauty and pain. Loss and hope.

Inside, I settle on the stool next to the old man.

"You think you'll ever retire, Gab?" I ask.

"I don't know. I can't do this forever. But I'd rather get wheeled off this boat than wait at home to die." Then, lighting another cigarette, he says slowly, "Off Cape Sable, heading west towards Seal Island, is about eighteen miles. Wasn't fifteen years ago we'd make that run and for that whole way, all you could see was pollock jumpin'. Big ones—three and four feet long, thirty and forty pounds each. Tens of thousands of 'em. They was chasin' the herring. Sky was full of gulls divin', screamin' their fuckin' racket. When the draggers first came, they were company boats, and they weren't sent for anything but cod. They'd tow and throw, tow and throw, until they got what they wanted. Few days of that, the sea was covered with dead fish far as you could see."

I say nothing.

"It's gone, Matt. What's been lost is beyond imagining."

In the dim light I watch his face. He begins to say something else, his toothless jaw moving, and I finally make it out.

"Man is cruel, isn't he."

6

Our tally after six days of fishing is twelve swordfish, weighing a total of 1,640 pounds. We offload the fish at the Newellton Wharf early on the morning of July 4, under the gaze of a DFO officer. The price per pound a few days ago was above $5, but it's dropping quickly with each new boat coming in. Now, at $4.50 per pound, Saul, Gabby, and Dwaine will clear about seven grand. Take out the costs of the boat, fuel, and food, and count something for the five days it took to rig the spotting tower and the stand, and it does not amount to much. They will head out next week for another try.

As promised, Saul has arranged for me to talk with another of the swordfishermen, Gilbert Devine, and his spotter, Jim Crawford. Gilbert has a sixty-foot tower on his boat, the tallest in the fleet, rigged like a schooner's mainmast. Having caught thirty fish on this trip, the boat will clear over $15,000. The following day, we drive over the causeway in Saul's pickup truck, past the scallop protesters, to Woods Harbour. Gilbert's property is clean and well tended—white house, modern storage building behind it, no clutter. We sit in Gilbert's living room as his girlfriend, Karen, serves tea. The house reminds me of my grandmother's: It has the same tidiness—the carpet shows the recent traces of a vacuum, and on the coffee table there's a glass candy bowl, pictures of family, not a speck of dust. Gilbert, in his late fifties, has a methodical, no-nonsense demeanor, which helps account for his being among the fleet's best captains. Crawford, who is taller, with dark hair, a square jaw, and a mustache, looks as if he just walked out of a Marlboro ad. If Gilbert patiently separates the wheat from the chaff, Crawford does so with a knife. Crawford has gone masthead for some of the best harpooners of the past forty years—Louie Larsen from Chilmark, the Mayhews from Menemsha, on Martha's Vineyard, the d'Entremonts.

"I've seen every one of them pull back from sticking an undersized fish," he tells me. "They fished with a conscience. We have a code of honor. Now, Larsen was one of the longline highliners in the sixties and seventies. He saw what he'd done and regretted it. He went back to harpooning, and that's when I went spotter for him."

"Saul filled me in on the longliners' high-grading and shacking," I tell them. "Bycatch looks like it can be pretty bad."

"Put it this way," Jim says. "If they record it in the logbooks, it's a lie. They're shacking way more than they record—juvenile swordfish, bluefin tuna, *and* they're taking shark fins. One guy told me they took seven hundred pounds of shark fins on the last trip. In '07, the DFO had 1 percent observer coverage on the longliners. According to the record books, they were dumping more than 40 percent of the catch, so you know it was way higher. By not observing at 100 percent, DFO is letting the longliners get away with murder, and both sides know it."

Crawford cites the example of the British Columbia groundfishery, which only recently was forced to switch all the boats over to video observation.

"The cameras go on when the lines are hauled back. DFO takes 10 percent of the recorded tapes and compares them to the captains' logbooks, but they have 100 percent of the tapes. I know the rep for the Area 4 halibut fishermen. He admitted to me that before observers, logbooks were lies. Now, with 100 percent video observation, it makes them better fishermen. He said those words. The cameras keep them honest and stop them from setting where they know they're going to get a lot of bycatch. If they reach their cap on bycatch, they're shut down."

Gilbert chimes in. "Without observers, it's carnage. I've seen turtles, dolphins, whales wrapped in gear. Even with observers, it's not as clean as harpooning. DFO does not reward any of the sustainable, traditional methods. They should."

Gilbert explains that in order to fish you must have a license, one that's either been purchased or handed down to you. There is an absurdity in the latter, in that you can own a license handed down through your family, earn money from it, and never set foot on a boat or work in the fishery. It's another way a public resource is privatized. The license gives permission to fish; the quota is the amount of fish you can catch with your license. Quota can be bought outright or it can be leased for a single trip. Canada has what's called an ITQ system—individual transferable quota. If you have a license and five thousand pounds of halibut quota, that's all you can catch; if you want to catch more, you must either buy or lease more quota. Because there is a limit on the total number of licenses and total quota available, the number of fishermen is also limited, as is the total amount of landed catch (discards and bycatch are another matter).

What does not make sense in this system, as Gilbert explains, is that the Canadians have no effective safeguards preventing the consolidation of licenses and quota into the hands of a few individuals. While the safeguards are on the books, enforcement is poor or nonexistent, and those who benefit have ways of getting around the restrictions. This is exactly what has happened in Maritime Canada, to disastrous effect.

"I call it the Rise of the Fish Lords," Saul says. "That's what these guys are. They're fish lords."

Saul explains that in a lot of cases these fish lords are fish-processing-plant owners or individuals who are able to buy license after license and amass significant amounts of quota. If they max on the quota they're allowed, they buy more through a proxy or a front organization. This consolidation of the wealth of the natural resource into the hands of a few in turn creates a range of problems: First, there is a significant stratification of wealth, cutting off entire communities from sharing in the benefits of what should be a communal resource. Instead of dozens of families making their living off a fish stock, you get a handful of wealthy men and women, with everyone else either cut out entirely or forced to work for a pittance if they want to fish at all. Saul has known dozens who have simply given up and sold their licenses and quota and gotten out of fishing. Under the stress and hardship, others have turned to drinking or drugs, leading to the collapse of families. Many of Cape Sable's younger generation have left for the tar sands of Alberta. They would rather live that life than try to make a go of it in fishing.

Globally, there is a huge overcapacity in fishing vessels, and the reduction of these fleets is a critical step in scaling down industrial fishing's overall impact. But this raises the question of what kind of fishing vessel— and what kind of fishing—should be promoted. Supporting a few corporate fleets with huge ships and massive fishing power (as well as destructive capacity) seems less in the interests of society than seeking to rebuild collapsed stocks (even to former geographic ranges), establishing sustainable levels of ship and fleet fishing power, and creating equitable means for the members of a community to share in access to the resource. Regardless of what economic term you apply to these notions of equitable division, the destruction of ecosystem balance and of community-based, independent fishing constitutes a loss of strength. Avoiding that destruction argues for solutions that guarantee the opposite outcome.

The concentration of wealth also creates a consolidation of power in the hands of the fish lords. They have been known to blackmail their crews, warning them that they won't be hired for the lucrative winter lobster fishery unless they work the summer groundfish season—an arrangement that is essentially feudal. Dwaine is routinely required to pay for a portion of the diesel and food costs on the boats on which he works, which never used to be the case. When you were hired on a boat, you worked for a share of the catch. The boat owner paid for everything else and took a percentage of the catch for the boat. Under the current system, food and fuel costs— sometimes even the costs of leased quota—are taken out of the deckhands' shares, and the boat continues to take its usual share in addition to that.

"It's how they stick it to ya," Dwaine says. "When you get down to it, it's hardly worth goin' out. I can work twelve-hour days for a week and make ten cents a pound, clear four or five hundred bucks take-home altogether, where the other fifty or sixty cents a pound is going to the guy who never steps onboard."

The consolidation of wealth and power supports another vector of influence: politics.

"One of the largest fishing corporations in Canada gets rid of all its halibut quota—500,000 pounds of it," Saul says. "The new buyer says he wants to apply that same quota to a new location. This would totally max out the fishing effort that is allowed to be applied to that area. But this buyer tells the DFO, 'I want it straightened out.' DFO granted him access to those grounds. I've tried to get more access in that area and have been denied every time. Everything they've put into conserving that zone—limits on number of trips and total poundage and hauls per week—it's all gonna be wiped out. Now how do you think that buyer worked it out?"

"I have no idea."

"The seller was one of the largest fishing corporations in Canada, remember. You think they had a stake in gettin' rid of that half-a-million-pounds-of-halibut quota? You think maybe a few strings got pulled over at the DFO to help cut that deal?"

"How are quotas set in the first place?" I ask.

"They're based on history. In our case, with harpooning, the DFO went back through the catch records and picked a bunch of years to average. After more than thirty years of longlinin', what kind of shape do you think the swordfish stock was in? There was nothin' left. There were still harpoon licenses but not many guys harpooning. We wanted to bring it back. But DFO gave 90 percent of the quota to the longliners and 10 percent to us."

7

Bobby Meacham* is a fishermen's representative from Mahone Bay,† fifty miles northeast from Cape Sable. He represents a few dozen small-scale ground-trawl (bottom-longline) fishermen in negotiations with the DFO, and he's agreed to talk to me on the condition that I maintain

---

*Not his real name.
† Not the real location.

his anonymity. He has been working within the fisheries management system for twenty years.

We meet in the parking lot of a gas station off Highway 103 outside Bridgewater. Meacham looks as if he just came out of the woods after lumberjacking for a few years. He's six foot three and has a thick black beard that reaches to the middle of his chest. He's dressed in jeans and steel-toed boots, a baseball cap, and an old tan Carhartt work jacket. His voice is a deep, slow burn.

Meacham is one of many people who have complained about DFO practices, and to the question of bluefin tuna bycatch in surface longlining he says simply, "A critical bycatch species that would close a fishery if the limit was reached gets discarded."

I ask him to give me his perception of how the DFO operates.

"There's a big difference in how DFO treats the big players versus the small ones," he says slowly and precisely. "In the offshore scallop fishery, DFO was pushed to figure out how much groundfish bycatch—cod, haddock—the big scallopers were killing. They needed it because of an agreement with the United States to monitor all groundfish catches. Took them five years to do it. Then, when they did, and they saw what the big boys were doing in bycatch, they turned around and took that amount off the small inshore groundfish fishermen's quota. They made the small longliners and mobile-gear guys take the hit for the big guys' problem. There's inshore and offshore scallop fleets. They ain't the same bird on almost every issue (bycatch, bottom impact, et cetera). Inshore fleet is small, tows small gear. Offshore fleet has ships that drag three dredges in tandem. Each dredge is twenty-two foot wide, weighs sixteen tons. That's gonna do some damage."

Meacham pauses to take a pull off his smoke.

"Now, the offshore scallop fishery is the largest corporate fishery in Canada. It's owned by Ocean Choice, Mersey Seafoods, Comeau's Sea Foods, Clearwater, and Himmelman. Bottom line is DFO is corporate controlled. The corporations don't give a shit about the habitat they're impacting or that they're killing groundfish. The suggestion was made that DFO give them a cap that would force innovation to reduce their fish bycatch. DFO refused to impose the change and just gave them more quota off the small guys' amount. Some of these companies have more codfish quota for bycatch than some whole communities have codfish quota, period. The waste could be almost entirely eliminated if they just managed better."

Meacham's eyes are expressionless, leaving me with the feeling that he's been involved with these issues for so long that his anger has hardened into something like a ten-ton block of lead.

"You got three levels—politics at the top, middle-management bureaucracy, and bottom-level enforcement. You got good people and fuckups on every level. At the top, a big part of the problem is the ministers. It's part of the system left over from the British. The minister is God, because the minister has what's called 'absolute discretion.' The minister can do pretty much whatever he wants, including change the rules when it suits him, particularly when it comes to doing favors for big players who can then help him get reelected."

"Do you know of cases where that's happened?"

He thinks about this for a moment. "Few years back, the lead candidate for prime minister comes to town, and the CEO of one of these major fishing corporations writes him a fifty-thousand-dollar check for his leadership run. Now, there are caps on individual donations when a party goes into an election, but there's no accountability in leadership funding. You can't tell me that much cash doesn't get you in. You should also know the illegalities and corruption happen not just with corporations; it happens with owner-operators too. Say a guy has a lot of debt and a big boat and a high life. He's going to fish to pay off that boat and stay ahead. He has to. Then you have the unions. The union in Newfoundland was the biggest whip hand in the industry for years. It had twenty-five thousand members. The fishermen bullied the pols into increasing their cod quota on the Grand Banks, and now they're reaping their own whirlwind."

"How about the other levels?"

"I also know of eight or nine cases where individuals in significant management positions within the DFO left and within days were working for the company they used to regulate. These are individuals who worked on determining quota and licenses. While they don't sign the document, they do write the briefing notes to make the argument for the allotment to the minister above them, so in that capacity they have enormous sway."

Meacham drops his cigarette butt and grinds it into the pavement. "With this shit you say to yourself, 'There's something walking across the road there. It looks like a duck. It quacks like a duck. What the fuck is it? Is it a duck?' "

"Why isn't the Canadian press covering any of this?" I ask.

"The press is dead," he tells me. "Fifteen years of reorganization and consolidation in the media, and we're left with local papers owned by an out-of-province company. They are barely able to publish, and don't have a high caliber of reporting. The days of free press in this province are ending. They don't want to get into complicated stories that might involve a little bit of science, a little bit of regulatory jargon, or some political intrigue. If you can't get the story out, then a lot of people give up or don't think there's a problem, because there's no coverage of it."

Meacham and I continue talking for close to an hour. He describes a litany of abuses including low- and high-level corruption, corporate favoritism, and incompetence. He describes the tendency of the DFO to closely control access to information, routinely blacking out large sections of official documentation. "They're so secretive you'd think we were in a fucking war," Meacham says. He also describes the devastating effect of large fishing corporations on local communities.

"One of the largest seafood companies in Canada comes down to Yarmouth and buys out a family scallop business. Promises to leave the jobs in the town. A month later, three hundred people are fired. Same company did the exact same thing down in Lockeport, in Port Mouton, and up here in Lunenberg. They did the same thing to the offshore lobster fleet. Now they berth their freezer trawlers at the cheapest ports they can find. They pay their crews very little money and drive them around in old school buses—guys who used to make $70,00 to $120,000 per year, depending on their position on the boat, are now making $30,000 to $60,000. Meanwhile, the owners are worth hundreds of millions. We're all going to be dead someday, but what's the point of screwing everybody you deal with?"

"Is all this the product of incompetence or corruption?" I ask.

"Both, and it depends on the fishery. There's plenty of incompetence, believe me. In our scallop fishery, we have the VMS (vessel monitoring system) that tracks the vessel and sends the DFO its location randomly once an hour. Down south, they have a big problem with some boats in the scallop fleet fishing in closed areas. They turn off their black boxes, run into a closed area, fish, come back out, and turn on the black box again, knowing they can hide behind the excuse that maybe just one signal was missed. So in the fisheries meeting in April, the reps from the area being poached forced the DFO to agree to ping every fifteen minutes instead of every hour. When the license conditions come out a few months later, what do they say? Ping every hour. And this is after the scallop fishermen themselves had agreed to it in the public meeting. At the eleventh hour, the head of enforcement for DFO in Halifax says, 'No, we don't want to do that because it would upset the national standard, which is one ping per hour.' Makes me think of that Aretha Franklin song."

"Which one's that?"

"'Chain of Fools.' That's the DFO."

Meacham digs inside his coat pocket for his lighter and pack of cigarettes. "What you gotta understand is, in the big picture, it isn't even a certain individual or a union or a company that's the problem; it's the mindset. We used to have a good mindset in most of these fisheries, where they said, 'If you treat Mother Nature gently and take a share but not too much and let the babies survive, you should have it forever.'"

"So where's it go from here?" I ask.

He inhales and takes a moment to consider this. "That depends. The reason we got together and rebuilt the Georges Bank groundfish is because of one critical person, a guy in the American system who was at our U.S.-Canada meetings. He said, 'Guys, we gotta stop this.' We said, 'What do you mean?' He said, 'We get together every four to six months and we lie to each other. I'm not gonna sit at the end of my career and bounce my grandchildren on my knee and when they ask me, 'What did you do for a living, Grampy?' tell them that I presided over the demise of the North Atlantic groundfish fishery. So we better fuckin' smarten up and save these stocks.' That's what it's gonna take—the balls to call it what it is, cut the bullshit, and get it right."

BOOK 2

DESTRUCTION

Introduction

Annihilation of a Fish

For Man is God
and man is eating the earth up
like a candy bar
and not one of them can be left alone with the ocean
for it is known he will gulp it all down.

—Anne Sexton, "The Earth Falls Down"

In 1986, a series of photographs called "The Chase" was taken by Paul Murray off Nomans Land Island, near Martha's Vineyard. The photos show a giant bluefin tuna, weighing over nine hundred pounds, leaping, missing, leaping again, and capturing an Atlantic bluefish about two feet long. The giant bluefin has all the design characteristics of a fighter jet: supremely tapered shape, short fins like abbreviated wings, extreme speed.

Murray's images offer a rare glimpse of the true majesty of these animals—creatures that most of us will never experience except as small, rectangular ruby chunks of flesh in sashimi and sushi, or as deep reddish-purple tuna steaks. The bluefin Murray photographed was about nine feet long, with a burst speed roughly ten times its body length—ninety feet per second (the distance from home to first base on a baseball diamond in the blink of an eye), or sixty miles per hour. Through *water*. Thanks to its remarkable physiology and immense strength, it was able to fly through its liquid medium at highway speed with a self-generated equivalent of over fifty horsepower.

Top ocean predators like bluefin play a critical role in structuring the overall balance of relationships throughout the food web below them. Much like wolves in the Rocky Mountains, the ocean's top predators are believed to exert a governing influence and a stabilizing effect on the ecosystems they inhabit. From a purely human-centric point of view, robust populations of these predators provide benefits to us in the form of healthy oceans, food, recreation, and jobs.

Varieties of bluefin tuna inhabit the Southern Ocean around Australia, the Indian Ocean, and the Pacific, but there is only one northern bluefin tuna. It is an Atlantic fish, the one Hemingway called "the king of all fish, the ruler of the Valhalla of fishermen." The northern bluefin has evolved unique physiological adaptations for speed, transoceanic migration, and rapid conversion of prey fish to accessible energy, enabling it to dominate as a top predator in the world's temperate oceans. The largest ever caught on rod and reel, which was landed off Nova Scotia in 1979, weighed 1,496 pounds and measured nearly eleven feet long.

Scientists have warned for years that the depletion in stocks has placed both northern and southern bluefin in jeopardy of commercial extinction.* While true extinction of an oceanic species is difficult (but not impossible) to bring about, commercial extinction is more easily achieved. Commercial extinction takes place when humans devastate a fish stock to the point that it loses its ability to recover and rebuild a population. The species often contracts in range, remains at very low numbers, and may even lose its functional niche in the ecosystem to other competing species. It is effectively displaced and marginalized, and the fate of the Grand Banks cod is proof that this scenario is feasible. We need only look at the history of bluefin tuna in the Atlantic to know that the species is approaching commercial extinction.

The fate of the bluefin has become reasonably well known through various documentaries and books. The salient facts are as follows: Japan consumes roughly 80 percent of the global catch in northern bluefin tuna and the lion's share of all other bluefin varieties. While the United States, Europe, China, and other nations eat increasing quantities of bluefin in sushi, Japan remains the main engine that drives the fish's destruction. To eat the raw, red flesh of the bluefin is viewed there as a sign that you are able to afford the very best in life, and it has a cachet that is equivalent to

---

*The Pacific bluefin, a related species, while still considered overfished, is not considered in danger of commercial extinction at this time.

that of the finest caviar. In Tokyo, the top-grade tuna at the highest-end sushi restaurants may fetch as much as $100 per serving.

A hundred years ago, however, bluefin tuna was not widely eaten in Japan, for lack of large-scale harvest and transport capacity. As recently as forty years ago, giant bluefin tuna caught in the Gulf of Maine and hoisted onto the wharf were hard to give away at five cents a pound.

What happened in the interim was that both technology and tastes changed. In the aftermath of World War II, Japanese longliners ranged the world's oceans to harvest fish to prevent starvation of the country's population. It was during this period that they developed a taste for the fatty belly meat—*chutoro* and *otoro*—the highest-grade part of the bluefin. Then, in 1972, with freezing and transport methods improving and costs dropping, the first North Atlantic bluefin tuna was successfully flown to Tokyo from the U.S. East Coast. By the 1980s, sushi and sashimi were becoming increasingly popular in the United States, the European Union, and other prosperous nations, generating even greater increases in harvesting.

Then, in the early 1990s, in a devastating but predictable development, the fishermen in Port Lincoln, South Australia, having laid waste to their own southern bluefin tuna populations and desperate to survive the impending economic storm, devised a way to "ranch" bluefin: They captured schools of southern bluefin, towed them back to the coast, and fattened them in pens before slaughtering them and shipping them to Japan. They had found a way to increase yield from a ravaged stock.

The idea quickly caught on. In the Mediterranean, ranching got under way in the mid-1990s as a means to make up the decreasing poundage of wild bluefin being harvested there. Ranches started popping up off the coasts of Spain, France, and Italy, with operations eventually spreading to Croatia, Turkey, Cyprus, and Malta. Soon there were more than fifty ranches dotting the coasts of the Mediterranean, with catches two to three times the quota limit of twenty-one thousand metric tons and the value of the illegal bluefin tuna trade estimated to exceed $400 million annually— one-third the value of the entire catch. Fleets of huge new purse seine ships were also built with EU taxpayer dollars delivered in the form of government subsidies, and these craft went into the Mediterranean to take all the bluefin they could find.

The Mediterranean, however, is the primary northern bluefin tuna breeding ground in the world, and the purse seiners were taking the fish as they aggregated to spawn. They were taking not only the big, fecund females but also the young that had not yet reached breeding maturity. They were capturing entire schools—thousands of bluefin tuna—in one encirclement of their nets.

By 2008 the seiners in the Mediterranean had reduced the population of breeding adults to less than one-fifth of what it had been only twenty years earlier. ICCAT warned of an impending stock collapse at the same time that it approved quota limits above the sustainable levels that its own scientific committee had defined. The message could not have been clearer, and yet they fished.

Whether out of disdain or indifference, the individuals responsible for this crime against Nature had no concern for these animals, and their attitude revealed itself in their denials, their political quibbling, and, for the more criminal among them, it revealed itself in their plotting, their illicit behavior, and their flouting of international law.

The eastern Atlantic spawning stock* of the northern bluefin tuna (whose primary habitat is in the eastern Atlantic off northwest Europe and in the Mediterranean) is estimated to have declined by more than 85 percent from its reference levels in the early 1970s. The western stock—native to the United States and Canada, and typically about one-tenth the size of the eastern Atlantic population—is in similar peril. To understand how and why these fish are being decimated on a global scale, I went to Tokyo to visit Tsukiji market, which processes 10 percent of the world's fresh seafood per day. I saw the thousands of frozen bluefin carcasses auctioned off daily and cataloged the vast array of living, dying, and dead oceanic life that flows through Tsukiji. From there I flew north to the small town of Oma, at the very northern tip of the main island of Honshu, where I spent several days with the small fleet of roughly forty fishing boats that still practice a traditional, sustainable single-hook method of harvesting blue-

---

* Stocks are referred to by their location in an ocean region rather than their location in relation to a body of land. Thus, the "western stock" of northern bluefin refers to the stock in the western Atlantic, off the East Coast of the United States and Canada.

fin. I saw the quick, humane way the fishermen killed their catch and the care they used in dressing the fish. I saw how hard they toiled and witnessed the reverence they still maintain toward these creatures. In recent years, however, the co-op of local fishermen in Oma has seen its catch fall from an average of three to four fish per boat per day to fewer than half a dozen fish per day for the entire forty-ship fleet.

After leaving Japan, I traveled to Port Lincoln, South Australia, to visit the place where tuna ranching originated. I spoke with members of the Stehr Group, a business descended from one of the first and most successful of the South Australia tuna barons, Hagen Stehr. I toured the Stehr Group's remote Arno Bay facility, where the company has invested millions of dollars attempting to induce wild southern bluefin to spawn in captivity.

Finally, I went to the front line of the struggle, the place where the fate of the northern bluefin will be decided: the small island nation of Malta, the epicenter of world bluefin tuna ranching. For years, only three organizations—the World Wildlife Fund, Oceana, and Greenpeace—had chosen to monitor the trade in the absence of any meaningful commitment of time, money, personnel, or matériel by EU governments. In July 2009, I joined the twenty-seven-person crew of the Greenpeace ship *Rainbow Warrior* as it set out from Malta's capital, Valletta, to patrol the southern Mediterranean in search of illegal, unregulated, and unreported (IUU) tuna operations.

Whirlwind

Tokyo and Oma, Japan

Port Lincoln, South Australia

1

The black asphalt and bright signs, the dark windows and light metal bridges of Tokyo's Narita Airport gleam in the cold night drizzle. Jet-lagged from the flight from California, I tow my luggage with slumped shoulders to the bus terminal, where I buy a ticket and take my seat aboard the coach. I watch the young baggage handlers load the passengers' bags, then line up and ceremonially bow to us as we depart. I drift off to sleep amid the sounds of travel—slapping wipers, the ring of the opening door, the diesel's whine, and the thump of fissures in the road.

I have come to Japan to witness a phenomenon unlike anything else on the planet: a fish market of colossal size, spread over fifty-five acres; a small city of sixty thousand workers that pumps and throbs in a cyclical influx and outflow of life as though it were some kind of gargantuan organism that climbed out of the sea to eat and die and be reborn each morning upon the shore of Tokyo Bay. The place is pronounced *Skee-jee*.

Tsukiji processes two thousand metric tons of seafood per day. One-tenth of the world's fresh catch. Four and a half million pounds. Fulton Fish Market in New York City—the second-largest seafood market in the world—takes almost a week to process what Tsukiji does in twenty-four hours. Tsukiji is an unchallenged behemoth, a black-hole vortex for sea life flying through the air by plane, steaming over the surface of the sea by ship, converging from around the world at this single spot on the globe.

At four in the morning, after having slept briefly at my hotel, I walk through the glimmering rainy darkness to a corner near Tsukiji's main gate, where I await Nick, the "Maido Man." ("Maido Man" translates roughly as "Mr. Thank You for Coming" or "Mr. Come Again" or simply "Mr. Welcome.") He arrives under a black umbrella, which he folds like a bat wing after greeting me. He's dressed in a tan waterproof jacket, a blue oxford shirt, and beige slacks. I detect subtle strands of gray in his black hair, which is swept back from his forehead, and I'm struck by how his unlined skin stretches taut over the planes of his face.

The Maido Man worked in the fish business for a dozen years and gives tours of Tsukiji two to three mornings a week. He speaks careful, well-enunciated English. We are joined on the corner by a young couple from Portugal and another from China. After paying our fee, we head off under the awnings of various storefronts, just now opening for business, their inside rooms casting dim, warm light into the black street as though it were firelight from the mouths of caves. Eventually we come to Namiyoke, a Shinto shrine. The Maido Man enters and pays his respects at an altar, bowing twice, clapping twice, lowering his head, praying, and bowing once again. He rejoins us and tells us he has prayed for a successful tour and has asked several Shinto gods to keep us safe. He brings us deeper into the shrine, where we encounter a large stone egg with perfectly folded chains of paper rectangles draped over it—prayers and benedictions from the egg suppliers of Tsukiji, to the supplier of all eggs. There are other totems and mementos, prayers, wishes, supplications to the Shinto deities—from the sushi restaurateurs and the tempura makers and the tuna middlemen—asking for continued success and expressing gratitude for the bounties of the past.

We leave the shrine and pass banks of Japanese lanterns, three high, nine across, glowing brightly above our heads on either side of the shrine entrance. They illuminate the sidewalk, each lantern displaying the name of a shrine patron written in black paintbrush script. The names include *Asahi Shimbun,* a major Japanese newspaper whose main offices are here in the Tsukiji area, and Ishimiya, a tuna "middleman" company, one of the main buyers, sellers, and distributors of bluefin tuna.

We turn a corner and I begin to feel something like a perceptible change in gravity. Small diesel trucks and workers on bicycles flash past us, joining crowds of other vehicles, white-coated workers, and men pulling handcarts, coming and going from all directions. A din pervades the atmosphere—the noise of throttling engines, tires, footsteps, human speech, horns, echoes, whistles and beeps, the tortured squeak of brakes, and the rapid aspirations of the propane-driven engines of a bizarre creation unique to Tsukiji, the turret cart. They are everywhere, passing at high speed, stopping in an instant, turning down alleyways and disappearing. Each has a short tower the size of a garbage barrel at its front, from which shines a single, bright headlight. The turret is topped by a steering ring, the engine inside the turret driving a small wheel below. The driver stands behind the turret, the flatbed section of the cart extending behind him, where myriad items are stacked and conveyed: wooden pallets, sacks of rice, boxes of knives, plastic bins, cardboard containers, water buckets, assorted crates, and piled Styrofoam squares wrapped in sheets of clear plastic. The turret carts race and dodge through the mayhem like mad little bright-eyed cyclopean robots, with their dry mechanical purr and their horns beeping with the urgency and panic of electronic game show buzzers.

Smoke mixes with mist from the rain, blurring the flashes of red, white, and yellow lights. By now I have lost my bearings as we enter a cavernous, cool, bright white hall. Using his hands like rakers, a man delicately fluffs piles of gray, dried, minuscule baby glass eels known as *shirasu*. The piles are contained within Styrofoam boxes—hundreds of them, stacked perfectly on tables. Cool air bearing the clean scent of brine permeates the room. Tables with boxes containing other types of dried fish stretch into the distance—thousands of boxes under banks of white rectangular lights hanging from the ceiling. Crowds of buyers, sellers, and inspectors mill about, examining the wares.

The Maido Man guides us out of the dried fish warehouses and we reenter the bustle of the box handlers and men moving pallets with forklifts, truck drivers smoking cigarettes by the cabs of their rigs, workers towing primitive-looking steel-wheeled wooden handcarts. We continue through the darkness, making our way deeper and deeper into this warren, each warehouse a separate, self-contained world.

At the sound of the dry, cold, echoing *thock!* of ax blows, the Maido Man takes us across a narrow lane into a warehouse where enormous blue plastic tarps cover row upon row of frozen tuna carcasses. The auction is being prepared. We cannot see the whole fish, but the stump where each animal's tail used to be protrudes from beneath the tarp. A man in black boots, carrying a large cleaving blade fastened to the end of a long wooden handle, lands blow after blow, chopping into the frozen tail stumps to expose a section of flesh for inspection. While I watch, he lands close to thirty blows without a single miss, each one falling in exactly the same narrow cleavage, no larger than an envelope's slit, deeper and deeper into the frozen, rock-hard flesh.

Our guide tells us we will return when it's time for the auction to begin, but before we depart, he directs our attention to an enormous swordfish, laid out on a green wooden pallet. Even with its tail, fins, and head removed, the trunk of its body is close to seven feet long and must measure five feet around. It is an enormous animal, five hundred pounds easily, with a massive sword that must exceed four feet in length.

We leave the tuna auction houses and proceed through the mechanized pandemonium of the lanes and alleys to a huge market space where goods are actually sold. There are over a thousand wooden stalls divided by pathways so narrow they force us into single file. Each unit is a small store, around ten feet wide by twenty or thirty feet deep. We pass rich cherry-red octopuses turned bottom up, white suckers exposed, as though they were spherical, white-nubbed mushrooms from an alien world. Their glistening opaque colors give them the appearance of blown glass. I gaze into a box of shiny ebony squid, packed so evenly they could pass for brightly enameled 100-millimeter cannon rounds. There are dozens of varieties of fish laid out in boxes stacked upon each other like the open drawers of a bureau. Immersed in ice and water, the fish gleam with freshness, and in a single glance I count orange roughy, redfish, pompano, bream, grunt, butterfish, parrot fish, sea bass, and snapper, their skins flashing gemstone colors—yellow citrine, vivid peridot green, pale amethyst lavender, paraiba tourmaline, fire opal. We walk past dozens and dozens of market stalls, past striped tiger shrimp, a pebbly beach of periwinkles, and a deepwater lancet fish, its thin, three-foot-long mirrored aluminum body circled upon itself, its dead face still fierce, needle teeth gleaming sharp.

We pass a bank of wooden crates filled with fine sawdust and tangled masses of small live lobsters. They appear feeble and confused, claws and antennae reaching weakly for the edge of the box, each one half buried in the dust and the bodies of its comrades. Each wooden crate has the appearance of a miniature mass grave, with half the victims still alive, struggling through the corpses for the surface.

At one corner stands a column of round black plastic bins, each containing several dozen desperately wriggling live eels, juveniles four inches long, from Hokkaido. They are a delicacy, eaten live, "to give energy," explains the Maido Man. They wriggle in a thin sheen of water, just enough to keep them moist.

Nearby is a cooler of what appear to be large rounds of beef tenderloin; this is actually whale meat, presented in marbled loaves. Our guide tells us that he ate this frequently in elementary school, where it was served for lunch. "Half the kids did not like it because it's so chewy," he explains. Then come tiny anchovies laid in exact, even rows, their flanks glimmering with a single metallic ribbon embedded within translucent flesh. There are fist-size abalone, their raw blanched undersides turned up, and cockles, then an overwhelming parade of clams and limpets, whelks, mussels, oysters, and a boxful of glistening brown, cone-shaped snails whose soft monopods protrude, dividing in two like butterfly wings. There are boxes containing massive, raw, slick sausages of pale, pinkish roe, densely packed in thin, organlike skeins, giving them the appearance of elongated brains. Near these lie thick, colorfully studded, phallic sea cucumbers in a range of colors, sizes, and textures.

We pass a station where a man seizes eight-inch eels one by one from a bucket, tacks each one's head to a board with a wooden peg, flays it, and extracts the spine in less than four seconds, as expertly as a surgeon. He uses a squat, curved knife no bigger than his thumb. We pass aquariums full of creatures that appear half dead, hypoxic, bewildered, catatonic.

I watch a man using a band saw to cut quartered tuna sections, four feet long, so frozen they appear to be covered in powdered sugar. The saw band screams the crescendo of an aria at every pass.

We stop at the entrance of a room that contains hundreds of small, blond wooden boxes, each of them no bigger than a man's palm and containing a sea urchin that will sell for $380. "The harvest is poor. That is why they are so expensive," observes the Maido Man.

Down one narrow alley we witness the preparation of *iki-jime* (*eekee-jeemay*). Two men work as a team, the first seizing live ten-pound yellowtail

amberjack from a tank. With two quick cleaver strikes, he opens the spine
behind the head and immediately in front of the tail. He passes the fish to
the next man, who takes it by the head, twists and opens the head wound
like a hinge, and inserts a long, stiff wire down the spinal cord, plunging it
in three or four times as the fish's body twitches with electric jerks. Holding
the fish by the tail, he repeats the process from the other end. The procedure
takes less than ten seconds from start to finish. By completely destroying
the spinal cord, the method delays rigor mortis for an additional eight
hours, allowing them to fetch a higher price per fish.

We now return to the open warehouses where the tuna auction is about
to begin. The bright blue tarps have been removed, and in a space the size
of a small aircraft hangar—one of many such spaces where the bluefin are
being auctioned—I see hundreds upon hundreds of perfectly arranged
bluefin carcasses, frozen solid, ghostly white, with gill plates, fins, and tails
removed.

An old brass bell begins to ring, filling the air, echoing through the
concrete chamber, while dark-blue-uniformed men, holding small flash-
lights and forged tuna picks called *tekagi,* whack at the exposed meat of
the tail sections, prying pieces off. They warm and roll the wads of flesh in
their hands, feeling their silky fat. They shine the light behind the meat,
gauging translucence and glow, then fling the flesh onto the floor. The bell
ringing suddenly stops, and a man standing on a wooden crate, clipboard
in hand, begins a rhythmic, barking shout. Lot after lot of tuna is speedily
sold, and soon the best-quality bluefin of the day, its dismembered tail fin
stuffed into its gills, is wheeled past me on one of the wooden handcarts.
It has been transported here from the North Atlantic, half a world away,
and must weigh close to three hundred pounds.

The Maido Man takes us from the bedlam of the auction house to
where the tuna are processed, back near the stalls. Here the high priests of
this art, assisted by teams of their attendants, use thin, gleaming swords to
butcher each fish in a slow, unrushed process. After an attendant positions
a fish on a wooden table, wipes it down, and lays a clean sword at its side,
an elderly gentleman approaches the fish, regards it, and then slowly takes
up his instrument. An attendant takes hold of the tip of the sword in a
towel as the old man positions it lengthwise against the fish, from head to

tail, and gives the signal. In one slow, smooth application of pressure, the sword sinks through the flesh to the spine, then slows as they make the turn around the spinal column, and with the blade now flat, the two men pull the sword out through the side of the fish. With one cut they have quartered the animal. Slabs of flesh are distributed to the attendants, who carefully trim the meat. The quartered piece is then divided into ever smaller pieces—thousands from one fish.

This goes on in stall after stall.

2

Two days later I am 350 miles north of Tokyo in the small fishing village of Oma, on the northernmost tip of the main island, Honshu. It has not been an easy trip. Mountain roads can bring you by land, but it's an arduous journey. The other alternative is to arrive by air, landing twelve miles away across the Tsugaru Strait in Hakodate, which I did the previous day with my translator, Wakao Hanaoka. Wakao is one of only a handful of employees of Greenpeace Japan and has volunteered to help me on this leg of my journey. It is because of him that I've come to Oma to meet these fishermen and to witness their traditional, sustainable single-hook method of fishing for bluefin, called *ippon zuri*.

I leave my hotel at 7:30 in the morning and begin my morning run, heading down the hill through the cool salt air toward the sea. The shore road is lined with small, neat, well-tended houses with nets hung in some of their yards. A few derelict fiberglass skiffs lie overturned and rotting in the marsh grass above the high-tide line. Oma is a modest community of fishers but is famous for catching the highest-quality bluefin tuna in all of Japan, if not the world. In Oma, bluefin are called "black diamonds." Fish of the best quality from this distant outpost have fetched prices at Tsukiji in excess of $250,000, with the highest being a 593-pound specimen that sold for $736,000 in January 2012.

Suddenly the air bursts with happy music from loudspeakers hung on the telephone poles, its childlike melody echoing into the hills. At first it has a communist, groupthink feel, but it begins to work on me. I run past a woman sweeping her front stoop. She stops her work to gaze at me, and

I say "Good morning" in Japanese. Nodding politely, she returns the greeting and resumes her work.

Half an hour later, I'm back in my hotel room, and after a quick shower I pack my gear and head to the lobby for a breakfast of scrambled egg, vegetables, rice, and marinated fish. Wakao joins me ten minutes before we're to be picked up. Wakao is stocky, about five foot eight, with a big, broad head and a thick vertical spray of black hair that makes him look as if he just stepped out of a wind tunnel. He attended college in Florida, speaks slightly lisping English, laughs easily, and has an excellent sense of humor. This morning his face is puffy from sleep, leaving him with a slightly bewildered look.

"I just woke up!" he explains. "My alarm didn't go off!"

As Wakao takes his seat, I notice Atsushi Sasaki entering the hotel lobby. Sasaki is a rod-and-reel bluefin tuna fisherman from the southern port of Sakai and one of the few fishermen in this nation of fishers to speak out publicly against the government's policies. It was Sasaki who picked up Wakao and me in Hakodate the previous day and ferried us across the strait in his narrow forty-foot fishing boat. Sasaki is sixty-one, with close-cropped salty gray hair, and his outgoing nature is overlaid with some unidentifiable combination of craftiness, drive, and self-assurance. Following immediately behind him is Takeichi Kikuchi, our captain for the day. About five foot eight, with jet-black hair, a thin build, and a serious face occasionally illuminated by a kind, open smile, he has a reserved manner that seems to be more a matter of shyness than of formality. I put him in his mid-forties. Kikuchi is one of the top three fishermen in Oma, with consistently high catches of bluefin. Both he and Sasaki are hard-core fishermen at the top of their respective games—Sasaki on rod and reel, Kikuchi with his single-hook *ippon zuri*.

Before we left Hakodate yesterday, Wakao and I sat with Sasaki in the lounge of one of the wharf offices, where he showed us pictures of some of his best bluefin catches, the largest tagged one being 318 kilos—about a seven-hundred-pound fish. He had landed even larger fish, but they had no weight tags.

Then Sasaki brought out a gleaming machined-aluminum reel. "This is a prototype," he said, explaining that the reel had been made by a friend of his, Ken Matsuura, who manufactures F1 and NASCAR racing parts. "Ducati, the Italian racing motorcycle company, uses a tapered drag bearing in the clutch of their racing bikes," Sasaki explained. "This reel has a drag system based on that design." He unscrewed and removed the side plate of the reel, revealing a conical series of plates. "This is called RDS, for Rolling Drag System. It has an even drag profile from the moment the fish strikes throughout the battle, through sudden runs, head shakes, everything. No matter what the fish is doing, the drag is the same. Heat, pressure, duration of fight—they do not matter. The drag is constant."

Maintaining even drag pressure on extremely powerful fish like bluefin tuna is critical, but many reel manufacturers' drag systems (which perform essentially like disks pressing against each other, applying pressure to the reel to slow it) lose effectiveness because of heat and wear. At a sudden run or shake of the fish's head, the drag may stick or bind, causing a sudden tightness in the line and a break. Sasaki handed me the Matsuura reel and I was immediately struck by how lightweight, simple, and gleamingly elegant it was—an impressive piece of engineering.

"There are only five reels like this," Sasaki continued. "Matsuura has made them for me in the one-hundred-thirty-pound, eighty-pound, and fifty-pound line classes."

Sasaki then produced a heavy tuna hook with a type of fabric leader that looked like a narrow sock scrunched up on the line above the hook. "This is a specialized shock leader of my own design. When the tuna strikes, it hits very hard. This system absorbs the impact." Sasaki handed me the hook and gave a violent tug on the line, and the compressed fabric leader made a small popping sound and lengthened from twelve inches to roughly two feet. Much of the initial energy of the strike was dissipated in the release. The key to the system is the fabric leader, which is made of Zylon, a synthetic liquid crystalline polymer used in military and police body armor, snowmobile engine belts, and other high-stress applications. It's exceedingly difficult to cut, even with the sharpest of knives or the best scissors. Knotted correctly to fishing line, it is all but unbreakable.

Our group heads to Kikuchi's car and makes its way from the hotel through Oma's awakening streets to the wharf. The weather looks favorable—clear skies, light wind. Already in the distance I can see the fishing boats gathered a few miles offshore, each one a long white sliver, slender from its flared bows through its streamlined fifty-foot length, narrow in the beam, with a bulbous bow below the waterline like an oil tanker. They are fast, nimble craft, roughly the same length but half the beam of the Novi boats.

On the way to the dock, Kikuchi says something to Wakao and decides to make a detour.

"Kikuchi asks if you would you like to see a bluefin tuna," Wakao says.

We pull up outside an industrial warehouse on a wharf several hundred yards from the marina. The facility is clean and well tended, lacking the typical fish-wharf stench of rotting bait and piles of detritus slung to the periphery in the tall grass—frayed rope, old bait barrels, rusting engine parts. A handful of workers stroll past wearing clean white rubber boots, aprons, and blue rubber gloves. Kikuchi enters the open warehouse hangar doors and talks to a young man who agrees to take us into the cold-storage facility. He leads us to a loading dock and then into a large concrete room where the temperature hovers around freezing. The vault is empty save for three large, bright-blue plastic containers about ten feet long by four wide by three tall. One of the container boxes is filled with a slurry of saltwater and ice. The worker maneuvers a small forklift to the edge of the box, reaches into the water to pull out a section of rope, which he loops around one of the forks, climbs back into the forklift, and slowly elevates the fork.

Out of the ice emerges the enormous head of a bluefin tuna. Its skull is larger than my entire upper body. As the entire fish rises out of the ice, I see that it surpasses even the largest tunas I saw at Tsukiji. I am struck in particular by the wedge-shaped, conical face. All the mass behind the fish drives that great bony skull through the water with a fury that is difficult to imagine. At maximum speed, a bluefin's tail moves so quickly that the human eye is incapable of perceiving it as anything but a blur.

"How much does it weigh?" I ask.

Wakao asks Kikuchi, who answers, "About 180 kilos."

I nod. "Four hundred pounds."

"How much bigger do they get?" Wakao asks.

"The rod-and-reel world record is four times this size," I tell him.

I realize that if this particular fish were judged to be of the highest quality and became the subject of a bidding war between buyers, it could fetch a price that equaled or exceeded the value of my home.

At the dock we board Kikuchi's boat, the dove-white, forty-seven-foot *Taiun Maru 35,* cast off, and head across the small marina toward the breakwater. Kikuchi gives a brief explanation of the boat's layout and gear. It has three pilot stations (one up front, one amidships in the wheelhouse, and one at the stern) and two electronics suites (one on the foredeck under a fiberglass storm cowling and one in the wheelhouse). In the wheelhouse alone I count nine different electronic screens.

The vessel, I realize, is brimming with redundant electronic and remote control technologies. Kikuchi fishes alone, in all weather, as much as eighteen hours per day, six days a week. During the season he fishes for tuna during daylight hours and for fresh mackerel and squid at night. For safety, to say nothing of successful fishing, he must remain in command of his vessel, with easy access to throttle, gear, and rudder controls, from nearly any location on the boat.

Kikuchi tells me the vessel cost thirty million yen (about $340,000) but adds, "The technology cost me more than the boat, about forty million yen," or about $450,000. In a good year, Kikuchi will earn almost $700,000 from fishing, enough to pay down the boat, the technology, and a good portion of fuel costs. If he does even half that well on average annually, he will pay off the boat and likely be a wealthy man in less than a decade.

From the wheelhouse forward to the bow are strung dozens of glass squid lights, each bulb about the size of a large eggplant. These, along with the array of bright flags festooning the rigging overhead, give the boat a celebratory feel as we head out through the breakwater. We pass a black-and-white-banded lighthouse to our starboard side and enter the Tsugaru Strait.

The nature of these waters contributes greatly to the quality of the bluefin tuna caught here. The Tsugaru Strait is the only connection for over nine hundred miles between the Sea of Japan (separating Japan from North Korea) and the Pacific Ocean. The currents here are strong, cold, and full of nutrients. As Kikuchi's brother explained to me, "Everything

has to fight for survival, the current is so strong and fresh. Even the abalone is better. It filters more cold water and has to hang on harder because
of the current."

Several miles ahead, the rest of the fleet has run together in a pack, and
as we steam to join them, Kikuchi rigs a single clear line coiled in a laundry basket at the stern of the *Taiun Maru*. The line is 130-pound test and
has the stiffness and glisten of fluorocarbon fishing line, specially formu-
lated to be nearly invisible in seawater. The many yards of line attach to a
heavy-duty swivel, which then joins the main line of Dacron backing. The
Dacron line runs up the port side of the boat to a large hydraulic spool
mounted on the side of the wheelhouse. After a fish hits, Kikuchi will set
the hook and apply pressure by hand until he can engage the hydraulic
spool, which will haul the fish in. The spool maintains only so much tension, to avoid the line breaking under the strain of the fish. The fishermen
of Oma use an electric shocking device to stun the fish, and in Kikuchi's
case it is a device of his own design, a kind of ring on an insulated wire
that he attaches and sends down the line to subdue the fish. It will sometimes take hours to get to the point that he can use the shock device and
engage the spool. Some of these men tell stories of battling large tunas by
hand for eight, ten, even twelve hours.

As we fall into the jockeying swirl of the fleet, Kikuchi signals for me
to come to the wheelhouse, where he describes the functions of the various
sounders, sonars, and gauges. The fleet, meanwhile, has positioned itself
above a school of bluefin tuna in several hundred feet of water, where they
are feeding on squid.

"At the right moment," Kikuchi says, "I will bait and drop the line over
the side."

Half an hour passes and then, at no sign that I can discern, Kikuchi
drops the *Taiun Maru*'s speed, walks to the back of the boat, flips open a
floor hatch, seizes a live brown squid about fifteen inches long, and runs
the hook through the hard part of its forward mantle fin. He throws it over
the side and lets the fluorocarbon line run out through his gloved fingers—
fifty yards, a hundred. Then he simply waits, holding the line between his
thumb and forefinger. After little more than a minute, he starts pulling in
the line, rapidly coiling it hand over hand in the laundry basket at his feet.

When it is halfway retrieved, he gives the line a hard yank, freeing the squid, and pulls in the bare hook.

Kikuchi explains, "If the tuna does not hit quickly, it will not hit at all. It means the tuna has detected that the squid is hooked or is not interested in the bait."

Boats steam past with foredecks festooned with flayed amber squid, row after row drying in the sun. I notice a few adolescent boys fishing with fathers or uncles, and several old men manning the helms of their vessels. Kikuchi tells me that there are many families out here, many generations of fishers.

"One man fishes with his wife," he says. "She drives, he fishes. They make a good team."

By noon the fleet has yet to catch a tuna, and Sasaki suggests that it's time for lunch. I gather with him and Wakao on the foredeck while Kikuchi pilots the boat. Sasaki offers me a can of cool ginger tea, dried squid, and several large balls of sticky rice.

"We call that *onigiri*," Wakao tells me. "It's Japanese soul food. You can mix anything into it—chicken, salmon eggs, seaweed. It will sustain you for hours."

"Have you always fished out of Sakai?" I ask Sasaki as we begin eating, continuing a conversation we started yesterday.

"No. I began fishing near Osaka in a semi-commercial manner, two hundred days per year," he tells me. "Osaka is near Sakai. I would catch seven hundred fish per night. These were not bluefin tuna but smaller fish, the size of mackerel. Purse seiners cut that catch by two-thirds—not just for me but for the other hook-and-line fishermen in the area. So eventually these fish were disappearing. I decided to move elsewhere to fish. I began traveling further away, and now I fish all over Japan, targeting bluefin, depending on the season, but only with rod and reel. One at a time."

"Are you against other methods?" I ask.

"Absolutely. Purse seiners should be banned and longliners restricted. They are simply too efficient. Currently there are no restrictions on longliners operating during spawning season in our waters. The Tsushima Current comes up by the Philippines and Taiwan and shoots between Korea and Hiroshima. Between April and May, bluefin spawn in this area.

Longliners and purse seiners sit in wait for them. Longliners are taking mostly adults; purse seiners are taking everything. I can see taking some adults, within reason, but not too many, and certainly not the young ones who have never spawned."

I share with Sasaki what I learned in Mexico and Nova Scotia about the relationship between industry, corporations, and government, and about illegal fishing. It comes as no surprise to him.

"Illegal fishing happens here, too, and there is the same corruption between government and industry. In fact, I strongly suspect that the big tuna corporations are among the major pirate fishing enterprises, not just abroad but here in Japan. There is no response from the government, which benefits from it."

"But you speak out," I remind him.

"Yes. I have seen the problem. I speak out because I must. Because what is happening is wrong."

The issue of the Japanese public's complacency regarding their nation's role in overfishing—especially in driving the destruction of bluefin tuna—is a subject I discussed with Wakao during my time in Tokyo. I remember saying to him, as we walked to an interview near Tsukiji market, "Japan seems like an exceedingly polite place. Nobody seems willing to ruffle anyone else's feathers."

"Yes. Well, this is true," he admitted. "Mostly, other approaches are preferred, like negotiation. We try to point out inconsistencies in policy, and ways policies have insufficient or negative results. We try to work with the government and industry to change how they operate, though that works only so well. It is difficult and takes a lot of time when there is a lot of money at stake."

"What incentive do they have to stop?" I asked.

"Not much," he acknowledged. "And the Japanese public tend to be less comfortable with direct confrontation. They take the perspective that the government probably knows what it's doing, or knows how best to handle the situation."

The interview we had scheduled was with the House of Hicho, one of the oldest and most respected of the intermediate wholesalers, or middlemen, of bluefin tuna in Tsukiji market. Hicho has been in business since 1861, when there were 108 wholesalers; today there are only 3 major wholesalers at Tsukiji. Tsunenori Iida, the current president of Hicho, has held that position for forty-two years, since the age of twenty-five.

Iida sat across from me, white-haired, reserved, and dignified almost to the point of severity. Over tea, Iida explained to me that the Japanese have eaten bluefin tuna for thousands of years, harvesting them in shore pens and with harpoon, as far back as the Jomon period.* "There is a coffin from the Jomon period made of tuna bones," he said. "Tokyo Bay used to have bluefin tuna in it. Those are gone now. Overfishing has changed the bluefin's migration around Japan. Bluefin used to come up from the south and split off, one group going to the Sea of Japan and the other going into the Pacific. Most now go into the Sea of Japan. Purse seiners wait there for them. The seiners can take five thousand fish at once. There are now other seiners from Japan and Korea interested in stationing themselves there."

"So how do you stop the bluefin stock from being ruined?" I asked.

"I believe purse seining and longlining need to be banned or reduced," he replied.

"Will the politicians do this?"

Iida's eyes clouded over. "Politicians need paper data; otherwise they cannot talk," he answered with disdain.

When I turned the conversation to tuna ranching, he said, "That, too, must be better regulated. Either limit the season or make the seine net hole size bigger, to allow the escape of juveniles. We get our ranched tuna primarily from the Mediterranean, then South Australia, then from Japan's own waters. Increasingly we are seeing product coming from Mexico."

"Have you seen a decrease in the size and number of bluefin tuna that you deal with?"

"Yes. A decrease in size and a decrease in number, everywhere." Iida paused a moment and said, "The whole scale of this business will decrease slowly. Not only our business, but everyone who has anything to do with bluefin."

---

*The Jomon period ran from 14,000 to 300 B.C.E., much of Japanese prehistory.

Here was a man confronting the end of eight generations of a family business that relied on this animal. I asked, "Is the collapse of bluefin tuna inevitable?"

Iida regarded me. "Yes," he said, and for the first time I detected a note of sadness in his voice. "It is, unless regulation is improved."

Not long afterward, I conducted another interview about the fate of the bluefin, this time with Hirofumi Hamabata, president of the Oma Fishermen's Co-op, at the group's headquarters, near the wharf. Hamabata, whose mouth sits low on his face and who tends to look at the world with a searing Clint Eastwood squint, is known throughout Japan for his fiery temperament and his outspokenness. He has appeared on television and in newspapers, and on every possible occasion he criticizes the government of Japan for its fisheries policies. As we talked, smoke rose out of Hamabata's mouth and nose, from a constant march of cigarettes, giving him a smoldering, volcanic look that matched his character. When Wakao, Sasaki, Kikuchi, and I first entered the room, his reserved gaze told me he was suspicious of me and my intentions. But as my position quickly became apparent, Hamabata's tone changed.

"I protest and raise my fist to the Fisheries Agency of Japan—as did my father!" he proclaimed, shaking his fist. "The government of Japan is saying we should protect the environment, yet they give permission to purse seiners and longliners to do what they are doing. The population of mackerel in Shikoku has crashed because of overfishing. Now those fishermen have to travel fifty or seventy-five miles to find bait. If there is no bait, the big fish will not come. There should be tight restrictions on purse seines and longlines for baitfish and bluefin tuna. The government pays subsidies to the industrial bait seiners to help them, but they do not offer the same to the small operator. When I complained, the Fisheries Agency suggested that the Oma co-op become a company to get the subsidy. But we know better. Once the co-op becomes a company, we would be vulnerable to a takeover by a larger company, thereby putting the bluefin tuna into the hands of the bastards once again."

"How does the co-op work?" I asked.

"The co-op allows Oma fishermen to exist and thrive as a community. Bluefin, yellowfin, flounder, are all taken here naturally. There are 780 people together in the co-op, and they survive together. Five and a half percent of the sale price of every fish goes to the co-op, which in turn provides the fishermen with a source of loans, insurance, wharf facilities, et cetera. The remaining 94.5 percent of the sale price goes to the captain who caught the fish. The co-op gives us all insurance against down times and strengthens the community as a whole."

"Would it be a successful strategy for the co-op to focus attention on the decision makers who favor large corporations over the small fishermen?"

Hamabata considered this. "The problem is that small communities like us have little power compared to the larger ports where industrial fishers are located. There is an upper-house cabinet member named [Tadamori] Oshima, from the Liberal [Democratic] Party in Hachinohe. Hachinohe is the base of operations for trawlers. If Oshima supports trawlers and purse seiners, he stays in power. He favors his cronies for his own benefit, rather than emphasizing sustainability for the fisheries."

"How is it possible that this continues?"

"I feel certain that bribe money is regularly paid to government officials to enable this to happen," Hamabata said plainly. Then, living up to his reputation, he began a blistering denunciation of what is happening in the Japanese fishing industry. "The purse seiners are terrible. I know of one purse seiner that had five tons of live sardines aboard and strategically placed the boat to let the sardines go all together, thereby stopping the migration of an entire school of bluefin. The ship then surrounded the school and bagged two thousand tuna in one shot. One purse seiner for squid can take in a day what our entire community of Oma can catch in a month, and the purse seiners don't take any days off! We decided to take one day off per week to put less pressure on the fish, but the seiners and the longliners don't do that. The largest of the seiners catch up to five hundred tons of baitfish at ten cents per kilogram. This is a waste, because the profit is so small and the value of those fish to other fisheries is so great. They should leave them! We have an expression in Japan: 'Farming is the mother of Japan; fishing is the father of Japan.' Individual fishermen *believe* this. They know this, and they have the same attitude in their hearts—preserve the fisheries! But the government and companies have only one desire: profit. This is fatal when you are dealing with the sea!"

Hamabata's outrage was palpable, and the other men in the room, all stone-faced, nodded in silent agreement. In a country where conformity and decorum are so highly valued and environmental causes have difficulty gaining any kind of wide public support, a man like Hamabata stands as an exception, while the overall outlook, unfortunately, remains poor.

✐✐✐✐✐

It is now approaching three in the afternoon, and the fleet has yet to catch a single tuna. Hamabata reiterated what I had heard previously—that on a typical day of fishing ten years ago, the Oma boats used to catch three or four tuna per boat daily. Now they are lucky if as a fleet they land a few fish, maybe half a dozen, every other day. Today does not look as if it will be one of those days—not because the tuna aren't present but because there are fewer of them. Sasaki pointed out a brief swirling bulge of water this morning and told me it was from a tuna. I have seen, from my seat on the deck, quick tear-shaped bullets leaping from the water in the distance.

Just when I think the day will pass without an *ippon zuri* harvest of bluefin, Kikuchi throttles up and we head to the periphery of the fleet, where one of his cousins has caught a fish. At the gunwale of the *Ryotoku Maru 38* stand two men greeting us with grins and shouts. Between them, a taut, silvery thread angles into the sea. One of the men hauls the line while the other stands beside him, ready with a long harpoon. They've already shocked the fish, but it is far from dead. The man hauling the line brings the fish up, the sharp prow of its face bobbing just clear of the surface, and with two quick jabs the harpooner strikes the tuna's skull. He drops the harpoon onto the deck, reaches over the side with a large flying gaff, and secures it under the tuna's chin. He gets a second gaff and secures it in the same place. Then, as the other fisherman uses a hydraulic winch to raise the fish, the harpooner takes a short five-inch knife and with quick, precise movements severs the arteries supplying the gills near the throat latch, as well as those running close to the surface behind the pectoral fins.

Wide crimson sheets of blood stream down the fish's gold and silver flanks. Finally, the harpooner takes an instrument that resembles an apple corer and cuts a round hole into the tuna's skull. He inserts a wire, running it through the brain and down the spine, and I watch in astonishment as the tuna's black back instantly goes pale gray as death washes over it.

3

From the second-floor balcony of the Grand Tasman Hotel, in Port Lincoln, South Australia, I watch a man in a motorized wheelchair go tearing up the street into the night, the orange pennant on his machine trailing him like a torch flame. In front of me lies the wide, lonely, windswept beach where the local seagulls establish yet again that they must have the ugliest cry of any seagull known—a sound that is more like the choking *graaaak* of an elephant seal than the plaintive call of a seabird.

What you notice first when coming into Port Lincoln are the enormous white wheat silos dominating the east end of town like Saturn V rocket boosters. Beneath them, a long jetty extends half a mile into the bay; it's so massive that entire grain freighters can line up against it to have their bellies pumped full of wheat from the golden fields shimmering behind the town and stretching to near infinity. The place has a distinctly off-season feel. During daylight, the beaches are empty, the breeze off the water cold; dogs off-leash chase the birds along the shore, barking incessantly, and the blue-green mottled bay lies devoid of all but a few boats. It is not a good sign that the hotel included earplugs with the room. The entertainment would start the following day, they warned me, but the earplugs would be useful against the dogs and the birds, as well as the karaoke I can hear starting up below like the wail of heartbroken cats.

The countryside of South Australia strikes me as the kind of place where you could hear stories of people being driven mad by the wind, where you could go months at a time without seeing another person or uttering a word, if that's what you chose to do. It's what the American Great Plains must have felt like to a homesteader 150 years ago, or the Russian Steppe during the time of the czars, except that this place borders the Southern Ocean. Two thousand miles straight south from here, across some of the harshest ocean on the planet, lies Antarctica. Between here and the ice sheet there is only frigid water, the world's largest population of whales, a plenitude of great white sharks, and all that is left of the wild southern bluefin tuna. The southern bluefin, cousin to the larger northern bluefin but a different species, has the distinction of having been the first ranched tuna, and the first tuna successfully bred in captivity. Both happened here in Port Lincoln.

In the morning, I cross town to the Port Lincoln Library to meet Sigi Veldhuyzen. Tall and tanned, in his early fifties, with close-cropped gray hair and a face lined from having spent years in the sun and wind, Sigi is immediately friendly and enthusiastic. He is a Port Lincoln native who at the age of seventeen went to sea to "fish the racks" on pole-and-line tuna boats. This method of fishing is no longer widely practiced but was popular after World War II and into the 1970s. Narrow metal racks were hung off the side of a boat just above water level. The crew lined up shoulder to shoulder in the racks, each man holding a stiff bamboo rod from which hung a single barbless, feathered hook at the end of eight feet of line. On the deck above, another crew member manned a live bait tank. When a school of tuna—a "patch"—was sighted, the boat would approach and the bait man would start slinging netfuls of live pilchards or other baitfish in the vicinity of the school, drawing them in. The tuna would erupt in a feeding frenzy, and the men in the racks would smack their rods down into the school, line and feathered hook flinging, as though they were beating swarms of ants with long sticks. The tuna snapped at anything that moved, and the fishermen would hook them, heave, and throw them overhead behind them in one fluid motion. Because the hooks were barbless, the tuna detached easily, flying into wooden pens on deck. The process would be repeated for as long as hours, until the school departed.* Poling was on the whole a sustainable method. Boats could catch only so many of the fish before the feeding frenzy died down and the school moved on. Even if another boat encountered the school the following day, not all of the fish could be caught.

---

* If you can tolerate the manly narration, a good example of poling from the racks can be seen on YouTube by searching "The Ironman of the Tuna Fishing," http://www.youtube.com/watch?v=lp_Rs75-5vI.

"Oh, tuna fishing in the seventies was the Rolls-Royce," Sigi tells me. "Nothing beats poling for tuna. I've been net-fishing for sharks, hoop-fishing, purse seining—there was nothing like poling for tuna. It was man and fish. It was only skill that kept them on the hook and got them into the boat. They say the best polers could have three fish in the air at the same time—one about to hit the deck, the second one on its way, and the third one hooked and coming out of the water."

He describes the adrenaline rush of approaching the patch as something like readying for battle. During one winter, his boat was up on the east coast of Australia, hardly catching any fish. They made their way back to Port Lincoln paired with a purse seiner and a spotter plane, and instead of turning to head into port, the spotter plane kept going, leading the ships to a patch of fish.

"We poled twenty tonnes," Sigi remembers. "The seiner got a hundred tonnes. A hundred and twenty tonnes from that one patch, and they were all large fish—fifty kilos. We were short crew, so we only had three sets of double poles going, and we still got twenty tonnes. I said two things to my mate that day, both of which came true. The first was 'I wonder if there's such a thing as a third wind?' The other thing was about the fish. We'd heard that when the purse seine net goes around the fish, they go mental. We wondered if that was going to happen. Well, it happened, all right. Ours were the only hooks left in the water, and when the net went around, we got our third wind, and sure enough, the fish went mental."

This happened in the early days of combining purse seiners with pole-line boats. The pole-line boats would lure the school in and start fishing, and the purse seiner would shoot its net around everything—the school and the pole boat. When Sigi began fishing, most of the boats were made of wood, but eventually the whole fleet changed to steel hulls. With the steel boats, the sound of hundreds of fish tails beating on the deck became a din as they thrashed in their final death throes. "I tell you," Sigi says, "if tuna screamed, there wouldn't be many people poling for them."

It was exhausting, bloody work. Legs and forearms felt the burn within minutes, and it was not uncommon for men to be completely spent within half an hour. On two occasions, Sigi witnessed men literally crawling from the racks on hands and knees, they were so exhausted. After a good run, the men would be soaked to the bone and crusted in salt, with hundreds of bloody, dead and dying tuna on deck, needing to be moved into the hold before they spent too much time in the sun.

Poling was not without its dangers, either. With so many weighted hooks flying around, accidents were bound to happen. Sigi knew of three men who'd lost an eye, and another man who fished beside him was hooked by an automatic poler (a later innovation) through the forearm. It yanked and yanked, trying to throw the hook back into the water with the man attached, until Sigi was able to grab his arm, hold him down, and unhook him. And then there were what the pole fishermen called "suicide" straps.

"The strap was on the rod and went around your hand. If you put it around your palm, you were all right, but if you put it around your wrist, that's when it became dangerous. If a big fish hit and pulled you over, well, that was it. It happened to me once. I wasn't using a strap, but I got pulled over. It was so quick, I opened my eyes and I was underwater with the fish towing me down. I saw him through the bubbles. I let go of my rod and was able to make it to the surface. They lowered a pole and pulled me out."

He tells the story of Keith Bellamy, killed in 1959 while practicing the double-pole technique with his twin brother on the vessel *Tacoma*. A large tuna hit, and Bellamy was torn from the racks and dragged behind the boat as he held on to his pole. He let go, and the captain, the legendary Bill Haldane, one of the earliest of the tuna captains, swung the boat around. Haldane threw himself from the upper bridge, diving thirty feet down into the clear water, where he could see Keith sinking into the depths, his waders having filled up with water. Haldane couldn't reach him, and Bellamy's body was never found.

Sigi recalls that in the heyday of tuna fishing from Port Lincoln, there were seven airplanes, five purse seiners, and thirty pole boats in the fleet, all fishing at once. "On a flat, calm day, every single patch would come up. With the planes and the fast boats, we'd just collect 'em up, collect 'em up, until we had every last fish in every patch. One time I saw a school of stripeys [skipjack tuna] that I reckon was a two-hundred-tonne school.

"One of the best sights I've ever seen was from up the mast, thirty meters above the water. We were following a school of bluefin trying to chum them up, and then every fish over this huge area just turned at one time. The color and the shine! Just the *shine,* iridescent golds and blues, shimmering in wave after wave—I'd never seen anything like it."

Then, with a note of poignancy, he adds, "It used to be nice out there. It was an adventure."

The history of commercial tuna fishing in Port Lincoln has undergone the same evolution as it has elsewhere in the world. In the 1940s and '50s, southern bluefin were harvested by trolling, a limited amount of purse seining, and pole and line. Most if not all tuna were destined for the cannery. Through the 1950s and early 1960s, government investment in shore facilities, along with improvements in methods and gear, led to more tuna being landed and more boats getting into the action. Spotter planes started being used. Record catches took place in 1964, 1965, and 1966, despite warnings about unrestricted access to the fishery. As predicted, the catch began to fall in 1967, and boats left the fishery. Throughout the 1970s, the catch rose and fell (reaching as high as nine thousand tons in 1977), and by the eighties the fishery had been pushed to its limits.

Like all tuna, southern bluefin are highly migratory and swim in international waters. During this period, other nations, especially Italy and Japan, took massive quantities of the fish from the Great Australian Bight, south of Port Lincoln, primarily using longline. With the establishment of the international two-hundred-mile exclusive economic zone (EEZ)* in 1979, the South Australians made the same mistake that was being repeated around the world: Instead of restricting and effectively managing the stock of southern bluefin in their now expanded waters, they went into overdrive to exploit it, building bigger ships that went farther out to sea for longer periods and with more powerful automated systems. By 1982 the catch had peaked at more than twice the record 1960s levels—over nineteen thousand metric tons per year for the Australians alone. Most boats had abandoned pole-and-line fishing for purse seining exclusively, and the market had shifted from canning to exporting frozen bluefin to Japan, as

---

*The EEZ gives any nation with a coastline exclusive rights to determine the use of the waters two hundred miles outward from its shores.

a southern bluefin destined for sashimi was on average *fifty times* more valuable than one destined for the cannery.

Listening to Sigi's account, and having heard similar stories in other cases of overfishing, I have come to understand that the factors that initially led to overfishing were not all based on greed. Economic and other realities worked against restraint and a conservative approach. Those realities included significant personal and government investment, expanding horizons of opportunity, jackpot catches, and the fact that these all occurred during a time when the widespread depletion of resources was not commonplace. In that atmosphere, it must have been difficult to imagine, much less truly appreciate, the limits of the natural world as well as the new, exponentially growing power of human technology. Straightforward economic concerns—like paying off your boat—would naturally have been foremost in fishermen's minds. Even in the early 1980s in Port Lincoln, fishing vessels cost hundreds of thousands to more than a million dollars. Because vessels are paid off in a currency whose value can fluctuate wildly, fishermen naturally choose to err on the side of catching as much as they can, while they can, in order to insulate themselves against disaster—a lost ship, a drop in fish prices, or bad weather.

But there is a point at which greed and not necessity becomes the driving force. There are too many instances in which fishermen keep fishing when the evidence is clear that there is a serious decline in stock and that continuing to fish actually jeopardizes their livelihood and the future. The refusal to restrict catches and the perpetual belief that the problem is overstated despite overwhelming scientific evidence to the contrary are warning signs that profit and self-interest have gained the upper hand.

"I poled for a couple of years, then I went on a purse seiner, the *Boston Bay*," Sigi says, resuming his history. "An American captain came over and skippered the boat. That was the first year the purse seiner really made inroads into catching tuna. We caught a thousand tonnes, and the same the next year. I remember asking this captain, 'Have you got a pole-line fishery in America?' And he said, 'Sig, we used to have a perfect pole-line fishery—much better than this one. We're not doing it anymore. We fished 'em out. From the time purse seiners came in, it took us five years before we'd wiped out our industry.' I thought, *That's interesting. I'm on a purse*

*seiner. I'm in the tuna industry. There's no controls on purse seine vessels—
more and more are coming in."*

Sigi looks at me and says, "Do you know, I believe it was five years
before the government slapped quotas on the tuna fishermen. That was the
beginning of the end. I spent twenty-three years in wild fisheries and saw
almost all of them collapse. During that time, I would have fought against
quotas tooth and nail. Quotas made me feel like you were trying to stop
me from being as good a hunter as I could be. My feeling was, if you just
let me fish, I can slay 'em. I can kill hundreds of them. It's the hunting
nature, but it's greed, pure greed—greed and a sort of ignorance. It was
only when I saw every industry I was a part of collapse that I accepted that
quotas were necessary. What pisses me off is that that captain said it to me:
'Five years it took us to wreck an industry.' The information was there! If
we'd had proper quotas years ago, we'd still have viable wild catch industries today."

Looking at his tan, lined face and the expression in his eyes, I realize
Sigi will live with that regret the rest of his life.* Then, as we're ending our
interview, he adds, "I sometimes think maybe we took the wrong branch
in evolution, you know? Like maybe it should have been a different line
that succeeded. But not us. We're too clever. And not clever enough."

<center>~~~~~</center>

This is where the story of Port Lincoln and the issues it raises become really
interesting.

When Sigi left the tuna industry in the mid-1980s, the most successful
of Port Lincoln's tuna captains had made millions off the fishery, as is
evidenced by the number of mansions around town and by Port Lincoln's
reputation as the home of the most millionaires per capita in Australia.
During the gold rush, these men had made serious investments in gear and
ships as well as freezer, packaging, and transport facilities. They had also
accumulated millions of dollars' worth of quota under an individual transferable quota system. Now, faced with ravaged natural stocks and extremely

---

* Sadly, nine months after I interviewed him, Sigi Veldhuyzen was diagnosed with
cancer, and he died less than a month later, at the end of August 2009.

tight quota limits, they were confronted with a new type of problem: They could no longer increase their effort or improve their technology to maintain wild harvest levels.

Faced with the severe contraction of their industry and an economically precarious future, the Port Lincoln tuna barons devised a way to circumvent the problem: If they couldn't increase the number of fish shipped, they'd increase the *poundage*. The fishermen of Port Lincoln developed the techniques and specialized gear for tuna ranching, which enabled them to catch and tow entire schools of fish back to offshore pens and fatten them there before slaughtering them and shipping them to Tokyo. With ranching, they found that they could double the weight of every fish they'd caught in six months' time, from an average of about thirty-seven pounds to between seventy and ninety pounds.*

It was an ingenious solution to a problem they viewed as economic in nature. In truth, though, the problem was never anything but an ecological one, and over time ranching demonstrated its shortcomings. Southern bluefin tuna require ten to fifteen pounds of forage fish to add a pound of weight. To double the weight of five thousand metric tons of wild-caught bluefin (the average amount ranched annually, representing most of the quota) would require feeding the tuna between *110 and 165 million pounds* of pilchards, a type of sardine. Under no naturally occurring circumstances would that many pilchards be eaten, digested, and defecated as waste in concentrated patches, as was now happening in the ecosystem of the Spencer Gulf, off Port Lincoln. Early tuna ranching, like salmon farming and other large-scale finfish aquaculture practices, failed to demonstrate that it was a truly "viable" solution, so long as that word included the connotation that it was actually ecologically sustainable. There were serious questions that needed to be addressed, involving feed (what should be used, where it would be harvested from, and the effects of that harvest on the ecosystem from which it was removed), waste (how much there would be and the impacts it would have), and stocking densities (how many tuna could be

---

*Aquaculturists in South Australia are now experimenting with "long-term holding," whereby tuna are fattened over the course of as much as eighteen months to increase yields even more (Aquafin CRC, "Achievements and Impacts [2001–2008]" booklet, page 7).

kept in a pen without leading to outbreaks of disease, and how those diseases would be controlled).

All of these are serious considerations. In 1995 and 1998, for example, a herpes virus in pilchards was responsible for the destruction of 70 percent of the tuna in Port Lincoln ranches and endangered the entire ecosystem of the Spencer Gulf. These pilchard die-offs were the "two largest single-species mass mortalities of fish ever recorded in Australian waters." To get a sense of their scale, both events moved in outward-spreading waves along the coast from their starting point off the Eyre Peninsula at a speed of 6 to 24 miles per day, eventually covering over 3,600 miles of the southern coast of the entire continent, from Western and South Australia to Victoria and New South Wales and, in the case of the 1995 event, spreading all the way to New Zealand. Tens of thousands of tons of pilchards died, covering the ocean floor and surface and beaches in the states affected. Scientists estimate that between 60 and 70 percent of the entire pilchard population died. These events had significant economic ramifications, about $9 million (U.S.) in both cases, although the full scale of the economic damages is not known. The 1998 die-off in Western Australia alone was the equivalent of three to five years' harvest in two months' time and closed the pilchard fishery in that state for a year.

The ecosystem impacts have been poorly studied, but several facts are understood. First, pilchards are a crucial species in the food webs in which they occur. The position they hold is called the "wasp's waist," because there are few other species that occupy the same niche and perform the same energy-transfer function up the food web as pilchards do. Scientists have linked increases in deaths and decreases in breeding of little penguins* to the 1995 event, anticipated similar impacts from the 1998 event on Australasian gannets, and estimate that these events will have long-term impacts on (and slow the recovery of) top-tier predators like sharks, southern bluefin tuna, whales, and other species.

It is important to acknowledge that a direct connection between imported pilchards as feed for the southern bluefin tuna ranching industry and the two major pilchard mortality events has never been definitively

---

Eudyptula minor.

established. Hypotheses put forward for the pilchard mass mortalities include that the virus was transported in ballast water in ships; that it was spread by seabirds; that it was latent in the native pilchard population and was activated by some kind of environmental stress; or that, in the case of the 1998 event, the cause was a mutation of the virus from the 1995 event. The qualitative evidence about the nature of this disease and how it spread, as well as probability and randomness calculations for where it occurred, dismiss these causes, leaving the imported-pilchard hypothesis as the most likely origin of these outbreaks and the most difficult one to reject.

Confronted with the history of overfishing and the challenges created by ranching, the Australian government and fisheries management authorities deserve credit for enforcing tight regulations on tuna quotas and stocking densities, and for making the tuna ranches in the Spencer Gulf among the most strictly monitored and "cleanest" in the world. The Port Lincoln tuna ranchers also deserve credit for their ingenuity and tenacity and for the fact that, on the whole, they seek to abide by the law and ensure that the environmental impact of the ranches is minimized as much as possible. In this regard, Port Lincoln ranks among the most successful examples of finfish aquaculture in the world.

Nonetheless, the difficulty with large-scale finfish aquaculture is that it effectively aspires to something like the alchemist's dream of converting lead into gold by seeking to use technology as a means of getting around the fundamental damage done by overfishing: the depletion of wild stocks and a decrease in the amount of protein available to humans as food.

As the commercial fisherman turned writer Paul Molyneaux states in *Swimming in Circles: Aquaculture and the End of Wild Oceans* (2007), the aquaculture industry "has almost a religious faith in technology" as a means of solving the underlying biological challenges of replacing complex, wild ecosystems with simplified, human-controlled mechanisms, in order to make up for the shortfalls created by the depletion of wild fish. Molyneaux makes the point that this faith in aquaculture is nothing more than a reconceived version of the belief that the ocean is inexhaustible. Aquaculturists admit that we now know the ocean *is* exhaustible, but to them there is nothing that technology can't solve or won't provide, now that we know Nature can't be relied on. Large-scale carnivorous finfish aquaculture continues to tax natural systems beyond their capacity and ignores the fact that you cannot extract resources at a rate that exceeds the natural system's ability to replenish them. Nor does this kind of aquaculture necessarily replenish wild stocks by easing pressure on them (the Atlantic salmon being a case in point).

Ironically, in Port Lincoln this misguided belief may have led to a method that could be sustainable, one that might help save the wild bluefin tuna.

~~~~

"Clean Seas Tuna"—a name that instantly conjures images of pristine, healthy fish or wiped-out oceans, depending on your political bent—is the brainchild of Hagen Stehr. Born in Germany in 1941, Stehr served in the French Foreign Legion in Africa in 1958, and at the age of eighteen landed in Port Lincoln fresh off a fishing boat. Over the next thirty years, through the boom years of the wild tuna fishery, he managed to work his way up from deckhand to captain to boat owner to magnate. One of the most successful of the Port Lincoln tuna barons, he is also, by all accounts, the most audacious of them—among the first to ranch tuna and the only one who has gone so far as to invest in trying to induce bluefin to breed in captivity.

Raising captive bluefin is different from tuna ranching. Clean Seas' breeding program begins with a captive wild brood stock. The company has succeeded in inducing this brood stock to spawn; the larvae are then carefully tended in an attempt to raise them to market weight and sell them. The attempt has succeeded only as far as raising fingerlings, but how far Clean Seas intends to go with this is unknown. The potential exists to raise successive generations of fish within a closed genetic loop, apart from any natural system. If these were essentially domesticated wild tuna, it could conceivably ease pressure on wild stocks. If the intention is to begin genetic modification, however, as has been done with salmon, the effort begins to migrate into different ethical and ecological territory.

The day after talking with Sigi Veldhuyzen, I drive out to the Stehr Group offices near the marina complex south of Kirton Point, where I meet with Hagen's son, Marcus, executive director of operations, and Morten Deichmann, general manager of hatcheries.

Waiting for Marcus to end a conference call, I fall into conversation with Deichmann in an office sitting area. He has the wiry frame and angular features of a cyclist, and behind his glasses I detect a patient if slightly skeptical manner. Born and raised in Denmark, he received his degree in aquaculture biology at the University of Copenhagen.

"Nature is an amazing animal," he says. "As long as you stay within boundaries, you can manipulate it."

I understand him to be talking about biology, not *Nature*—not manipulation on the scale of entire ecosystems, but of smaller systems. "Can people really understand the complexity of natural systems to manipulate them without negative effects?" I ask.

"People think Nature is somehow fixed. This is not the case. Nature is constantly changing. And human beings have always influenced ecosystems. Often, we destroy systems to the extent they're not beautiful anymore, but a lot of Nature is not beautiful, and not nice. But it is robust and resilient. Some systems you have to stay away from—a mountain lake, for example. If you put energy in, you will tip the balance. Nature has its own disasters, don't forget."

Applying his argument to his own business, I ask, "Are you concerned that some of your tuna may escape the pens, get into the wild stock?"

"Infiltrating wild genes with our brood stock is not a problem, because our brood stock are wild fish. We aren't interbreeding them. We're at the point of wanting to *create* the life cycle, not truly close it. At any rate, captive fish are not good at natural behaviors. The Norwegians, who produce a million metric tons of farmed salmon per year, are not finding genetic crossovers.* Nature will take care of itself. If we go too far, it will become exhausted and shut humans down."

We talk for a while about the overfishing of northern bluefin, and he shares his concern that places like China and Mexico, which practice

---

*Farmed-salmon escapes actually have a serious negative effect on wild populations, threatening their genetic makeup, among other things. See http://www.bellona.org/aquaculture/artikler/Genetic_ effects.

large-scale aquaculture but lack strong monitoring and protective measures, could end up as environmental disasters.

"What do you think of this process of applying aquaculture to bluefin?" I ask. "What will be the impact on wild stocks?"

He clearly understands the thrust of my question—whether or not there will be wild stocks left in the future—but dodges it. "That's up to consumers, not business. If people demand wild tuna, wild tuna will continue to be caught."

Deichmann now tells a story meant to illustrate the futility of preserving rare wildlife. "Denmark is a garden, you know. The whole country is a garden. Every square meter is managed. There's no real 'wild' left at all. When I was a student, our professor took us to a forest preserve. 'Do you think this is wild, untouched?' he asked us. We answered that we did. Then he explained how heavily it was maintained. His point was that Nature, if left to its own devices, would have overrun the place, that eventually nonnative species would have come in, and that what we saw as the beauty of it—its 'natural state'—was an illusion. Nature is constantly changing."

The professor then described a certain rare wild orchid that was supposed to grow in the reserve and told his students to spread out and look for it. A student found one and called the professor and the other students over. The professor, upon seeing the flower, reached down and tore it out by the root, to the shock of his class.

"The professor said, 'If you have to set aside ten acres to protect four or five orchids that may or may not be there, it is too late.' He held up the orchid in front of us. 'It is too late for this. Take a good look.' "

I see Deichmann's—and the professor's—point: If wilderness exists only within ten-acre plots, carefully tended, it is no longer wilderness but merely the illusion of it. We should not be so easily fooled, or so easily contented, by false simulations of wilderness.

Taking his point further, I ask Deichmann what he thinks of the possibility of rebuilding wild ecosystems to reverse the harm we've done.

He answers, "Well, it's a massive system," without further comment.

Oceans are indeed massive ecological systems, but something is lost in reducing them to such clinical terms. Biologists are trained to understand

The author's great-grandfather Martin "Big Pomp" Arens at Cuttyhunk, Massachusetts, circa 1954. The fish is a striped bass weighing over fifty pounds.

The author, age four, learning to fish with his father.

The *Adriana* crossing Medano Bay, Cabo San Lucas, Mexico.

OPPOSITE: A striped marlin on the hunt in the waters off Baja, Mexico.

PHOTOGRAPH COPYRIGHT © BRANDON COLE

Depending on location, broadbill swordfish are usually found between 600 and 1,800 feet deep during the day (between 100 and 300 feet at night) but have been known to hunt as deep as 3,000 feet or more. (Painting: *Deep Hunter* by Al Barnes.)

Dwaine d'Eon taking aim at a broadbill swordfish.

A Nova Scotia swordfish harpoon boat on Georges Bank.

Captain Saul Newell of the harpoon boat *Brittany & Brothers,* out of Cape Sable Island, Nova Scotia.

Pure power: a nine-hundred-pound giant bluefin tuna hunting an Atlantic bluefish off Nomans Land Island, Massachusetts, in 1986. This tuna was over nine feet long and capable of speeds through water of nearly sixty miles per hour.

The morgue of a species: bluefin tuna being prepared for auction, Tsukiji market, Tokyo, Japan.

Oma, Japan: Captain Takeichi Kikuchi practicing the sustainable single-hook method of catching bluefin tuna called *ippon zuri*.

Large bluefin tuna being harvested by the *Ryotoku Maru 38* off Oma, Japan.

A juvenile southern bluefin tuna.

Leaving the *Rainbow
Warrior* en route to an
inspection.

The *Saint Antoine Marie II*, out of Marseille, France, one of the latest generation of high-tech purse seiners operating in the Mediterranean.

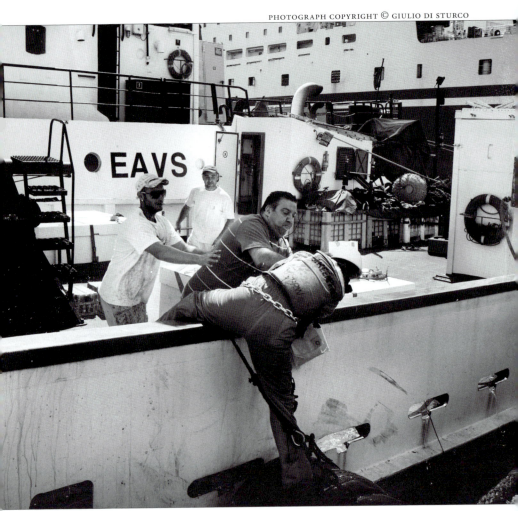

Greenpeace campaigner Emma Briggs being punched by Massimo Cappitta of MareBlu Tuna Farm as she attempts to board the *Santina*.

Off Ribbon Reef Number 10, near Lizard Island on the Great Barrier Reef, Australia. The second thousand-pounder: this fish weighed approximately eleven hundred pounds and was about twelve feet long. It flew over sixty feet and reached a height of fifteen feet in its jump.

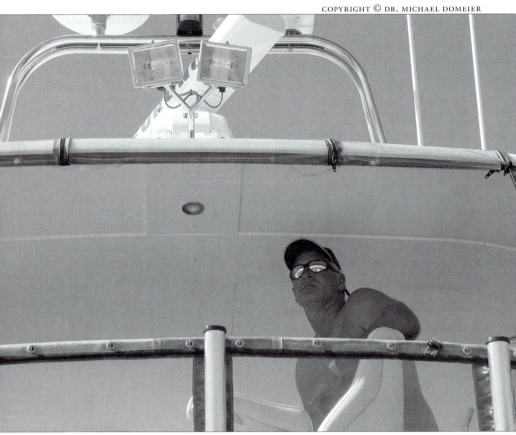

Captain John Gregory at the helm of *Primetime.*

Primetime angler Michel Marchandise with a swordfish weighing over 600 pounds. The weight is an estimate because of fluid loss of 10 percent after one week in an insulated bag in the vessel's cooler. The final weight at the dock was 545 pounds.

Primetime in a storm: twenty-foot waves, fifty-knot winds, and they will be fishing in it.

Nature as a system with inputs and outputs of energy, but there comes a point at which this view runs the risk of reducing the vibrancy and wonder of life to inert objectivity, where actual living beings become unitized pounds of flesh, packets of energy that can be converted from one form to another—pilchard to tuna to human—in a simple mathematical equivalency. The same is true of seeing Nature as constantly changing, and human influence as being equal to all other forms of change. It is difficult to accept the presumption that our impacts on Nature constitute only one of a series of energy inputs or extractions.

Neither of these rational perspectives can take into account what happened, for example, to Sigi—*in* Sigi—when he witnessed that massive school of bluefin turn beneath the waves. This is beyond the ability of science to touch, systematize, harness, or control, and to me it is one of the strongest arguments for why our goal must be balanced ecosystems rich in diversity of life. What happened in Sigi falls within the province of the soul. This is the true home and refuge of wilderness, and it cannot be quantified. It is also why wilderness—Nature unchained—must continue to exist, in wholeness, not by the parcel. It is necessary to our survival on many levels, spiritual and otherwise. Wilderness—a wild, functioning ecosystem—is our greatest guarantee against disaster. Every square mile of estuary lost on the Mississippi delta means more hurricane storm surge that smashes New Orleans and floods the houses of the delta towns to their rooftops. Every striped marlin or dorado in the waters off Cabo San Lucas, every swordfish and shark off Nova Scotia, every wild tuna off Oma, Japan, and South Australia, contributes to the health of the ecosystem beyond their mere value as meat.

Some minutes later, I move with Deichmann to meet with Marcus Stehr in a cluttered, well-used executive office, the condition of which reveals an organization focused more on working than on appearances.

Stehr stands about five foot eight, with dark hair and a passing resemblance to Robert De Niro. His muscular build and flat eyes and the gold chain around his neck create the effect of a low-level mobster. He swears liberally and often prefaces what he says with "Look," then peppers his responses with rhetorical questions.

"Look," he says to me, "I've been out there every year harvesting blue-fin for the past twenty years. The only year I missed was two years ago when I got my divorce. Every other year I've been out there seeing the wild stock, fishing them, so I know their health and I don't need no fucking scientists or the Greenpeace types to be telling me what the stock is doing. It's healthy. Did we overfish them? Yes. It was out of control. But with the quotas, and because they've finally stopped the Japanese overfishing, those fish have come back. There are thousands of tonnes of juvenile bluefin tuna out there. Not only that," he adds, "but at the end of the day, unless the weather is absolutely perfect, it's a surface fishery, so that's going to limit how many you can catch. I know pilots who have counted five thousand tonnes—two hundred patches—in one day."

Stehr's complaints about the Japanese are justified: In 2006, the Japanese were proven to have illegally caught—by official figures—approximately twenty thousand metric tons above their approved quota of southern bluefin tuna between 1986 and 2006. The actual figure for that period, as estimated by environmentalists and commercial fishermen both, is believed to be greater than ten times that amount. The value of this illegal overcatch is in the vicinity of $6 billion, but what's more striking is how this overfishing has affected the stock. By hiding its illegal overfishing, Japan skewed the fisheries management science, making management regimes and projections worthless. Taking into account Japan's overfished amount, adjusted scientific projections showed that if Japan had stuck to its allocated quota, the southern bluefin tuna population in 2006 would have been five times as large. Instead, as of 2006, southern bluefin had spent ten years on the IUCN* Red List as a critically endangered species.

Turning the subject to Stehr's ranching operations, I ask him what problems he's had with issues like disease and feed.

"Disease? We haven't had problems with disease except for that one year. We can't go above a stocking density of four kilos per cubic meter. The bloody government won't allow it. Do I think we could go higher without problems? Yes. But they make us keep it down, and we abide by

---

*The International Union for Conservation of Nature (IUCN) is the body that rates the conservation status of species.

it. They've got bloody cameras counting the fish as they're unloaded from the tow pontoon! Look: We live under the strictest fucking environmental regulations for aquaculture in the *world*. We just got certified as meeting ISO 14001.* That's bloody tough. My personal opinion is the level of regulation is ridiculous. We can't bloody sneeze if it isn't in the regulations."

I switch my tack and ask, "Let's suppose for a moment the breeding stock of southern bluefin is actually as low as the scientists say it is: 3 to 7 percent of the historical maximum. Doesn't harvesting from the wild to support the ranches pose a problem, especially when the minimum safe limit for the breeding stock is 20 percent, and given that even if a total moratorium were placed on the fish at this point, they would not attain that minimum safe level until at least 2020?"

"Look," Marcus says, "I don't know about 20 percent. All I know is, there are plenty of juveniles out there, and we only harvest juveniles for the pens."

Deichmann jumps in, adding, "We harvest juveniles because they offer more capacity for adding weight. They add more weight more quickly than adult fish. There's also fairly high natural mortality among juveniles. It makes more sense to take them than breeding-age adults."

I turn back to Marcus. "I understand you recently closed the life cycle on bluefin at Arno Bay," I say, eager to learn more about the thousand-acre property ninety miles up the coast from Port Lincoln in the direction of Adelaide. It is Clean Seas' crowning gem, a controlled-access facility where they propagate mulloway and yellowtail kingfish and are seeking to do the same with bluefin tuna in commercial quantities they hope will eventually reach ten thousand metric tons per year. They're still a long way from that goal, but several months before my arrival, scientists at the facility succeeded in inducing southern bluefin tuna to spawn, resulting in a world first: human-propagated southern bluefin larvae. The larvae eventually died, but it was a significant milestone all the same.

"That was a hell of a feat," Stehr says proudly. "It's only a matter of time

---

*ISO 14001 is an environmental management framework that helps companies develop and continually improve their environmental management systems in order to adhere to all applicable laws and limit their products' impacts on the environment.

before we get the larvae to fingerlings, and then to harvest weight. It's not a matter of *if,* but *when.*"

In the late 1990s, the Stehr Group decided to put aside 2,200 bluefin from their quota. They held the fish in pens and fed them, letting them mature year after year. After more than a decade—and millions of dollars invested—the Stehr Group and Clean Seas Tuna had 350 adult bluefin of breeding age in pens offshore. Then, in what Hagen Stehr is fond of calling a "military-style operation," Clean Seas sedated and airlifted individual adult bluefin by helicopter to the Arno Bay facility, where they were lowered through a retractable roof into a large indoor tank. It took several years to get the variables of hormones, light, feed, and temperature correct, but in March 2008 the tuna successfully spawned, resulting in fertilized eggs and hatched larvae.

"You will be a true king of kings if you can close the life cycle," Marcus Stehr says.

To "close the life cycle" on bluefin would mean that Clean Seas had mastered the techniques to reliably induce spawning, raise larvae to adults, and presumably induce that second generation to spawn as well.* This has already been accomplished with a number of fish species, including salmon and kingfish. If Clean Seas is able to achieve this with the bluefin, it may offer hope for wild tuna by taking pressure off the harvest of wild stocks, but the question remains whether this will really mean a significant decrease in the harvest of wild fish by other countries in time to rebuild the stocks to the minimum safe level of breeding adults. There is also the question of whether such a breeding operation should be done in the wild. As it stands, the brood stock itself is genetically wild, as are its fingerlings. Once the tuna are hatched and raised to a large enough size, they will be transported back to pens in the open ocean, where the only thing separating them from the wild ecosystem will be a net. If Clean Seas begins modifying the fish genetically, then the same concerns about escapes, impact on wild fish, and so on that apply to the salmon industry could apply here. Given that the eventual goal is to raise and sell ten thousand

---

*The full intent of Clean Seas' breeding program is not clear and is guarded as a trade secret.

metric tons of bluefin, the questions regarding what they will be fed, what impact their waste will have, and how disease will be managed remain causes for concern.

I look at Marcus and pause for a second before asking my question. "What are the chances I can drive up to Arno Bay and have a look?"

With his flat eyes, Marcus looks back at me and says nothing. Then he answers, "Well, I think it would be good for you. If you didn't see it, it wouldn't do you justice, and you wouldn't do *it* justice. Do I want to let you? No, I don't. But I will, because I think you should see it."

~~~~~

I had been told, prior to arriving in town, that the drive along the coast highway east of Port Lincoln was "as boring as bat shit."

The next morning, I'm on the road by nine o'clock and within minutes am speeding along a gray ribbon of asphalt toward a point on the horizon that never comes any closer. The landscape is all but treeless, and the limitless spaciousness extending away from me on all sides makes it feel as if the horizon line has been dropped. Brief seconds pass in which I am aware of a kind of reverse claustrophobia. I've driven through the southwestern United States, the Great Plains, and Big Sky Country; I've been far out at sea on flat, calm days; but South Australia is the only place I've ever experienced this warping effect of space.

Dead kangaroos lie on the roadside like giant squirrels blackening in the sun. I see signs for towns purported to exist between the highway and the coast, which remains in view, and yet there are no towns. Dirt trails shoot up mile-long hillsides then disappear at the lip, and I wonder what I'd see if I drove up to the ridge and peered over. What windswept barrenness would come into view? The sky is a blinding galvanized plate with wispy island cloud forms etched across it. On a ridge two miles away, a massive, solitary combine lumbers like a slow red mammoth. I pass only three cars in almost a hundred miles and am reminded frequently by road signs that to fall asleep is to die.

Finally I see the sign for Clean Seas Tuna and turn down a dirt road to cross a blasted stretch of salt pan, still-water ponds, and fringes of thorny scrub the color and texture of steel wool. Past a sign that reads PERMISSION

NEEDED TO ENTER. CAMERAS NOT PERMITTED, a series of tan warehouses rises into view. I pass through a concrete gateway to a complex of buildings and an open dirt lot where huge purse seine nets are piled in mounds beneath a crane.

A swarm of small black flies accumulates around my head as soon as I step out of the car and make my way to a low office building, where I'm soon joined by Adam Miller, whose sandy hair and tall, thin build are reminiscent of a midwestern farmhand. Miller, in his early twenties, was trained in aquaculture in Adelaide, and his main task on the site is to tend the bluefin tank. After crossing the dirt lot, we enter one of the tan warehouse buildings, where I'm given a pair of rubber boots and follow Miller as he steps into a shallow tray of iodine, a quarantine measure against the infiltration of pathogens. As we walk through an area of humming pumps and piping systems, Miller explains that all the water in the bluefin tank system—3.8 million liters—is filtered every three hours, removing solids and carbon dioxide, running through aerators and ultraviolet screens, and then returned to the tank.

As we step into a control room equipped with computer monitors and scientific equipment, Miller says, "We have some video of them actually spawning last spring," and he brings up a video on one of the screens.

"The females release their eggs at night," he explains as we watch the video of the bluefin in a kind of promenade. "They'll go along like this, then one of the females will just shoot off and the males will go after her. She'll spin to the top, releasing her eggs, and the males will rocket past her, trailing these smoky plumes. It's something to see."

I picture the spawning multitudes running at night in the Straits of Florida or south of the Balearics off of Spain, the females pirouetting toward the surface and the males chasing them, blazing their milky contrails. I realize how lucky I am to be able to see this footage. There are other universities and industry groups working on breeding bluefin in captivity, but as of this writing Arno Bay is the only place on the planet where the southern bluefin has been successfully spawned under controlled conditions.

"Let's have a look at the fish," Miller says, and he takes me through a door into a large room, half of which is taken up by an enormous circular tank, with high walls and a walkway running along its upper circumference. As we climb to the top, I see that the tank is roughly twenty-five feet across, and when I look down I see, swimming in endless circles, fifteen medium bluefin tuna, five feet long and about 250 pounds each. Their bodies are dark on top, with sides of burnished silver that appears rubbed off in places. They seem very relaxed.

"That's our goal, actually," Miller tells me. "We want to make them as comfortable as possible. We try to mimic their natural surroundings in water temperature and light. And we feed them very well—frozen pilchards and squid, which we get locally."

"Actually, they're about due for a feeding," he says. He goes down the ladder, then reappears with a white five-gallon bucket and offers me the ladle. I scoop the thawed squid and sling it out over the fish. The tuna, with little discernible change in tail-beat speed, smoothly accelerate to each morsel. Bluefin glide unlike any fish I've seen; theirs is a quintessential hydrodynamic shape, letting them slip through the water with little effort.

After feeding the tuna, Miller gives me a tour of the mulloway and yellowtail kingfish facilities. Clean Seas has already closed the life cycle on both of these species and successfully raises hundreds of metric tons per year for domestic use and export. The fish are bred, hatched, and raised on land and, when old enough, are transported out to offshore pens.

We head outside and pass several men transferring kingfish fingerlings, and I am amazed to see the fish—two and a half inches long, sixty days old—swimming upstream against the flow coming through a clear lavender ribbed plastic pipe, about five inches around. It is a hose full of swimming fish—tens of thousands of them.

Miller then takes me to where their feed is manufactured. The room looks like a sophisticated home-brewing operation, with plastic tanks, hoses, and pumps and a smell both organic and yeasty. For the first ten days, the kingfish and mulloway larvae are fed zooplankton—rotifers, specifically—which look like translucent swimming grocery bags stuffed with food. Indicating a large, open-topped plastic tank containing an opaque, yellowy liquid, he says, "There are two thousand rotifers per drop of water. We raise six billion per batch." After ten days on the rotifers, the kingfish are switched to brine shrimp—*Artemia salina,* a.k.a. sea monkeys—from Utah's Great Salt Lake. A few months later, they begin eating pelletized food, which is typically a mix of grains and fish protein.

After we complete the tour of the facilities, Miller takes me by jeep to show me the rest of Clean Seas' site, traveling over sandy, rocky roads scraped out of the hard ground of the barren coast. A short distance offshore, I see the yellow booms encircling the tops of several fish pens. Most of Clean Seas' tuna pens are much farther out—more than twenty miles—but these are the brood stock pens.

We stop at a gate, and Miller exits the jeep to undo the wrap of wire keeping the gate shut. Apparently—although they are nowhere in sight—there are herds of sheep that, given the opportunity, will storm the Clean Seas base. After another half-mile of road, we begin to sink into heavy sands behind a line of dunes, and we get out and begin to walk. All around are strange vegetal forms—shore plants, succulents, odd flowers, and grasses—and the ocean that now comes into view is an unfamiliar one. Bronze whalers and great whites frequent the cold, desolate offshore waters here, where the wind blows hard and steady.

"You do any fishing out here?" I ask Miller.

"Sure, yeah. We come down here at the end of the day with a few beers and a rod, throw something out there, see what we get."

"I was going to ask what you do for entertainment. Seems a bit short on options out here."

He laughs. "Yeah, well. We mostly do our shifts, work and live here for a chunk of time, then head back to Port Lincoln or Adelaide. It's all right."

"You could do worse," I say, looking over the long beach and the deserted sea.

~~~~~

It is late July 2010 before I finally have the opportunity to speak by phone to Hagen Stehr, who is on vacation in New Zealand. He has an Austrian accent reminiscent of Arnold Schwarzenegger's, overlaid with Australian. Stehr is a genial straight shooter and has the engaging air of a man motivated by an evangelical vision of the future.

"I hate the concept that 'it can't be done,'" he tells me. "Everything can be done as long as you have the will to be successful and the desire to do something. Give me a spoon and I can shift a mountain."

Stehr prefers to think of himself as a Christian (although, by his own admission, he does not always behave like one), and he is an aficionado of General George Patton. He's visited Patton's birthplace and owns the general's entire published works.

Stehr is open to discussing the challenges he's faced trying to breed bluefin, to keep his company together, to keep investors satisfied that they aren't pouring money into a bottomless hole. It's been a titanic effort to overcome the technical and financial hurdles of trying to close the breeding cycle on this fish.

"My claim to fame is to pull the scientists by the nose and kick them in the ass and have them all singing off the same songbook," Stehr tells me. "They're all prima donnas! They don't care about anything else but writing another paper to foster their own careers. If that's happening, you're running wrong. You've got to keep very close control. They're like a herd of wild cats. If someone doesn't call me a bastard once a day, I feel lonely," he says with a laugh.

I ask Stehr if he feels any responsibility for having contributed to the decline of the southern bluefin during the years of overfishing.

"I do, absolutely. We didn't know what we were doing. It was insane. I had a vessel that had fifty-five-tonne capacity. I remember once I had close to a hundred tonnes on it, with a foot and a half of freeboard left. It was ludicrous.

"Look, I am not a greenie, but to have an ocean where my grandkids can make a living from it, we need to have a strong management system, to look after the environment. The fishing industry helped the demise of the resource around the world, and there ought to be leaders in the various sectors who step forward to take a different stance. All of us need to take some sort of responsibility, not only for us but so that we have a resource in a hundred years, two hundred years."

"You're starting to sound like you have a little bit of environmentalist blood in you," I point out.

"Hey! You would not be the first to slander me like that! I am very right-wing—I am to the right of Genghis Khan! But I tell you, Australia has got it right with the strict regulations and the quotas and how hard they manage aquaculture."

Stehr explains that South Australia is the only place in the world practicing true offshore aquaculture, which makes a significant difference environmentally.* Much aquaculture around the world takes place within short boating distance of shore, in fjords, bays, and coves. True offshore aquaculture is done in comparatively deep water in areas of significant current or tides.

As far as the wild stock is concerned, Stehr tells me that in nearly fifty years of fishing he's never seen more juveniles. "There are thousands and thousands of tonnes out there."

This echoes what his son, Marcus, reported, but it belies the Commission for the Conservation of Southern Bluefin Tuna's 2011 stock assessment, which shows that the wild stocks are in severe trouble—anywhere from 13 to 17 percent below the minimum safe level in the breeding population—despite Australia's strict management. The damage from those years of overfishing in the sixties, seventies, and eighties (and by Japan more recently) was so severe that it is still being felt, and the measures to restrict it have not been strict enough. In South Australia, as off the East Coast of the United States and certainly in the Mediterranean, the precautionary approach would indicate that a moratorium—or at least a severe reduction in all bluefin harvesting—would be in order until the minimum safe level of adult breeders is achieved. While bluefin tuna are incredibly fecund (an adult female can produce fifteen to twenty million eggs during one spawning season), the mortality of those eggs and larvae is so high, and so much remains unknown about their spawning and reproductive success, that bluefin are considered a low-to-moderate-reproductivity species. Given these facts and their depleted numbers, a moratorium or a drastic reduction in fishing seems the safest way to ensure that bluefin tuna populations are rebuilt to safe levels as soon as possible.

Stehr agrees that the imposed quota limits are responsible for what he reports as this glut of juvenile fish. I ask him if the halting of the recently

---

*There are actually other locations practicing offshore aquaculture, including Kona, Hawaii.

revealed overfishing of southern bluefin by the Japanese might also have contributed to the numbers of juveniles seen.

"It is absolutely criminal what Japan has done," Stehr says hotly. "I write an article every month for AusMarine, where they call me the Kaiser. I mentioned it in there. Foreign Affairs rung me from Canberra, asking me, 'Please, Mr. Stehr, would you [speak more gently about this],' and I said, 'No, I won't. Because it's a fact of life.' The Japanese have routed the system absolutely chronically. They get away with it because nobody is prepared to stand up."

The total spawning stock for all the southern bluefin in existence is believed to be between 45,000 and 49,000 metric tons—which sounds like a lot of fish. But consider that the high-end estimate of 49,000 metric tons is thought to represent, at most, *only 7 percent* of what the spawning stock used to be. The Japanese alone illegally overfished more than 200,000 metric tons of southern bluefin between 1986 and 2006. And while the Japanese might have been stopped, illegal fishing continues in countries like Indonesia, where catches are not well tracked.

Considering all these factors, one realizes that 49,000 metric tons of adult southern bluefin—somewhere between half a million and a million adult fish, spread out over their vast range, at the mercy of modern industrialized fishing from many countries, some of it illegal—represents a slim toehold for a species rather than a stronghold.

Given these conditions, are tuna ranching and breeding helping wild fish or hurting them? Should we be focused on rebuilding wild stocks instead of breeding the fish in captivity? Stehr's answer is sobering: Wild fish stocks, he explains, are almost all at maximum utilization levels. There is no more room for increasing wild catches. And going to sea remains costly, risky, and without guaranteed returns, at the same time the human population and demand for protein are only forecasted to grow. All these factors make the propagation of tuna and other species through aquaculture seem inevitable, and pressure on wild stocks unlikely to let up.

"We don't hunt anymore with spears, do we? We raise our beef," he tells me. "It will be the same with tuna and other ocean fish. Australia imports 79 percent of its fish now. What is the moral of the story? Wild seafood will become impossibly expensive, or we will go to offshore aquaculture."

If Hagen Stehr is to be believed, it would seem there is nothing we humans cannot do if we put our minds to it. But so little of what we put our minds to is for the protection of not just wilderness but of wild ecosystems. The difference is not just semantic. "Wilderness" is often thought of as something we protect for the sake of its beauty or for recreational purposes. The idea of "wild ecosystems," on the other hand, emphasizes the fact that our lives depend on vast interconnected systems whose complexity remains beyond our control. As we diminish wild ecosystems, we put ourselves at great risk by jeopardizing our food supply, our sources of freshwater, the diversity of plant and animal life, and whatever else is compromised by our unlimited or poorly regulated activity in the system. The Australian government deserves recognition for its strict enforcement of regulations that attempt to preserve what little is left of the wild southern bluefin stock in its waters. But given the extremely low adult breeding population, the fact that other countries do not have such stringent oversights, and the fact that the southern bluefin tuna has been listed as an endangered species for years, one must ask why any fishing is allowed to continue. Jobs are clearly at stake, and Morten Deichmann's comment that only juveniles are harvested would seem to indicate that breeding adults are conserved, but juveniles become adults, and the recruitment of the young to the breeding population is a high-risk affair. The chance that a southern bluefin tuna larva will reach maturity is on the order of one in several million. Consider, too, the role bluefin play as top-tier predators and their poor match as candidates for efficient aquaculture (requiring high feed ratios of forage fish for every pound of weight gained) and it would seem that the intentional rebuilding of the stock as soon as possible should be a top priority.

Aquaculture will, as Stehr suggests, be practiced more and more widely. But elsewhere, in countries struggling with fewer resources, the move toward aquaculture in the context of pervasive corruption, continued industrial fishing, and an inability to enforce even the most basic measures will only spell greater environmental destruction. The mindset that led to overfishing—that the ocean would provide infinite resources—will indeed be replaced by the mindset that aquaculture in all its forms can provide us with infinite resources where Nature cannot. But in the meantime, what will happen to wilderness? Does it not have a value other than as a source of animal protein?

Tuna ranching and captive breeding still rely on removing thousands of metric tons of juvenile bluefin from the wild stock, and so it will continue for years, until (in the case of captive breeding) Hagen Stehr's organization and others like it succeed in their quest to close the life cycle on bluefin.

In some near or distant future, Hagen Stehr might be able to realize his dream of breeding bluefin tuna like cattle without having to rely on wild tuna. And maybe that will mean that Australia won't have to fish the wild oceans anymore. The more likely scenario, however, is that as the global human population grows, the demand for protein will increase and various parties—whether poor nations, unscrupulous corporations, or pirate industries—will continue to fish using industrial commercial gear at sea. The cascade of change caused by these illegal, unregulated, and unreported factors in natural ecosystems will continue until wild stocks are exhausted. At that point, as in the case of the Atlantic salmon, aquaculture may provide the only remaining viable stock. This might satisfy the demand for protein, but it will have done nothing to keep wild oceans intact.

As I end my conversation with Stehr, the only answer I come to is this: If we want to have wild oceans and all the ways they provide for us, we will need to protect them. There is only one way to do this: legally, correctly, scientifically, with full transparency and with strict enforcement. Preserving the oceans should not eliminate commercial fishing in the wild, but if commercial fishing goes so far as to exceed the minimum safe threshold for the breeding stock in any species, it should be suspended until that stock recovers. Anything short of this is simply the appearance of management, not management, and without it, the challenge of controlling human ambition is simply impossible.

There is no better example of this in the world than what is happening in the Mediterranean to what remains there of the northern bluefin tuna.

The *Warrior* in Malta

Greenpeace and the Battle in the Mediterranean

No ecological problem will ever be solved until it becomes a political problem and it will never become a political problem until public opinion demands it.

—Paul Armond, as spoken to Mike McGettigan

1

Early on the morning of June 15, 2009, I wake up in my seat on a Delta Airlines flight somewhere over western France. The light coming in the window sends blinding golden flares off the wing. In about an hour we are due in Milan, where I will board another plane and fly south over the Tyrrhenian Sea—between the shin of Italy and Sardinia—and over the desiccated landscape of Sicily to the small island nation of Malta, for thousands of years a crossroads and way station for travelers in the Mediterranean.

Only four days ago, on June 11, I received an e-mail from Yesim Aslan, a communications officer for Greenpeace out of Istanbul, notifying me that there was a berth for me aboard the *Rainbow Warrior* if I could get to the dock in Malta by the fifteenth.

Apart from knowing it was an island in the Mediterranean Sea, I realized I had no idea where Malta actually was. There on Google Maps lay the country—a tight cluster of three small islands like a scattering of pebbles sixty miles south of Sicily.

I had already digested a substantial amount of information from various sources—books, scientific papers, interviews, conservation publications, and documentaries about the bluefin tuna trade in the Mediterranean. But with funds low and only French as a backup to my English, the challenge of finding a way to directly experience and understand the situation was a daunting prospect. Overtures to the region's largest tuna-ranching company—the Spanish corporation Ricardo Fuentes e Hijos—had yielded no response, nor did my attempts to gain access to anyone at Maruha Nichiro, a Japanese company and one of the world's largest seafood corporations, with substantial interests in Mediterranean bluefin. My prospects had dwindled to almost nothing when Yesim's invitation arrived.

How one views Greenpeace and organizations like it depends on where one gets one's information about them. Are they rational conservationists, fundamentalist "greenies," the last great hope for humanity, or something in between? My own impressions of Greenpeace up to this point have been generally positive, for two reasons: First, I agree with its commitment to a nonviolent, albeit confrontational, approach to issues related to the environment, which has enabled it to maintain integrity in its mission; second, I support most of the causes to which it has devoted its resources. Since its founding in 1971, Greenpeace has successfully opposed the dumping of enormous quantities of radioactive and poisonous industrial waste into the ocean; fought to stop whales from being hunted when many of those species were on the threshold of extinction; and protested underground and surface nuclear tests, overfishing, and the most destructive types of industrial fishing gear, including bottom trawls and gill nets. It has also lent its support to alternative and sustainable forms of energy.

The plane comes in low over patchwork fields and lands on the outskirts of Milan. I pass the three hours of my layover downing multiple cups of espresso, eating prosciutto-and-provolone sandwiches, and reading through a series of reports by the three major environmental groups at work on the bluefin issue—Greenpeace, the World Wildlife Fund, and Oceana—as well as stock assessments by the International Commission for the Conservation of Atlantic Tunas and bluefin trade analyses by a consulting firm called Advanced Tuna Ranching Technologies (ATRT).

ATRT is run by Roberto Mielgo Bregazzi, a Spaniard now based in Madrid and Paris, who used to work for TFM–Grupo Antalba, one of the largest Spanish tuna-ranching operations in the Mediterranean, with hundreds of metric tons of bluefin in pens off the Murcia coast. Bregazzi began as a diver and helped design some of the first towable pens, but he got religion after he saw the bluefin trade spiraling out of control. In 2003, he left the business and began working covertly, setting up a network of informants in major Mediterranean ports. He has attempted to account for every known, reported, illegal, unreported, and obscured source of harvest and trade of bluefin tuna in the Mediterranean dating back to the early 1990s. His network has documented and photographed ship movements, offloading of bluefin, ranching operations, transport of feedstock, and more—an effort that has resulted in one of the most comprehensive views of the bluefin trade across the entire Mediterranean since ranching began there. He has cross-checked and verified his information against ICCAT data, nation-specific export and import records, the Eurostat statistical database, scientific reports, and Lloyd's Marine Intelligence Unit, which tracks vessel movements.

What Bregazzi has found is both staggering and disheartening. The destruction of the bluefin tuna fishery in the Mediterranean since 1996 has laid waste to a resource that supported the local cultures for over nine thousand years. The fishery is routinely overfished above ICCAT quota levels—sometimes by more than double—with impunity. The history of bluefin tuna in the Mediterranean since ranching began, and in the Atlantic in the past fifty years, is a tale of unmitigated disaster, involving the plunder of one stock after another.

Fishing in the 1950s was focused in the North Sea and the Mediterranean, and in the 1960s it expanded to include the western Atlantic stock, off the coasts of the United States, Canada, and Brazil. By the 1970s, the North Sea stock was much reduced, and the western stock off Brazil had ceased to exist. Throughout the seventies, heavy fishing continued on the western stock off the United States and Canada, with the eastern stock off Europe, the Mediterranean, and northwest Africa continuing to be heavily exploited. By the 1980s, the North Sea stock was completely destroyed and the western stock off the United States and Canada had crashed.

The 1990s saw a steep increase in fishing pressure on the one remaining robust population: the Mediterranean stock, which historically has been the stronghold of Atlantic bluefin. From the mid-1970s until 1996, the annual catch of the Mediterranean stock was around 21,000 metric tons. Between 1994 and 1997, the haul more than doubled to between 45,000 and 50,000 metric tons per year. Despite estimates in 1999 that the population of spawning adults was down by more than 80 percent since the early

1970s, fishing at the rate of 50,000 to 60,000 metric tons per year continued for the next decade, in the face of increasingly dire warnings of impending collapse. The bluefin haul was notoriously and massively underreported by a purse seine fleet that grew without limitation or enforcement of any kind. Fattening ratios were faked to launder unreported catches, there was widespread use of illegal spotting aircraft, seiners caught huge amounts of illegal juvenile bluefin under thirty kilos, and catch reports were falsified, throwing off ICCAT stock assessments. By 2007, eleven nations, with an estimated ranching capacity of more than 60,000 metric tons of tuna per year, were wiping out what little was left of bluefin in the Mediterranean.

As I pack these reports and board the plane for Malta, I realize that the question weighing heavily on my mind is no longer "What happened?" but "How is this allowed to continue?"

2

The deep blue of the Mediterranean Sea gives way to the turquoise of coastal shallows; then Malta suddenly slides into view beneath the wing. The swimming pools of residential homes flash in the sun in a landscape that looks blasted and parched, with the soft, dry texture of old chalk.

Exiting the plane on the tarmac, I'm hit with a thick blast of heat and white sunlight so bright it pains the eyes. I'm pressed for time to make the early transport out to the ship, and if I miss it I will have to wait seven hours for the next one. I find a taxi and ask the driver to take me quickly to the sea passenger terminal in Valletta Harbor. Taking me at my word, he drives like a madman through the crumbling streets of the capital.

Arriving at the terminal, I'm approached by a woman in her late twenties with long, curly brown hair and Turkish features. It is Yesim, my communications contact, who introduces me to the others. Among them are another American from Greenpeace in Washington, D.C.; a Frenchman who I suspect is blind; and a tall, curly-haired Italian man, who smokes profusely and whose bearing suggests a combination of wariness, skepticism, and mirth. He introduces himself as Marcello Conti.*

---

*Not his real name.

Eventually we are taken by our Maltese ship's agent to the transport vessel, a simple open-decked industrial tug. We pull away from the dock and head down the main leg of Valletta Harbor, lined by rock cliffs and topped on almost every promontory by the angular, thick stone walls of fortresses. The Germans bombed Malta to rubble in the early years of World War II, but they were unable to take the island. It's no wonder.

We clear the breakwater at the mouth of the harbor, with its small stone lighthouse looking like a chess piece, and begin to head offshore. In the distance, perhaps two miles away, I see the *Rainbow Warrior* at anchor. She lies upon the placid sea like a great sailing ship, her three tall masts reaching into the sky, her rainbow stripes and the white dove carrying an olive branch in its beak visible on the forward bow from even this distance. She's 180 feet long and 28 feet wide, with masts reaching over 80 feet tall. She is indeed a true ship—a refitted North Sea fishing trawler, cut in half and lengthened in the middle, with masts added to give her a second means of power. This ship is the replacement for the original *Rainbow Warrior,* sunk in Auckland Harbour, New Zealand, in 1985 by French agents. In that attack, a Portuguese-Dutch photographer, Fernando Pereira, was killed, leaving behind a wife and two small children. It is a sober reminder that, despite its peaceful mission, the *Rainbow Warrior*'s work is dangerous. Greenpeace boats have had huge drums of radioactive waste dropped on them; they've been rammed and run over. Greenpeace volunteers have been beaten and stabbed, their skulls cracked, bones broken. (In 2010, a Greenpeace campaigner on the same mission we are about to go on was hooked through the calf by a grappling hook thrown by a tuna boat crew member and nearly dragged off the Zodiac inflatable he was riding in.*)

The ship itself has the heavy prow of a fishing vessel, with a low midship section. Here, welded racks hold the gray Zodiacs, with their stocky two-hundred-horsepower outboard engines. To the rear, the *Warrior* has a high aft deck with a broad, flat wheelhouse up top and a rounded stern. As the tug draws up alongside, I notice the old steel-plate hull, fastened with large rivets and coated with heavy, chipped layers of green paint.

---

*YouTube, "Greenpeace Activists Violently Attacked at Sea," http://www.youtube.com/watch?v=sCb4TqjwWKQ.

We haul our gear off the tug and step onto the *Warrior* through a heavy steel door amidships. The low middle deck here is neat but crowded with equipment, including industrial storage barrels, hoses, toolboxes, and a hydraulic crane folded upon itself. The crew members have a look that is a blend of woodsy trail hiker and bottom-of-the-ladder deckhand: T-shirts and shorts, sunglasses, and sneakers, wearing caps or with heads wrapped in bandannas. They move with confidence and sureness. I watch them on deck for a few minutes, and they seem to know their work. Those who are not involved in our transfer pay no attention to us but remain focused on their tasks. The campaigners greet one another with a note of strong, upbeat morale. Across one of the Zodiac's big engines I notice what at first appears to be a series of bullet holes, but I realize they're stickers imitating them—the same kind I've seen adorning the rear gates of pickup trucks. It's a touch of positive bravado.

My bunk is belowdecks in a room I will share with an Australian cameraman, a young Brazilian cook, and an Englishman in his early thirties who holds one of the ship's two boatswain (pronounced *bosun*) posts. I stow my gear and head back up to the aft deck, where I encounter the Italian, Conti, discussing with several Greenpeace campaigners whether they should head back to St. Paul's Bay to observe two transship boats—the *Tirana* and the *Almatea*—which he believes may have made their drops already.

Transship boats move tuna between purse seine and ranch pen, or from ranch pen to refrigerated ("reefer") vessels, on which they are taken to Japan. Transshipments are allowed only under certain circumstances, and this year, for the first time, transshipment of dead fish has been ruled illegal. Still, transshipments at sea remain routine and difficult to monitor and enforce, and they are a significant means by which the number and origin of tuna are obscured from authorities trying to monitor the trade.

I draw closer to the conversation and hear Conti explaining that another ship, the *Kyung Yang I,* a former Korean longliner that used to be known as *Astraea 101,* is now serving as a reefer ship. It was spotted outside Malta five days ago, headed south toward Tunisia, with its anticollision system (which tracks its position by satellite) turned off for twenty-four hours. It then reappeared south of Malta, heading back north.

"She was low in the water," Conti says to me. "I believe she was carrying a full load of Tunisian bluefin. She's just south of here, alongside another ship. If they're transferring tuna, it'll be almost impossible to tell where those fish came from. The only way to be certain it is carrying illegal bluefin is to get actual observer footage of the transshipment as it happens. But there are other ways you can put the pieces together. It takes three to four days to freeze tuna solid at negative 60 degrees centigrade. You can tell how long the fish has been freezing, within that window, by its color. Then you can retrace the ship's movements to get a sense of where the fish might have been loaded into the freezers. If it was in Tunisian waters but the ship's records show that the fish are labeled as Maltese bluefin, or if the load exceeds the country's allocated quota, you know it's illegal."

These few moments of conversation—describing illegal transshipments, renamed and reflagged vessels, and cut satellite links—demonstrate only a few of the ways bluefin are smuggled or laundered.

After the Greenpeace campaigners step away for a meeting in the wheelhouse, Conti points to a scattering of ships and a series of large buoys and explains that we're anchored within a mile of the largest bluefin tuna farming operation in the world. The buoys demarcate Malta's exclusive fisheries zone,* an area of roughly one square mile in which are contained numerous floating cages, forty meters (130 feet) wide, evident from their spherical surface floats.

"Those cages were planned to accommodate a capacity of nine thousand metric tons of bluefin tuna," Conti observes. "They actually hold closer to eleven thousand metric tons."

This is an impressive amount, especially when you consider that the entire western Atlantic quota for bluefin is roughly 1,900 metric tons. Consider, too, that Malta's farmed-tuna capacity represents 80 percent of the total approved quota for the entire Mediterranean and eastern Atlantic in 2010, nearly all of the ICCAT science committee's recommended quota.

Conti speaks in heavily accented English. I'm not clear about his role until he tells me he is not affiliated with Greenpeace or any other group or agency. "I am an investigator," he tells me simply.

---

*The official name of the tuna-ranching zone is the Aquaculture Zone off Xorb I-Ghagin. Three different tuna-ranching companies operate within it: MareBlu Tuna Farm, Ta'Mattew Tuna Farm, and Deep Sea Aquaculture.

"Are you sailing with us?" I ask.

"No. I return to Palermo in the morning."

Realizing that this is probably my only chance to talk with him, I cut immediately to what I really want to know. "What I haven't figured out is how the corruption works. You have all this money being made, you have quotas being smashed, and I keep asking myself, *Where's all the money going? Who's benefiting?*"

Conti answers me in the form of a story: "Say you're a prominent fishing captain in your community—say Marseille, in southern France. In the early 1990s, you begin to see an increase in the profitability of bluefin tuna. You hear about this ranching idea they're trying in Spain. You go to your local politician, the guy who runs the port, called the *prudhomme,* and say to him, 'A new purse seine vessel would make me more competitive. The government is providing subsidies. I would like a new ship and would like you to pay the government share.' This is about 38 percent. The politician says, 'Yes, I think I can do that. What might you be able to do for me?' The fisherman says, 'You build me my ship with a 38 percent subsidy, and I can guarantee you five hundred votes next election.' The captain can do this because, as a prominent fisherman, he has major economic impact on his community. So the captain goes fishing with the new ship and does extremely well, because it's the gold rush years of tuna fishing in the Mediterranean. With these faster ships, weather and locale are no longer issues. You have satellite images showing the temperature breaks, the plankton blooms, and you have spotter planes locating the schools of tuna. You have a banner year, and you go back to the politician and say, 'I'd like another ship,' and this time the politician says, 'That might be possible, but what can you do for me?' The captain says, 'I can give you a thousand votes.' The politician answers, 'That's good. But I will need more.' The captain thinks about it and says, 'I can give you 100,000 euros for your political purposes. We could move it through Switzerland or Monte Carlo,' and they agree on the deal. They might even cement it with a weekend in Spain, with good Spanish food and wine and Spanish women. So as the infrastructure builds—for jobs, for the tuna ranches, for the community—the incentive to look away from what is happening to the bluefin stock itself gets stronger and stronger. The politician in charge of the port might say, a few years later, 'You were over your quota of a thousand metric tons by a factor of three. What can you give me to help me obscure those figures?' And on it goes. The public knows little or nothing, the conservation organizations are not inside the game, so they don't have the contacts or know the loopholes. They are trying to pin tags on a thousand cats running in all directions, and they are outnumbered three hundred to one. It all happens, and the damage is done by the time you try to put controls on it. We are now at the point where there are seiners that cannot harvest enough bluefin to pay their loans. So what do they do but go back to the government for a bailout? And this after they've made millions with a government subsidy—taxpayer money—to build the boat in the first place."

After absorbing this, I ask, "But didn't people see it coming?"

"Yes, of course. But they only see what they want to see, and how would it have mattered anyway? Look at it from another angle: You're a tuna rancher from southern Spain. You make a ton of money in a very tight bunch of years, but by the third year of heavy harvesting you see that the tuna around the Balearic Islands, where they breed and where you have always caught them, are smaller and harder to find. The next year it's almost what you'd call 'bad,' and you begin to do the math in your head. You look at all the ships and ranches and you know it's ruined. You also know, farther south, off the coast of Libya and Tunisia, there are tuna. So you take a gamble and send one of your guys down there. He knows a little Arabic, enough to understand when the translator is not translating everything. He goes down to Libya and finds himself in this port director's office, and it is his job to secure access to their tuna grounds from this man. The port director says to the envoy, 'We are tired of Europeans coming down here offering us projects that never come to pass.' The envoy tells him, 'You are still blockaded, and yet I came, I am here. So you know I mean business.' The Libyan regards him a little more thoughtfully. 'If you are to have access to the tuna in these waters,' he says, 'I will give you a credit of one million dollars to front the operation. If you do not actually create or succeed with this operation, I keep the million and you owe it.' The envoy tells him flatly that a million U.S. is out of the question, but he says, 'I am a European. I deal in euros. And even though the euro is below the dollar, it will be at 1.5 in two years, and strong again the next year after that. I don't want a credit of one million U.S., but a credit of one million euros I will take.' So that is how the Spaniards got their hands on a new tuna ground ahead of everyone else. That is also how the competition for tuna spread across the Mediterranean. The Spaniards made their deal with the Libyans, and three years later that port director was doing very well, because he had a stake in the ranch they had set up."

I realize I've been down this road before—in other discussions, in reading the reports—and that the formal, public structures don't matter because they have no real teeth and are uncoordinated. They have no ability to control any of this, especially if the politicians are involved the way Conti indicates and the public is asleep or unaware, and therefore unable to apply any pressure to keep the process honest.

"There is one other piece," Conti says. "The role of the Japanese. When it all started, the Japanese would fly their Spanish friends to Tokyo, where they would take them to dine at the most expensive restaurants in the Ginza district. They'd ply them with the best sushi and sashimi, still quivering, and they would get uproariously drunk. That's how they operate, friends and gangsters all of them. But then they'd put the screws to the Spaniards on the negotiated price. 'We will give you eight euros per kilo,' they'd say. It's robbery—the Spaniards knew it, the Japanese knew it—but it was impossible to protest. Who else will buy the volume of tuna the Japanese will? No one. No nation can import eighteen thousand metric tons of the highest-grade tuna and consume it as they do at their prices. The Spaniards ended up agreeing to eleven euros per kilo. The only thing that saved them that year was the falling value of the yen and the fact that they had the Libyan access.

"The Japanese have such total dominance, and there is so much money to be made, that any incentive toward restraint is overrun. Plus, economic factors and competition play a role. The year after the one I just mentioned, the Spaniards faced new challenges. Stronger yen, higher fuel prices, scarcer fish, more countries fishing. Everyone starts to push the boundaries. You overshoot your quota by fifteen hundred metric tons, you start offloading directly at sea to Japanese reefers, you fish beyond the closure date and score another two hundred metric tons and quickly transfer it to a ranch north of Turkey. Everyone has heard of the so-called Japanese strategic reserve—that they have actually stockpiled frozen bluefin tuna in warehouses to sell at higher prices when the wild fish are gone. Some say it's twenty thousand metric tons.* I have evidence that it's more likely sixty or seventy thousand metric tons, socked away at negative sixty degrees centigrade, where it's good for five or six years.

"In 2008, the endgame had been run. The tuna were way down, and they were all small—less than ninety kilos, with a full third under thirty kilos. Now it's the summer of 2009, and how many Japanese longliners do you think are operating here in the Mediterranean? I'll tell you: There are only six Japanese longliners operating here this summer, where before there were dozens. But there are sixty longliners—sixty!—now operating off Cape Verde, on the African coast, hooking every bigeye tuna there is to hook in those waters. The writing is on the wall. They moved on to Africa and bigeye because the Mediterranean bluefin are done. Our fishery, a mainstay of the cultures surrounding this sea for thousands of years, has been annihilated in less than two decades."

3

Later that evening, with the ship under way, the crew and passengers gather in the mess for the mission briefing. The main strategic overview is given by François Provost, one of the lead campaigners, who's in his early thirties and of medium height, with close-cut dark hair, unshaven jaw, and an olive drab cap. He could pass for a French Che Guevara. Like many on board, he smokes a running chain of thin, dark hand-rolled cigarettes. Provost explains that teams of campaigners—the strategists and tacticians—will be on a rotation schedule, with someone on the bridge at all times. They will identify ships, check them against official ICCAT rosters, determine when to launch the Zodiacs, and decide what actions should be taken, if any.

The other campaigners, sitting nearby, include John Hocevar from Greenpeace in Washington, D.C., and Alain Combémorel, a gentleman philosopher, photographer, and chemist who first became involved with

---

*A portion of these "reserves" was ruined after the power that supplied the freezers was cut by the tsunamis that hit Japan on March 11, 2011, and led to the Fukushima Daiichi nuclear power plant disaster.

Greenpeace in its campaign against toxic anti-fouling paint, which had contaminated the harbor bottom in Marseille. The other representative from Greenpeace France is François Chartier, whom I first met in Valletta and who is indeed blind. Chartier has a gentle bearing and is an expert in EU fisheries and the Mediterranean bluefin trade. Dave Roberts is a red-haired John Lennon look-alike from Greenpeace UK. The captain, Pete Bouquet, is a thirty-year veteran and a pilot of the original *Rainbow Warrior,* and his patience, experience, and humor come through in his easygoing, fatherly manner.

Provost describes a complicating factor in the operation: Waves of refugees from Tunisia and Libya have been crossing in overcrowded boats from North Africa to the Italian island of Lampedusa. If the *Warrior* should encounter a vessel in distress, the priority will shift from patrolling for illegal fishing to rendering assistance. Provost also explains that, for the first time—and because of the pressure exerted by nongovernmental organizations like Greenpeace, Oceana, and the World Wildlife Fund—the European Union has agreed to a joint military deployment of ships from France, Spain, Cyprus, and Italy to monitor this summer's tuna fishing.

"So we are likely to encounter military patrols, which is positive. They are finally trying to oversee what is happening. We also have our own spotter planes up looking for targets," he adds, and then he details the target priorities. Reefer vessels will be first, because these are the critical link that enables the illegal trade. "If we come across a transshipment at sea, we will ask to board the reefer to inspect. If we find they are in possession of illegal fish, we will occupy the vessel and notify the authorities."

The second priority is purse seiners in the process of encircling fish. Given the rampant overharvesting (typically ten thousand to thirty thousand metric tons above the official seasonal quota), it is Greenpeace's strategy to interrupt and inspect all harvesting, based on the premise that the official ICCAT monitoring and enforcement systems have proven to be completely inadequate to the task of correctly managing and conserving the stocks. The strategy is to force transparency on a system that has so far succeeded in completely blocking it. Greenpeace's tactics are not arrived at lightly but are the product of years of monitoring and smaller, less disruptive protests that have increased in intensity and risk only as the situation has become more dire. To board and occupy a vessel or to block the harvest of tuna as it's happening is a provocative act, and safety is a real concern.

The meeting ends, and as people clear out, I fall into conversation with John Hocevar, the American. In his late thirties, he's tall, with aquiline features and a thick, dark stubble on his head. He has the thin, lanky angularity of a vegetarian and the most intense green hawk eyes I've ever seen. He has a patient and quiet manner, but after getting to know him better, I understand that Hocevar is fundamentally a hunter, his quarry all the ways stupidity manifests in human beings, whether as greed, shortsightedness, or brutality. All I pick up at this point, though, is that the guy is calculating behind his patient exterior and that he has a subtle but intense blue-flame burn.

I ask him about the crew. During the briefing, I heard at least eight different accents, counted a third as many women as men, and put the age range from the early twenties to the mid-sixties.

"You ought to talk to the chief engineer, Vlad," Hocevar tells me. "He's former Russian navy. Worked on nuclear subs. He's got some good stories. He told me one about how they used to shadow those huge cruise ships all the way into U.S. ports—they'd come in right under the keel. They'd also follow U.S. Navy boats and check out their jettisoned trash. Figured it might be good for intelligence. Apparently the only thing they found was that the U.S. guys had far better porn."

When I ask him how he got started, Hocevar proceeds to spin out a long history of activism dating back to high school, when he protested being forced to register for the draft. He then went on to an undergrad degree in biology and graduate work in marine biology in Florida, where he founded and led the organization Students for a Free Tibet. Most of his work since has focused on the oceans. He has fought to protect sea turtle breeding habitat, helped formulate a coastal conservation plan for the country of Belize, and piloted a one-man submersible two thousand feet deep in the Bering Sea off Alaska, where he explored a series of underwater canyons for the purposes of conservation. Hocevar has been with Greenpeace for six years and is an expert in both U.S. fisheries policy and history and in the strategies and tactics of nonviolent civil disobedience. Only later will I come to understand how much this philosophy of nonviolence is a keystone in the identity not only of Hocevar but of pretty much everyone on the crew.

Despite their varied personalities and exteriors, their one unifying trait is how willing they are to step into situations most of us would avoid.

↗↗↗↗↗

The next morning, we're roughly sixty-three miles southwest of Malta when the word comes down that one of the Zodiacs is being launched. From the bridge deck, I see laid out upon the sea half a mile away a large, white, high-tech purse seiner with attendant cage and net boats. Several hundred yards behind these sits the imposing, rakish form of a French warship, the *Surcouf.* The purse seiner is in the process of transferring tuna from its net to a towable sea cage.

The midships deck of the *Warrior* is a flurry of activity. Mehdi Moujbani, the small-boat mechanic, takes the hook dangling from the crane cable overhead and latches it to the hoist straps on the port-side Zodiac. Emma Briggs, the ship's second boatswain, hands me a life jacket and in minutes I am over the side and into the Zodiac with Chartier, Provost, Moujbani, the Australian cameraman Chris Lewis, and a Milanese photographer, Giulio di Sturco. We cover the half-mile between our ship and the seiner at low speed to avoid giving the impression that we are launching some kind of attack.

The purse seiner is the *Saint Antoine Marie II,* out of Marseille, France—one of the new generation: large, fast, with advanced sonar, electronics, and satellite technology. This ship is well known, as is its captain, Perez. Both were part of the blockade of the port of Marseille in 2006, when more than thirty fishing boats and purse seiners surrounded the *Rainbow Warrior* as she tried to enter port, preventing her from anchoring. They boxed her in, pelted her with fruit and eggs, doused the decks and crew with firehoses, and made an attempt at boarding, which was stopped by French police. The blockade only helped secure wide media coverage for Greenpeace's position on the overfishing of bluefin tuna, and what would have been merely a local story about the arrival of the *Rainbow Warrior* in Marseille became international news.

As we approach the concentration of ships, the purse seiner slowly lifts its enormous net in sections out of the water with the aid of a large stern crane, which has the thin, segmented appearance of a spider leg. It piles the net in a huge mound on the stern of the ship, with crewmen crawling over it, securing it in place. The net has already transferred most of its catch into the towable cage, which is visible only as a large ring of surface floats forty meters across. Dropping in a circular wall beneath the floats is the cage itself, which descends another forty meters. Hundreds of metric tons of tuna can be contained within the walls of such cages. A second, smaller purse seiner, acting as the cage tug, waits outside the ring while several smaller motorboats zoom around, their pilots regarding us with disdain. One in particular positions himself between us and a good view of what is coming up in the net. Despite his efforts we can see several bluefin tangled in the webbing.

Losses during transfers are not uncommon. As the space within the net closes, the tuna become more and more crowded. Most shoot out of the net into the cage, but those that are entangled often begin to asphyxiate, unable to flow enough water over their gills. These fish are in the three-hundred-pound range: teardrop-shaped, metallic blue and silver, and as long and broad as a bed. I watch them being lifted out but cannot see onto the decks above, where they are lowered down and summarily slaughtered.

On the upper bridge decks of the seiner, French naval personnel are watching the operation, which I take as a welcome sign until Provost mentions that the season officially closed two days ago. "It's another loophole. This particular ship has not fulfilled the quota assigned to it. So they are allowed to keep fishing until they do."

This seems counter to the purpose of a season deadline, especially given how much illegal fishing goes on in addition to the legal quota. What this additional few days' fishing represents is the fact that the "official" seiners have negotiated a way to make sure they are allowed to catch their quota regardless of the true total catch or of any deadline. Provost points out that the quota for the *Saint Antoine Marie II* is 184 metric tons. At this season's going rate of approximately five euros per kilo, the ship is not likely to meet its running costs even if it fills its entire quota. From what Greenpeace and ATRT have been able to glean so far, the average weight of the fish in this season's catch is between seventy and ninety kilos.

"This makes achieving their quota of 184 metric tons more difficult," Provost explains, "because they have to catch a greater number of fish. So they have three problems, really: Market price is too low, the fish are harder to find, and the fish they do find tend to be small. They are screwed. They made their money in previous years—millions. Now they are trying not to lose money, and they are willing to completely exhaust the stock to do it."

Moujbani steers us away from the stern of the ship and around the cage perimeter to the bow of the seiner, where Provost hails the bridge in French. Several men appear, one of whom is the captain, Perez. He has an oval face, several days' stubble, a receding hairline, and a shrugging, cool demeanor. He regards us amicably enough from twenty feet overhead, and he and Provost exchange pleasantries. When Provost asks about the catch, the captain admits to greater difficulty this year in locating fish. "Are you aware of any illegal activity—transshipments, that sort of thing?" asks Provost. The captain seems to ponder this, then tells us he has some suspicion about three Moroccan vessels and one Turkish vessel thirty kilometers to the east of our position.

When Provost ends his conversation with Perez, we head off in the direction of the *Surcouf,* a La Fayette–class light frigate, over four hundred feet long, with the beveled, radar-dampening angles of a modern warship—simplified boxy superstructure, no railings, almost no windows to speak of, and a cluster of tech hardware in a stack aft of the bridge. Forward, there is a 100-millimeter gun battery, and amidships there is what appears to be a kind of retractable screen, sixty feet wide, perhaps two stories tall, like a huge hangar door. Provost again hails the bridge until some crew members finally appear, and though he conducts a conversation similar to the one he had with Perez, the crew of the *Surcouf* reveals little. We conclude our business and head back to the *Warrior.*

It is here on our return that I first become aware of a creeping sense of futility. We were late to this seine operation, and it was only a transfer to a towable sea cage, not an illegal transshipment at sea or an actual attempt to capture a school. We are only one ship trying to monitor hundreds of ships involved in the tuna trade in the Med. The *Surcouf* is a second ship, yes, with far more capabilities, and there are perhaps a dozen other military vessels involved this year in addition to aircraft, yet altogether the monitoring capacity is far short of the number of boats harvesting. I think about Perez resting his elbows on the rail, seemingly untouchable. Here is a man—a fisherman—who has been one of the more successful captains in the past decade in this intensely competitive fishery. His one ship has the fishing power of a whole community, a whole fleet of fishing vessels. I wonder, how does he regard his role in all this? Does he rationalize his part by saying he is merely a cog in the larger machine, or does he justify his actions by citing economic necessity? Is his perspective more cynical, reflecting the universal defense of commercial fishermen around the world who continue to overfish despite witnessing firsthand what their actions do to the environment on which their livelihoods depend ("If I don't catch it, someone else will")? That defense brings to mind a statement from one of ATRT's reports that summarizes the rationale of many Mediterranean purse seine captains:

> Suppose that I stick to my quota, but others do not. In this case Blue-Fins will get fished out, and everyone will be the [loser] in the long term. But I will be a [loser] in the short term as well, since by confining myself to the quota allocated to me I will suffer an immediate drop in income that others do not. Suppose on the other hand that I break my quota. Then, if others break theirs, BlueFins get fished out, certainly, but I am not a special loser. Contrariwise, if others keep to their quotas while I break mine, the stock will be preserved to my long-term benefit as well as theirs, but unlike them, I will not suffer an immediate drop in income either. So, whether other BlueFin Tuna fishing states ignore or observe their quotas, my best strategy is to ignore mine, while blaming others for doing so.

This year, 2009, is the first in which there has been any meaningful oversight of the bluefin trade by authorities outside of ICCAT, and while the presence of the *Surcouf* is certainly welcome, even it operates within the parameters established by international agreement. This year's quota is a perfect example: In the context of more than a decade of rampant illegal overfishing, three times the sustainable fleet capacity, and destroyed spawning stocks at less than 15 percent of what they were in the 1970s, ICCAT has nevertheless set the quota at 22,000 metric tons, despite its own scientists' recommendations (in 2007) that the quota should be no more than 12,000 metric tons to avoid collapse of the stock. The *Surcouf* will merely enforce the quota, but what is the quota if not an arbitrary figure, especially since it's detached from science? The real power, I realize, lies not in the *Surcouf* or in Perez or in the technology of the huge purse seiners. The real power lies in controlling the rules by which the game is played. The real power lies in the law, in defining what is legal and what is not, *and in enforcing it.*

If in this context Greenpeace's efforts seem futile, they are also an absolute necessity. The organization's intent is not to stop the trade—an impossible goal, given the circumstances and the organization's limited capacity—but rather to confront the premise of the activity itself, to challenge its very continuance in the face of all the evidence pointing to the ruin of this species in the Atlantic and the Mediterranean.

Indeed, there comes a time when, regardless of whether an activity has legal protection or not, one is obligated to challenge it, as long as it fails to satisfy the enduring principles of "eternal justice."*

<center>~~~~</center>

Lunch in the *Warrior*'s mess answers any question about vegetarianism among the ship's crew, at least half of whom are enthusiastic omnivores, taking heaps of chicken in a Thai peanut sauce and strips of beef in a savory, dark gravy. The cooking is far above what one might expect from ship's fare.

I take my plate and sit at a table with several other crew members and Moujbani, the small-boat mechanic in charge of keeping the Zodiacs in top running condition. Moujbani has a classic Arabic face—full lips, long, arching nose, black irises, cocoa-toned skin. There is a gentle, pedantic quality to his voice, as though he seeks to explain things that his listener does not understand. He rolls his *r*'s with a short, soft burr and uses few if any contractions. "I am a Tunisian—in other words, not from Afghanistan," he offers. "I am a tourist, not a terrorist," he adds, laughing, then looks around the table to gauge the reaction.

"I am actually from La Marsa," he says, more warmly. "It is a small town three kilometers from Carthage. My family are all fishermen—cousins,

---

*Lydia Maria Child fought for the abolition of slavery, for women's rights, and for Native American rights in the first half of the nineteenth century. She is quoted as saying, "Law is not law, if it violates the principles of eternal justice."

grandfather. We fished a lot when I was a boy. That was the mid-eighties. The fish were abundant then. By the age of twelve I had built my first boat—six and a half meters, wooden-hulled—and by fourteen I employed two men, a thirty-eight-year-old and a forty-seven-year-old. I watched the Tunisian fleet grow. Now it exceeds the capacity of the ports. As a boy I caught squid at night with my bare hands, standing waist-deep in the water, with two lamps hung off my shoulders. This would be impossible now! There are no more squid there. It is the same with the urchins: They are gone. You can find them only at ten meters or deeper."

I ask him how long he's worked for Greenpeace.

"How long have I worked for them, or how long have I *wanted* to work for them? I first volunteered when I was fourteen. 'Stay in school,' they told me, so I finished university and went to sea. I worked on trawlers and purse seiners, on tuna support vessels, on merchant ships. Then, in 1997, I started with them and I have been here ever since. Twelve years. I say to myself, *It is time to go, Mehdi. You have stayed here too long.* But still I stay. I go home after a rotation and then I long to come back. Sometimes I think I will go crazy."

During the slow afternoon hours, the ship seems to lie still while the entire tableau of the world scrolls by as though upon a screen. Late in the day, a white, heavily rusted stern trawler with the sharp prow and blunt face of many southern Mediterranean craft comes into view, towing a tuna cage. It is the *Karim,* from Tunisia, headed south-southwest for the Tunisia-Libya border. Moujbani speaks with the crew via radio on the bridge. They claim the cage is empty, which the three campaigners on duty—Combé-morel, Chartier, and Roberts—agree is likely the case. The suspicion is that the *Karim* might be headed for the Libyan border to receive tuna. Depending on the circumstances—the origin of the tuna and whether it exceeds the quota—the drop could constitute an illegal transshipment at sea.

As Moujbani explains, "If they are not going to get a drop, and they cross into Libyan waters, the Libyans will seize the boat and jail the crew. They will beat them daily until they get another crew. So if you are the crew, being beaten daily, you pray they seize another boat so that crew can take your place as entertainment."

The radio squawks and Moujbani answers. A number of voices are audible—some from the *Karim* and that of the captain of another boat, which we suspect to be the *Karim*'s rendezvous beyond the horizon. The captain of this boat asks the *Karim*, "What the fuck are they doing there?"—meaning us.

"Let them come," says a third captain. "We'll fuck them up."

"No. It is best to let them be," says the voice from the *Karim*. "Let's see what they do."

The *Karim* is still a long way from the boundary. Combémorel, Roberts, and Chartier decide to set a course to the east, away from the *Karim*'s heading. Then, sometime this evening, we will reverse course in order to arrive at the suspected drop coordinates at midday tomorrow. Moujbani suggests we monitor channels 14 and 12, which are used by fishermen in this area.

Some hours later, the word comes from Combémorel on the bridge that Perez, the captain of the French seiner, has sent us on a wild goose chase. There are no Moroccan or Turkish vessels in the area he indicated.

I sit on the bridge deck as the Mediterranean sun sets and, reflecting on the day's events, find myself wondering what it must have been like to travel the Mediterranean by sail, on a Greek trireme or a Tunisian xebec. What was it like not to know what lay over the horizon, to navigate by the stars, to be unaware of what tomorrow's weather would be? To take for granted the fullness and abundance of Nature? Spawning bluefin were once so numerous, they forced the warships of Alexander the Great into battle formation. What was it like to live in a world where the powers of humankind were still limited in scale, in time, by geography?

I scan the faces of the crew, sitting on the bench seats in front of the bridge windows, smoking and talking. It is the end of the workday, and the captain has permitted them a few beers. François Provost looks sleep-deprived and drawn; François Chartier has his head cocked to one side, eyes tracking nothingness; Dave Roberts vehemently argues politics with Alain Combémorel, the more patient diplomat. Lesley from New Zealand, in her sixties and living a new adventure after having worked in medicine, sips from her bottle and chats with dark-haired, pretty Liz from England. Gentle Yesim's face is touched with the waning light as tendrils of her long, curly hair dance about her face. They come from walks of life as diverse as the military, nonprofit work, nursing, merchant marine, commercial fishing, teaching, catering, subsistence fishing, and olive oil smuggling. And yet they have chosen to place themselves in the service of a worthy cause in which the current battle is all but lost, while the broader war remains as yet undecided.

4

The following day we make repeated launches to inspect and interview a range of vessels—longliners, cage tugs, trawlers. We do not find the *Karim* again, and if it has indeed made a rendezvous for a tuna drop, we have missed it. As we approach the *Azzurra II* from Valletta, towing a sea cage, its crew declines to speak with us, claiming no English; its Zodiac crew—whom I take to be a Serb and a Maltese—divulge that the tuna have indeed been hard to find this year. The *Azzurra II* is soon met by an older-style seiner whose transom reads *Sajomelita,* its home base in Pusan, South Korea; the *Surcouf* quickly appears to send out an inspection team to both vessels. By midmorning, all appears to be in order, and we move on. Afternoon launches are made to a French trawler, a Maltese tug, and a Maltese longliner. In the evening we encounter the trawler *Bartolomeo Asaro,* whose gregarious Italian crew cracks jokes and offers us food from a brightly lit starboard hatch.

The most memorable vessel that we encounter, however, is the *Maria Assunta II,* from Valletta. It is a small, run-down forty-foot longliner fished by a single Maltese fisherman. As we approach in the dark, he emerges from the forward cud, looking vulnerable in shorts and a smeared T-shirt. We explain our purpose and ask him his. He's fishing for swordfish with roughly eighteen miles of line, which he has only just set. He will not know what he has caught until morning. In response to Hocevar's technical questions, the fisherman answers that he is fishing 1.2-millimeter branch line, J-hooks size 3/0—"not strong enough to hold tuna."

He is a welcoming presence and continues talking with us until we eventually bid him good night. As we pull away, he calls out in the darkness behind us: "Please take care of our tuna. They are fishing them to extinction."

Hocevar later remarks, "He knows what's going on. His livelihood is at stake. How can that guy possibly compete with a modern seiner?" This is much the same observation that had been made to me by Alain Combémorel before dinner.

"It happened in Malta recently like it happened elsewhere in the Mediterranean," he explained. "The government approaches the fisherman and tells him, 'Replace your old boat. Get a government subsidy to build a newer, faster boat.' But it is essentially blackmail, because what if the fisherman says no? He will be less competitive, at a disadvantage, and perhaps the money will not be there for him in five or ten years, when he does need to replace his boat, which for now is serviceable. Replace it, mind you, with something equivalent, not with something with fifty times the fishing power, as the government would have him do. So what can he do but decide to accept the offer?"

Most small-scale fishermen—certainly the more traditional ones—are independent operators. Many are poorly educated and lack the knowledge and the connections to influence the political process. While they are not entirely powerless, the likelihood of their organizing sufficiently is slim. Combémorel also pointed out how many of the boats handling cages or providing support are former fishing boats.

"To a fisherman this must be like a bad dream," he said. "They love the pursuit, the challenge of finding fish. If they had wanted to be in the business of transporting goods, they would have hauled cargo for the merchant marine or maybe they would drive a bus. But you see how the industry has reorganized fishing. The little guy doesn't stand a chance. He will become extinct. The income of a hundred or a thousand families will be concentrated in the hands of a few, and we all suffer for that."

After dinner, I'm joined at the table by Vlad, the Russian chief engineer. Vlad is, like much of the crew, in his thirties and has the thick, muscular body of a man accustomed to the clang of heavy iron in the form of weights as well as machines. His head has the squarish proportions of a cinder block. I have seen him on deck wearing a pair of sleek gold-rimmed, amber-tinted Euro mafia sunglasses, which he carried off well. His hair is cut in the Russian version of the high-and-tight, with the addition of a thin strip of a mohawk at the back of his head. His voice is a classic Russian bass, resonant and deep.

Vlad grew up in Sebastopol, on the Black Sea. "Everything around me was the sea. My people come from the sea. I have tried to escape, but without luck. Now, I have decided this is my place." He has done long stints in commercial fishing—on Ukrainian, German, and Norwegian ships and on krill trawlers sieving the waters off the South Orkney Islands, near Antarctica. "Trawling krill is quite difficult," he says. "We bring eighty tonnes on deck; machinery only can process so much. We throw over many tonnes of fish. I think, *This is outrage.* I am just a man, you know? A son of this world. I come on commercial fishing boat from Russian nuclear submarine. And yes, I am fighter, but I was surprised to see what they do. They act like chimpanzee. No: Chimpanzee smarter. They bring up flat skate and they take out its eye and make jokes with it. This is animal behavior. They are like children. In Russian navy, this would not be tolerated. I was very upset. I started to fight with them, and I make lots of enemies. Some part of crew was with me, some part against me, but I was leader against the idiots.

"For food, I see why we kill. But a person do this for fun, I do not respect him as a man. In big fishing trawler, there is the slip, where net comes up. We were close to Namibia, and big sea lion enter through the slip to trawler deck. His neck is damaged by rope. Big damage, blood coming out. He was tired, almost dead, and the stupid sailors started to joke with him, to play with him. He stood himself up on his flippers. They try to put fish in his mouth. Idiots. They have no respect. No respect for life.

"This waste is problem with trawlers. I saw same thing off Namibia as in Antarctica. Krill is krill. But when you catch eighty tonnes of little fish and you cannot sell them because it is not what company wants and you have to throw them over into the sea again, this cannot be right. We sell many, many young fish to Africa, where they are hungry. But how many trawlers—big fishing trawlers—are patrolling those waters? Hundreds! And do you know, each big fishing trawler, it is doing the same as we are doing—pushing fish over side. Sort and throw."

From commercial fishing, Vlad went into merchant shipping, where he worked on a variety of ships. The picture he paints of life in those fleets, crewed by boorish drunks and unhappy men with lonely lives, adds new meaning to notions of misery. He joined Greenpeace only recently.

"I was hired to work on a cement carrier in Amsterdam a few months

ago. The ship was a mess. Everything was out of maintenance. We were in
the shipyard, and I saw how much had to be done and I said to them, 'My
dear gentlemen, fuck you.' The *Rainbow Warrior* was docked nearby, and
they invited our crew over. The captain of the *Warrior* at that time was a
Spaniard with Russian roots, also named Vlad. He told me to come work
on the *Warrior*. It is good here. I like the strikes. I want to fight against
fucking idiots. This is my internal feeling. Salary is fine; salary is not life.
Before this journey we had nice tour around Spain. So many beautiful
Spanish girls, such a beautiful atmosphere. For me, a seafarer, this is most
important. Well, there is food, and then there is comradeship. This is what
makes ship tolerable. *Rainbow Warrior* is very good. Without comradeship, it is impossible, like in merchant fleet, where everyone is angry." He
makes a face and grunts. "But here, there is special spirit on this boat. It is
Rainbow Warrior, after all, yes?"

We continue westward. Near midnight, unable to sleep, I make my way to
the bridge, where I talk briefly with the second mate, Fernando, a diminutive, calm Spaniard who has consistently impressed me with his reason-
ableness. He shows me our course. We're headed for a location near
Chergui, off the Tunisian coast, and should reach it by morning. I walk
out on deck to stand in the night breeze. Over the horizon to the south I
discern a faint, semicircular glow that, according to the charts, must be
Tripoli, 115 miles away. Before morning we will pass just north of the
Bouri oil field and within about 70 miles of the self-declared Libyan Fisheries Protection Zone.

   Then, as my eyes adjust, I see the extraordinary sight of the Milky Way
banding the sky in a dazzling spray of stars. There is so little light out here
that the star field reveals new complexities and levels of detail. It is vastly
more populated than I've ever been able to see and appears to have fissures
and cracks running through it, so densely packed are its billions of suns. I
stare at it, through the silhouetted masts and rigging of the *Warrior*, and
am suddenly aware of perceiving depth to the galaxy itself, as though I can
see the star cloud in three dimensions. This is an illusion, of course, but a
remarkable one. It is the first time in my life that I've perceived the total
absence of sky, as though the blue of day were a dome that night had rolled

back, revealing the splendor of the heavens. And I know then how absurd the idea is that we are alone, the only diamond in a universe of jewels.

5

On the morning of the third day, we all take part in maintenance tasks, which are never-ending. Winches for the sailing lines are taken apart, inspected, greased, and reassembled. The various types of intake covers and electrical boxes on deck are freed of their heavy crust of paint, innards are inspected, bolts swapped out, seals greased, and covers rebolted. If a bolt seizes or snaps, it is drilled out and the hole is retapped, a tedious job. Every day, Moujbani works on the inflatables, maintaining electronics, steering, wiring, cables, fuel lines, engines. I join John Hocevar in knotting eight-inch lengths of severed nylon rope onto four-foot sections of string, weaving what are called "baggywrinkles." Each woven section results in a fringe three or four inches thick; each segment is then tied together in a bunch resembling a caterpillar, and these are mounted on the shrouds (mast tension wires) to prevent the sails from wearing out as they smack the shrouds in the wind.

By 6:00 P.M., our position is 35°26.4'N by 12°12.7'E. This puts us eighteen miles west of Lampedusa and sixty-five miles east of Cap Afrique, Tunisia. As the air begins to cool, the sea holds a blinding, metallic-orange sheen as though it were hot oil. An hour later, we come upon a midsize Tunisian trawler, the *Salmen,* towing a tuna cage. We launch one of the Zodiacs and approach the vessel, which seems to have more rust than paint on its blue-and-white hull. At the forward section of the ship, its battered skin becomes apparent. It has been indelicately handled, scraping along quays and larger vessels without the benefit of tires or the massive inflated bumpers seen on better-equipped ships. Pumps spew water from seven different ports and scuppers on the port side alone. Chartier hails the vessel, and the Tunisian captain, a slightly round man with fleshy cheeks and baggy eyes, appears. Chartier explains our purpose and asks if we may come aboard. The captain shrugs as though he does not have the right to refuse and directs us to the stern, where we are met by half a dozen expressionless men. Moujbani draws the Zodiac closer and we board awkwardly over the high transom, stepping onto the *Salmen*'s wooden deck. There are gaps in the decking where rotten pieces have given way, and the metal walls and gunwales of the ship are awash in orange-brown smears of rust. A single massive nylon rope, faded teal green and thick as a man's calf, extends from anchor points on the superstructure out to the tuna cage, a hundred yards off the stern. We are led through a kind of open fish-processing room dominated by a massive industrial longline spool and cutting tables, then down a passageway in which I notice a teakettle on the floor next to packets of spices, plastic gallon jerry cans of cooking oil, and a plastic bin holding onions, peppers, potatoes, and dozens of garlic cloves.

On the bridge, Hocevar and Chartier collect information from the captain's paperwork—port of call, ownership of the tuna, quota, and permit identification numbers. The ship has been at sea sixty-six days and plans to drop its cargo at Mahdia, Tunisia. Greenpeace will check this data against official records to determine whether the ship is fishing legally and whether the tuna it is carrying are legal and within the quota.

The captain, reading off the paperwork, says, "For the tuna, we have a weight of 187,000 kilograms, about 2,800 fish, caught off Algeria." When Chartier asks what size fish they are holding in their cage, the captain tells him, "We have a mix. Large and small."

After answering a few more routine questions, the captain invites us to dinner, telling us, "I can offer you some nice lamb or goat."

Chartier declines. "Thank you. We have just come from dinner."

"I would like to send you off with some shrimp, then. Jumbo—very good. I would like you to have it."

Chartier accepts graciously, and we begin walking off the bridge. I miss a turn and find myself in a common area with a bunk room off to one side. Gloomy and cramped, it holds a square table covered in felt, and lining the walls are bench seats whose torn padding protrudes in great tufts. There is a desultory, exhausted spirit to this ship and its men, whose poverty was apparent in their threadbare clothing, missing teeth, and emaciated legs the moment we boarded.

On the rear deck, three of the *Salmen*'s crew members are relaxing in the corner with a small cookstove, a teakettle, and a three-foot-tall hookah containing a large, smoldering wad. One of the men, noticing me eyeing the contraption, holds out the long emerald-tubed pipe, inviting me to smoke.

"Tobacco?" I ask in French.

He shrugs. "More or less."

I take a few tokes from the pipe and taste a mild, sweet flavor, like a cigar laced with sugar. I hand the pipe back and thank my host, who now smiles, amused.

When we are back on the Zodiac, Moujbani explains. "It was only *shisha,* flavored tobacco. They are Muslim, remember. Drugs, alcohol, all of those are forbidden. Not to mention very illegal. In Tunisia, the penalty in jail time is not worth the risk. They offered the pipe in friendship and hospitality. It is also why they gave us shrimp."

Back on the bridge, John shares the information from the *Salmen,* and Dave says incredulously, "That one boat is towing 187 metric tons of blue-fin? What's that worth?" There is some debate, but the campaigners agree that even at a conservative estimate of five euros per kilo, the value of the *Salmen*'s cargo is north of $1.5 million. It is more money than the six crew members, combined, are likely to earn in twenty years of work.

Chartier asks, "If it is 187 tonnes, is there not a limit for the ship? And what is the quota for Tunisia?"

The *Salmen* is acting only as a tug, a cage hauler, but his question is directed more toward the circumstances in which the tuna were caught. Were they caught by one seiner or several? If only one, it's possible that the seiner exceeded its quota. It's also possible that the estimated size or number of fish is inaccurate. Perhaps there are more fish but they weigh less, or vice versa. How accurate is the estimated weight? The fish are not actually weighed until after they are slaughtered. And why, if the tuna were caught off Algeria, is the *Salmen* now heading west? Once again I am made aware of the challenge of accuracy and oversight in a fishery of such enormous scope, divided among more than a dozen countries, with so much money at stake and such meager capacity for monitoring.

~~~~~

The next afternoon, I climb the ladder to the foredeck, where Rita is servicing another of the sailing winches. We expect an increase in wind overnight and may actually sail tomorrow.

Rita is the ship's official "garbologist"—responsible for processing every kind of refuse the ship's crew produces, separating items into recyclable metals, plastics, and biodegradables. A little over five feet tall, with buzz-cut black hair, she has a lovely, clear voice and a ready smile and laugh, and is broad-shouldered and strong.

"I am from Beirut," she tells me. "Formerly East Beirut—that is what they called it in the war." She was a year old when the Lebanese civil war started, and seventeen when it ended. She knew plenty of people who were killed, including friends, and was nearly killed herself three times. "It started with the Palestinians, and then it became different parties fighting each other, and finally it was everyone fighting everyone. It was politics. I hate politics.

"I always wanted to be a sailor," she says when I ask how she came to be on the *Warrior*. "I used to work in food services and events, but after the assassination of Hariri,* the economy went to shit, and finally I quit. A friend who had worked for Greenpeace said they needed volunteers to crew. I said, *Why not?* My first tour was in 2008. I was on the *Arctic Sunrise* when it was attacked by the Turkish seiners.† They were quite violent. Quite angry. We had an early wake-up call that morning. I was on the helicopter fire crew [the *Arctic Sunrise* has a helicopter pad on the stern deck], so we launched the heli, and it returned sometime later, and then there appeared over the horizon this one yellow ship speeding toward us. And then another and another appeared, and soon we were surrounded by a number of large Turkish purse seiners. Their crews appeared on deck and one had a shotgun and began firing at the copter. The other men began throwing heavy lead fishing weights. Our engineer at the time was a Canadian woman who yelled for us to take cover. 'They're sending missiles!' she said, and I thought to myself, *Oh God, not missiles,* thinking she meant real ones. The Turks disabled the helicopter and did a lot of damage to the ship."

The video of the 2008 Turkish attack shows the aggression of the Turkish ships. They come at the *Arctic Sunrise* with clear intent and hold as close

---

* Rafik Hariri, former prime minister of Lebanon, was assassinated in an explosion on February 14, 2005, in Beirut.

† YouTube, "Greenpeace Vessel Attacked," http://www.youtube.com/watch?v= ivr3xnDsFn4.

as fifty feet to both the port and starboard sides. One of the seiners actually collides with the *Arctic Sunrise* amidships. The fishing weights they throw are roughly half-pound, sausage-shaped leads, about four inches long. Hurled from sixty or eighty feet away, they hit with enough force to shatter the helicopter's Plexiglas windows and dent the ship's steel-plate walls and decking. Had they hit a person, they could have killed him. The attack lasted over an hour.

The Turks had good reason to be alarmed: At that time, they had two hundred purse seiners and only a nine-hundred-metric-ton quota. The Turkish fleet alone had enough capacity to catch all fifteen thousand metric tons of the ICCAT scientists' recommended quota for the entire Mediterranean.

"I could not have been a sailor had I not come here," Rita continues. "I have always wanted to be on a ship, but in Lebanon a girl cannot be a sailor. I never fit the system anyhow. This has given me a chance. This is right for me. I think I belong to the sea now. I will go back to Beirut when I am not sailing, but from now on I will sail. I am doing what I was meant to do."

That afternoon, I get into a conversation with Emma, the Australian boatswain, as she works painting the port rail. The water in the Mediterranean is the clearest I have ever seen—clearer even than the waters off Cabo San Lucas. As the ship slides forward through the sea, rods of light shimmer and switch in the water, appearing and disappearing in different hues of blue. The water is so clear that if you see a plastic bag floating, it is not uncommon to wonder whether it's actually on the surface or under the water, or somehow levitating above the surface, hovering there with liquid softness.

Emma is thirty-nine years old, shy and very quiet, plain in appearance, with sandy blond hair tied back in a ponytail. She does not often make eye contact while speaking and is not one for small talk. She spends large parts of every day in near total silence, chipping paint, cleaning showers, greasing the mast shrouds, inspecting equipment and ropes. I wonder whether life on board offers her respite from a world that is too bombastic for her temperament. Emma has been on Greenpeace ships for six years doing three-month rotations. When she is off rotation, she and Gianni, the *Warrior*'s tall, scruffy, mellow Italian radioman, go home to Italy or Australia. At the end of each rotation, she is ready to return to the other extreme. Sea to land, land to sea. Prior to her six years on Greenpeace ships, she spent four years canvassing and doing other work for the organization in Australia.

"How long do you think you'll continue?" I ask her.

"Oh, I don't know. Forever, I suppose," she says.

Beneath her quiet exterior there is something else. I perceive it in the way she moves through the passageways of the ship, up ladders or rappelling into the rigging, at meals in the mess with everyone else, or after hours on the midship deck. It's a kind of quiet force, something stubborn—not driven, necessarily, but strong, hard. Maybe it is her reticence, contrasted with strong interior convictions, levels of commitment to a purpose many of us do not know.

Then I see something down in the water off the starboard rail.

"Look," I tell her, pointing.

There, twenty feet down, an enormous sphere of silver sardines spins in the crystalline silence.

That evening, the campaigners receive word of increased activity near Malta, with two new reefer ships anchoring at the boundary of the exclusive fisheries zone, and a third reefer, heavily laden, bound for Valletta from Libyan waters. The decision is made to put the *Warrior* back on a heading toward the island.

In the course of the next twenty-four hours, more intel is gathered about the reefer vessels' bait loads (or lack thereof) and the fact that the ship from Libya is carrying frozen tuna. Targets are chosen, investigated, and prioritized or dismissed based on a range of factors. Routine approaches on the morning of our arrival to two of the reefer ships yield information that will help in constructing a picture of the overall industrial scale of the fishery.

At 4:00 P.M., a strategy briefing is held in the mess, and the entire crew assembles to hear Dave Roberts and François Provost's status report. There are enough targets, they announce, and a high enough likelihood of illegal activity, that the *Warrior* herself will dock in one of the branch anchorages in Valletta—a strategic repositioning that will enable its Zodiac crews to strike any target quickly.

Roberts asks for volunteers for the first strike boat. Before he can even finish his sentence, three hands go up—Liz, from the UK, Rita, from Lebanon, and Emma, the quiet boatswain from Australia. They sit near one another, and I wonder whether their volunteering en masse was planned. (Rita tells me later that it was not.) They beat out a number of other raised hands—Alain, Gianni, Lesley, Alex—who will be in the second Zodiac with rudimentary painting equipment (rollers on long poles, roller pans, paint, and a tarp to protect the Zodiac). Two other smaller craft will carry members of the local Maltese press, along with me, the photographer di Sturco, cameraman Chris Lewis, and others.

With the crews selected and the general plan of action outlined, I realize that the likelihood of a direct encounter has just gone up significantly. There is a wired feeling in the room. Roberts covers news cycles and other issues of timing, then tells us simply, "Good. Monday morning we go."

◜◜◜◜◜

On Monday, the twenty-second of June 2009, our small flotilla of inflatables departs the *Rainbow Warrior* at 9:00 A.M., moving to a staging area at the base of the promontory on which sits one of the massive stone forts. The first Zodiac, with the boarders, and a second Zodiac, with the painting equipment, hold position there. The third boat, carrying crew member Marta Ibáñez, me, several campaigners, and a cameraman and photographer, moves forward alone, crossing a half-mile of open water to the targets at one of the industrial wharves in the harbor.

Our objectives this morning are two ranch support vessels—the *Cabontiñoso Dos,* from Cartagena, and the *Santina,* from Malta. Both ships are roughly sixty feet long and outfitted with deck cranes and freezer storage, and both are operated by Fuentes in support of Malta's MareBlu ranch, the largest in the world, whose enormous tuna pens dominate the fisheries zone outside the harbor. Because of their freezer capacity, either of these support vessels could be used to move illegal tuna.

When we approach the *Cabontiñoso Dos* and attempt to make contact, we are completely ignored, apart from being glared at by one of the men walking past on the deck with a box of stores. This goes on for minutes until finally a smaller, young, clean-shaven man holding a sheaf of pink shipping invoices approaches us from the other side of the deck, looking irritated. As he and Ibáñez converse in Spanish, Hocevar, Provost, and Roberts start to climb aboard.

"No," the younger man says. "You must leave. We are not interested." He is polite but unequivocal. "Go. You must go. Get off the boat."

We withdraw to the staging area, where Dave Roberts describes the first interaction and briefs the pilots of the other boats—Alex in the paint boat and Dan, the British first mate, who will be driving the lead Zodiac with the boarders. The boarders—Liz, Emma, and Rita—are wearing bright orange coveralls with heavy galvanized chain around their waists, hard hats, life vests, and handcuffs attached to one wrist, with the other shackle free to be attached to a part of the ship. The plan will be to move the boarders in quickly and get them onto the deck of the *Cabontiñoso*.

The three boats move out in tandem, and when the first Zodiac pulls in under a high section of the *Cabontiñoso*'s starboard quarter, in one efficient motion Emma leaps onto the gunwale, swings a leg up and over, and is on deck. She moves quickly forward to a ladder, where she attempts to handcuff herself to the rail but is intercepted by the young man who prevented our boarding earlier, now followed by an enormous man with the build of a weightlifter and wearing a distinctive red-and-blue-striped shirt. Before Emma can get the shackle on the rail he is upon her, smashing his fists down on her hands, then grabbing her by the hair and shoulders. He spins her around and pushes her onto a tarpaulin covering a deck boat. An older man now approaches her aggressively, shoving her toward the gunwale. Together the two men bodily haul Emma to the rail and fling her headfirst over the side. She falls close to ten feet into the water, landing next to the first Zodiac. As she is hauled onto the boat, narrowly avoiding the Zodiac's spinning propeller, something comes flying a few feet from our heads: a shipping pallet has been heaved at us.

A number of the crew members from the *Cabontiñoso* have meanwhile armed themselves with fifteen-foot-long boat hooks and taken up stations along the starboard rail. Two brandish the hooks up forward near the bow, lowering them to within inches of the Zodiac and its occupants. From the reactions of the Greenpeace crew, it is clear that the swiftness and level of violence is unusual.

As our boat pulls back from the side of the *Cabontiñoso*, the old man in the blue shirt calls out to us from the deck. He unfastens his belt from beneath his large drum of a gut, drops his trousers, and, yelling insults all the while, moons us, eliciting incredulous laughter from Ibáñez.

Dave Roberts radios the bridge of the *Rainbow Warrior,* informing them that the response to the boarding attempt was violent. The bridge answers that they have notified the authorities (a matter of procedure); they, in turn, will alert the Maltese navy. Roberts then begins a series of short exchanges with the leaders of the other Zodiacs.

"Are you guys willing to try it again?" he asks.

The crews of both boats confirm that they are. The plan is to send two boats—one in between the docked ships to paint, the other to try to find a place to board near the stern.

Alex pilots the paint boat around the front of the *Cabontiñoso Dos* but is prevented by sailors with boat hooks from getting anywhere near the hull of either ship. Dan, who has run the other Zodiac toward the stern of the *Cabontiñoso,* is similarly blocked.

The next option is to circle all the way around both ships and land the boarders on the concrete wharf. Dan steers the lead boat to the quayside and offloads Rita, Liz, and Emma, who approach the *Santina* but do not attempt to board. Rita pulls out a three-by-three-foot banner that reads BLUEFIN TUNA MASSACRE, while back on the paint boat, which is still positioned in front of the *Santina,* Lesley and Alain hold up a larger banner bearing the same slogan. Giulio is snapping stills when Marta calls out, "Watch out! Watch out! They're going to throw something!" and I look up to see a crewman run forward on the *Santina* and hurl a full, open gallon can of green paint into the air. It comes crashing down into the paint boat, nearly hitting Alain in the head. The burly man in the red-and-blue shirt now appears on the bow of the *Santina*. Behind his right forearm, with the butt of its handle concealed in his palm, he wields a foot-long *tekagi,* the same kind of forged tuna pick I saw used at Tsukiji market to seize and drag frozen tuna carcasses.

On the wharf, Liz has engaged crew members of the *Santina,* telling them that Greenpeace only wants to inspect the boat as representatives of the public interest. She asks them to consider the future of their livelihoods and the fact that it doesn't make sense to push the stock to collapse. As we join the boarders, the crewmen from the fishing vessels run water hoses up from belowdecks as another means of repelling a boarding attempt. Several private security officers in fluorescent yellow vests now appear on the wharf, asking the Greenpeace protesters to leave, informing them that they are on private property.

Dave Roberts is engaged in a conversation with one of the *Santina*'s crew, explaining, "We simply asked to see the ship's manifest. We want to see the paperwork. If everything is in order, we'll leave."

Then a commotion draws our attention back to the *Santina*. Liz has moved aft as a deflection, pulling a number of crew members after her, and with their attention drawn away, Emma attempts to board, leaping across the gap between the concrete quay and the boat's gunwale. The burly man charges her, spraying her with a hose. Then he drops the hose, sets his feet, and starts smashing her in the face and helmet with huge roundhouse punches. Emma slumps back, still holding the gunwale, and he picks up the spraying hose and shoves it in her face. Two crewmen have grabbed his arms, but they are too late in restraining him. Twenty feet forward, Rita makes another attempt, leaping off the quay onto the *Santina*'s gunwale, but is shoved off by crew members and soaked with hoses. Marta steps forward and takes Emma by the arm, helping her back and away from the boat, and finally Rita retreats.*

6

The action in Valletta Harbor makes the international news. The footage of Emma being thrown off the *Cabontiñoso Dos* and punched as she tries to board the *Santina* receives heavy coverage throughout Italy and the rest of Europe, in print and on television and the Web. She survives the incident with only a swollen neck and a black eye.

In the aftermath of the incident on the wharf, the Greenpeace members and several of the fishermen are asked to report to the police station to give

---

*YouTube, "Attivisti aggrediti da un peschereccio," http://www.youtube.com /watch?v=967u1NmLw_k&feature=player_embedded.

statements. Greenpeace decides that it serves no campaign purpose to press charges, and in turn the ranching company, MareBlu, decides not to press charges against Greenpeace.

Inspectors from the Maltese Fisheries Conservation and Control Division (FCCD) board the *Santina* and the *Cabontiñoso Dos* to examine the paperwork and the contents of the holds. They report that the ships are carrying tuna caught in the Libyan Fisheries Protection Zone. All paperwork is reported to be in order and the fish legal. Greenpeace attempts to reach the FCCD several times to get more specific information about the cargo of tuna, the locations where it was caught, and the names of the seiners that caught and delivered the fish. After several calls, the FCCD representative tells Greenpeace to stop calling, as he has been instructed not to speak with the organization, and refers it to Malta's fisheries minister, Joe Borg, but calls to the minister's office are not returned. Borg, another controversial figure in the Mediterranean tuna trade, is also the European Union fisheries commissioner* and as such is charged with representing the collective interests of EU nations and with overseeing the sustainable management of EU fisheries. As of 2009, an estimated 88 percent of EU fisheries were considered to be overfished.

The legality of the bluefin tuna in the holds of the *Cabontiñoso Dos* and *Santina* is never substantiated by any third party. The paperwork and the contents of the holds are never viewed, photographed, or otherwise verified by Greenpeace or by any of the newspaper or television journalists present at the scene.

It also comes to light that the man who threw Emma overboard and punched her in the face is Massimo Cappitta, a director of MareBlu Tuna Farm. MareBlu is a joint venture with Ricardo Fuentes e Hijos, the Spanish company that controls 60 percent of the Mediterranean tuna market, with annual revenues of approximately $346 million.

The public's reaction to the incident is mixed, but most people respond with outrage at the violence of the fishermen. Others feel that Greenpeace's actions were provocative and question the legitimacy of an attempted forced boarding, arguing that it was a violation of private property. Some

---

*Borg no longer holds this post.

question the role of women in the potentially violent circumstances of boarding. Several ask by what legal, sanctioned authority Greenpeace undertook such actions.

John Hocevar, charged with responding to these questions, answers:

We boarded these vessels because illegal activity is a serious threat to the survival of bluefin tuna. . . . The vessels may be privately owned, but the tuna are a public resource. Greenpeace has been instrumental in gathering information on illegal activity in the fishery for the last several years, sharing evidence with governments, which have then acted on our documentation. Further complicating the situation is the fact that the Maltese fisheries authorities are among the most corrupt in the world, so enforcement of the laws left in official hands is unlikely to happen at all.

He adds:

It doesn't make the newspapers very often, but a large portion of Greenpeace's work involves providing technical reports and testimony at policy meetings, lobbying, grassroots organizing, scientific research, and collaboration with businesses. Sometimes, though, quiet diplomacy is not enough, and unsustainable or illegal activities must be confronted and exposed. Action of this nature often carries with it a certain amount of risk, as we saw. . . . Unfortunately for those who put their own greed above the health of our planet, that is a risk we are prepared to take.

That evening, the campaigners hold a post-action briefing in the mess. Such meetings are standard procedure, a way for the organization to review its policies and decision making and to determine whether the actions adopted achieved the desired goals or whether different strategies and tactics should have been used.

It is generally agreed upon by those at the meeting that Greenpeace was lucky that the various incidents—the tossed paint can and shipping pallet, the boat hooks, and Emma's being attacked—did not result in serious injury. Given the clear aggressiveness of the fishermen, some question whether the group should have waited for the authorities to arrive before any subsequent boarding attempts.

After lengthy debate, Captain Pete observes, "I can understand why that adrenaline momentum wants to carry on. From my perspective, it went more or less according to plan. The general way the whole thing was approached was successful. I can't see anything that could have been done differently or better."

After the meeting, I speak with Emma, a veteran of dozens of similar actions, about her second boarding attempt. "Dave asked me to do it, and I was fine doing it. I agreed to do it," she acknowledges. "This is how Greenpeace is able to influence issues like this: by standing up for what is right and not being suppressed by the threat of violence. I really believe in nonviolence. Not only is it the right thing to do; I also believe it's the most effective way to get your message across. But I was surprised by the level of violence from the fishermen, especially the second time. I was in a bit of shock afterward."

In later communications with me, John Hocevar would clarify the difference between civil disobedience and nonviolent confrontation, and their underlying strategic rationale.

Boarding vessels without permission is definitely a bit controversial. Personally, it doesn't surprise me when fishermen refuse permission to board. It doesn't really surprise me when they get angry when we board anyway. It IS provocative, but when the reaction is completely out of proportion to the action, like we saw with Cappitta, it's well beyond what most people are willing to accept. At that point, they lose any moral high ground they may have been able to claim, and support swings back to us. This wasn't our intention, but we always know it's a possibility. Boarding is one of those tactics where most of the likely foreseeable outcomes are positive. If they allow us to board, we get the information we want. If not, we can highlight the lack of transparency, corruption, and illegal fishing that have contributed to the demise of the bluefin. If we are able to stay on board with banners until the police come, the pictures will help tell the story.

Civil disobedience is a bit different, but related. Civil disobedience involves breaking an unjust law, for example the bus and lunch counter sit-ins [during the Civil Rights era], or much of what Gandhi did. These are also win-win tactics similar to boarding: either the law is not enforced, and your actions directly chip away at an unjust law, or you are arrested—which puts a strain on the authorities, shines a spotlight on the issue, and/or builds momentum for the effort.

~~~~

Two days later, I'm due to depart Malta for home. In my cabin, packing my gear, I'm joined by Alex, the boatswain.

"Would you like a souvenir from the ship?" he asks. He reaches into his locker and presents me with a "monkey's fist," a carefully woven ball of rope secured to the end of a throwing line to give it weight. It is a testament to a boatswain's skill with knots and a true memento for me from my time aboard this famous ship. I thank him and tuck it among my things.

I spend my remaining hours on the island walking in the warm sunshine through the streets of the old city, making my way to the waterfront and the Upper Barracca Gardens. Over lunch at a café, I gaze out upon the broad port, the dry dock and shipyards across the harbor, the promontories topped by their stone fortresses and, rising up behind these, the many red-domed churches, each flying brightly colored flags signifying the pride of Kalkara, Birgu, Isla, and Bormla.

I recall a conversation I had with Alex yesterday, when I asked him if he ever felt frustrated at the pace of change.

"I am," he told me. "So much is at stake, and so much is lost in a process that moves as slowly as this does. And part of me wonders how effective it is."

"What are the alternatives?" I asked.

"There's violence," he says, though not condoning it.

"Violence could have been used," I acknowledged. "You blow up one ship and kill someone, you make eternal enemies of his brothers and family and friends, and next time they'll come back armed to the teeth. Then you come back more heavily armed, and it goes on from there. You may achieve more in five years' time than Greenpeace will, but you will never achieve what they have in twenty years, or thirty. The only way to stop this is to confront it, forcefully but nonviolently, and draw them out into the light. In the long term, it's more powerful."

I realize, sitting in the café in old Valletta, that I was attempting to give myself, as much as Alex, a sense of hope. The truth is, some battles are waged too late, when the damage done is too great to be reversed. I remain hopeful for the bluefin tuna, if only because of the sea's incredible resilience.

The breeze blows, surprisingly cool. Far below the cliffs, the buzz of a small Maltese luzzu comes to me. The luzzu is one of Malta's traditional, colorful fishing boats, narrow and high-prowed, like a gondola. The boat makes its way down the harbor to the sea, where dozens more like it dot the waters. On the prow of each luzzu is painted the Eye of Osiris, an ancient symbol meant to ward off evil spirits for sailors and fishermen as they ply the great waters. I find myself wondering whether the incantatory powers of such symbols have waned or if they have no power when the spirit of evil arises from the fishermen themselves.

7

In July 2009, less than a month after my voyage with the *Rainbow Warrior*, Prince Albert II of Monaco called for the Atlantic bluefin tuna to be listed as an endangered species under Appendix I of the Convention on International Trade in Endangered Species of Wild Fauna and Flora (CITES). A CITES Appendix I listing is the most urgent, requiring a ban on international (but not domestic) trade of the species in question. The call was hailed as long overdue and was supported by a number of European nations, including Germany and the United Kingdom, as well as by the European Commission and French president Nicolas Sarkozy, who said, "It is against this great responsibility that we will be judged by our children and the generations to come."

After Monaco's announcement, the European Commission's Directorate-General for the Environment confirmed that "from a scientific and technical point of view, the criteria for the listing of Atlantic bluefin tuna appear to be met. . . . There is no doubt about the link between inter-national trade and overexploitation of the species." By September, all but six of the twenty-seven European Union member states supported a ban, and yet they were blocked by the six nations that opposed it. Those six—Spain, France (despite its president's support), Italy, Malta, Cyprus, and Greece—are among the largest bluefin-tuna-fishing states in the Mediter-ranean. The ban was strongly opposed by Malta and the EU fisheries com-missioner, Joe Borg. (Although the Maltese bluefin industry employs only about a thousand of the country's four hundred thousand citizens, it is worth $131 million a year.) Borg eventually capitulated to the mounting pressure and came out in support of a CITES ban in October, and that same month Monaco made a formal submission to the CITES commis-sion. The Japanese, meanwhile, had already publicly made it clear that they would not abide by any CITES ban and would keep their markets open to the import of bluefin. With that they provided the only incentive needed by bluefin smugglers and pirates to continue illegal fishing of the most economically valuable fish in the sea.

Monaco's formal application meant that the 175 contracting parties to the convention would have to vote on the issue in Doha, Qatar, in March 2010, with a two-thirds majority confirming the global ban. The ICCAT scientific committee, the UN Food and Agriculture Organization ad hoc expert panel, and the CITES Secretariat all publicly acknowledged that the level of decline suffered by the northern bluefin satisfied the criteria for endangered species status, putting this fish in the same category as the African black rhino and the Himalayan snow leopard.

In September, the UK's *Guardian* published an article based on confi-dential information from the French navy about its inspections of the tuna fishery the previous May. The French patrol ship *Arago* had inspected twenty-four vessels from Spain, Italy, Greece, Turkey, and Cyprus that were fishing for tuna in the eastern Mediterranean. The report cited the Turks as showing no adherence to ICCAT regulations whatsoever—no completed paperwork, and in some cases no paperwork at all, in addition to a nearly complete lack of ICCAT observers on board. The single ICCAT observer in evidence among the twenty-four international ships was reported by the *Arago* to find "all sorts of explanations or false arguments to try to justify noncompliance with ICCAT recommendations. Moreover, the estimations of the amount of fish in the cages given by him were on average 10-times lower than those estimated by the divers of the *Arago*." In all, the *Arago* found twenty-two violations of ICCAT regulations among the vessels inspected, including "fishing without licenses, poor or absent recordkeeping and taking fish below the allowed size."

A separate incident reported by the Lebanese newspaper the *Daily Star* in October 2009 detailed the indictment of five Turkish and two Algerian shipowners, as well as the general secretary and the director of the Algerian Ministry of Fisheries, in a criminal conspiracy involving the illegal capture, laundering, and cover-up of 210 metric tons of bluefin caught during the 2009 season. (The approximate value of that amount of bluefin is over $1.3 million.) The government officials named in the indictment were to be paid to ignore illegal fishing by, and to prevent coast guard inspection of, the Turkish purse seiner *Akuadem II* and its ancillary support tugs, the *El Djazaïr II* and *Chahid Rais Hasni,* which were used to launder the tuna.

At the CITES meeting in Qatar on March 18, 2010, members voted *not* to list the bluefin tuna as endangered. In the months leading up to the vote, Japan had lobbied aggressively, garnering support from poor island nations in exchange for fishing industry investment—the same tactic that had proven successful years earlier in International Whaling Committee meetings. Its efforts also succeeded in defeating measures that would have protected endangered species of coral and several kinds of shark. The Japanese embassy went so far as to serve bluefin tuna to its delegates the night before the vote.

In the period before the vote, the media had also been filled with stories about the impending CITES meeting, and opponents used misinformation and half-truths to obscure the real issue. One document circulated was the 2008 ICCAT stock assessment of all northern bluefin in the Atlantic, which put the estimated population at roughly five million fish. With a population of that size, was there any danger of the fish's becoming commercially—much less actually—extinct?

As always, the devil was in the details: The 2008 ICCAT stock assessment estimated the population across all age groups of the stock. The purported population of five million bluefin would naturally have included a majority of immature fish, ranging in size from very small juveniles to ones near sexual maturity. But most of these fish would never live to reproduce, when all forms of mortality were considered. It is the breeding-stock numbers that matter when gauging the bluefin's viability, not the total population figures, because it is only those that live to breed that offer hope for the species. And it is precisely that group that has declined so precipitately.

For the 2010 fishing year, ICCAT lowered the total allowable catch (TAC) to 13,500 metric tons. At the November 2011 ICCAT meeting in Istanbul, member nations agreed to institute a requirement that every nation supply fishing data in order to be permitted to fish the following year. Members also agreed to an electronic catch-document scheme to replace the largely fraudulent paper one. But the electronic-document scheme is a half measure, still easily circumvented. It does not trace each tuna from harvest to the plate in full transparency, nor does the scheme require the tracking of tuna through the dozens of ranches in the Mediterranean, which leaves an enormous blind spot in monitoring and an easy means to launder the fish. In fact, the World Wildlife Fund reported that fishing capacity in the purse seine fleet is *twice* what can be profitable within the limits of the ICCAT quota—a huge incentive for poaching. A recent study by the ICCAT scientific committee demonstrated that output from the tuna industry is 70 to 80 percent higher than what it should be, based on inputs. Related to this, a study presented by an independent expert at the Istanbul meeting showed that growth in ranched bluefin tuna is typically on the order of only 20 to 30 percent, as opposed to the industry's figures of 100 percent or more increase in weight. This continues to signal the likelihood that exports from tuna farms include many illegally poached fish. The Pew Environment Group, in its 2010 report *Mind the Gap: An Analysis of the Mediterranean Bluefin Tuna Trade,* found that the amount of bluefin tuna traded globally exceeded the official quota by 141 percent, which also indicates that illegal, unreported, and unregulated (IUU) fishing continues unabated. This was nowhere worse in 2011 than in the southern Mediterranean and particularly off the coast of Libya, where, during that country's civil war, Italy and other nations were alleged to have fished for bluefin despite a clear ban by ICCAT and the European Commission.

The destruction of the bluefin fishery in the Mediterranean over the past decade represents both the loss of income to tens of thousands of fishermen and hundreds of local communities (at an estimated annual cost of $400 million per year) and the concentration of wealth in the hands of a few— some $16.4 billion between 1998 and 2008. The value of the Mediterranean bluefin hunt during this time dwarfs the estimated value of the global trade in shark fins between 1996 and 2006 ($8.3 billion), the global trade in whale meat between 1990 and 2000 ($8.2 billion), and the global trade in elephant ivory at its peak, between 1978 and 1988 ($1.02 billion).

The bluefin heist in the Mediterranean has been called "an international disgrace governed by a looting rationale" and an operation run by "an international tuna cartel." An investigation by the International Consortium of Investigative Journalists (ICIJ) found in 2010 that there is a "complex international black market in East Atlantic bluefin tuna worth an estimated $4 billion" and that allegations of Mafia involvement in the trade are rampant. Personnel from the World Wildlife Fund and other conservation organizations have received death threats in the form of bullets sent through the mail and a bouquet of lilies and chrysanthemums— Sicilian funeral flowers—laid on the desk of a WWF media liaison at a 2006 ICCAT meeting in Dubrovnik.

However it is measured, whether economically, politically, or morally, what is happening and will continue to happen in the Mediterranean tuna industry brings shame upon every nation and every individual participating in it.

There should be a category of international law under the heading "Crimes Against Nature," enforced by international police, intelligence, and military agencies, in a manner similar to how crimes against humanity are enforced and prosecuted by the international tribunal in the Hague.

What has happened to the bluefin tuna would qualify, along with what has been done to myriad other life-forms that have been driven to the brink, or over it, by unrestrained human ambition.

Morality demands this. Nature demands this. The future of this planet and our own survival demand this.

BOOK 3

THE PRIMAL WILD

Introduction

In Pursuit of Giants

Why should all the major religions of the modern world include a crucial encounter with wilderness—Moses, Jesus, and Mohammed in the desert mountains, Siddhartha in the jungle? And why should the predominant modern view of the origin and development of life have arisen from the five-year wilderness voyage of a Victorian amateur naturalist named Charles Darwin? There evidently is more to wilderness than meets the eye—more than water, timber, minerals, the materials of physical civilized existence . . . [These individuals] wrenched their respective cultures out of a complacency that amounted to self-worship and thrust them in new directions that (if not always entirely beneficial) enlarged the human perspective. Moses forced his society to accept a unifying law; Jesus forced his to accept the unity of all humanity; Darwin forced his to accept the unity of all life. I doubt whether any of the three would have been able to influence his society if he had not been fortified by a season in the wilderness.

—David Rains Wallace, *The Klamath Knot*

O ur understanding of the world is incomplete if we accept only what can be validated by science, law, numbers, or any other empirical determination of "fact." There are types of knowing and experience that exist beyond these—truths that only intuition can perceive, truths that only the raw, harsh, crushing beauty of Nature can evoke in us. There is a realm of experience where the direct encounter with Nature strips you bare emotionally, rakes you clean of artifice, and tears down the walls surrounding your civilized self to connect you with that place inside where intuition and instinct were born.

It is easy in contemporary society to become detached from those types of knowing, to have them become atrophied and even foreign to us. To lose them, though, is to lose some of the most powerful forms of intelligence we have. They are the means through which we come to know justice, sense our purpose, envision the impossible and achieve it, and become more fully human through connection with the soul. They are the seat of courage, our source of wisdom and vision, and our vehicle for transcendence. There is no technology of any kind that can match them, and there never will be.

We as human beings must confront a confounding factor that lies at the heart of everything we are and all that we do. We have reached a point in our evolution where we are able to shape the world at will, but we do so haphazardly and without forethought. The results, as we are seeing with increasing frequency, are ruinous—first to other species, and eventually to ourselves. We will soon have the ability to guide and control our own evolution through the manipulation of biology and the integration of our physical selves with the machine. The extension of our powers forces us to confront, now more than ever, the morality of our actions and choices. We are obliged in this as creatures who can conceive of a universe in which right and wrong operate not as abstract concepts but as realities as unassailable as gravity and the speed of light. We are bound by our conscience to act in accordance with the irrevocable truths of a moral universe, and though we can choose to ignore these truths, doing so betrays what makes us truly and most extraordinarily human.

Exploring our relationship with Nature has informed humankind's deepest quests into philosophy, science, and religion. But now, with the natural world at a point of crisis matched only by the five previous extinction events in the history of this planet, we can no longer entrust the determination of our moral behavior to philosophers or scientists, economists, corporations, governments, or anyone else. We *as individuals* must take responsibility for our own actions and choices with respect to their impact on the natural world. We must do so if we expect Nature to endure. Without it we have no security, for we will have endangered the complex system by which all forms of life—and every aspect of our own lives—thrive and multiply.

The opportunity to experience ocean wilderness and explore what it means to be human in the context of that world is why many venture out on the sea in pursuit of giants. Those who are compelled to fish for these reasons are sometimes misunderstood by people who regard fishing, for any purpose other than to obtain food, as a form of torture. That there is an element of pain in any kind of fishing is undeniable, and to seek to minimize this as much as possible is a moral imperative. But having fished for decades, I know how much my own life has been enriched by my encounters with the wild ocean, and it would be disingenuous of me to argue that there is not a place for angling. That said, I understand that, as our perception of the world and other species changes, the consideration of our role in the world—and especially our treatment of other creatures—deserves to be reexamined. Many people fish because they yearn to touch and be touched by the divine in Nature, if only for an afternoon, and even if they are unconscious of it. Perhaps it's true, as a friend insisted to me, that "fishing as a means of encountering the divine in wilderness only shows a lack of imagination." In answering him, I can only rely on my own experience, which assures me that what I've seen and felt in the presence of the ocean's great fish has compelled my soul and my imagination to places I never would have reached had I not gone out on a boat.

When I set out on this journey to understand what we have done to the world's great fish, it was my hope that I might be able to encounter one of them firsthand. To experience in its natural habitat any creature of great size is to appreciate one's own insignificance and the unfathomable processes of the natural world that have given rise to such a thing. But size alone is not what makes a fish "great." They are great because they live in fierceness, because they are at the mercy of so much, and because they show such courage and will to live in the face of it. In the presence of these largest and fastest of all fish, one must acknowledge a certain awe and humility, for in them the forces of creation have massed their energies, building girth and heft and length, as well as great power and speed with age, creating something that is more than the sum of its statistical data. Well hooked in the corner of its mouth, it will demonstrate to you what grandeur is, tearing line off from your heavy-duty reel as though it were a toy, rendering you and your little boat insignificant in the totality of its blue kingdom.

Granders in the Coral Sea

Lizard Island, Great Barrier Reef, Australia

We must be refreshed by the sight of inexhaustible vigor, vast and titanic features, the sea-coast with its wrecks, the wilderness with its living and its decaying trees, the thunder-cloud . . . We need to witness our own limits transgressed, and some life pasturing freely where we never wander.

—Henry David Thoreau, *Walden*

1

In fishing, the chances of seeing, much less catching, a fish over a thousand pounds are less than one in many million. Of the hundreds of millions of fish caught annually by anglers around the world, fewer than 150 are likely to tip the scales at over half a ton. The state lottery is a better investment of a hard-earned dollar than going fishing in the hopes of seeing or catching a grander marlin.

As in any kind of gambling, there are ways to increase your chances of coming out ahead. If you hope to see a thousand-pound marlin, the best way is to save your money, pack your bags, carve out at least a week's time—longer if possible—and then in October or November fly halfway around the world to the northeast coast of Australia, to a place called Cairns (pronounced *Cans* in the local dialect). Offshore of this town, you have a better chance than anywhere on Earth of seeing a grander in action. Every year, twenty, maybe thirty fish, but certainly fewer than fifty of this size are caught off Cairns on the Great Barrier Reef, and the vast majority of them, I am happy to report, are freed.

In Cairns there is a lovely boardwalk that traces the curve of the sand flats bordering the broad bay, with rainforested hills rising dark green and lush in the distance. The bay and the flats fill at high tide and would look inviting for a swim were it not for signs erected along the boardwalk announcing that the world's largest variety of crocodile—the saltwater croc—is routinely spotted thereabouts.

Along the boardwalk is birdlife of all sorts—pelicans flying in formation, several varieties of specialized spoonbills (poor things with that kitchen spatula attached to their faces), and little surgical dowitchers and curlews with their twitchy, quick bodies and long, curved instruments stitching the mud back and forth with the action of sewing machines. In the nearby trees are hundreds of birds, the most raucous and quarrelsome being the pied currawongs. One of them jogs along the boardwalk, big-hipped, armless, running like a fit duck after a square of sparkly cellophane blowing ahead of it. It catches the cellophane in its beak and carries it off, the bright rag of its prize flapping about its face. They have the ambition of crows, these currawongs, and that blotch of yellow around their eyes gives them the appearance of having donned war paint before heading out for the day's raids.

Off to the north, just beyond the edge of town, the great Qantas airliners rise up, rumbling through the heat shimmer like white-winged phoenixes, and turn northeast out over the Great Barrier Reef. Then, toward evening, a line of clouds builds far out at the mouth of the bay like a wall of smoke curling back on itself, and then the color washes down from the top, a soft chalky red darkening to lavenders and blues, and then the cloud wall goes slate-dark with night soaking through all heavy and thick, like ink through cloth, and then the day is over. The darkness soaks through the air itself but not the birds, and in stark contrast to the gloomy backdrop flights of bright white ibises drift overhead like slender origami kites, and the currawongs have a huge family row in the trees to end the day.

On the way back to the hotel, the sky fills with massive shadowy seagulls. At least they look like gulls until I notice the scalloped trailing edge of their wings and realize they are gargantuan fruit bats the size of winged Chihuahuas.

This is when I recall that it is near here, in Chillagoe, ninety miles west of Mareeba, that fossils of great marine reptiles—plesiosaurs, with four paddles for legs, and a long neck and tail—were found, and into my mind they come swimming in pods over the shallows of the ancient Apian Sea. Sawfish up to ten feet long lie out in the bay off Cairns, with their strange toothed weapon of a snout like a flat ceremonial club. In the balmy night air and with the tops of the palm trees tossing like horse heads and all the rest of it, I feel, even though I have just arrived, that I've already come to love this place.

At the airport the next morning I wait in the lounge of a small regional charter service running turboprop aircraft out to various points on the GBR. My destination is Lizard Island, 150 miles up the coast and twenty miles offshore of the Munburra Resource Reserve. Eventually eight other passengers and I walk out into the heat and bright sunshine of the tarmac to board the plane, and we all watch as a boy who looks to be about sixteen years old, dressed in a uniform with blue cardboard epaulets, takes the wheel. When an equally young copilot takes his place beside him, the three Aussies in the seat behind me start saying things like "I wonder if his mommy knows he flies planes" and "Is he sitting on a book? My God, I think he's sitting on a book!"

The pilot is, in fact, perched upon a book so that he can see over the instrument panel.

At the go-ahead from the tower, he runs the throttle up wide-open, and we tear off down the runway, airborne in an instant and banking away from Cairns. In no time, we have left the coast behind and are out over the Coral Sea, flying through cloud islands at three thousand feet. Below us the water is turquoise and emerald, with the shallows yellow tourmaline and the reefs horseshoe-shaped and flattening out as they run off in a chain into the distance. I can feel my heart cracking open at the sight of it, the sheer coral cliffs plunging into deep-blue depths, dark channels harboring streaming schools of colored fish, and beaches whose sand may never have felt the imprint of a human footfall.

More than an hour later, a strong crosswind bucks the plane as we bank hard to line up for the Lizard Island runway from several miles out. As we pitch and yaw, dip and leap, I look down at the bay nestled behind the island's long, high ridge and wonder which among the scattering of boats is ours. The boy pilot brings us in with admirable skill, holding the plane steady despite the crosswind and touching down gently.

What is immediately noticeable after the engine is shut down and the bags offloaded is the silence: It is blessedly quiet, with the wind the only sound in the hot, heavy air. We make our way down a sandy path, past the staff cottages of a luxury resort, and through a line of palm trees to the beach, where we kick off our shoes and walk to a small boat waiting for us. It is attended by two tall, rail-thin, grinning and tanned Australian deckhands.

They take our bags, load us aboard, and with cheerful banter run us out over the crystal shallows of the lagoon to our ship, the *Odyssey,* an eighty-foot aluminum catamaran, with aft deck consisting of a bar and chairs under a roof, inside galley kitchen attended by a good cook, three long tables with bench seating, and, toward the bow, bunk cabins and showers. At the stern and flanks of the ship are tied a number of smaller fishing boats and Zodiacs ranging from eighteen to twenty-five feet, but my eye goes from these to the real objects of my desire: two sleek sportfishing boats, *Nomad* and *Saltaire*—thirty-four and thirty-six feet, respectively, with flybridges and outriggers and brushed gold reels the size of coffee cans on the heavy tackle rods, fully equipped to venture beyond the edge of the reef to the deep water to find and count coup on some truly massive black marlin.

After dropping my bags in my cabin, I set out for the aft deck, where I meet a number of the other guests. There are two Bobs from Fort Lauderdale—one a vet, the other a chiropractor—who have fished before with this operation, the last time being the previous year, when the latter Bob got a grander to the back of the boat before releasing it. The veterinarian Bob is tall, with a certain heaviness around the eyes and in the midsection, and, though not exceedingly talkative, he is friendly. The chiropractor Bob is shorter and leaner, with curly hair and a touch of boyishness in his face. He has such an enviable straightness to his spine and neck that I can't help but wonder if a chiropractor can self-adjust. Unlike his friend, he is loquacious and talks about the fishing and how hit-or-miss it can be with marlin, but worth it if you find them, and then he moves on to the

GTs—giant trevallies—and what it's like to have one of them attack a surface popper over the shallow reefs.

"It's sick what they do to you," he says. "I mean, it's fun, don't get me wrong. It's a blast. It's everything you'd want. Hard hit—God, they hit hard. They're exhausting. They're like . . . vicious. It's punishing. You stand up with the rod, you're not in a chair. The action is crazy. Totally brutal. I'm here to relax so I'll probably focus more on the marlin."

The Bobs have known each other for many years, and though they go fishing whenever they can, it sounds as if they do little out of Fort Lauderdale. Chiro Bob has a condo at a resort in Costa Rica, and in the coming days I will enjoy being regaled with his stories of striped marlin and sailfish offshore of that country blessed with an overabundance of natural beauty.

There are two father-son teams, one a very tall, very large, gray-haired Canadian named Ken and his shorter, white-haired father, John, whose eyes and smile retain a youthful spirit and verve. The other is an Australian father in his forties, a doctor, tall, slight of build, with a somewhat worried expression. His son, Will, is the picture of boyhood—small for his age (which I put at about ten), blond, with his father's light frame and exuding a shy, wide-eyed joy, barely kept under wraps, to be on such an adventure. In the coming days he will do titanic battle with a GT that outweighs him by forty pounds and could tow him on water skis. He will fight that fish with the courage and spunk of Peter Pan facing Hook, and he will return to the *Odyssey* grinning and triumphant, with a tale to tell that will last him the rest of his life.

There are also the three Australians who sat behind me on the plane. The first one, Clarkie, is a heavy-duty, dark-haired bear of a man with hound-dog eyes and one of those hugely resonant bass voices. Before the journey is over, Clarkie, feeling "crook" (Australian for nauseated) on the fourth day out in fifteen-foot seas and thirty-knot winds, and with the boat backing up into the waves and the waves coming over onto him in the chair as though they wanted to body-slam him, will nonetheless battle an 850-pound electric purple marlin to the transom. This marlin, as it curves up to the boat and lies out flat just under the surface for a moment before disappearing, will offer a brief close-up glimpse of just how huge and intensely purple it is, glimmering in the gray windy sea.

Clarkie will get out of the chair, promptly puke, smile sheepishly, and feel fantastic.

One of the other two Aussies, Brett, in a rakish pair of silver sunglasses, has the good-natured bearing and wry humor of a man accustomed to and happily ensconced in family life. He runs a company that makes soft trim for boats—cushy thigh rails and seats and the like. The third man, Chris, is broad-shouldered with an athletic build and a comfortable, relaxed grin that invites anyone in his vicinity to bring it on. He runs a company that does large-scale electrical systems design and installation. The three of them have fished together for years down in their home territory off Melbourne.

The last to come aboard this afternoon is Darren, a blond, shaggy, straw-haired plumber from far north Queensland. His wife surprised him only a few days before with the gift of this voyage, and he arrives on board looking happily dazed and ready for a good time. The first thing he does after dropping his bags is lean an elbow on the bar and ask the hostess, Tara, for a Bundaberg and Coke.

Little do I know at the time, but Darren will become my tour guide into the world of the Square Bear. Bundaberg is Aussie rum. It comes in a square bottle with a tapered bottom and a label showing a polar bear. If you ever get in a bar fight, reach for this bottle. It's the size of a bowling pin and looks like it would swing well. But make sure it's empty before you waste its golden cane juice on some Aussie's thick skull. Bundaberg is very good stuff and to waste more of it than is absolutely necessary would be a shame. It goes by several names including "Cane Champagne" and "Queensland Diesel," and is available in four varieties—underproof, overproof, extra smooth, and reserve. It is worth noting that before the advent of scientifically calibrated instruments, the strength of Bundy was gauged by pouring it into a handful of gunpowder and lighting it. If it blew up, it was overproof. If it didn't, it was underproof. It was people with this kind of ingenuity who first created Bundy in the harsh environment of the Australian bush.

As the sun goes red and sinks to the horizon, a few of us gather at the rail to watch Will, in one of the sportfishing boats, getting a lesson in how to fight a marlin from the chair. Standing next to me, Brett of the plush cushions says, "That's like having bait on both ends." Indeed, little Will should be battened down, lashed to the chair, or surely he will be yanked clear out of the boat if anything over 150 pounds hits his line.

The conversation turns to the subject of GTs. Damon, the Aussie owner of the operation, confident and very able but surprisingly young to be running a multi-million-dollar sportfishing adventure outfit, smiles and says wryly in his attenuated Australian accent, "Yeah, we start the Americans out on the GTs until they cry. That way they behave themselves."

Little trays of hors d'oeuvres float past, from which we snatch gobbets of food: fluffy pillows stuffed with cheese, tangy grilled beef strips.

Brett tells the story of a man he knows who lost both arms—mangled beyond recognition—in an industrial accident. They were going to sew new arms on, and he asked that one of them be a woman's. "For selfish pleasures," he told the doctor.

"True story," Brett says as another round of Bundaberg and Cokes is delivered.

Soon it is dark and I am on one of the Zodiacs heading across the lagoon through the twinkling night, passing huge anchored sportfishing yachts floating on fogs of glowing blue light, sleek shadows cruising in the water underneath.

Darren says to me, "I think you've taken a liking to the Bear, mate."

We disembark on the beach like a landing party and make our way to the line of palm trees, behind which stands a bar. The bar is just a palm thatch roof on heavy timber stanchions, no walls, with good liquor at only $5 Australian per drink. This is about $3.50 American at the going rate. There is a giant marlin hanging from the rafters, with the top four inches of its tail snapped off, wearing a little cowboy hat on its dorsal fin, giving it a jaunty, fun-loving air. The bartender tells us it weighed 950 pounds. I turn to Chris.

"Can I get you a rum?" I ask.

"Does a marlin have a pointy nose?"

Unknowingly, I am into a "shout"—Australian slang for buying rounds—with Darren, Brett, and Chris. Certain terms are explained to me. A "gobby" is a blow job. To "cark it" is to die. And in a land as parched as the Arctic is snowy, the inhabitants of Oz have developed a rich vocabulary with which to describe drought, most expressions taking the form of comparison: *It's as dry as . . .* a dead dingo's donger, or a nun's nasty.

All cares slip away, and I swim in warm waters of laughter and camaraderie. Gradually I become aware of the darkness beyond our sphere of light. Past the silhouette of palm trees, beyond the boats in the lagoon, lies the sea, shadowy, dark, and restless under a high overcast. Through the vapors of the Bundaberg I feel it out there, brooding and indifferent to us.

2

In the morning we leave the *Odyssey* in the fishing boats, which disperse in a fan pattern, the smaller ones heading to the shallows behind the reef to fish for GTs, yellowfin, wahoo, and maybe a big dogtooth tuna that's come up from the coral ledges. The bigger boats—*Saltaire* and *Nomad*—head out ten miles to the rampart wall of the reef and the deep water. I'm on *Saltaire* with Darren and the two Bobs. As we round the northern point of Lizard, the wind hits us full in the face, blowing at twenty to twenty-five knots and the sea running in tightly packed, ten-foot-tall corrugated swells. *Saltaire,* broad-beamed and heavy, crashes through them, sending arcing shrouds of spray up over the flybridge and behind us in a sheeting rain. Fifty yards back I watch *Nomad,* at thirty-four feet long, leap clear off the top of a wave, props screaming. She comes down hard, and a white chrysanthemum, big as a parachute, blooms in front of her.

I watch our mates, Glanville and Pat, as they prep the baits: fresh wahoo and queenfish, caught the day before by the crew, with bonito or yellowfin or barracuda also used if that's what comes up. The baits have been gutted, weighted in the head, and sewn with waxed rigging line starting at the nose, going back under the chin and along the belly in a perfect crisscross pattern. The hooks are huge 20/0 Mustad Duratin circle hooks the size of hamburger patties, tied with a flemish eye and crimped. The baits are three to fifteen pounds or more in weight and anywhere from one to four feet long; if we had bigger we'd use them. I've heard of a live, bridle-rigged thirty-eight-pound yellowfin tuna swallowed whole by a black marlin in these very waters. The marlin weighed only 650 pounds.

Up on the flybridge I join Tim, our South African captain—soft-spoken, thoughtful, reader of books, lover of fish and all things fishing. He talks about Scott Bannerot of *Marlin* magazine, who used to mate on the boats out here. Tim relates a Bannerot story of a marlin he saw come up on a longline, which after being gutted still weighed 2,200 pounds.

Ahead, along the powdery mint green edge of the reef, with its fringe of white waves like an ermine collar, is the kingdom of the giants itself. We head through a gap between the coral and watch the waters shift to indigo blue as the bottom drops away and the swells open up, with broadening troughs between the crests. We run up and down over the heaving, shimmering blue hills, with the engines generating a kind of harmonic whining song, while 150 feet behind us the baits skip and leap over the waves. Tim recalls that he's seen five marlin at once appear behind trolled baits such as these, like a squadron in the swell.

"There was one large one and four small ones. The large one rolled under the bait, had a look, and peeled off. Then one of the smaller ones came up and had a look and took it. The angler hooked the fish, got it to the boat, and wanted to keep it. It weighed over a thousand pounds. The large one that looked first and peeled off was bigger than it by an order of magnitude—an entirely different scale. It had to have topped fifteen hundred."

As large as the marlin grow out here, occasionally one comes to the surface having lost everything back of the gill plates—that is to say, it comes up as a head, the rest of it having been taken by a shark.* These predators are called great whites for a reason: Topping five thousand pounds and growing to more than twenty feet long, they are the ultimate rulers of this kingdom. Our location on the Great Barrier Reef is supposedly north of their preferred temperature range, but barely so. Yet it hardly matters whether it's a great white or a huge tiger shark or a pack of bronze whalers that can do this to the trailing eight or nine feet of a giant marlin. What matters is that it happens in the great wide world, and should always happen, in what has been called "the sportive brutality of the sea," and that

---

*YouTube, "Giant Black Marlin Attacked by Monster Sharks," http://www.youtube.com/watch?v=qjdEohdYcvQ. Used courtesy of *The Ultimate Fishing Show* presented by Matt Watson.

no matter how good video games become, they will never be this good, and will in fact never touch the wildness of real life in the physical world.

We are one of only four boats I count running on the outside of the reefs within the whole of the horizon. Through the course of hours we troll up and back along the reefs, running off as far as five miles, staying near Day and Carter reefs in the south, and moving as far north as Hicks Reef. We do half-hour rotations in the chair, and during one of mine, sometime around midmorning, I see behind me, at just under a hundred yards, a sleek black marlin with my bait in its mouth. By his small size he could be a male, greyhound long and lean, flashing silver with shiny black patent leather topsides. He's running with the bait, tasting it, and I'm waiting for him to swallow it, waiting to apply pressure on the line to turn the hook, when I feel it go slack. Tim puts the fish at around four hundred pounds, which would mean it was likely a small female and a good deal heavier than I estimated. Shortly thereafter, *Nomad* runs past with a marlin tail-walking behind it. The marlin looks to be about 350 pounds, a beautiful fish, with the starry night of its back sharp against the silver ice sheet of its flanks. It's up vertical with its nose in the air, directly behind *Nomad,* then flips over and dives. Then it's up again, and I can see the big Canadian, Ken, lean forward and reel hard, with his platinum gray hair blowing. The fish comes out, thrashing its head, glinting spray flinging off it in a semi-circular arc, and then it dives again. Then the fish comes out right behind their boat, seven or eight feet long, and it goes on like this until the boat is out of sight, lost in the troughs.

The wind keeps up all day, running shivers up the backsides of the waves and rolling the tops over. After hours in wind like this, I feel as though it has penetrated my skin, gotten into my hair and mouth, under my clothes, and it's a strange feeling having the wind under your skin, moving through fat and muscles, rippling your hide and blowing through the chasms of your mind with its reedy vesper song. The waves, too, have gotten into my body, all day long in the rocking and tilting, the lift and drop of the boat running over the sea. Whether or not you're catching fish, being out in the weather like this and having the weather *in* you makes you feel vibrantly alive. The salt spray has coated me with a greasy mineral distillate; I can taste its clean, bright flavor on my lips. Colors seem

heightened here, from a moody eggplant-dark storm front passing to the
south, all bruised and beat up, to the stunning variety of shades of green
in the fringe of the reef (limes, spring leaves, chartreuses, and sherbet) to
the ocean's hues of violet, plum, midnight, and topaz. Then flying fish, no
bigger than locusts, suddenly emerge and scatter over the waves, a fragile
light gleaming off the twittering glassine membranes of their wings, as
though they were made of mica. They flick silver blue over the wave tops,
gliding hundreds of feet, and I feel as though I'm witnessing flights of fairy
craft engaged in simultaneous aerial and submarine battle, in an ancient
unknown war waged among tinsel-winged beings, whose technology
reflects evolution's apogee in the primitive mechanical artistry of the
Gilded Age. They have the appearance of small, intricate devices with flapping splined surfaces, handwrought gilded scales, superfluous but lovely
stylized adornments. They glide away, wings clicking, gears whirring,
goggled and scattering bravely to the wind, and while I have envied birds
all my life, I envy flying fish more. Aside from the myriad rare and common species of butterfly and moth—the fritillaries and elfins, heliconians
and metalmarks—there is nothing in the natural world, that I know of, so
ephemeral as flying fish. There are species yet to be identified, and how
could it be otherwise? They exist in a world between worlds, in the inner
space between the whitewater of crumbling waves and the misty cloud
banks hovering over the sea, and in the blue sunlit realm at the top of the
water column. They fly among the froth and the salt spray, in the margins
of elemental transition, across seascapes too small for us to perceive but
which to them appear as towering blue ranges heaving overhead, torn by
hurricanes. They are like hummingbirds, a phenomenon visible to the
naked eye, fascinating and fleet-winged, dazzling in greens and blues and
clear windowpane wings. They have names like sailfin and beautyfin, spot-
fin and blotchwing, but I'll be damned if one of them shouldn't be called
the coral victory or the tinselwing spitfire. They are the jeweler's absolute
masterpiece in diminutive fish.

After hours of sensations and visions like these, I'm left in a kind of
brimming quiet awe at the beauty of the world. There are other fish brought
aboard—wahoo with their snapping triangular jaws, and a nice bonito of
about twelve or thirteen pounds that the deckhands keep for bait. We talk

about all manner of things in the camaraderie of men at sea, and though we come from distant parts of the globe and disparate lives, the one thing we share is that we are alive and happy riding this big white elephant over the blue and windy wilderness.

Without many fish to count for our efforts and caring not in the least, we return in the golden late-afternoon light, back to the ship moored in the lagoon at Lizard Island. Tara delivers Bundaberg and Cokes, and we swap stories with the three Australians who spent the day being abused in the small boats by violent gangs of giant trevallies that came up over the gunwales swinging at them, leaving them with smashed poppers and broken rods.

At this point in the day, the mates from the boats are going on ten hours on their feet, and they still have several hours of work ahead of them, prepping baits, washing down and refueling the boats, repairing damaged gear. To be a crew member in a sportfishing operation like this, especially if you are in your early or mid-twenties and crazy about fish, is to live a kind of waking dream. You spend all your days outside in the weather tending lines, serving clients politely, smiling for pictures with strangers, and gutting and cleaning fish, and though some of this is difficult and tedious, every bit of it is worth it because of the opportunities it offers. Most people never realize that to be the fisherman in the chair is one thing, but it is another thing entirely to be the mate who reaches over the transom and takes the leader in his gloved hand when the fish is so close he can look it in the eye. It is the mate who gets to feel, better than anyone, the heartbeat and character of the creature on the other end of the line. Sometimes, of course, that creature will be a thousand-pound animal coming vertically out of the water, like a log shot out of a cannon within arm's reach.

Among the other hardships they endure is not eating enough, not drinking enough beer, living in close quarters with little or no privacy, and long stretches of time without female companionship (the one female aboard, Tara, being off-limits). In many ways, theirs is a monkish existence, forgoing the lifestyle of their land-based counterparts in favor of a kind of spiritual calling to bear witness to the great fish of the world. Nevertheless, they remain boys with energy that must be expended, and they do this in the evening by feeding the day's spent bait to the wildlife that lives in the lagoon.

The lagoon where *Odyssey* lies at anchor is part of a nature preserve and as such is closed to fishing. The result is one of the best reasons that I know of for setting aside parts of the ocean as reserves, because if you have never seen an untouched ocean ecosystem, you have never really seen the sea. I have not really, truly seen the sea, I realize, until I watch the fish come running from all across the lagoon when the dinner bell is rung.

From the waterline deck where the sportfishing boats are tied, several of the mates knot rope around pieces of old bait and slap the wads of meat down on the water. In seconds it is as though the hounds of hell had been summoned. Black crescent-winged shadows come speeding at us from under the distant ripples, zipping under the boats, slicing and turning in their flybys. I have finally laid eyes on the demonic GTs. Charcoal gray, with muscular rectangular bodies, their big faces far forward on their heads, with downturned mouths, they can grow as long as a man and weigh over 150 pounds. The ones in the lagoon are the size of Labrador retrievers and come in at about 60 to 80 pounds, some as low as 40, the big ones topping a 100. They are fast as whippets, with the brawn and disposition of pit bulls. All the dog analogies come naturally to an animal that moves and hunts in wild, rangy packs like these do. In Japanese they are called the ronin jack—"jack" from among the species that make up the family Carangidae, and "ronin" after maverick samurai, the masterless rogue warriors of the shogun period. The big ones are on the bait and running with it before their image registers on your retina. With their crescent-shaped, back-curving pectoral fins, they look like something designed by a 1920s art deco artist with a studio in the underworld.

Then lemon sharks appear, six and eight feet long, curious and docile as cows, their suede hides the color of lemony honey. They glide lazily along the surface, appearing to merely nose and gum the bait. Myriad other fish that I cannot make out circle deeper down, including shark forms that are thick and heavy through the head and shoulders. These are bronze whalers, a member of the requiem shark family, which includes hammerhead, bull, and tiger sharks—a clan not to be trifled with. A particularly beautiful small tuna is tied on and flung out by Karl, the young engineer in charge of all the *Odyssey*'s mechanical functions, and the GTs are on it with snarls and teeth bared, beating the water to a froth. The tuna flies up in tatters and we are all laughing, the chunk of meat hanging limply now at Karl's feet, right at the edge of the decking, when I see a massive form slide out stealthily from beneath him. Before I can say anything, a void has appeared in the water, a sinkhole into which what remains of the tuna disappears with a resonant gulp, and after a massive jerk, Karl is lucky to be left standing. The culprit is a four-hundred-pound, six-foot-long grouper named Gerald, with a head the size of a wheelbarrow.

3

Somewhere between the first and second days of fishing, life seems to become disengaged from the flywheel of time. I realize this as I sit in the fighting chair on *Saltaire* gazing out over the wave-swept sea, lines running out silvery in the sunlight from the outriggers, baits flopping lively down the wave fronts, gold reels flashing on either side of me, the reefs far off to starboard, and the brown pyramid of Lizard Island hazy in the distance. It may be lingering jet lag or the fact that I haven't laid eyes on a clock, digital or analog, since I left the mainland. It's as though my heart and mind have somehow settled into perfect alignment, a harmony of time and place and being and purpose.

Behind the dark screen of my sunglasses, with the wind in my mind, over tractless miles on the surface of the sea, I find myself pondering certain questions—how they know they're marlin, for example. Here is a creature that never speaks, never sees its own reflection, and yet knows its own kind. What is it like to live in a three-dimensional world of water with few, if any, reference points except the perpetually morphing surface, a piece of plastic flotsam, a red-hulled ship, a floating mass of pulsing pink jellyfish, a white shark arching its back at you? What is it like to inhabit that magnificent body, so powerful and fast? What is it like to feel mating initiated by the ocean's caress, by the mere proximity of male and female— to have the ocean's bidding done through you, via you, with you as the instrument of larger things, and all volition taken from you?

What do marlin think of the world above the waves? What do they make of clouds, of the cool bite of air across their gills, of the white-hot sun, of green islands? Do they ever lie on their sides, far out on a calm sea at night, and look at the moon?

And what dramas take place in the heart of the ocean beyond the view of humankind? What rhapsodies of life, colorful and multitudinous, course through the alien sea, unknown to us and forever to remain so?

These are the thoughts that occupy an angler's mind as the hours pass, and, unconscious of myself, I begin praying to the powers that be to send a great marlin up, up out of the sea to show herself. To pass within proximity of my bait and take it in her jaws back there in the clear water of the swell, coming down the front of the wave so I can see her purple back and how long she is—to take my bait in her jaws and turn and run, letting me see her grandeur and her greatness on display and marvel at it, because I, with my pale flesh, my heavy legs and weak eyes, will never know such things.

Come up from the deep, I pray. *Just come up. Just once, come up.*

But she does not.

On *Saltaire,* the winds remain steady at twenty-five knots, the seas ten feet or better, and we move south along the reef line, focusing on the south end of Carter and the full length of Yonge Reef. We have lost Vet Bob to queasiness, so it is only me, Darren, and Chiro Bob rotating at forty-five-minute intervals in the chair, with Glanville, the South African mate, and Pat, the silent deckhand trainee, tending lines, with Tim piloting from the flybridge. Over the morning hours, we catch barracuda and queenfish and another small tuna, which we keep for bait. The queenfish is close to three feet long, with large half-dollar gray spots and a long midline streak. The queenies are the best swimmers of any bait, pulsing and beating over the surface of the waves as though reawakened to life. With one of them flopping and swimming through the swells behind the boat, you can't help but feel that your chances of seeing a marlin come up on it are increased by a factor of at least two or three. "Aw, yeah," Glanville confirms, "queenies are like chocolates for marlin. They're like lollies. They love 'em!"

At one point we put out the small tuna, and it falls back in line opposite the queenfish, where it suddenly vanishes. The only clue to its disappearance is a fleeting shadow, which leaves no way of gauging the size of the marlin that just took the fish. The way the rigger pops and the reel starts going off, however, suggests that it's not small. Glanville shouts, "Port rigger! She's taken it!" He lets the fish run a good thirty seconds, maybe forty-five, and then he throws the reel into gear and starts to apply pressure. At this point he should feel something, maybe even see the fish come up out of a wave, but something's off. A moment passes, then another, and Glanville stands looking out over the sea, hand on the reel, until finally he shakes his head.

"Spit it," he says, and reels in the line.

He brings aboard the tuna, which is limp and blanched white, its meat pulped and a section of its back missing. Glan and Tim examine it.

"That went all the way to the belly, didn't it?" Glanville asks.

Tim nods. "She folded it," he says. "Mashed it, folded it over in her mouth, then swallowed it. Hook couldn't set because the barb was covered."

〜〜〜〜〜

Before fishing for marlin the next day, we motor out in one of the small boats to a section of reef known as the Cod Hole. We anchor and don our dive vests, and after Tim, the South African captain turned divemaster, gives us a speech about avoiding sea snakes, he takes me and two of the three Australians, Chris and Brett, and we go over the side. Glanville and Pat remain on deck with Clarkie, who understands that to enter the water is to become a link in the food chain, which in Australia is no joke. The water is so clear that it registers only as a liquid warmth against the skin and a flat blue murk in the distance. Behind the boat, we are met by a loose aggregation of forty or fifty large fish—potato groupers, the white-on-crimson polka-dot bommie cod, coral trout, and red-lipped emperors. They look at us with large, round eyes, curious and seemingly docile, but their twitching bodies make it clear that their curiosity has a purpose: not so much "What is it?" as "Is there something on it I can eat?"

We dive down forty feet to the white coral sand bottom tilting off into the deep, and cruise around large coral heads that have broken away and tumbled from the reef wall. The heads are covered with life—algae and

soft corals, sea horses, anemones, shrimp and crabs, and myriad little dam-
selfish flying in golden echelons. In the sand are blennies, fingerling little
bulldogs defending their turf with belligerent courage and disgruntled
little faces. We see triggerfish with their serrated white teeth, and a hump-
head Maori wrasse whose pompadour gives it the appearance of a 1950s
greaser in strange blue-green makeup. There is so much life packed into
every square foot of the reef that an entire day could be devoted to exploring a single patch of coral. In the space of only five minutes, my senses are
overwhelmed by the variety of life I see—clown fish pairs tending their
fleshy anemones, delicate white leather coral with a surface of Irish lace, a
bright yellow nudibranch with blue racing stripes, hard staghorn corals
like a patch of brambles, table corals, pastel pink gorgonian sea fans, and
crinoids like bouquets of feathery worms.

Tim shows us a moray eel inflating and deflating in its coral tunnel,
with menacing mouth and bright, alert eyes. Off in the murky distance I
notice the lazy sentinel presence of sharks—whitetip and gray reef. Then,
swimming between two large coral heads, I look down and see that the
bottom of the small gulley is lined with giant clams, a dozen of them, each
two to three feet wide from one side of its wrinkled smile to the other.
Each is lined on the inside with what looks like rich purple-blue velvet, in
the middle of which is a single pulsating ventricle through which it takes
in and expels seawater. Lining the outer rim of velvet along both sides of
the wrinkled lips are hundreds of eye dots, brilliant electric green. By now
I understand what is not written in any of the holy books: that Paradise,
so long sought after, never was on land. It was beneath the sea, and remnants of it can still be found off the Great Barrier Reef.

Our small group fans out, and we explore on our own. I glimpse below
me, six or eight feet down on the coral sand, a large snail encrusted in algae
and waving green grasses. I swim down and pick it up, and upon turning
it over I see its fleshy occupant withdrawing to the interior. Not wishing
to disturb it, I return it gently.

Back on the boat, Tim says to me, "When I saw you pick up that snail,
I came swimming at you at full speed to tell you to put it down. That was
a cone snail. It shoots out a small harpoon with a neurotoxin. You probably
would have made it to the boat, but then your heart would have stopped,

and you'd have died on deck. We would have tried to keep you going with CPR, but it takes half an hour or longer for the toxin to wear off, and by that time you'd have to wonder what would have been left of you. I probably should have mentioned it with the sea snakes."

Brett looks at me with a smile. "Today's your lucky day, mate!"

My smile is somewhat weaker than his as I contemplate the branching short road my life could be taking in these very moments. Feeling a breeze through my hair, as though the great ax in the sky has just missed my head, I laugh uneasily, looking nervously at my hand.

During that evening's ritual of feeding the wildlife of the lagoon, Karl the engineer goes so far as to put on a diving mask and stick his head under the water, after which he comes up sputtering and exclaiming at the monstrous size of the GTs. This in turn inspires Glanville, who knows no fear and, being South African, thinks nothing of large sharks—he's swum with and filmed great whites off his native Durban coast. Glan grabs the underwater video camera and, throwing on fins and a snorkel in addition to the mask, actually gets into the water with the fish.

The other mates begin seeding the area with bloody chunks, and the trevallies start coming in fast and hard, the larger ones as big as 120 pounds. When the mates begin tossing chunks of meat directly at Glanville's head, the game is on. Those of us on deck spy a bronze whaler out on the periphery. It cruises in slowly, skirting quickly past Glan, who gives him a poke with the camera, then slinks away.

At about seven feet long, a bronze whaler cruising smoothly by may seem a contemplative animal, but its languid movements and calm demeanor belie its speed and seriousness when excited.

As Glanville films the GTs, we spy another bronzie out on the periphery, then a second and a third at spaced intervals along the edge, and before we know what is happening the ambush is on. At some signal we do not perceive, all three whalers turn at once and race at Glanville from different directions. He spins underwater in time to see the first one on top of him and shoves the camera in the shark's face, then drops it and flees at high speed over the surface of the water, cartoon style—legs kicking, arms pinwheeling—straight for the swim deck off the back of the *Odyssey*. The camera floats away and slowly sinks. The crew on board, Glanville the most urgent among them, determine that they will have to salvage the camera immediately, and after rethinking doing it with snorkel and mask, they suit up with scuba gear and take one of the Zodiacs to find it.

When the camera, still running, is brought back on deck, it is immediately hooked up to the flatscreen monitor. It has recorded not only the initial shark hit and Glanville's quick retreat, but the aftermath as well: dozens of whalers blazing toward the camera, bumping and mouthing it to determine whether it is edible.

And so we pass our time upon the Coral Sea. We watch the sun set, we are well fed and watered, and we spend our days fishing on the windy ocean. As we watch the baits lay their tracks over the miles, Tim shares stories with me on the flybridge of *Saltaire:* the tale of the Thai fishing vessel illegally poaching fish from Australian waters, which made the mistake of brandishing weapons at the Aussie coast guard, who in turn called in the navy, who proved less understanding. And of the trawler that went down with captain and mate clinging to the wreckage, and the two tiger sharks that found them and circled, closing in gradually over the course of seventeen hours, and on the morning of the second day took and ate the mate before the captain's eyes.

I sit with Glanville one evening as he runs through the underwater photographs stored on his laptop—all pictures he has taken, of great fish and white sharks off Durban; of his small boat and his mates, a chronicle in pictures of months, long seasons, a life spent cavorting in the sea—more in his short years than I will ever do. He tells me a story of fishing with rod and reel—underwater—for giant grouper on his home reefs, and hooking one and being taken for a ride up and over the coral hills, through the life-rich rocky corridors of the sea. How I envy him. He is young, yes, and a blessed clown, but he is far from stupid. He is only braver and more carefree than I am, in daring to live unfettered in relation to the sea, loving it and throwing himself at it and, especially where sharks are concerned, striving to understand their innate curiosity and cautiousness, which far exceeds their menace, and being willing to encounter them in their world, on their terms, rather than on his own. The enduring image I have of

Glanville comes to me as I sit in the chair on *Saltaire,* and it could be a vision of any of these deckhands: I see a great marlin break free behind the boat, coming out glistening and huge, black and sparkling in the sunlight, and I see Glanville take the leader in hand like a bridle, cut the line with a flick of his wrist, and, in one smooth, slow motion, step up onto the stern and throw himself off the boat onto the back of the fish as it sails past, and he rides the fish bareback into the sea.

4

The wind has been blowing a steady twenty-five knots for three days, sculpting the seas off the rim of reefs into a glorious tableau of whipped peaks, indigo blue. I head out on the sportfisher *Nomad* with Damon at the helm, the two mates—Deano and Ed—tending the lines, and the three Australians as my shipmates. We beat our way out through a garden of giant chrysanthemums, and I feel something in me, an inkling: *Maybe today is the day.*

We are armed with the equivalent of a marlin smorgasbord: a number of truly beautiful queenfish, each close to thirty-five inches, and several wahoo four feet long, and a medium Spanish mackerel, and a tuna. We settle in, trolling south along Yonge and No Name reefs under zinc cloud patches moving offshore, the blue sky opening up and the ocean becoming a dazzling field of sequins and pearls. Flying fish—half a foot long and larger than the first ones I saw—emerge in whole schools with the sound of sudden rain.

While Brett sits in the chair through the first round, I talk with Chris under the flybridge about his diving adventures in South Asia, including a trip to Truk Lagoon, in Micronesia, site of one of World War II's worst naval defeats for the Japanese.

"The lagoon is formed by a circle of reefs," Chris explains. "The Japs used it for protection from the weather, but it was a disaster. The Americans found them and bombed them to hell for two days. We went diving with a charter, and there were wrecks everywhere, absolutely smashed. We dove down to some kind of Japanese cruiser and went inside with our guide, who lit the way with his flashlight. There were human bones, and in the engine room he shone the light up into the overhead piping, where a human skull was lodged up in the corner. The man it had belonged to had been blown to pieces by the detonation of the bombs coming through the hull. Back on deck, the guide told us a story about an American coming out to dive with him who had been present at the battle. He'd been a bomber and had torpedoed one of the boats, and it was this boat he wanted to dive on. The guide said, 'We took him in there with a party and had a good dive and we headed back, and only when we got to the boat did I realize he had turned back. We dove back down to try to locate him, and we found him inside the boat. He was neutrally buoyant, the tip of his fins on the deck, and he was just sort of leaning forward there, dead. He had breathed his air out and died there among the men he'd killed. His daughter told us later it had bothered him his whole life, ever since the war. He could never come to terms with it.'"

By eleven in the morning we've come south of No Name Reef to the top corner of Ribbon Reef Number 10, running down toward the horizon more than twenty miles. The swells move under us in great heaving ridges, broad on both sides, with fifty feet between the crests. *Saltaire* passes us two hundred yards to starboard, cream-colored on the blue, Vet Bob in the chair working a fish we can't yet see, and then it's out on its side in a froth coming at us, pushing whitewater. It goes under and we watch *Saltaire* bob and totter, at a near standstill close to the reef, working the fish. The sun catches *Saltaire* beautifully, showing her lovely plumpness and curves, and then Tim's backing up hard on the fish, bulldozing a four-foot wall of rolling whitewater with the stern of the boat, up and down the swells. We can hear the engines on the wind from here, and we see Vet Bob in the chair leaning forward with the neck shroud of his desert hat whipping like a towel. Then the fish comes straight up and out behind the boat, quivering like an arrow. *Saltaire* comes up on her and slows its backward chase until Glanville leans over, grabs the leader, and cuts her loose.

By this time we have done one complete rotation and are into our second; I have come up skunked twice now, and it's Chris's turn in the chair. The breeze is strong and the sun—hard white and nearly overhead—has pushed the indigo into the depths and brought up the azure, the *bleu de France,* the royal blue, and the colors are singing, absolutely singing, until

I think the fuse in my eyeballs is going to pop, just fizzle and blow because it's too much. And then, right then, that is when the fish hits.

The fish hits like a gorilla grabbing a candy bar from the grocery rack. It's a slow-moving, patient gorilla, but with gorillas you know that when that big mitt comes out for that candy bar, it's going to take that candy bar with a smooth swiping force that will not be denied, and that's what this fish does. It takes the bait in its mouth and moves off with it, the reel in free spool clicking like a tin drum with a ratchet in it, and Damon tells Ed and Deano to bring in the other lines—*"Bring 'em in. Get 'em in"*—and Brett hops on the center rod and reels, with Ed on the starboard, the port line having got the fish, and the remaining baits come flopping back to the boat as the big fish keeps taking out line while we sit still drifting in the swell.

Now the lines are in and the fish has had her chance to sit down and start her meal, and that's when Damon puts the boat in gear. A sound comes up from under the decks like the deep vibrating bass from a synthesizer. It's like a building symphony of electronic kettledrums and basses, and I have not heard this sound before out of *Nomad,* but neither have I heard her growl before, starting hard from a flat standstill with a big marlin on the line. Roiling whitewater churns out the back of her, and we pick up speed moving forward, the reel starting to go, a moment passing as the bait pulls out of her gullet into her mouth and the hook turns in the corner of her jaw, and now she's hooked—hooked and feeling the pull on her right side for the first time in her life, and off she goes. Damon slows the boat to a stop. She's running at a quick jog under the surface, shaking her bill, the permutations running through her mind as to what might be happening, and then she decides she doesn't need to know and starts to run, really run, going for Wonga north of Cairns, going for Dingo Beach and that's three hundred miles away.

A feeling comes over me as I watch from the flybridge next to Damon: intuition. The way that line is going out, the way that fish is running, this is a big fish. A *big* fish. Holy shit, this is a big fish.

It is at this point that Ed shows his colors, and why he's the top mate on *Nomad.* What comes out of Ed now is the fusion of a Game 7, bottom-of-the-ninth-inning World Series radio announcer and your head corner coach in a boxing match for the heavyweight title. He stands beside Chris, cheering him on, narrating the action, coaching him on what to do—"Wind it on, wind it on! Wind, wind, wind!" and "Get into her, get into her"—and we have not yet seen the fish, but the line is a long, long way out, halfway to the horizon, and so tight you could play "Foggy Mountain Breakdown" on it if you knew how.

Big swells ride toward us, pulsing through like cavalry, leaving nothing in their wake. One of them hits, coming up and over the transom, and Ed hollers, "Hello vicar! That stern the bum!"

The wind is beating tin sheets in our ears.

Then Damon, sighting the fish way out, yells: "Whoa! There it is! It's jumping!" and I look, but all I see is a distant splash at over four hundred yards, no fish.

Now Damon's got the engines going, with a deep-throated, heavy saw-ing sound, backing down on her as Chris reels, pushing stern-first through the swells, backing down. Damon's holding back, gauging what the fish will do—run at us, maybe, or go off to one side—but she keeps going straight back of us, the bright neon line angling out almost flat. She's on the surface and staying there.

Ed continues to urge Chris on, shouting, "That's it, that's it, get into it! Give it to her now, give it to her! Into it, into it! Big wind, big wind! That's it, come on!" and he sees Chris sucking wind and says to him, "Oh, you're having fun now, aren't you!" Chris sits back in the chair, taking a moment, and Ed keeps on him: "Now get yourself up on over that reel and *wind!* Come on mate, you're doing really well! Wind! Wind! Wind! You've only got nine hundred yards to go!"

Whitewater comes over the transom again and Ed is soaked, shouting, "Yeah! That's what we like!" and Clarkie and Brett howl for their mate. I'm up on the flybridge with Damon and I can see Chris bent over in the chair, straining against the reel, winding, winding, as though he's wrestling one pissed-off badger on his lap.

Chris is winding what is affectionately known as "the square reel." With any big fish, the round reel becomes difficult to crank around so that all you can do is push up, push forward, push down, and pull back as though following the outline of a square. Right now he feels as if fire ants are marching in long, torchlit processions deep inside his forearms.

Damon calls down to Chris, "If he goes and starts to jump or anything and you need to get the line back quick, go into high." The reels have two speeds, controlled by a lever that engages one gear or the other. Damon couldn't have warned him sooner. "Whoa, there he is!" he shouts, and I look out to see, about two hundred yards back, a broad spume of whitewater as though someone had just driven a car at high speed off the end of a pier. Now Damon drops the hammer on the engines, their deep kettledrum song rising up even louder.

Somewhere back of the stern, men are throwing garbage barrels of water at us. Ed shouts, "I can see the top-shot marker!" which means the fish is off about a hundred yards. "You're doing beautiful work! You're going to be stuffed before you get out of that chair!"

"I can see him!" Damon says, spotting a tar-brown smear through the water way out, and Ed confirms, "He's out on the surface, not far now, keep it going—"

The engines drive, drive the boat stern-down, and then Ed calls out, "I can see the leader; keep it coming!" and that's when I see the smear, about eighty feet back under the waves, brown as a Tootsie Roll, just a glimpse, and now Ed gets loud: *"Wind it on! Wind it on!"*

Damon has the throttles flat knackered, and it sounds like an orchestra of nothing but those big basses and kettledrums, the music growing terrible and dark, and the fish continues to pull and we keep coming back on it, and now the line is tilting in a steepening angle as we gain on her. When the leader comes out of the water, Ed leans over with his gloved hand to take it, and that's when, for the first time, we get a sense of her.

"That's a good fish—that's a *big* fish!" Damon yells, and he's seen plenty of them.

We all see it, down there smeared and brown, looking like a log fifteen feet under.

Damon shouts, "Look at the size of this one!" as Ed hauls on the line with both hands, trying to bring her closer. The boys on deck are hollering and shouting, and I'm braying like a mule. Damon exclaims, "That's *big!*

That's a *good fish!* That's bloody eight hundred!" and under the water the fish snaps her mighty head.

Then, that is when it all unfolds. The fish angles her head up, tail lowering, dorsal fin clearing the surface, and turns on the full power. All of her, all the girth and length of half a ton, comes up out of the water as she stands on her tail, head throttling back and forth, her body like a great black tower rising up out of the sea. Her bill is like a long black truncheon, thick as a man's arm, her scimitar pectoral fins out stiff to the side and all the dichroic and diffusing scintillations of light coming off her skin, which no camera, no matter how good, will ever capture. She is jade green, violet, and tar brown across her heavy back, silver ingot flashing on her sides, with a fistful of glistening, thin black tubes (*Pennella* parasites) crowded at the base of her dorsal fin, giving her the appearance of being encrusted with age. The rays of her dorsal fin are black with glowing purple in between, and as she reaches her full height she begins to crumble, the tower falling over to the right, and down she splashes, beating her tail, plowing a deep, curving furrow through the sea, driving whitewater like a speedboat. She surges out and dives under again, and from there, with the boat in a state of utter pandemonium, all of us hollering, she lights out full bore for the other end of the world. Damon revises his estimate up to nine hundred as the top-shot marker fires out of the rod like a shell followed by a hundred yards of neon green line, and then she blows out of the water way back, up and out, head snapping at an all-out sprint. Damon jams on the throttles, nearly snapping the shafts, and Ed yells, *"Get those turbos humming!"* as the bass cellos and kettles start going again, fierce and ominous, but the fish is leaving us behind, way behind, and Ed shouts in sheer glee, "She's having a go!"

We can see off in the distance the sportfisher *Ningaloo* out at seven hundred yards, rocking and tilting obliquely as she comes across, long white outriggers whipping as she rides the swells. The fish is headed for her, blazing under the surface. Ed yells in Chris's ear, *"Just think what you'll tell all the kids in school!"* but then cries out, "He's headed for the bow of that other bastard! Get him back! Come on, get him!" You can't help but feel as if you're at the track and the ponies have come around the bend headed for home and you've got the second mortgage riding on the winner.

"Wiiiiiind!" Ed roars and we are all cheering Chris on. The brown blur of the fish continues running toward *Ningaloo,* and Ed says in alarm, "She's gonna jump in their spread!" but *Ningaloo* runs past, dragging her baits and lines away, and the fish is clear. How Chris's arm hasn't fallen off I don't know, but he keeps at it, winding, winding, bent over the reel, pulling back, and unbelievably we now begin to gain on her. The turbos are going full-throated now, drawing pure oxygen, the gears grinding like a tractor trailer's, and slowly, slowly, we close on her. She's twenty feet under, sixty feet back, now only forty feet back, and now she's twenty feet, she's there—right there, for chrissake—ten feet back, and Ed leans over again, grabs the leader, and hauls. She floats up level from fifteen feet down like a great brown waterlogged sequoia coming up from the bottom of a lake.

Good Lord, she's huge. I couldn't for the life of me get my arms around her head. She pauses for a moment under the surface as Ed grabs another four feet of line and hauls, but she'll have none of it. Up, up she comes, head thrashing, body writhing, plowing out and around in a big semicircle, pink bubblegum of her mouth showing, and she's curving now, coming back at the boat. "Watch out!" I yell to Damon (I think, or the guys on deck—somebody), but she stops ten feet shy of smashing through the starboard windows and goes under. She goes down eight feet, rights herself, and runs parallel to the boat. With *Nomad*'s stern swinging away and blocking the wind, a window opens up into the sea and I see her down there in all her beauty—eleven, twelve feet long, fins lit up brilliant electric blue, big hump under her dorsal, long razorback fin running down toward her tail, and next to me Damon says, "That's a big fish. That's huge!" She goes under and then, with two massive tail beats, strokes off into the depths, bending the rod over and nearly taking Ed with her, and putting a brutal crunch on the bearings in the reel. "Let him go, Ed," Damon says, then adds, "That thing's huge! That's got to be pretty well close to a grand!"

For all the imagining, all the dreaming I have done about the sea, for all the books read and images absorbed, there is nothing, simply nothing, like seeing the living thing. I feel as if I have been whisked to a mountaintop where, against all probability, the sky has opened above me, illuminating the earth and sea below, and one—just one, just a single mystery of the great fish—has been revealed to me.

Ed turns to face us on the flybridge, raising his two arms in victory, and screams, "*Yeah!* If we hadn't seen that little one this morning, we might not be on this one now," he says. "That's cool!"

On deck, Clarkie is doing his happy giant laugh while Brett, Deano, and Chris are all howling and carrying on. Somebody get the champagne. The fish is still on, taking out line, the reel clicking slower as it dives to a depth of about eighty feet.

Ed looks out at the line and says, "All right now, he's gone far, and I want to have another go at him. Wind!" and we are back into the game. The boat and the fish circle each other, pirouetting in a slow dance until Damon finally says, "We should probably take our next opportunity—"

"Cut her off?" Ed asks.

"Yeah. Our luck has served us well so far."

The power of this fish strains credibility. Forty minutes into the fight, she has run out and back, well over a thousand yards, dozens of times, against the braking power of the reel, against a healthy man, against this boat, and still she takes line. It goes on and on, the fish seeming never to tire while we—and Chris—certainly do. We are no match for her, and it would take us hours to bring her to the transom so we could cut her off. Then there is a sudden release of tension as she breaks the line. Chris reels in the tag end, which comes up severed midway on the leader. Ed takes hold of it, inspects it, and says, "Tail": She got a turn of the five-hundred-pound clear monofilament line wrapped around her scythe of a tail and simply cut through it.

We all gather around, congratulating and shaking hands with Chris, who looks like he's gone the full twelve rounds. He is sweating and exhausted, right arm stiff, hand frozen in a claw, but the look on his face—on all our faces—is one of pure joy. He slides out of the chair, pretending to collapse on weak legs, and slides over to the gunwale where he sits, cap back, smiling and spent.

What I will probably never understand is why I should have been so blessed as to witness what happens some forty-five minutes later, after Brett has assumed the chair. As the queenies track like ice-skaters down the waves, a marlin suddenly comes across onto one of them in a blur—a marlin bigger even than the one Chris just spent an hour fighting. The marlin takes the bait full bore, having charged it from maybe a hundred feet off. As it roars away with the queenie in its mouth, the boat instantly descends into chaos. The line streams and streams away, steady and hard as though no drag were on it, and then there she is looking at us from five football fields away, her great truck-door head coming out of the waves, tossing back and forth, wind blowing water off of her in streamers like silver tresses. She dives and comes out again eight times, and after coming across four hundred yards, she turns back in the other direction and shows us what the full afterburners on a marlin can do. That fish, that incredible fish, flees with the green line to the right, fifteen or twenty feet under the surface, a quarter of a mile away, and we watch the line traverse parallel to the horizon at blistering, unfathomable speed. I raise my old Nikon with the long, heavy lens on it, thinking, *I've missed every one of her head shakes so far, but I will be damned if I miss this shot,* and I dial it in on the end of the line, way the hell out, because the line is coming up and I know she's going to jump. Then in an explosion of spray, she bursts clear out of the sea like a gleaming silver missile and I fire my shot and I get her, and as she leaps, a chasm opens up under her, the deep trough of a wave, and with that yawning gap she breaks the bonds of the Earth and is flying.

The belly of that fish hits at a minimum fifteen feet in the air. She is eleven hundred pounds, over twelve feet long, and easily flies sixty feet. In my mind this is how I will always see her: rising out of the windy sea, fins spread, mouth open, tail beating, head wagging side to side as she arcs up, whole body undulating as she hits the apex of her jump—glorious, supreme, the queen of the ocean, shining in the absolute divine power of Nature.

And it is at that moment that I feel my own soul open its wings, throw itself against its bony cage, and escape out of me in a rush to fly after that fish. Part of me, I know, will remain out there somewhere off Ribbon Reef Number 10 until the end of my days.

For there, before my eyes, was the fish I had dreamed of since I was a boy, coming out of the sea like a flying horse—free, resplendent, dreamlike, untouchable.

She had spat the hook, and she was free.

The Last Voyage of *Primetime*

Two Hundred Miles off the Coast of New Zealand

> Greet yourself
> In your thousand other forms
> As you mount the hidden tide and travel
> Back home.
>
> —Hafiz
> (translated by Daniel Ladinsky),
> "All the Hemispheres"

1

The faces of the sea are infinite, and we shall never know its story, nor its fate, nor all its myriad dispositions, and if we think we know it because we have walked upon its shores, fished its depths, survived its storms, studied and collected it or spent seasons in its embrace, still we cannot say we truly "know the sea," because it is, indeed, as Lovecraft wrote, "more ancient than the mountains, and freighted with the memories and the dreams of Time," and such things are not for humankind to know.

But if time dreams, and if time has memories, then time knows, as only we can guess, that the greatest of all fish still living in the sea is not the bluefin tuna, for all its power and sublime racing design, or any of the clan of marlin, for all their delicate rapier beauty, their titanic size, their shimmering colors, and their ability to fly. I believe, as do many others, that they are all overshadowed by the broadbill swordfish—the gladiator, old *Xiphias*—in whom greatness is expressed not by speed or size or color or beauty but by spirit and deed.

In the far southern corner of the globe lives a man who is likely the greatest swordfishing captain on rod and reel who has ever lived. John Gregory has put his clients on—and landed—more five-hundred-pound-or-greater swordfish in the world than anyone. Since 2001, he has landed 138 swordfish, 40 percent of them over a quarter-ton in weight, the largest of them just under eight hundred pounds. There is no one else fishing in New Zealand, much less the world, who has achieved anything close to this record. One of the best places on the globe to fish for swordfish on rod and reel is off Florida, but there the fish are generally in the one-hundred-to-three-hundred-pound range, and caught within view of the lights of Miami. The great captains off Peru and Chile in the 1950s and 1960s landed many swordfish, among them some of the largest that have ever been taken. They fished in wooden boats with linen line and hickory rods, within relative proximity of the shore, often within view of the coast. But the seas they fished were not yet besieged, as today's are, and in all likelihood there were more huge swordfish to be caught then than there are now.

All factors considered, there is no one on Earth today who can touch John Gregory. There is no other captain I know of who will take a fifty-eight-foot sportfisher with a crew of two, plus one or maybe two anglers, three hundred miles from port, two hundred miles offshore from the far northern tip of New Zealand, out into unmapped, unnamed nowhere, well beyond the reach of help should problems arise, and who will fish literally twenty-four hours a day for a week, and sometimes as long as ten days. Who will load five hundred gallons of extra diesel fuel in three large bladders on deck for the journey. Who will, after fishing through the night, start at dawn trolling jet heads for marlin just to pass the time until night comes again, because it is night—and specifically swordfish—that is the real purpose of the campaign. And who, after playing and releasing marlin and anything else that comes up during the day, will switch back over with squid at dusk to fish for swordfish in the night sea, his real workday having begun. He and his clients and crew will come back in not because they have finished, but only to refuel and resupply, and then they will turn around within a day, head back out, and do it all over again.

There is fishing, and then there is swordfishing in the black heart of the sea, in the mighty ocean, and the only boat you will find out there, pale in the moonlight, is *Primetime,* with John Gregory at her helm.

There are not many people hard-core enough to go with him. There is no retreat out there; there is nowhere to hide. If they get caught in the weather then they ride the weather out, and it has to be extremely bad and unpromising weather for John Gregory to even think of steaming for the outskirts of it to wait until it blows through. He will not only ride out bad weather—twenty-foot waves in fifty-knot winds or worse—he will ride it out *and keep fishing in it,* and it is only a very hardy few who will want to be out in that kind of blow, a very few who have that special, rare thing in them that turns on at the thought of leaving the civilized, controlled world behind and going into the wild. If a person is built like this, if he feels this in relation to the sea, and especially in relation to going fishing offshore, then there is simply no one else to choose. He must go with John Gregory.

I am determined to join Gregory on one of his trips, but the problem is how. When I first talk with him, he is on his cell phone within range of the coast, steering from the helm on the flybridge of *Primetime.* He makes it clear that he is through with his business, because to keep the operation going has simply become impossible: Insurance costs him $700 per week and higher when he goes to sea, and it costs $25,000 just to get the boat ready with all the permits, permissions, licenses, maintenance, and systems checks. That sum doesn't even include the payments on the boat, the crew expenses, food, fuel, and everything else. The past year, he has been stricken with a tunneling growth, a tumor that affects the deep, fleshy parts of his back and buttocks and extends deep into his legs. It was diagnosed as benign, but he is fighting it with everything he's got, including drugs and multiple surgeries. He's done the math and decided he's through and is going to sell the boat. He's had a good run, but it's over.

After hanging up with Gregory, I accept the fact that my longed-for trip isn't going to happen, that it was simply not my fate. In any case, I would never have had enough money to fund it. Under the circumstances, the best I can do is talk to people who have gone out with him and tell their stories. I get names from John and exchange e-mails with a few of them, and I have a few chats by phone. One man in particular, a Belgian—Michel—has fished all over the world for swordfish, from Venezuela to Florida and a number of times off New Zealand, with *Primetime* and other boats. He has fished for black marlin off the Great Barrier Reef and for striped marlin off Manzanillo, but it is swordfish that he sees when he closes his eyes. A giant six-hundred-pound swordfish, which he caught on *Primetime*, is mounted on the wall leading to his study, his "fishing room," where he keeps the books, artifacts, and memorabilia of all his thirty-five years of involvement in the sport, and especially of his pursuit of swordfish. When he tells me why he fishes, what draws him to the sea and why he goes with John Gregory as far out as he does, I hear it in his voice—that he is drawn to it for the same reasons I am. I can tell he knows the pure joy of going out there and being in the weather and seeing the fish, and so I decide it will be Michel that I interview. We exchange letters and he sends me video from his last trip, and I get enough information for a portrait of Gregory.

When it is nearly finished, however, I learn from John that Michel has decided to go out a final time to see if he can break the fifteen-kilogram-line world record for swordfish.

I am thrilled for Michel and send him my good wishes and congratulations. A few days later, though, an idea has wormed its way into my head—an idea that is presumptuous and out of character for me. But these are swordfish and I can't rid myself of it. I send an e-mail to Michel with a simple proposal: Let me come with you. Take me fishing with you on this last voyage of *Primetime*. All I can promise is to get myself to New Zealand and shoot the best video I can as a record of the trip.

I do not hear from Michel for a few days, and when he writes back he expresses a completely understandable hesitation. I am an unknown quantity, and to spend a week on a fifty-eight-foot boat with a stranger, whose seaworthiness and moods and disposition he does not know, is a huge gamble, especially when he's paying a king's ransom for this last opportunity to fish with men he has grown close to. In my e-mail I had written, "I hope it is not too forward of me to propose this," and in his response he writes, "We are on the limit actually" and "I am very reluctant to take chances to spoil the expedition."

Regret burns in me. I write back to Michel: "That we are on the limit, I think suggests it is best that you take this last journey in the companionship of familiar friends. I would not want to jeopardize that for you, even for a short period of time." I send the e-mail and consider that I have very likely lost the positive regard of a man I respect.

He, however, responds with the kindness and generosity for which I will always remember him: "Thank you very much for your answer and for your understanding," he writes. "Actually, I appreciate it very much. So much that now, when I know you realize the meaning of all this, I'm ready to 'take the risk' to have you on board with us."

And with that I realize the impossible is going to happen: I am going to New Zealand, to that lonely paradise in the corner of the ocean hemisphere, and I am going to fish on *Primetime* with John Gregory.

2

I land in Auckland thirty-two hours after I started my journey from the East Coast of the United States, having covered more than a third of the distance around the planet, and immediately I make my way to the short regional turboprop link from Auckland to Kerikeri. From ten thousand feet up I see the Poor Knights, an offshore marine reserve surrounding a cluster of islands where on a previous trip I dived and saw the incredible fecundity of life within its protected boundaries. This included a massive school of jack crevalle ten thousand strong, feeding on small shrimp at the surface.

I arrive at my lodging at the Kerikeri Homestead Motel, fall into bed, and promptly sleep seven hours, waking to the cool, early-evening breeze finding its way through the blinds. Out on the terrace, I marvel at the overwhelming lush greenness of this country, the air literally sweet with mild, warm, earthen fragrances. A faint haze is discernible against the rolling ridgeline in the distance. The squat, plunging hills of Kerikeri, with their mottling of open field and pasture, punctuated by stands of native New Zealand cedars and tall, thin-leaved rimu trees, are refreshingly, gratifyingly quiet. I hear the chortling of birds, something that sounds like a cricket but with more of a hollow wood pop, and the comforting rustle of a light breeze through the leaves. After a quick dinner at a nearby restaurant, I head back to bed.

I wake the next day at 7:00 A.M., shower, make coffee, and begin cleaning and repacking my equipment, readying for our departure later in the day. A high-pressure system sits over the whole country, promising good weather for the next half a week, if not longer. The weather is sunny, with patches of cloud hugging the coast, the temperature again in the high fifties. The threat of a last-minute disaster will loom in my mind until I am on the boat with Michel and John and we are leaving Whangaroa Harbour.

Just before noon, I'm picked up by a local taxi driver, Alec, and taken to the Kerikeri airport to meet Michel. I watch as his flight angles down and lands, then see him emerge from the doorway of the plane, an unassuming man, gray-haired, sturdy at about five-eight, and with few bags, having packed lightly for the journey.

After he greets me warmly, we load our things into the taxi and set off on the forty-minute drive to Whangaroa, passing through forests and patches of recently clear-cut hillsides between Te Whau and Orotere, with vistas of lumpy ridgelines opening and closing, and steep green hillsides towering beside us as we drop in elevation to the coast. Alec tells us about Minerva Reef and the abundance of nine-foot sharks that swarm in over the shallows in pursuit of the large crayfish that live there. When we reach the small town of Whangaroa, he tells us they are thinking about moving it. Silting of the river and overcutting of the steep hillside forests have resulted in six-foot-high floodwaters coursing through the town twice in the previous year. The road runs on the right bank of the brackish river, and off in the bay we see the acres of oyster racks that are partly to blame for the flooding. They've slowed the river's flow, causing its silt load to drop out, almost damming the mouth and pushing floodwaters onto the plain and into Whangaroa.

Lovely wooden sailing vessels and pleasure boats are moored in the river, and behind them the steep hills rise and fall into the distance, round-topped, green and yellow, with patches of red cliffs showing through. At the harbor we unload our bags, bidding good-bye to Alec, who will pick us up in a week's time, and we wheel our things down onto the wide dock. There, standing off a ways, turning slowly in the bay, is *Primetime,* looking as big as a locomotive. From the flybridge helm, facing us and working the controls behind his back, John Gregory delicately reverses her to within six inches of the wharf without touching it. The two mates, Mike and Jimmy, take our things, and we step lightly aboard. Then we begin our run out of Whangaroa, past Waihi and Ranfurly bays, and as John increases the throttle I feel the swell and the force of the breeze increase. We are at sea.

Primetime is not a production-line sportfisher. She was custom-built in 2000 to John Gregory's specifications by New Zealand's Salthouse

Boatbuilders. She is fifty-eight feet long, with an extra meter in the cockpit, almost seventeen feet wide, and built like a tank. The cockpit where the fighting chair sits is huge—two hundred square feet—and has enormous underdeck chillers to accommodate whole fish. She cruises at twenty-two knots, draws only three feet, weighs sixty thousand pounds, and is as nimble as a cat. Her agility is due to her twin 695-horsepower Scania diesels. The engines cost $110,000 each and are so exceptional that Gregory has put eighteen thousand hours on them and has yet to have them overhauled. Every time the oil is changed, he has it chemically analyzed. They do not roar. They sing with power.

The boat took a year to build. The hull alone took four months to lay. It has four huge laminated stringers running from bow to stern and a massive central keel, the entire structural framework overlaid in fiberglass mesh interwoven with carbon fiber for strength. Other, production-line boatbuilders will typically lay a hull in a few days, spray chopped-strand fiberglass over it and be done.

The quality on *Primetime* is evident everywhere. The forward-cockpit gunwale and aft-corner cleats, for example, are solid one-piece, fourteen-inch-long anvils cut by water jets from one-and-a-half-inch stainless steel plate. They fold down into slots, out of the way so as not to snag a fishing line when they're not needed, but when folded up and put into service they have a minimum holding strength of thirty tons. They are anchored in rock-hard kauri wood wrapped in carbon fiber. When Gregory ties his heavy fuel bladders onto these, the last thing he wants is for them to pull loose in heavy seas. The majority of production-line cleats, screwed into the gunwale top beam, would tear out like a rotten tooth under a fraction of that strain. The custom stainless cleats cost $3,600 each.

The finger pulls on the stern hatches are longer and wider than stock pulls, so that deckies wearing gloves can more easily work them. They are not entirely recessed for the same reason.

The two tuna tubes on the top of the transom, for live skipjack, are each fed by four-thousand-gallon-per-hour pumps. The tubes are painted black inside to calm the fish, which go in headfirst.

The helm and captain's chair are situated far aft on the flybridge so that Gregory can steer and maneuver the boat during a fight. He has no intention of being "a bus driver," piloting the boat from a useless station too far forward. When desired, however, he can steer the boat and control the throttle from anywhere on deck, using a handheld remote unit.

The fish door at the stern, which allows the mates to bring a fish aboard the boat, is not of the typical design that swings back inside and fastens against the transom. It is a custom-made pocket slider door, extra wide, that recesses and locks into the transom itself. This is the most efficient and least cumbersome design. Gregory has learned from the experience of swordfish smashing the fiberglass of the stern that he needs to line the outside of it with stainless steel plate.

The aft slider door to the main cabin weighs several hundred pounds and is fitted with ten-millimeter-thick armored glass, as are the cabin side windows. This was a refit after *Primetime* took a series of three enormous breaking waves over her when she was out beyond the Three Kings. The waves smashed the boat over on her side, ramming through an air intake, punching in four inches of laminated fiberglass, and tearing everything out of the cockpit, including the fighting chair, until the boat finally righted herself.

Primetime is rated to Lloyd's of London's highest standard for this kind of offshore vessel. Its wiring is all offshore-survey-rated. It has Furuno computer navigation, redundant GPS, Furuno sixty-four-nautical-mile radar, and long-distance reader. Gregory takes extensive precautionary measures in running and maintaining her. He replaces the thermostats on the engines every other year, even though the manufacturer recommends every five years. He has a proper life raft that cost him $7,500 and will accommodate twelve men, has double floors, and carries supplies that would last his typical complement of four or five men a third of a year at sea. Every year he opens it, inspects it, and repacks it, and he replaces the hydrostatic releases every twelve months rather than the recommended thirty-six.

The boat has the complete complement of correct fire equipment and pumping systems, all of which are redundant, and Gregory has obtained all the proper permits, licenses, and insurance, none of which is cheap. He has the right radios and even the right 406 EPIRBs—emergency radio beacons—which provide superb accuracy and dependability in satellite linking, as opposed to the older (and cheaper) 243 EPIRBs, which may or may not get the satellite fix.

John Gregory is a big man—burly at about six foot four and 275 pounds or better, with a shock of white-gray hair somewhat darker at the back. During the day he wears bug-eye sunglasses with an electric blue mirror tint, but when he takes them off he's got chestnut brown eyes, tender as a girl's. He has absolutely no tolerance for mediocrity, slovenliness, carelessness, or incompetence in dealing with these waters, for the simple reason that people's lives are at stake and because any kind of inattentiveness shows a profound lack of respect for where we're going. No one else ventures there, apart from commercial fishing boats. Charters out of Whangaroa and Bay of Islands go only partway out. John has observed, "If a lot of those guys' clients knew the boats were not well maintained and that they lacked the proper safety equipment to be in these waters, they'd never come out here with them. Nor should they. They are not prepared."

Our destination is the area in which the Tasman Sea and the Pacific Ocean converge. We are heading to the northwest out from Whangaroa toward the Three Kings, a small group of islands thirty-five miles north of Cape Reinga, the extreme northern tip of New Zealand. A thousand miles farther are the islands of New Caledonia. Twelve hundred miles west is New South Wales, Australia. Six thousand miles east is Santiago, Chile.

Suffice it to say that beyond the Three Kings there is nothing. We are going to the Three Kings, and then we are going 150 miles beyond.

As land recedes, I talk fishing with Mike, the first mate, who has been with *Primetime* seven years. "Striped marlin will hit your bait inside out," he says. "Blues will do the opposite, coming from the outside in. You can also hear the difference by the sound the reel makes. Blues make it scream like a Ferrari; stripeys don't. Also, on a large stripey the dorsal will be tall, like a sail. On a big blue, the dorsal almost looks undersized."

Mike has developed a theory about the population of swordfish in the area we'll be fishing. There are those that stay in the vicinity of the deep ridges and those that pass through. The ones that stay are beset by a small deepwater shark called a cookiecutter, which takes three-inch-wide, nearly inch-deep circular chunks off the flanks of the swordfish with its sawlike lower jaw. These resident swordfish tend to be squatter and thicker and are battle-scarred. The swordfish that Mike believes pass through the ridges area are smoother, longer, leaner, and unscarred.

When we are about twenty-five miles out, Jimmy reports that the water maker is not functioning correctly, despite having been checked and confirmed before leaving and despite having just been overhauled, with new seals and bearings in the pump unit.

John is not happy. Attempts are made to ascertain and fix the source of the problem, but to no avail. He decides to turn back and is on the cell phone talking to the mechanic the second we are in range. He does so in polite tones, but his orders to the crew are a bit more curt. John Gregory, more than any captain I've sailed with, absolutely commands his vessel. He is clear, concise, and firm, and his crew jumps to it, partly out of fear, largely out of respect, and because they themselves are absolute professionals. Gregory decides to top off our fuel when we are in the harbor, even though we've burned only a hundred gallons of a maximum capacity of 1,800. This is not a necessary step. We could even continue without the water maker, rationing water and limiting showers, but in both cases it is most prudent to deal with the problems, to be conservative, to be prepared. Being the captain he is, this is exactly what John Gregory does.

3

We get the water-maker pump fixed late that afternoon and again take off from Whangaroa. As we steam out of port, through the islands and out the mouth, the crew and John are on edge, eager to begin fishing and anxious to please Michel. He is *Primetime*'s best client, the one who has returned more than any other, and the one with whom they most enjoy being at sea. He is a true gentleman, soft-spoken, considerate, thoughtful, and exceedingly generous. Each night he and I will sit down to dinner together and split a bottle of his wine, discussing books he's reading and my own past and family. At this point in his life he takes more pleasure in letting others have the experience of catching and releasing marlin than he does in fishing for them himself. He not only permits but insists that Jimmy, Mike, and I get in the chair and fish and enjoy ourselves while he plays the role of mate, handling the leader, tagging* the fish, cutting them off.

Michel appreciates how fortunate he is to have been able to pursue this dream, to travel around the world and live long periods of his life at sea, in some of the most remote corners of the globe. He has voyaged through French Polynesia, Tonga, Samoa, Papua New Guinea, the Solomons, Vanuatu, and the Cook Islands. He has fished off South America and Africa, in the Mediterranean, and off the southern shore of Cuba; off the San Blas Islands—the Pearls of Panama—and off Costa Rica to far, remote Cocos. In the past two years he's been several times to Micronesia, which he counts as the most beautiful islands he has ever seen. He's an avid diver and now, finally, after relinquishing control over the daily operations of his company, he has more time to spend with his family and takes the opportunity every chance he gets to cruise the waters of the world with them. He has pursued and caught all the great fish of the sea—black and blue marlin, striped marlin, sailfish, bluefin tuna. Michel started pursuing swordfish twenty-five years ago and has caught twenty-four in his life so far.

"Swordfish are not the same," he explains. "They are erratic, unpredictable. They will come back at you, then reverse in an instant and go off in the other direction, and you cannot stop it. Swordfish have more moves than a bluefin, more power than a bluefin or a marlin, and will outlast anything. They are the most difficult and the rarest to encounter. First of all, they are usually so deep. If you fish during the day, you have to fish way down, or you have to fish at night. In Florida we were fishing sixteen hundred to eighteen hundred feet deep during the day using just a strip of bonito with two hooks in it. Off Venezuela we fished two hundred meters deep and used octopus or sablefish or squid. Or you have to go in cold water, and the weather is usually unpredictable and can get very bad. Here with John, fishing for swordfish is not a day trip; it is truly an expedition. There is little comfort because of the weather. Another obstacle is the price, how expensive it is to run the operation. I am lucky to be able to afford it,

---

*Many sportfishers tag as a way of helping scientists and conservation organizations compile data on species, location, and travel of fish.

but this is one part of John's problem: The season is short, the weather can be nasty, New Zealand is far, and it is expensive."

Michel first came to New Zealand in 2004 after having read a report that a Kiwi boat, *Striker,* had caught a new world-record swordfish on eighty-pound line. The fish weighed 739 pounds and was caught using the technique of slow trolling at night, which was developed off the coast of Kenya. *Striker* broke the record on its first attempt with this method. Michel tried to book the boat but was unable to reach the captain, so he contacted the IGFA, which gave him the name of Geoff Stone, the captain of *Major Tom II* and the current world-record holder, with a fish of 811.8 pounds on eighty-pound line. Michel went fishing on the boat and had three good fights, but the fish all pulled the hook. The captain told him, "With my boat, a forty-footer, I have to stay in the lee of Cape Reinga. We all know the best area is farther north around the Three Kings. I don't dare go out there because of the weather, which can get so bad so quick we would be in trouble. If you really want to catch a record swordfish, you should book *Primetime.*" The morning Michel was leaving Whangaroa, he saw *Primetime* in her berth. He made a phone call, and John came down and showed him the boat and explained how he fished.

On his first trip with John the following year, Michel caught two swordfish weighing 350 pounds and 440 pounds, respectively. The experience changed his life. After returning the next year and catching his 600-pound fish, he got it in his mind to try for the fifteen-kilogram-line world record. He and John realized that, given the average size of the swordfish caught beyond the Kings, and given the current record for the fifteen-kilogram-line category—392 pounds—they had a fairly good chance of beating it. As Michel figures, "There is only a very narrow opportunity if you are thinking about trying to better the record for eighty-pound line, and even more rare if you are thinking of trying to best the heavy-tackle all-class world record." That record has stood at 1,182 pounds since 1953, when Louis Marron landed the fish off Inquique, Chile. "And how many trips, and how many swordfish would you have to fight and perhaps kill to try to beat those records?" Michel asks. "No, the window for those categories is very small. But in this fifteen-kilogram category we have a chance.

Last year we were very close, but missed the gaff shot. Last spring, one broke the line after a fight of eight hours forty-five minutes."

As regards the ocean beyond the Three Kings, Michel says, "The conditions can be frightening. You have to rely on a good boat and a good captain or you are in trouble. We go as far as 180 miles beyond the Kings, and even the Kings are not a refuge. You cannot land there, and there is no good anchorage. We are even farther out from the northern tip of New Zealand, and even there you're a hundred miles from the harbor, and there are no decent harbors between the Kings and Whangaroa.

"I rely on John Gregory absolutely," he says. "He has a way to find the fish and to adapt the fishing according to the weather and the conditions. I've witnessed some very good decisions he's made. Sometimes we took risks and it worked very well, and other times we did not take risks and we were right not to. He also knows the bottom like the bottom of his pocket.

"When you see the hard hours the crew puts in, pushing every day and every night, a crew of three, twenty-four hours per day, you realize they are really tough, really passionate men. They like what they do—the crew is sensational and are absolutely dedicated, you cannot imagine to what point. And they are after broadbill first and foremost."

～～～～

With daylight nearly gone, we are twenty-two miles east of the Cape Karikari Light, heading into the southern end of Great Expedition Bay on our way to a location known as the Garden Patch. At around 9:00 P.M., Mike and Jimmy start putting the swordfish baits together. They use a large squid with a sparkly skirt hung over it, with two green Cyalume sticks several feet in front to illuminate the bait and attract the fish. Banks of cloud move across the half-moon; the whole night is infused with a deep indigo blue as foreign stars shine overhead. As Mike lowers the Cyalumes, their green chemical glow trails astern, first bright and focused near the surface, then widening and diffusing as they sink to between two and three hundred feet deep. He calls out "Fire in the hole!" to signal that the baits are down. We troll slowly forward at about two knots.

I sit with John on the flybridge in the soft hush of waves, with the pure, fresh-smelling breeze washing over us. John describes how, when he used to night-dive, he could spot the Cyalume glow of the other divers seventy or eighty meters away in the absolute blackness.

"You take a swordfish," he says, "with that giant, fantastic eye, made for these depths and much greater, made for absolute darkness, and you imagine it can pick up that glow from, what, half a kilometer or more? Much more, I suspect."

On our way out this evening, we received news from two other boats coming in that they got only two marlin in six days. The Kings have been hot all year, but the water temperature has dropped significantly in the past forty-eight hours. I ask John what might have caused this.

"Who knows," he says. "It's the Three Kings. They do what they want."

There are three major banks beyond the Kings—Middlesex, King, and Coby. There the water depth goes from nearly five thousand feet to sixty-five feet in the space of a few miles.

"Middlesex is the worst," John says. "It can get bloody shitty on Middlesex."

There are also deep ocean ridges—the Maria Ridges—running north–south, while far to the east, beyond the South Fiji Basin, is the Havre Trough and then the Kermadec Trench, one of the deepest places on Earth, at just shy of 33,000 feet straight down.

The temperature change and the poor fishing reported by the incoming boats may be due to the wind, which is blowing out of the south and southeast. "We call these southerlies and southeasterlies 'the Kiss of Death,'" John says. "Anything from the south, especially the southeast, it's like turning the fishing off with a light switch."

John knew from the age of ten that he wanted to be a commercial fisherman. At fifteen he went to sea crayfishing and working bottom draggers.

"My father was a staff sergeant major in the New Zealand army, and the family used to vacation down near Coromandel. I would fish all day, every day, down at the wharves and watch the commercial boats come in and unload their catch. Out on the banks trawling sometimes, we would get a large swordfish in the cod end of the net. You have to bring the net up over a large roller at the back of the boat to get it in, and oftentimes the swordfish would have worked its sword out the side of the net and be whacking it around. Bloody dangerous. You'd be a fool to approach a fish like that. It would kill you."

John recalls a video, shot by a commercial fisherman, of two massive tiger sharks attacking a broadbill on the surface. The tigers had taken its tail off, and then one of them made the mistake of coming at the swordfish from the front. It opened the shark up from front to back with one massive swipe of its sword and sent it, according to John, "a bleeding, screaming mess to the bottom." The other shark decided it was no longer interested in the swordfish and moved off.

Another of John's stories concerns a massive swordfish caught on a longline. The fishermen took the section of main line with the fish on it and attached it to a separate fighting line so that they could bring the rest of the longline sections in while they tried to land this fish. They wrapped the fighting line—a rope with a breaking strength of eight hundred pounds—around a hydraulic capstan, the mechanism used to raise the anchors on a ship. Even with the aid of the capstan, it took five hours to bring the fish to the boat. When they brought it up out of the darkness into the light cast by the ship, the fish was gargantuan—by some estimates over a thousand kilos—and promptly broke the line.

John has seen swordfish bills six feet long.

"I've seen monsters come up in the nets when I was commercial fishing," he says. "Swordfish definitely go over 850 kilos. Among the largest I've see was 524 kilos, and that was trunked."

This fish was thirty pounds shy of the all-tackle world record, without its head, tail, fins, and guts.

Swordfish are distinctive not only for their size and strength but for their ferocity and courage, their willingness to turn on an aggressor. On one trip, John and his crew had a 650-pound swordfish on the leader in five minutes and quickly swung two gaffs into it. Mike opened the transom door, and the fish propelled itself into the cockpit area.

"This was a mistake," recalls John. "The fish was totally green, and when it touched the deck, it went absolutely berserk. Its tail smashed in the teak-and-aluminum bait hatches on the cockpit floor—just punched them in."

The fish got its sword under the fighting chair and proceeded to break the welds. It broke free and swung wildly, the sword like a machine scythe slicing back and forth on deck, cutting into the fiberglass gunwales. The crew and clients fled the cockpit area, some running up the stairway to the flybridge, others into the main cabin.

After tearing the place to pieces, the fish ran its sword clear through a large, insulated, custom-made fiberglass storage cooler—easily 125 pounds in weight—and thrashed around with the cooler impaled on its sword until the front part of its face tore completely off under the strain. It bled out and died.

"It was on the leader in five, on the boat in six, and dead in fourteen minutes," recalls Mike. "It was eight minutes of bedlam. That fish—three hundred kilos mind you—nearly threw itself off the boat. It was jumping three feet off the deck."

John tells me, "In those few short moments it did $25,000 worth of damage to the cockpit. It was sobering to see. They are absolutely fearless. I had one come alongside *Primetime*—which is nearly sixty feet long—and lift its head out of the water and smash the side of the boat with its sword. It inflicted several thousand dollars' worth of damage to the air intake. Their power and agility is unparalleled. Marlin are pussycats by comparison. They're just Christmas trees."

Swordfish are not the only extraordinary creature in these waters. John has seen huge thresher sharks, orcas, and colossal and giant squid whose mantles (the bomb-shaped part of the head) were over eight feet long. He has seen marlin come up with their gut cavities completely cleaned out and has heard of sportfishers off this end of New Zealand who have brought up only a head and backbone of a marlin, the rest having been taken by squid.* "The colossal squids hunt in packs," he explains. "That marlin that came up, just head and backbone, might have had three or four colossal squid feeding on it before it was done. Their beaks can cut you apart. I've seen it with the small ones in the tanks with the fresh bait. You get the blue-water spearfishers out here trying to spear marlin underwater. I think they're bloody stupid. I wouldn't want to be in the water with squid that are capable of doing that to you."

---

* For video, see: http://www.youtube.com/watch?v=7f1UQOvblO8. Used courtesy of *The Ultimate Fishing Show* presented by Matt Watson.

The number-one predator of the swordfish is the mako shark, which John, being a Kiwi, pronounces *mock-o*.

"The one thing you have to worry about when you get a sword on the line out here is whether a bloody mako will come after it."

For these instances, John uses tuna bombs, small explosives about the size of an M-80 firework, which ignite underwater after they are lit. Tuna bombs are used by purse seiners to keep sharks away after the tuna are in the net.

There are a lot of makos out here, too.

Where we're going is so far from anywhere, and comparatively so untouched by humans, that it is alive with life. It's as the sea should be: completely wild.

4

I am to bed early but have been assured by Mike and Jimmy that they will wake me if there is any action. My sleep still off because of travel, I wake late at night and wander out onto the back deck. I stay out on deck for hours and see the moon rise. Next to me, behind a fiberglass wall, the cockpit head gurgles and clicks like an old man asleep. Occasionally the reel in the fighting chair ticks once or twice as we ride up a swell and the line tightens. Dim red and white lights glow high on the flybridge mast behind me like candles, and I gaze out over miles of gently heaving moon-lit sea. At one point I look up into the sky and see the moon at the far end of a long, clear tunnel through the clouds, like a faded star deep within a nebula. Michel and Mike have gone to bed, Jimmy is up on the flybridge with John, and I sit on a step over on the starboard gunwale, behind the overhang of the flybridge, out of sight.

Something happens to the sea in darkness. It's as though the sea comes back to itself, as though it were a ghost that returns to where it once lived only in the absence of the living. It is a primordial loneliness, the loneliness of the sea. It's the loneliness of something that has existed for so long, through so many ages, through the reign and demise of so many of its great and fearsome, beautiful and dreamlike children, that it is beyond the grief of it. It's as though it accepted its loneliness and separateness eons ago so that the rise and fall of life no longer pains it, and perhaps no longer even interests it. It breathes, and the wind blows and the waves roll, and the sea gazes at its only real companions: the occasional moon, the passing clouds, the eternal stars, and the blackness of space between all.

We get no hits overnight, but within half an hour of daybreak a big striped marlin hits the right rigger as though it came racing under the boat from the opposite direction and hit the lure full bore. The sea is a confusion of swells fifteen feet high, with about seventy-five feet between the crests, all coming from different directions, the water an ice-pack blue behind the boat but the rest of it a heavily furred, heaving mass the color of carbon steel. The sun is as bright as the open door of a blast furnace. John calls out that he can see the fish jumping—and there, way back, the marlin leaps from a hilltop, silver and silent.

It takes Michel a good fifteen minutes of steady winding, with *Primetime* in reverse, to bring the fish to the boat. Mike leans and grabs the leader, Jimmy quickly tags the marlin, and then Mike guides it to the starboard gunwale and takes it by the bill in his gloved left hand. He uses pliers to remove the hook from its bill, then lets the fish rest, taking in water over its gills. It's a beautiful fish, about 180 pounds, and highly alert. New Zealand probably has the highest average weight of striped marlin in the world and holds a number of records for this fish. It does look like a Christmas tree, as John said, with blazing purples and blues.

Jimmy and Mike working in tandem are extremely well coordinated, with Jimmy on the extra-long tag stick lowering it, never hesitating, and getting his shot in quick and sure to the side of the dorsal. The two men grab and clear lines, switch rods, tag the fish, and orchestrate the action in the cockpit with the precise choreography of chefs in a kitchen during a dinnertime rush. Mike makes sure the fish is ready, eyes angling down into the water before releasing it; then he guides its head away from the boat and watches it take off. In this muted light, the stripey positively shines under water with that preternatural blue glow.

By late that afternoon we can see the Kings in the distance, and the cockpit is soon awash in the scents of brine and sea life as Mike takes out and begins preparing the squid for the night's fishing. They are over a foot long and weigh a pound or two each. He cleans out extraneous tissue from the inside and cuts the tentacles partway back. He sews a large 14/0 J-hook* into the mantle, securing the shank of the hook to the tough flesh at just the right location in the body so that there is nothing anomalous in its appearance. Mike fits the sparkly skirt over the top and rechecks all his work—knots, sewn portions, hook location. It takes him close to half an hour to complete each piece from start to finish.

Mike has the pasty-white pallor and doughy softness of an Englishman raised on fish and chips. He wears a thin gold chain around his neck and a black Jack Daniel's moppy hat that sits tight on his head. Soft midsection notwithstanding, he is the kind of guy to jump into the middle of a fray without a moment's thought. He is possessed of a true gentility, with a touch of the artful dodger. His politeness and appearance belie the fact that he is as hard-core as they come—a 100 percent perfectionistic competitor.

With the Three Kings only five miles off, I climb the stairs to the flybridge to take in the view. The air is filled with the warm, dry scent of herbs and flowers, the perfume of these islands. As we draw within a quarter-mile, I can see that they are, apart from the cliff faces, completely covered in thick, faded green, yellow, and ocher scrub. We steam on, coming along the western side of Great Island and then the northern side of East Island, drawing within a hundred yards of the cliffs. Surf heaves up on the exposed rocks, the seaweed harvest gold and rusty orange. Some of the cliffs are 150 feet tall, ash gray in the higher elevations and with a burnt, aged-charcoal appearance above the water. The place has a Jurassic feel. John explains that the Kings are a reserve, that no one is allowed to set foot on them.

The islands were inhabited by a small band of Maori until 1840, and they figure prominently in traditional Maori beliefs as the final way station for the dead on their return to their mythical homeland of Hawaiki. The Maori believe that the spirits of the dead voyage to the tip of Cape Reinga,

---

*Gregory has chosen to use J-hooks for the swordfish this time because the hookup is more certain and because of the record attempt.

to an ancient pohutukawa tree there. They descend through this gateway to the underworld and travel the seabed, emerging on Great Island, their final opportunity to bid farewell to New Zealand before continuing on.

Eventually we ourselves turn northwest, leaving the Three Kings in our wake. We are fortunate in that the weather, which through midday was windy from the southeast at twenty-five to thirty knots, with waves building, has since improved, and by nightfall the wind has calmed and the sea has settled.

After dinner Mike again carefully lays the Cyalumes and the squid in the water, attaching the downrigger weight and letting the whole apparatus sink behind us. We are now thirty miles northwest of the Kings, heading into blackness.

5

When Mike and Jimmy bring up the gear the next morning, there's a gash from one side of the fifteen-pound lead outrigger weight to the other. The weight is the size of a small Frisbee, and at the point of impact, the swordfish blade went in a good quarter-inch, with the traces of its strike tapering and fading all the way across to the other edge of the disk. On the weight Mike and Jimmy have drawn little eyes and a downturned mouth like that of an unhappy fish, with a message on the tailfin that reads, DO NOT EAT.

Moments later, at about 8:15 A.M., there is massive hit on the port rigger, and the fish proceeds to burn off five hundred yards of line straight to stern, with blistering speed. Then it turns to starboard and sounds but does not jump, which is unusual but not unheard of. Because of its speed I wonder aloud whether it's a blue marlin, and Mike answers, "Oh, yeah. Only a blue can make a reel scream like that."

Jimmy is on this one and quickly finds himself in a protracted tug-of-war. He doesn't bother going harder on the drag but just lets the fish run when it wants to, winding for all he's worth when it comes to a stop. After half an hour we finally see the fish, and it is indeed a blue marlin— a large one, around five hundred pounds and a good eight or nine feet long. It is a far heavier fish than a striped marlin—muscular and broad, more like the build of a black marlin—and has none of the stripey's slender lines.

Michel is on the tag pole this time, wearing the line cutter and pliers on a belt around his waist like a deckhand in the event the fish gets tangled in the line or he has to go for the hook. Michel tags the fish; then Mike, with leader in hand, steers the blue to the starboard gunwale, unhooks it, and pushes the fish off. We have a little celebration for Jimmy—it's the largest blue he's ever caught. Smiling, and barely breathing after the half-hour fight, his only comment is, "Took off like a bloody nut. Did you see that?"

After breakfast, I finally get a chance to talk with Jimmy. He is taller and leaner than Mike, twenty-nine years old, with a strong face of angular planes and a defined jaw. He has the rugged good looks, politeness, and gentle bearing of a cowboy. He owns a small aluminum boat with a small engine that he bought from John, which he uses to fish along the coast off Whangaroa. I can tell by the way he talks that the sea has become his obsession, and he is at that point in his life where he faces the conundrum of choosing whether to live his life at sea or on land. If *Primetime* were going full time, Jimmy would almost certainly work the deck and never look back until he was ready for retirement. For Mike, who has a wife and daughter, that decision has been made.

During the off-season, Jimmy lives in Broome, Western Australia, a coastal town on the edge of the Western Desert, and installs steel roofing on houses and small businesses. The money is very good but the work is brutal, as the temperature can reach 115 degrees Fahrenheit. "On concrete tile roofing, if you slip, you can grab your hammer, turn, and drive the claw into the tiles to stop yourself," Jimmy explains. "Not the case with steel roofing. If you get going on a steel roof, you quickly gain speed and have no chance of getting your claw in. And there are razor-sharp edges to contend with on your way down. If the I-beam gets wet and you slip, well, you're catching it in the nuts or you're going down onto the floor below. The money is so good because other crews from elsewhere in Australia will bid on the jobs, start them, and simply abandon the site halfway through because of the heat, not even look to get paid. Our crew, we do our own jobs and we also do all the cleanup on the other unfinished jobs."

Jimmy began working with John after they were introduced by his sister, who is John's wife's hairdresser. John needed a new crew member—there was a period when he went through a lot of them. As Jimmy recalls, "John asked me, 'Do you have any experience?' I told him what I knew how to do. And he says to me, 'So you don't have any experience.' He thought the lack could actually be a good thing. No undoing bad habits."

John has in fact been irascible the first few days out, although he keeps it under wraps. He is in pain (though not on painkillers) from the wound that is healing from his most recent surgery, which left a void in the flesh of his thigh large enough to hold an aerosol can. He sits on the flybridge in his mirrored blue sunglasses wearing an Aussie-style outback hat, his eyes fixed either on the water behind the boat or on the instrument panel in front of him. He used to smoke four hundred cigarettes a week and drink twenty cups of coffee a day, but he's changed his habits and is down to 269 pounds, from a high of 368.

John does not miss a single detail in the operation and maintenance of his boat. Coming down the stairs, he looks down and sees a chunk the size of a large raisin missing on the bullnose of one of the teak steps. He points to it and says to Mike, "That's happened in the last two days. Do you know what happened?" Mike doesn't. "Yes, last two days," John says to himself, and moves off. You can sense the mild disturbance, the notation in the long, constantly updated checklist on the running condition of his boat. *Primetime* is eight years old and has seen some of the hardest service a craft of its kind can see, and yet it looks as if it came off the production floor the day we set sail.

Gregory is the sort of man, I realize, that you would never want to face in battle. He would be an absolutely formidable adversary—concrete, tactical, strategic, unhesitating, and completely without mercy. If this were a different time, you would find John Gregory at the rank of admiral, commanding a wooden ship of the line in the Royal Navy during the age of Nelson. And he would have been absolutely deadly if you found him opposite you, his ship turning to bring his cannons to bear against you in a broadside. It'd be the last thing you saw.

However daunting his standards, John can look at a young man like Jimmy and see the raw talent and the advantage of being able to shape him into exactly what he wants in a mate. And this is precisely what he's done. Mike and Jimmy are the only crew John uses now, and they are never at rest. They are always alert, either standing on deck watching the lures, in the kitchen prepping the next meal, or chatting with the clients, which is part of their job. Other times they are checking in with John about whether now is a good time to transfer fuel from one of the bladders to the inboard tanks, or they're cleaning the deck, or oiling something, or prepping fresh swordfish bait, or tying on a new leader. They keep a record of each rod and lure, time on reel, wear on the line. At the end of each night, if there has been any action whatsoever on the fifteen-kilogram rod and reel, they will change out the line and leader completely so as to preclude any kind of gear failure getting in the way of Michel's fifteen-kilogram record attempt. The rods have roller guides and are regularly lubed. On the 14/0 swordfish hooks, Mike files flat the inside edge of the hook facing the shank so that the hook will not cut its way out of the fish. John uses only Mustad Demon circle hooks for the marlin, and only Momoi Hi-Catch line.

"We have tested Momoi to destruction," he tells me. "The leaders are all Momoi. They take all the abrasion of the sword and the marlin bills. We have never popped a line on a swordfish."

The reels are Shimano Tiagra 80-wides, one of the best reels in the world. During the day they use the 80s on the chair rods out to the riggers, with Tiagra 50-wides on the gunwale rods. The 80s are cranked all the way down. The only time John lost a fish because of equipment was when they were using Penn reels. Their drags heated up and seized, and the line snapped; it was the last time John used Penns.

John takes no pleasure in killing any of the fish he lands and has all the right tools and gear to prevent injury wherever possible—dehooking devices, line cutters, pliers, etc.—but if a fish has to be killed, then he is unsentimental about it and sees to it that it will be killed safely and correctly. The gaffs Mike and Jimmy bring out for swordfish, should Michel decide to take one rather than release it, are as long as pikes—the longest being eight feet—and they have a single enormous half-inch-diameter stainless-steel-reinforced chrome gaff hook at the end, with a gap between the shank and point of the hook of about twelve inches. They could be confused with weapons from a museum of medieval armament. Jimmy will reach out over the transom and sink them into a swordfish as it flies past. The gaffs are flying gaffs, meaning the entire hook detaches from the pole and remains attached to the boat by an eighteen-foot length of rope anchored to the base of the fighting chair, which is anchored to the cockpit floor and to the hull itself.

Knowing something about offshore fishing and having watched this crew, I think it's fair to say both mates and captain are among the best in the world, if not *the* best. They have a fastidiousness, a vigilance, and an attention to detail that are very difficult to maintain over time, and yet they maintain them. It is these very qualities that make the difference between whether you actually catch fish or spend most of your time soaking line in the water—or lose fish because of avoidable mistakes.

6

I am awakened later that night by the sound of the fifteen-kilogram reel going off. I fly out of bed, grab my camera gear, and get out on deck, where Michel is by the fighting chair, working his arm through his dark green rain jacket. In the low light I see him look at me and smile, eager, while Mike and Jimmy make sure everything is set. The reel is still going. It is four in the morning, with no hint of dawn in the sky.

John flips on the cockpit lights, revealing Jimmy and Mike dressed in short-sleeved, high-collared, long-waisted blue rubber tunics. Mike also wears his special swordfish gear—black stretch pants striped in rings of midnight blue and a faded red hoodie that he wears under the tunic, hood pulled up over his head. The outfit, he swears, has caught a lot of swordfish. The light tool belt carrying pliers and a line cutter is cinched around his waist. Jimmy, likewise wearing the tunic and the belt, also wields the giant gaff. They look like squires attending their knight. Michel has by now taken the chair, and the reel has stopped. Mike keeps the chair turned in the right direction as Michel reels and Jimmy keeps himself poised by the starboard corner, ready to strike with the gaff. When the fish runs in the other direction, Jimmy maneuvers around behind the chair and positions himself in the same crouched stance by the port corner. This goes on for twenty minutes until, behind the boat, there's a flash of bluish silver in the dark. John calls out "Shark," and everything in the cockpit instantly relaxes. Michel reels, and the mako comes up twisting in the prop wash, its eyes glowing green dots. The fish is solid at about 250 pounds. Mike reaches over and with Jimmy's help cuts it loose.

Dawn comes, and the day is completely fresh, with the air crisp and the sun blindingly bright. At precisely 8:00 A.M., a 250-pound striped marlin hits the gear and immediately goes bounding off 150 yards oblique to port, executing fifteen skimming leaps in a row, then taking an additional 200 yards of line. Mike is on this one, reeling with the cold early-morning breeze blowing over him.

At 10:30, another striped marlin, this one even larger, takes one of the lures and executes a great series of half-out-of-the-water jumps and flips against the dazzling sunshine, coming out on the starboard side and leaping beside the boat, high up off the top of a wave. It then swings around and goes under, the reel zinging as it takes line. Then it's up again, 125 yards behind us, leaping and twisting in our direction. This one is Michel's, and both it and the previous marlin are to the transom in less than fifteen minutes. They are very green, and they snap their heads and thrash and beat the water to a froth before Jimmy or Mike can grab their bills and cut them loose.

During the typical midday lull, I sit next to Mike and Jimmy in the cockpit, watching the lines.

"Quickest sword we took was gaffed in six minutes," Mike says. "Fish came up and immediately charged the boat but would turn off at the last second about five meters out. It did this repeatedly, and then it made the mistake of turning in toward the boat, and Stretch—the mate at the time—swung a gaff into it. The fish pulled out five or six gaff shots as quick as we could put them in. We finally got one that stuck and hauled the fish on board, and it was all hands on deck. I took one of the ax handles and began smashing the fish on the head—and they were on the money, too, right over the eyes—and it didn't even slow him down. Not a bit. I must have hit him forty or fifty times, and finally we had him subdued. Fish weighed about 450."

Jimmy relates a similar experience in which he handled the gaff on a fish weighing over five hundred pounds: "I sunk it fourteen times—all good shots—and as soon as I had them in, it tore them out."

Mike recalls one incident in which he grabbed the leader but the fish hauled back so hard that the five-hundred-pound-test stainless steel swivel exploded. Mike rolls up his sleeve to reveal a starburst scar on his forearm. "It just blew apart, little pieces of shrapnel flying."

Mike remembers one fish they had on for ten hours. "It was a good one, over five hundred pounds, and it absolutely routed the angler. The thing is, he wouldn't piss himself. That's what did him in. You can't fight a fish that hard for that long and not have a piss. We kept telling him, 'Just piss yourself, mate, we'll hose you off,' but he wouldn't do it. Of course, this put him in the position of not wanting to take more fluids. He then got dehydrated and slid down from there. At eight and a half hours he was done, absolutely routed, and had to pass off the fish to the next man. At ten hours, we had that fish up behind the transom and gaffed him, but every time I'd lean over to try to get the small gaff in to steer his bill and head into the cockpit, he'd take a shot at my head with his sword, just like that. It was like a guillotine. He was waiting for me."

At just after four in the afternoon, we get a double hit. It is my turn in the chair and I take the rod and see the marlin skittering off behind the boat, and then it's under the surface, running. It's only the second marlin I've ever caught, the first being in Cabo San Lucas, but this one is very different—far stronger and about twice as large. It's on the eighty-pound gear but still it makes me work, and it comes in like the others, fresh and green, and Mike lets it tire itself for a moment before quickly removing the hook and freeing it.

Less than half an hour later, there is yet another strike, and this one is Jimmy's. The sea has settled considerably, and the fish goes long and deep for the end zone, taking hundreds of yards of line, and now it's John's turn to have some fun. He drops the hammers on the Scanias, and we back up hard, the transom bashing walls of water up and over onto Jimmy and into the cockpit. Jimmy is soaked, reeling like crazy, trying to keep up with the belly in the line, bent over the reel while Mike calls out to him, "What've you done, Jimmy? Have you been a bad boy, Jimmy?" We get to the fish quickly—a stripey of about 180 pounds—and it does a beautiful slow-motion leap left to right from one side of the transom to the other, all lit up blue and slender, and then takes off in another burst in the direction of the setting sun.

We have had more fish today than we've had in all the preceding days put together. I am aware of the good mood on the boat, the laughter, the fact that I hardly know what day it is, the feeling that this group of five has come together—or rather, that the four of them, who have fished together so many times before, are back together again enjoying the smooth synchronicity of their team, and that they have welcomed me into their midst.

7

Soon after dinner that evening, the fifteen-kilogram reel suddenly goes off in the cockpit. It is fully dark now, the squid and Cyalumes and downrigger weight have gone down, and the entire atmosphere of the sea has changed from the exuberance of daylight to the hushed, waiting, primordial quality of night. I grab my gear and head out on deck. Mike and Jim are in their blue tunics, kicking gaff ropes under the chair. Michel comes out in his dark blue rubberized pants with the red suspenders, climbs in the chair, clips the harness to the reel, sets himself, and begins to wind. John flips on the cockpit lights and calls out to Michel, "All right to back up?"

"Yeah, yeah, you can run—"

"Back door is open at the moment, John, just so you're aware," Mike calls out. (Jimmy is inside the cabin, so the door is left open until he exits.) It is essential that John know whether the heavy cabin door is open or closed. Anything can happen during a fight: A heavy wave coming in could wreak havoc in the cabin or, worse, endanger the very survival of the boat if it was bad enough. The door is either shut closed or locked open. It is so heavy that if it were left open but unsecured, it would pose a very real danger, easily breaking an arm or smashing a femur if it slid shut as someone was moving through it. The door is always closed during a fight.

Mike looks up at John on the flybridge and says, "That thing was *hemorrhaging*, man—"

"He's got a lot of line out now—"

Jimmy comes out of the cabin, closes the door, and calls out to John, "Closed!"

John starts driving the boat hard back in pulses, and Michel stands up and is leaning over the reel, pumping hard, gaining yards as we barrel into darkness. Spume and mist are flying up into the air from the waves bashing into the transom, mixing with intermittent fogs of smoke from the engines.

The fish is not running like a mako and has made no jumps. Given its driving power, it is very likely that Michel has a good-size swordfish on the line. We can see only thirty feet, maximum, with any clarity, behind the boat. The moon is mostly covered, but when it comes out the atmosphere brightens to a deep blue black, and I can see wave crests and ridges and the far moonlit meadows running in an endless sawtoothed seascape. The seas have calmed from some nights before and are in the four-to-six-foot range, mostly on the lower end.

"This ain't no shark," John calls down.

"No. It certainly isn't," Mike agrees, and then, noticing that Michel's got the line tightened up hard, tells him, "We're on the double, chap, so take it easy." It is more a reminder than a warning, and it's part of Mike's job to make sure Michel is aware of any detail that may require his attention. Any good mate will coach the angler as a reminder to pay attention to the myriad factors and conditions that can make the difference between a successful catch and a loss.

Mike, looking out as far as he can see, suddenly shouts, "He's coming back at us!" Michel stands up and begins to reel furiously, taking in the line as the fish turns and charges in our direction. "He wants a piece of the action," Mike shouts, and about fifty feet back, a green glow appears under the water. Jimmy moves back and forth behind the chair to starboard and port, positioning and repositioning himself, gaff held high.

Mike shouts, "We might get a chance here!" and instantly I hear the Scanias drop an octave from their high, smooth song to a digging burn as John throws the gears from forward to hard reverse. Thirty tons of boat go from churning forward to stopping, then jumping backward. John calls out from overhead, "There he is! I see him in the lights over there!"

Now Michel is pumping on the reel, watching the tension on the line, gathering it all in as fast as he can, and Jimmy has run over on Mike's right, the gaff glinting high in the darkness as Mike ducks under the front of the fighting chair, under Michel's line, turning the chair in the direction of the fish as he goes past, and shouts, "He's coming straight at us, John!" and I hear the engines go from reverse into forward again and we leap ahead, whitewater spewing behind us. The fish is dodging in on us, zigzagging, coming left then right then straight at us.

"Oh, nice fish!" Mike shouts, and ducks under Michel's rod and goes all the way to the port corner. I'm behind Mike at the foot of the spiral stairway to the flybridge. I watch as the fish comes blistering across the back of the boat, forty feet off the stern. Mike cries out, "Look at the speed of it!" and at that second the swordfish turns, as easily and quickly as if it had only thought about turning. It turns at top speed, having covered a distance of about sixty feet in about a second. That fish, cranking from side to side, head and tail moving in that characteristic opposite bending motion of swordfish, turns so quickly I am barely able to keep the video camera on it. The animal flies within three feet of where I stand, shooting under the boat, throwing us into chaos and making a bid to catch the line in the running gear.

I have never in my life seen anything move like that, not even that second grander marlin in Australia. The image that swordfish leaves in my mind is of a gray ghost—long, very heavy through the shoulders, with a beautiful, straight sword over three feet long, lit up faintly to one side of its face in the green glow of the Cyalumes.

When he first sees it turn, Mike cries out, "John, it's running up! It's running up toward the front!" and practically dives at the line as it spins behind Michel and threatens to hang up in the port outrigger stanchion and in the two rods stored in the port-gunwale rod holders.

John yells, "I can't! I can't!" meaning, "I can't do anything, I can't turn in time, I can't move out of the way," but Mike succeeds in getting a hand on the leader and keeping it off the boat and out of the gear. He yells to Michel, "Ease the brake, ease the brake!" meaning, "Come off the drag on the reel or the fish will use the boat to shred the line. Give it slack and let it take the line."

Unbelievably, Mike is able to keep the leader off the boat and out of the gear, and the swordfish does not run under the boat close enough to snag the line in the props or the rudders. It has shot across behind us, turned, shot under, turned again, and rocketed out two hundred feet behind the boat in roughly six seconds. Mike, back at the transom, sights the line out behind the boat and shouts, "Cleared! We're good!" and then turns and says, "Whoa! How did we make that? Check the speed out on that! That was all in one piece! My God! All in one piece, out and back!"

From up top John calls out, "Here he comes again!"

Between the sounds of the transmission clutches mashing, the engines bearing down, the props churning and the sight of the boys in their gear, the spotlights and the maw of darkness, the spray from the transom, the mist, and the smoke from the exhausts, what I see before me looks like a scene of battle.

Now the swordfish begins making repeated runs at us, shooting in, turning, diving, and surfacing far back in an instant at blistering speed. Then it decides to sound and goes down and stays there at about 120 feet deep. Mike comes back and stands halfway up the spiral staircase to the flybridge and says to John, "It's some kind of miracle, mate, that we didn't get chopped off. And shit he was fast! He was like a rocket ship!"

We laugh in disbelief and awe at what we have just witnessed. Mike returns to his post at the transom, and John says to me, "It was like I was saying to you: If the marlin are on the bite, then the swordfish will be, too. And the marlin were on the bite today."

From the deck, Mike calls back to John, "Did you get an idea of size?"

"I was too busy bloody moving, mate."

There is a rubber band on the line marking the fifty-meter point, meaning from that point out, there is fifty meters to the leader, and for the next three-quarters of an hour Michel and the swordfish battle over this marker. This rubber band goes back and forth dozens of times, the fish pulling it out, then stopping, and Michel working the line back on the reel. The fish has dug in and is anywhere from 40 to 120 feet down, and from 10 feet to 80 or 90 feet off the transom. The line twangs as it comes slowly off the reel, sounding like a guitar string being pulled tighter and tighter. It is only fifteen-kilogram line and must be near its breaking strength. But Michel is patient. He lets the fish take line, and when it stops, he reels it in as far as he can and leans back against the rod, pulling. Jimmy feeds water and grapes to him to keep him hydrated and energized. A fight like this could go on for four hours, or six, or twice that long, and the key is to stay ahead of fatigue.

After an hour, the fish starts running up on the surface again, out and back, challenging us. He runs at us and we move away, and he turns. We go back on him and he runs, then turns to come at us, his trajectory traced by the faint green glow. John brings out a cardboard box filled with tuna bombs, each about three inches long, with waterproof fuses and sealed caps so they can be thrown in the water and detonate at depth after sinking. He will use them in the event a shark shows up.

Another fifteen minutes of patient struggle between Michel and the fish, and Mike comes back to discuss with John whether they should make the call now to take the fish if they happen to get a gaff shot. The fish is not an obvious record breaker, although it may be very close, and it is better to make the decision now rather than wait and try to make it in the confusion of the moment. Ultimately it is Michel's call.

John says, "Just tell Michel we're not sure. If we gaff it and it doesn't make it . . . well, we won't get a second chance."

The fish is closer behind the boat now, Michel having gained a good fifty feet and kept it, and it has become a battle of wills. Michel eases the fish up, and the glow is a bright green lurid sphere thirty feet down, and we can see the shape of the swordfish moving in it, blurry and large.

Jimmy confirms the strategy: "I'm just going for it, right?"

Mike says, "It's quite a good size, John—"

"Right. Let's go for it, if we can get him up on top. I can't see him properly—"

Michel brings the swordfish up to twenty feet, but it powers away again, bending the tip of the rod.

This back-and-forth goes on for another forty-five minutes, at which point John says, "I hope he hasn't been hassled." He senses something odd in the way the rod tip moved, and Michel is hauling up on the line, and the glow is rising, and we see the silver shape. Mike reaches for the line, telling Michel to drop the tip of the rod—"Down, Michel! Down!"—and then John's shouting, "It's taken! There's a shark's got him! A bloody shark's got him!"

The swordfish rises to within five feet of the surface, and where its tail used to be is now a stump. Mike is reaching for the line overhead, Jimmy is to his right with the gaff, and then to the port side, thirty feet out, I see something float up from the darkness of the deep. It is gray and as long as a minisub.

"Here's our shark right behind us!" John shouts.

Jimmy reaches over, gets the gaff in the swordfish, and is pulling the pole out, releasing the flying gaff head, when the shark turns toward the boat, coming for the swordfish. Jimmy's got the gaff pole off and throws it behind him, and he's holding the rope with all 350 pounds of the sword-fish as best he can, knowing there's a mako of 900 to 1,000 pounds, ten feet long, coming directly at it. Mike pulls with both hands on the leader and it goes slack. "The hook's pulled, Jimmy! Watch that sword!" Mike opens the transom door as Jimmy struggles with the weight of the sword-fish. I get a look at it and am amazed again at the distortions that happen at sea. It looked small—maybe 150 or 175 pounds—as it first came up thirty feet behind the boat without its tail. But now its sword, the top of its head, and its dorsal fin lurch past the open door, Jimmy struggling to hold its weight, and the sword itself is huge, the dorsal close to twenty inches tall. Jimmy shouts, "Where's that shark gone? Somebody bloody give me a hand!"

Mike hears him and slides quickly between Michel and the chair and jumps to the rear of the cockpit to get the other gaff. Jimmy is a slip away from being in the water, and the fear in his voice is audible. The shark is huge and is still under the stern of the boat. Jimmy turns and shoves his butt against the transom to use his body as a lever against the weight on the rope, and to avoid being dragged in if the shark hits the swordfish again, and then behind him begins the first detonation of the tuna bombs. They have a sharp, steely concussion—*crunk!*—and explode with a blind-ing white flash beneath the water. Jimmy leans forward toward the fighting chair, holding the rope in one hand and reaching under the chair for the hand gaff, and he turns and is about to sink the gaff into the swordfish's head when he looks over the edge and shouts again, "Where's that shark?" Another of the tuna bombs explodes about three feet down—*crunk!*—and Jimmy decides to sink the gaff into the base of the swordfish's bill. As the bombs are going off left and right, Mike gets to the transom with the long gaff and sinks it into the flank of the swordfish. Jimmy pulls with the rope in his left hand and the gaff in his right, and as he heaves, the whole head of the swordfish comes up into the gap of the transom door, and in that instant another tuna bomb detonates immediately behind it, four feet down, lighting up the entire scene in silhouette, revealing that the sword is long and straight, over three and a half feet long. Michel is groaning *"Ohh"* at the shame that it ended this way—that the fish has been killed and has no shot at the record because of the shark. With brute strength, Jimmy twists and heaves the 350-pound fish onto the deck through the door, the last of its life ebbing out of it, the blood pouring out of its stump, thick red oxygenated blood like paint, red and opaque and quickly clotting over the deck. I move onto the deck from the flybridge and watch the swordfish slowly gape its mouth open and shut as it bleeds out. The shark has shredded its back to ribbons, the enormous toothed mouth first sinking in behind the dorsal, then sliding down, shredding flesh until it reached the tail, lopping it off. The silver talons of the two gaffs are in it, the fish is dead, and we stand around the corpse. I know the others feel regret for the swordfish, for the way this ended. So do I. I also feel the counterbalance to what I experienced in Australia. There, I was changed by joy and the beauty of what I saw. Here, here I am struck with awe and quieted by sorrow at the loss of this animal.

Later Mike will say to me: "Marlin, when they come to the surface and see the boat, say to themselves, 'I must flee the great white elephant.' The swordfish is different. When the swordfish sees the boat it says to itself, 'I must confront the great white elephant—and kill it.' They have the heart of warriors."

⌐⌐⌐⌐⌐

We fished through a good part of that night. On the next drop, the squid was hit by another mako before it was even down, and we saw the shark coming vertically out of the water eight times in the moonlight, 150 feet back. It leapt and splashed silently in its wildness across the moonlit sea, and I admired it no less than the swordfish or any of the marlin I'd seen, and there was yet another mako after that.

In the following days, we got another striped marlin, and Mike caught a beautiful blue marlin at over five hundred pounds that got its tail wrapped and died on the line, and it took Mike more than two hours to bring the fish to the surface. I remember feeling something was off, the way the line angled straight down without movement, and Mike saying, "I don't like this," and John saying, "Something's off. Something's wrong. Bloody thing's tail-wrapped." Still I waited, thinking, *No, it's just digging in. It's just a strong fish, it's got its head down,* and I maintained that hope over the hours it took to get the fish up. Still I hoped when I saw the fish on the surface floating like a bronze log, and even when we brought it to the side of the boat I looked for some flicker in its eye, some movement of the jaw, and I thought I saw something as we tried to revive it. But I hadn't seen anything; it was dead. I could feel the regret and the pity move through all of us. None of us wanted this. It's not what we intended. And then I was angry with myself because the idea crossed my mind that if the animal was dead, perhaps I could take the bill as a way of remembering it, as something I could use to show people, and then I was disgusted with myself. *Just let it go,* I thought. We pushed the fish off and watched it sink, going back into the cycle to become shark food or squid fodder, but back into the cycle nonetheless, and the boat was quiet as the lines were put back out.

The loss of this fish, added to all I'd seen in my travels, left a sick feeling in me. The weather turned at the end of the week and we headed back to Whangaroa. Michel invited me to stay and go out on the final leg of the voyage, and every part of me wanted to, but I had to get back to my job in the States.

I got a note later from Michel saying that when they went back out the next week, they encountered a pod of orcas over one of the banks where they'd gone to catch a bottom fish called a bluenose. The orcas snacked on the bluenose as they pulled them up, and never touched the hooks. Michel wrote that he got into the longest fight of his life, one that lasted almost sixteen hours, but ultimately the swordfish was simply too large to bring in. When I talked to Mike about it later, he told me they got only two glimpses of it, and he had no doubt it would have been the record on fifteen-kilogram line for decades, maybe forever. When I asked him how big it was, he said he hated to guess weights and normally wouldn't do it. "But on the record, conservative," he said, "it was 650 pounds easy— 650 all day long."

Off the record, he said it was more. A lot more.

Epilogue

In his essay "Death All Day," Richard Rhodes describes his experience as a young man in Kansas, hunting down and shooting coyotes for sport, and then attending a cockfight in the evening. There he witnesses men, women, and children enjoying the spectacle of bloodletting. By the end of it he is nearly sick from all he has seen. He writes:

> There is no darkness of nature so dark as the darkness of men . . . We stare, unblinking eyes, at dying beasts and see only casual transformations . . . *The plains of Kansas are even lonelier than the sea.* They are lonely as men are lonely who seek, as we seek beyond all civility, blood to freshen us, wounds to warm our hands . . . We would eat the moon, rape the sun if we could. Hemingway did well to apologize, but not to the Christians.

Rhodes's reference to the famous author's apology draws from the opening of Hemingway's classic book on bullfighting in Spain, *Death in the Afternoon,* in which Hemingway acknowledges that modern Christian morality will likely judge the bullfight to be indefensible for its cruelty. Rhodes reads this as an ironic and disingenuous apology on Hemingway's part. While there is evidence to support this interpretation, one can also argue that Hemingway had sincere intentions to "tell honestly the things I have found true" about bullfighting. Hemingway asserts that "whoever reads this can only make such a judgment when he, or she, has seen the things that are spoken of and knows truly what their reactions to them would be." Rhodes's response, after his day of witnessing the slaughter in Kansas, is that it is not the Christians to whom Hemingway owes an apology, but rather, it is all of us who owe an apology to the animals of the Earth, for all that we inflict on them.

Entering the second decade of the twenty-first century, we are in danger of fulfilling all the terrible portent of the name that Australian paleontologist and environmentalist Tim Flannery suggests for us: "the beast that eats its future." We are, in the history of evolution and in the long story of this planet, the most striking anomaly: Stage by stage, we overthrow Nature's dominion. We have done this so pervasively that we now exceed the restrictions of distance and geography, as well as the magnitude and sheer scale of ecosystems and animal populations, to the point that we overwhelm each of these on a global scale, largely through technology and as a result of our own exploding numbers, but very much as the result of our own ignorance and lack of ability to cooperate to achieve a different outcome.

We might ask how the threshold that has been crossed in the last half-century is any different from the normal processes of evolution and extinction, in which species rise and fall as ecosystems shift and change. The relevant consideration here is not whether it's normal for species to live and die, but whether it is acceptable for us to be the agents of that obliteration. Few of us would argue that it is morally defensible that we degrade ecosystems to the point that they risk or actually result in the extinction of species. From an angle that considers only our own survival, however, one must ask, "Are we not also putting ourselves in grave danger by these actions?"

Of course we are. The evidence has been building for decades that we have entered a dangerous, new, and unstable age, and yet we continue to conduct ourselves as if this were not the case.

The fundamental question at the heart of commercial or sportfishing, fish farming, establishing (or not establishing) marine reserves or national parks, or using animals or animal products in any way is not simply the question of what our right, moral relationship to wilderness and wild creatures should be. It is first and foremost a question of what our relationship *must* be if we intend to survive. Short of a nuclear war or an asteroid strike, the human species is very likely to survive in some way, at some level, in some part of the globe, well into the future, even in the event of massive climate change, famine, war, or pandemic.

But is base survival all we aspire to? How lonely and forsaken will the world be if we are all that remains, staring at one another in our cities, beyond the outskirts of which there exist only the exhausted land and the barren sea, and the forlorn remnants of the once beautiful parade of creatures that shared this world with us?

All the scenarios of doom we encounter on a daily basis numb us with their intensity and frequency and by the fact that for the most part they remain abstract. It is hard enough to picture and mentally grasp a ten-foot-long tuna and what its loss really means in the world, much less get our minds around the import and magnitude of melting ice caps.

But if we intend to do more than just survive, we must contemplate and begin to understand what these things mean. There is no other choice. We must push ourselves to confront and deal with what is happening in the destruction of species and of this Earth.

The central challenge in this is the fact that most of us live in near-total separation from the act and the necessity of killing the food we eat. We have little connection to or understanding of our relationship to other creatures, how we rely on them, and the fact that they are actually sentient beings as opposed to just "resources." We live in near-total isolation from the truth of our reliance not only on other animals but on the relationship *between* animals—on ecosystems, fresh water, clean air; on Nature itself. Given this, can we truly claim to understand Nature, much less act in relation to it in a way that ensures more than just our base survival? And, if what we mean when we talk about Nature is wilderness, then what do we really mean by "wilderness"?

If we think of "true" wilderness as being wild ecosystems that exist free of a governing human influence, then there are many who believe "true wilderness" no longer exists. Jeremy Jackson, director of the Center for Marine Biodiversity and Conservation at the Scripps Institution of Oceanography and one of the preeminent voices in ocean science and conservation, refers to "the myth of oceans as wilderness." Likewise, in *The Unnatural History of the Sea,* marine scientist Callum Roberts discusses how human impacts on local and regional marine ecosystems have been occurring for centuries, and how the seas we know now bear little resemblance to the raucously wild and abundant ocean that existed not so long ago.

There are certainly still wild places on Earth, and I hope this book has succeeded in evoking the richness of some of them—the North Atlantic off Nova Scotia, the Great Barrier Reef, the waters north of New Zealand, the Sea of Cortez. They are "wild" because the creatures that inhabit them are themselves untamed and exist outside human control. True wilderness, however, is wildness that extends across entire ecosystems and involves not just groups of animals but entire landscapes and seascapes, complete cycles of life across generations and throughout the entire web of relationships among creatures. This kind of wilderness, free from our influence—or in which our influence operates within the balance of other species—has largely vanished in the past fifty or sixty years. The disappearance of wilderness has meant not only the loss of an entire world but with it, an essential part of who we were and who we might have been.

It serves no purpose to offer the usual platitudes that if only we commit ourselves, we can reverse this situation. This situation will not be turned around, because the point of no return has already passed. We have changed the world. Nor will I suggest that a long road lies ahead for the dedicated to re-create that world. This will not happen.

What remains is for us to fashion a new world, and the only way the world will be new and different is if we are. We simply must change how we think and how we conduct ourselves if we expect a more hopeful and promising future than the one that presently awaits us.

We are capable of this. We are not only "the beast that eats its future"; we are also the creature that dreams the world into being. We create great works of art, we understand and can learn from history, we can dream of and then create the means to dive seven miles to the bottom of the ocean or exceed the gravitational pull of the planet. We can believe in peace, work toward it, and achieve it. We are capable of compassion, self-sacrifice, and forgiveness. We love our children and have proven again and again that we have the power and the courage to overcome the seemingly impossible not merely for the sake of our own survival but for the sake of what is right. In our behavior toward Nature, we have mistaken "dominion" for "free rein." But our ability to dominate the life-forms of this planet does not release us from responsibility; rather, it entrusts us with the obligation to act wisely in stewardship of the natural world. We have the capacity to extend our affection and our empathy to those beyond our ken, and we have the power to choose to cultivate it.

In the course of my travels and research to understand the causes of overfishing and its impact on the great fish, a consistent pattern emerged: the pattern of corporate/government collusion to exploit resources without regard to science or strict adherence to the precautionary principle. Each of the cases I refer to (Mexico, Nova Scotia, Japan, and the Mediterranean) differs in its specific details, but the overall pattern is one of continuing high-impact exploitation, carried out by corporate industrial fleets, sanctioned by governments, in the face of evident ruin. This process is typically not initiated by design but rather emerges over time as a series of responses to an evolving, complex problem that includes demand for protein, diminishing fish stocks, social and economic factors, scientific misapprehension of the problem, and inadequacy in enforcement and oversight.

Underlying all of these, however, are deep institutional flaws in how some governments operate. They fail to protect against internal corruption and influence by outside private interests, they fail to maintain the defense of common resources and provide for the protection of the common good, and they fail to institute meaningful and effective oversight of fisheries.

The problems of overfishing and the failures of fisheries management are now at an advanced stage and require a sophisticated, coordinated, and dedicated response. The problems continue or worsen in those places where business as usual persists, where science and the precautionary principle are secondary (if they are considered at all), and where governments and corporations work together to uphold the industrial fallacy. The trend tends toward improvement where science and the precautionary principle are used to determine a rebuilding plan, and where a strong mandate, sufficient funding, and adequate enforcement support this plan.

The destruction of the oceans is also very much a result of how we, the general public, collectively think about and behave toward the natural world and how we behave in our role as citizens. Whether it's a dragger captain who fishes while aware of the damage his gear inflicts and still resistant to attempts to find a new way, a recreational angler who doesn't consider how plastic lures and lead weights affect the environments he or she fishes in, a jogger who tosses a plastic bottle he can't be bothered to recycle and which ends up floating in the Great Pacific Garbage Patch, or a homeowner who cares more about having a weedless lawn than about the health of the estuary downstream, we all bear responsibility for the impacts of how we live. We also bear responsibility as citizens for whether or not we hold our governments accountable for their actions and hold ourselves and one another accountable for ethical behavior when it comes to the treatment of other creatures in the exercise of our power.

We must accept accountability where the stability of species and whole ecosystems are endangered because of us. In this new age, one of the most important things to achieve is an understanding of the consequences of the many deaths we inflict, as a means of learning to value again the sanctity of life. This includes a deeper understanding of how our actions inflict pain and suffering on other animals, including fish.

By the same token, we must consider that the creatures of the world have a value in and of themselves, separate from us. They are born to this Earth just as we are, and are children of it no less than we are. We must move away from thinking of other life-forms as "resources" and consider that they are not merely to be used for our entertainment, nourishment, or other benefit, but that they are, indeed, cohabitants of this planet—a planet we do not own but have the privilege of inhabiting, as well as the very real responsibility of protecting.

You could, like me, be unfortunate enough to stumble on a silent war. The trouble is that once you see it, you can't unsee it. And once you've seen it, keeping quiet, saying nothing, becomes as political an act as speaking out. There's no innocence. Either way, you're accountable.

—Arundhati Roy, *Power Politics*

Solutions

There are solutions to the destruction now being wrought upon the world's oceans and their inhabitants. We have, first and foremost as an ally, the incredible fecundity of the oceans themselves and the regenerative powers of Nature. We have also proven in the past that we ourselves are not a lost cause. What follow are a number of policy considerations that apply to fisheries management, commercial fisheries, government, and consumers. Then come specific steps that each of us as consumers can take to decrease our impact on the oceans. Finally, I discuss how sportfishing can be made more humane and offer recommendations for its improvement.

Policy Recommendations

The Fish First: The principle of "The Fish First" means that any harvesting of marine populations that have been determined by independent science to be at or below the critical minimum safe threshold for breeding population should be closed until the stock rebuilds.

To place the health of fish stocks first is not just a responsible environmental stance but also a sound economic one. It recognizes that recreational fishing, commercial fishing, and all associated sectors of the economy rely upon the continued existence of healthy, stable stocks of marine life. The technology that has been applied to harvesting ocean species has not stayed within the realm of what ecosystems can sustain. A policy of "The Fish First" either would involve using intensive industrial methods more sparingly or would support the use of less intensive technologies like handlining.

Rebuild fish stocks beyond MSY: Fisheries have traditionally been managed according to the concept of maximum sustainable yield (MSY), which seeks to maximize the amount of fish that can be extracted from a stock while stopping short of causing the collapse of the stock. This policy hasn't worked for a number of reasons, including flaws in fish reproduction science and stock calculations, a failure to look at entire ecosystems rather than just a single species, and a failure in the political process to adhere to the precautionary principle and the best available third-party science. Given that so many stocks are now rated as heavily fished or overfished, the priority must be on rebuilding them and, where possible, on reestablishing the health of fishing grounds that have been devastated. More equitable distribution of access (possibly facilitated by the buyout of quotas and licenses), paired with the linkage of community ownership of resources, would support the stewardship and sustenance of marine life rather than the exploitation of it for the greatest possible economic gain in the short term. A second phase would involve science-based rebuilding plans that reconstitute fish populations based on whole-ecosystem models. As a complement to the rebuilding plan, it will be critical to set sustained target population figures for fish species not at MSY but at higher levels. This would provide for a margin of error against the unforeseen, including corruption, IUU fishing, disease, and other factors. It makes sense to seek to reestablish fish populations to their former ranges and to fish those stocks at levels that actually support stable, higher populations and higher yields.

Prioritize the northern bluefin tuna: Factors including high market demand and exceptionally high prices are driving the northern bluefin tuna to annihilation. More effective action needs to be taken to shut down breeding grounds during the spawning season in the Gulf of Mexico and the Mediterranean. Organizations like Greenpeace are right to institute campaigns to raise consumer awareness of how the consumption of bluefin tuna is driving the destruction of this species around the world. Canada continues to fail to account for the significant number of northern bluefin that are "shacked" by its longline fleet, and the United States, likewise, continues to allow the commercial harvest of bluefin tuna when the numbers are clearly low enough to indicate that harvesting should stop until the population is rebuilt.

Establish more marine reserves: One of the most powerful measures we can take as stewards of marine life is to protect it against ourselves. This includes guarding it against the failures of our political mechanisms, as well as against simple greed, the unforeseen consequences of new technologies, disease, global warming, and more. The establishment of a robust system of different types of marine reserves—whose configuration, placement, and specific operation are determined by local populations of stakeholders—promises to create local stewards of vital ecosystem areas. The specific goal of protection—for example, a particular rare species of fish or the rejuvenation of cod breeding habitat in the Gulf of Maine—will determine the requirements of size, location, and security. Protective measures could include what are called "time/area closures"—parts of the ocean that are shut down during specific periods, such as breeding season. In some cases, setting aside strict no-fishing reserves is absolutely critical.

Address conflicts of interest and corruption in government management of fisheries: The relationships between governments and corporations in many places in the world undermine the basic concept of the role of democratic government in protecting the common good. An ethical framework and a process of ethics review should be established, and nations held accountable to one another for their ethical management of fisheries—much as nations are held accountable for child labor practices, to use one example. The organization best suited to bring together international members to establish this framework of ethically sound and environmentally sustainable fisheries would be the United Nations Food and Agriculture Organization.

The problem of government-corporate collusion to exploit resources at the expense of the common good and the environment is a more complex issue. International organizations like the UN are not likely to be effective in exerting control over government-corporate relations, nor would this necessarily be desirable. In those countries where the government-corporate relationships are at the heart of the overexploitation of fisheries, it is likely up to the people and the democratic institutions of that country to take on the challenge of confronting this type of corruption.

Practical Steps for Consumers: Know and Go Low

Given the range and severity of environmental and resource issues facing us in the twenty-first century, the argument can be made that it is no longer acceptable to remain ignorant and uninvolved. Choose the issue that means the most to you, get informed about it, and take action to support what you believe is right. The power of a well-informed public engaged in civilized debate is the generative power of democracy and is vital to any significant change.

Where making informed choices about seafood, people often want to know what they can eat responsibly, which requires that the consumer be well informed. Consumers also have the power to use their spending as a means of influencing markets, especially locally. Here are some simple ways to achieve outcomes that are positive for the ocean.

Find a trusted rating source: Find a rating source you can depend on, and know why you can. There are several excellent sources that, as of this writing, emphasize placing the fish first and that I believe are excellent guides. Among the best of these is Monterey Bay Aquarium's Seafood Watch guide,* which you can download by region in the United States. I do not recommend supporting Marine Stewardship Council (MSC) certification because, among other factors, its process allows for some conflicts of interest, and its criteria for approval still allow the use of damaging gear types.

Don't know/Don't buy: Educate yourself about the types of seafood you like to eat. Then, when spending your money, ask for information about the origin, conservation status, and catch method used for the specific product you want to buy. If no information can be given, inform your fishmonger or restaurant server that you're interested in sustainable, high-quality seafood, but you will not buy it without being assured of its origin, its conservation status, and the method by which it was caught. This is a simple but powerful means to influence the economic supply chain.

A cornerstone of being a more powerful consumer is to know your seafood and learn about what you're eating. Bycatch in wild shrimp harvesting, for example, ranges between five and ten pounds of other life killed for every pound of shrimp. If it's farm-raised shrimp, where was it raised? How were the issues of disease and parasites handled? Most farm-raised shrimp comes from Asian countries, and many have poor environmental regulations. Are you willing to eat shrimp whose origin you do not

---

*http://www.montereybayaquarium.org/cr/cr_seafoodwatch/download.aspx.

know, whose quality you cannot be assured of, and whose impact on the environment is likely negative?

Decide which items you're willing to pay more for. Dredges used to harvest scallops, for example, tear up the ocean bottom, but farmed scallops are available, as well as scallops harvested by divers. Both methods involve no bycatch.

Are you willing to eat longlined swordfish, considering the likelihood that bluefin tuna, leatherback sea turtles, and other species were killed in harvesting it? Would you be willing to support and pay a little extra for harpooned swordfish? It's worth the health of marine ecosystems to inform yourself about such issues.

Go low: If you intend to eat seafood, it's important to recognize that not all fish are created equal. Each level of the food chain is known as a "trophic" level. Apex predators like sharks, bluefin tuna, and swordfish are high-trophic-level species, at the top of the food chain. As described in the chapters on South Australia and the Mediterranean, adding a pound of weight to bluefin tuna requires ten to fifteen pounds of other species, like sardines, mackerel, or herring.

By eating lower on the food chain, you are eating from a level that regenerates rapidly, as opposed to the higher trophic levels, which turn over generations at a slower rate. The advantage of "going low" on the trophic level, therefore, is that your consumer choice contributes to the preservation of ecosystem balance by allowing predator populations to recover and by taking energy out of those parts of the system that have a greater ability to withstand the impact (as long as they're not overfished). Species lower on the food chain (lower trophic levels) include sardines, anchovies, mackerel, mollusks like clams and mussels, and also "vegetarian" fish (fish that eat plants rather than other creatures); these include tilapia and barramundi.

Give up eating bluefin tuna: Despite the fact that Japan consumes 80 percent of the world's bluefin tuna and that it remains a delicacy in high demand in that country, it still makes sense to take a stand and not eat this fish no matter where you encounter it. Nowhere in its range—and regardless of whether southern or northern varieties are considered—is the population of bluefin robust enough to warrant consumption. Bluefin tuna simply does not meet "The Fish First" requirement of a healthy population baseline that would make it acceptable to consume.

There is also symbolic power in refusing to eat bluefin. Already, we have effectively lost wild Atlantic salmon and, across much of its range, Atlantic cod. It's time to take a stand against eating bluefin tuna.

Recommendations for the Improvement of Sportfishing

Every year in the United States alone, hundreds of tons of plastic lures and soft baits are produced for the recreational fishing sector. Millions of miles of fishing line are manufactured and sold, as well as thousands of tons of lead fishing weights. This is unconscionable for an industry that purports to care about fish and the environments in which they live, and which is the basis of their customers' recreation. It is also time we look at the fact that hooks as they are now designed still fail to dissolve in fresh or salt water in meaningfully short time periods, so fish that have been released with hooks still attached continue to be at risk. There should also be solutions devised to solve the issue of inadvertently killing large fish by tail wrapping. Finally, recreational fishers should understand that they constitute a fishing force that has a significant impact on freshwater and marine ecosystems and that the ability to fish is a privilege made possible by the abundance of Nature—and earned by our effective stewardship—rather than a right that we can exercise without the burden of responsibility. What follow are specific recommendations to recreational fishers, sportfishing gear manufacturers, and fishing tournament operators to help reduce the negative impacts of recreational fishing on fish populations and their environments.

Recommendations to Sportfishers

Put the sport back in sportfishing: With the advanced technologies in fishing line, reels, rods, boats, electronics, and almost every aspect of recreational fishing, the case can be made that not much of the element of "sport" remains in this endeavor as it was originally conceived of by Charles Frederick Holder on Catalina Island in 1898. After witnessing a crowd of men and women hooking and hauling out of the water hundreds of yellowtail that had come close to the beach to feed on squid, Holder sought to reverse this meaningless slaughter by supporting the idea that there should be guidelines for ethical conduct in the pursuit of angling. Eventually, through these first actions, the International Game Fish Association (IGFA) was born. To its great credit, the sportfishing community has shown itself to be one of the most flexible and conscientious groups in voluntarily adopting improved devices and practices. It is time to go one step further and put the sport back in sportfishing.

Get rid of treble hooks: There are lures available that have as many as three treble hooks (for a total of nine hooks) per lure body. These can cause significant damage to a fish, hooking it in multiple locations and making it very difficult to unhook. Treble hooks are far too damaging and should be done away with.

Use barbless hooks: If you intend to test your skill or give the fish a "sporting" chance, use barbless hooks. There are plenty of designs that ensure reliable corner-of-the-mouth hooking, and without the barb they are easily and quickly removed and do very little damage. An alternative is to compress the barb yourself.

Use the right size hook, and err on the small side: Know what you're fishing for and use the proper size hook. The gap between shank and tip point, the overall shape of the hook, and the depth of the bend all make a difference in how the hook sets in the fish. Hooks that are outsize for a particular type of prey have a tendency to do more damage than small hooks because the tip of the hook can come out through the gills or the orbit of the eye. This can be avoided by erring on the small side in choice of hook size.

Know how to handle the fish: Whenever possible, do not put your hands (even gloved hands) on a fish, which removes the mucous slime protecting its body. Use a fish-gripping device that grabs the fish around the bottom jaw. Have a pair of pliers or a hook-removal device handy. With very large fish or fish with teeth, spend the money on the right gear, which is sturdy enough to give you control over the fish's head.

If you are taking a fish to eat, know how to properly kill it, quickly and humanely: There is no excuse for not knowing how to quickly dispatch a fish if you intend to eat it. A common method is a blow to the head, and while this is usually sufficient to stun the fish, it may not kill it. The best way to kill any fish is to sever the spinal column behind the head and then bleed it by cutting its throat. Know where these access points are on any species you intend to catch. Make sure the knife is sharp. Under no circumstances allow a fish to expire by suffocation, thrashing around on deck or in a fish box. This is unnecessarily cruel and likely degrades the meat.

Keep only what you will eat within seventy-two hours: There is no reason to catch and keep "the legal limit" merely because it is legal. Fish refrigerated any longer than seventy-two hours is not fresh. Frozen fish is a personal choice, but consider whether you really need it and will really eat it. Reconsider whether or not you want to give fish to neighbors; some species are like zucchini, for which the recipient will not always be grateful. (Bluefish is one such fish.)

Forgo keeping fish for trophies: An easy way around this is to make sure you keep a tape measure and a camera with you when you're fishing. If you catch a fish you'd like to remember, take its measurements, snap a photo, and release the fish. Some fish-grabbing devices have a scale built in so that when you lift the fish, you can determine its weight. If you really want the fish on the wall, there are plenty of companies that can make quality fiberglass reproductions from your measurements and your picture. More anglers are choosing this, and while some may at first balk at the idea of a reproduction, consider that by choosing this route, you are not only preserving the fish, but leaving it in the ecosystem to be caught again or to pass on its presumably good genes for future generations.

"Fish green" means "Go biodegradable": There are plenty of biodegradable, ecologically friendly alternatives to plastic lures and soft baits that are available through domestic and international suppliers. Get rid of your old plastic lures and baits and change over. Fish that ingest soft baits often die as a result, and plastic lures eventually degrade, releasing their various chemical constituents (phthalates, etc.) into the environment.

The same goes for traditional monofilament fishing line: Recycle your old line and convert to biodegradable products. Biodegradable line is easily purchased online or at a good-quality local retailer and comes in standard test strengths, and most kinds will decompose in two to five years (as opposed to up to six hundred years for traditional monofilament).

Devise better hook and line technologies: There have been many debates about whether fishhooks dissolve, rust out, or rot depending on whether they're left in freshwater, salt water, a fish's mouth, or a fish's gut. Tests and studies have been conducted, and the reality is that fishhooks take months if not years to degrade. Fishhooks that degrade quickly or are digestible will ultimately serve both fish and anglers by doing only what they're designed to do and not causing unintended harm.

The industry would also do well to create a device—perhaps a swivel at the juncture of main line and leader—that could separate the fish from the line on command, such as by radio signal. This would allow fishermen to release the fish without touching it, and in cases where the fish is in danger—either by tail wrapping or at the appearance of sharks—the angler could decide to instantly free it. The option has always existed to simply cut the line, but in the case of a large, tail-wrapped fish, this might not remedy the problem. Also, a fish with a hook in its mouth, trailing several or perhaps dozens of yards of line, is a fish with a serious liability and a limited chance of survival.

Don't buy lead weights, and support measures to ban them: There are ecologically friendly alternatives to lead weights. Lead in the environment has significant negative neurological and reproductive effects on mammals, birds, and humans. Why contribute to this? Tungsten weights are not an acceptable alternative, because tungsten's effects in ecosystems are unknown. Brass and steel weights are the safest bets.

Also, support measures to ban the sale and to phase out the use of lead weights in fishing. Certain "pro-fishing" organizations stand against this, but the arguments do not hold up against the simple consideration that we throw thousands of tons of lead into our fresh and salt waterways every year, that lead has known negative impacts, and that there are equally effective alternatives.

Get beyond "kill" tournaments: Tournaments that permit or require participants to kill fish—especially fish that are not eaten—are an outdated concept. Kill tournaments typically incentivize taking the largest fish, often the most fecund females, which is counterintuitive to the spirit of preservation in angling and counterproductive to the goal of conserving and rebuilding fish populations.

Give back: Do something to benefit the waters you fish. It's worth taking the time to learn about the ecological health of your favorite fishing spot. Whether it's a pond, a lake, a river, an estuary, or an area of open ocean, educate yourself about the status of its health and the health of the species that live in it and around it. If you don't protect it against overfishing, pollution, and overdevelopment, who will?

Learn to dive: If you have any interest in the sea or freshwater habitats or the species that live in them, learn to scuba dive. You'll realize how little you really knew about the world below the water's surface.

Support marine reserves: One of the most important things any angler can do is understand that the "right" to fish is actually a privilege made possible by the abundance of Nature, regardless of the regulations, permissions, or limits imposed by a particular state or country. As an angler, if you care first and foremost about the fish, do something about it. Learn about the value of marine reserves—including, especially, no-fish reserves. If you have never been to a marine reserve or protected area, go to one that is well established and, if possible, dive there. You will get a privileged glimpse of what's been lost, and you will see what can be regained. Inform your legislators and representatives of your support, use your power to vote, and use your consumer dollar where it counts.

ACKNOWLEDGMENTS

The journey recounted in this book took five years, around ten thousand hours of research, interviews, reading, and writing, and nearly seventy-five thousand miles of travel—the equivalent of almost three times around the globe. The journey was possible only because of the effort, goodwill, and contributions of dozens of individuals. I received no financial support except from my publisher and family. I received no money from fishing organizations, environmental groups, or commercial fishing groups. I did receive nonmonetary support from the International Game Fish Association, the Blue Water Fishermen's Association (a commercial-fishing lobbying group), the Billfish Foundation, Greenpeace International, and private individuals and commercial and sportfishing captains—in each case, typically in the form of free access to their operations or events, staff, or in-house experts.

I would like to thank Rick Kot, my editor at Viking Penguin, for making me a far better writer, as well as Laura Tisdel and Kyle Davis for their assistance and insights, and the rest of the publishing team for their hard work. Thanks to my agent, Richard Abate, for believing in me for over fifteen years and for suggesting that this topic, which I originally envisioned as a magazine article, should instead be a book. All of these people, and those who follow, helped in some way to make not one but several lifelong dreams come true.

Mexico: I want to single out Russ Nelson, Guillermo Alvarez, Wallace "J." Nichols, Vince Radice, and Minerva Saenz de Smith for their critical input and help in understanding the complexity of the fishing issues in Cabo San Lucas. I want to thank Juan Beltran, Adriana Moya, Captain Enrique Martinez, and First Mate Ernesto Moyron Reyes of Pisces Sportfishing for their patience and tolerance of my questions; R. Wayne Bisbee and Julia Brakhage of Bisbee's Offshore Tournaments for sharing their catch data; Byron Bernard, Gricelda Mendez Castro, Oscar Ortiz, and Flavio Campos Reis for sharing their stories; and David Phillip of the Fisheries Conservation Foundation, Debra Losey of the Southwest Fisheries Science Center, Dale Jones and Todd Dubois of the NOAA Office of Law Enforcement, and, from the International Game Fish Association, Rob Kramer, Jason Schratwieser, Becky Wright, Lesley Arico, Eric Combast, Mike Myatt, Emily Collins, Gail Morchower, and Grant Larson. Thank you as well to Olaf Jensen for walking me through the details of the striped marlin population figures. Finally, I would like to recognize the outstanding work of Mike McGettigan and SeaWeb in defending the Sea of Cortez; his work was pivotal in broadening my understanding of the scale of the issues in Mexico.

Nova Scotia: Special thanks are due to Saul and Dianne Newell who put me up, befriended me, and welcomed me into the life of a Nova Scotia fishing community. To Saul especially, I owe a lifelong debt of gratitude for taking me out onto Georges Bank and showing me a new world. I want to thank Gabby Newell, who shared his stories, and for his and his wife Linda's hospitality, as well as Dwaine d'Eon, who welcomed me aboard as one of the crew and let me see him miss. I want to thank Ronnie Newell for insights into the flaws of Canada's Atlantic fisheries management process, and Ken Hinman and Pamela Lyons Gromen of the National Coalition of Marine Conservation and Glenn Delaney of the Blue Water Fishermen's Association for offering their views on the Give Swordfish a Break campaign and the health of the Atlantic swordfish stock. Thank you to scientist Don Grady for his review of parts of the Nova Scotia section. Thank you to Jay Lugar of the Marine Stewardship Council and to Derek Jones, who put me in touch with Saul in the first place. Thanks go to Franklyn d'Entremont for his oral histories, and to Jim Crawford for his stories and insights, for reading early drafts of the Nova Scotia section, and for a sample of the best view on Georges. Thanks also to Gilbert Devine for his hospitality and views on the controversies plaguing Nova Scotia's fisheries. I owe a special debt to Susanna Fuller, Alexandra Curtis, and Shannon Arnold of the Ecology Action Centre for their assistance in reviewing data and drafts. I also want to thank Brian Giroux for his critiques and insights; Boris Worm, Catherine Muir, and graduate students of the Worm Lab at Dalhousie University for their feedback; Christine Annand and David Jennings of the Canadian Department of Fisheries and Oceans; Troy Atkinson of Hi-Liner; and of course Bobby Meacham for giving me an insider's view.

Japan: Very special thanks are due to Wakao Hanaoka, who took it upon himself to connect me with the fishermen of Oma, Japan, flew with me there, acted as translator and travel companion, and made the Japan portion of this book feasible and productive. Without him it could not have happened. I want to thank Tomonori Higashi of the Japan Game Fish Association, Naoto Naka-mura for the tour of Tsukiji, and Lionel Dersot for his generosity. I especially want to thank Atsushi Sasaki and Takeichi Kikuchi for their welcome, their stories and insights, and their expertise. Thank you to Hirofumi Hamabata of the Oma Fishermen's Co-op and Tsunenori Iida of the House of Hicho.

South Australia: David Ellis of the Australian Southern Bluefin Tuna Industry Association provided critical insights, information, and debate. I want to thank Craig Foster, Morten Deichmann, Marcus Stehr, and Hagen Stehr for opening their doors to me and providing a view of their significant efforts toward breeding bluefin tuna in captivity. I want to thank Michael Braden and Louise Mrdjen and the staff of the Port Lincoln Library for their assistance, as well as Dan Gaughan and Tim Ward for their insights into the South Australia pilchard mass mortalities of 1995 and 1998, and Peter Trott of the World Wildlife Fund for Nature, Fisheries Program, Australia, for his insights and data related to current southern bluefin breeding population numbers. Special thanks go to Sigi Veldhuyzen's wife, Cathy, and their daughters, for their generosity in sharing family stories and for the review of the draft of my interview with Sigi.

Mediterranean: I owe a significant debt of gratitude to John Hocevar for his tireless assistance in understanding the issues of fisheries management and conservation of bluefin tuna in the Mediterranean. He has devoted his life to the protection of wild creatures and yet retains enough openness and balance to consider as legitimate the views of a recreational fisherman toward those same creatures. I want to thank Roberto Mielgo Bregazzi of Advanced Tuna Ranching Technologies for his courage and resourcefulness in using data to expose the corruption and criminality of the bluefin tuna trade in the Med, and for sharing that information with me. He deserves recognition for his efforts. I want to thank Marcello Conti as well as the crew of the *Rainbow Warrior* for their time, personal stories, and interviews, especially Mehdi Mouj-bani, Chris Lewis, Alex Holmes, François Provost, Alain Combémorel, Liz Cronin, Emma Briggs, Vlad Lobin, Rita Ghanem, François Chartier, and

Yesim Aslan for their assistance. Special thanks are due to Gemma Parkes and Chantal Menard of the World Wildlife Fund in Rome, and Marta Madina of Oceana Madrid, for sharing information and for their efforts toward coordination.

Cairns and Great Barrier Reef: Big thanks go to Damon Olson and Claire Gobe of Nomad Sportfishing and to the crew of *Odyssey, Saltaire,* and *Nomad* for the memories of a lifetime. I especially want to thank Glanville Heydenrych, Ed Lester, Dean Dibeler, and Tim Baker for their patience, expertise, companionship, and good humor. Thanks to Tara Mote and Brett Hanlon; to Brett Vorhauer and Chris Carthew for their generosity in using photos; and to Andrew Clark, Darren Bundaberg, and the Fort Lauderdale Bobs for a hell of a good time.

New Zealand: There are debts of gratitude, and then there are things you could never pay back. To Michel Marchandise from Belgium, I owe one of these. His generosity in allowing me to accompany him off New Zealand brought me further into the heart of wildness than I ever hoped to go, and in many ways made the conclusions of this book possible. I want to thank Captain John Gregory and his wife, Samantha, for their hospitality and for John's willingness to welcome me aboard *Primetime.* I want to thank Mike Harris and Jimmy Gigger for all they shared, and acknowledge their dedication and the absolute professionalism of their work. Thanks also to Kerry Strongman and his wife, Monique, of the Arts Factory, in Te Hana, and to Karli Thomas of Greenpeace New Zealand for all her work and the information she shared in support of this project.

Scientists: The insights of the best possible objective science are the hope for the future of the oceans, for understanding our impact on them, and for being in a position to improve their condition. My understanding of the seas was immeasurably deepened by the information the following men and women took the time to explain to me. Thanks go to Barbara Block, Andy Rosenberg, and Molly Lutcavage for their insights on bluefin tuna stock health and migrations. Special thanks go to Bill Leavenworth and Karen Alexander for taking me back in time to realize just how much has been lost in the Gulf of Maine and the North Atlantic. Thanks also to Bruce Bourque for walking me back into the prehistory of coastal Maine and digging out some very cool four-thousand-year-old swordfish rostra. Thanks to Bob Steneck for sharing his views on the necessity of understanding the differences among types of marine reserves and the importance of local determination of their design. Special thanks go to Bill Ballantine, father of New Zealand's marine reserves, for opening his home to me and for sharing his enormous wealth of experience; Callum Roberts for his work on humanity's long history of interaction with the sea; Victoria Braithwaite for her work on pain receptivity in fish and for her balanced view; and Carl Safina for responding to my inquiries and for sharing his papers, opinions, and privileged information. Thanks to Ellen Peel of the Billfish Foundation for contacts, interviews, and moral support. I want to thank Sylvia Earle for taking the time to speak with me; her sensitivity to the ocean's creatures greatly deepened my own. Thanks as well to Ron O'Dor of the Census of Marine Life, Ben Halpern of the National Center for Ecological Analysis and Synthesis, and Jeremy Jackson of Scripps for in-depth interviews and contacts and for their illuminating work. If I have made errors in portraying any of the science in this book, they are my own.

Environmental groups and foundations: I want to express my gratitude to Mark Spalding of the Ocean Foundation; Ben Freitas, Michael Hirschfield, Elizabeth Griffin, and David Allison of Oceana in Washington, D.C.; Phil Kline and Frank Hewetson of Greenpeace; Mark Stevens and Jill Hepp of the World Wildlife Fund; and Ayelet Hines and Doug Rader of Environmental Defense for information on the catch shares system. I want to thank Geoff Smith of the Nature Conservancy in Maine and Charles Curtin of the MIT-USGS Global Climate Change Collaborative for their insights on the benefits and limits of marine reserves.

Commercial fishing: I want to thank Rich Ruais of the East Coast Tuna Association, Captain Gary Grenier, Jeff Reid, Keper Connell, and Steve Merrill for their stories about the waters off Kennebunkport, Maine. And thanks to writer Paul Molyneaux for his time, his books, and his vital insights into the truth about the limits of aquaculture.

Sportfishing: Captain David Preble influenced this book through his own work on yellowfin tuna and the history of commercial fishing and sportfishing in New England. Thank you for sharing your insights and opinions about the state of pelagic fish populations and the necessity of taking action. I want to thank Gary Cannell of *Tuna Hunter,* in Gloucester, for sharing his time and opinions, and "Black Bart" Miller for interviews and his story of the Hawaiian queen. I want to thank Captain John McMurray of the Mid-Atlantic Fishery Management Council for interviews and articles and for continuing to have the courage to speak the truth to commercial and sportfishing interests alike: that the only sane course of action is not self-interest but preservation of the fish first. I want to thank Michael Fowlkes and his wife, Kim, for their generosity and hospitality in our encounter on Catalina.

Various fields: Thanks go to Tim Choate for the interview and for his work in pioneering the use of circle hooks, and to Jim Chambers for speaking with me and for his work in compiling documentation and photographs of some of the largest fish ever caught by any method. Thanks to Heather Tausig of the New England Aquarium and Charles Clover for his landmark work on overfishing and for his assistance. Heartfelt thanks go to Diana Udel for believing in me and in this effort since day one. You've been a moral support and a great friend. I want to thank Paul Murray of Murray Products for permission to use the sequence of photographs of bluefin tuna, Enric Sala and Brian Skerry of the National Geographic Society for their enthusiasm, and Jeannine Pedersen, curator of the Catalina Island Museum, for help in locating resources. Thank you, too, to Lee Crockett and Tom Wheatley of the Pew Environmental Group for the latest population figures on North Atlantic bluefin tuna. I want to thank Bob Arbib and Joan Schuman of the Collaborative for Educational Services, as well as Dr. Ann Southworth, Ann Ferriter, Justin Hurst, and Sheila Hoffman of Striving Readers for their flexibility and for offering their support of this work while also trying to complete other jobs.

Interns: Thanks go to research interns Emily Hart, Annie Alquist, Janet Guo, Lauren Braccio, Kristine Salters, Angela Oliverio, Rebecca Benson, and Kassia Rudd for their help in locating critical papers and doing summary reading on a wide range of topics. I want to thank Chris Cabot for the preliminary interviews and reading, Lela Schlenker for her work on bluefin, Elisabeth Brasington for historical background information, and especially Julia Beaty for her interest, dedication, and assistance over many months. Though she's not an intern, I want to thank Julie Goldman for her moral support, dinners, and printing of hundreds of pages of research notes, reports, and papers. I want to also thank Melanie D. G. Kaplan for her hospitality and moral support and for reading early chapters.

Travel assistance and family: I want to thank Dennis Maloney for the last-minute use of his pickup truck for the drive to Nova Scotia, Mike Rigney for cash and airline miles at exactly the right moment, Brian Rigney for hotel rooms and airline miles, John Rigney for the many hours fishing, and Sarah Rigney for her enthusiastic support over the years. Thank you to my mother, Sue LaVoie, for the many ways in which she challenged me to think more deeply about my role in the world. Thank you to my father, Brian Rigney, for his support and for teaching me to think big, and to Joe Cuticelli for helping me out with lodging in Tokyo and for his decades of faith in my writing.

Readers: My thanks to Liz Beal for her many years of faithful readership and encouragement. Bill Randolph deserves significant thanks for being a reader of early drafts, as well as an adviser and a supporter. I want to thank Jen Iba for her many years of encouragement and friendship, and I especially want to thank Joe Gannon for his friendship, critical commentary, and incredibly thorough reviews of all the sections. His insights and unsparing honesty were absolutely essential in bringing out the best in the book. I could not have done it without him. Special thanks are also due to Paul Newlin and Claudia Ciano-Boyce for their friendship, hospitality, and sustained encouragement.

I want to give special thanks to Holly Wren Spaulding for her precision with language and her keen editorial eye in reading sections of this, as well as for her support and faith in me and for believing in this project and in us.

Finally, I want to thank my father and mother for taking the risk thirty years ago that a summer house in distant Maine might offer us new opportunities to know the sea. It changed my life.

NOTES

Prologue

1 **sole member of the family Xiphiidae:** Swordfish are considered members of the billfish family because they have an elongated upper jaw, called a rostrum, although it is quite different in shape from those of the other billfishes.

2 **The largest of these nets can haul in more than three thousand tons:** The largest purse seiner in the world is the Spanish *Albatun Tres,* at 115 meters long, with a haul capacity of three thousand metric tons (6.6 million pounds). It primarily hunts smaller tuna species in the Pacific.

3 **circle the globe 550 times:** Charles Clover, *The End of the Line.* Documentary, directed by Rupert Murray (2009).

3 **wasted sea life:** This figure comes from a United Nations Food and Agricultural Organization report released in 2009. The report is an update of an older report going back to 1994. The updated report calculates the average annual global bycatch in metric tons between 1992 and 2001. FAO, "World Inventory of Fisheries: Reduction of Bycatch and Discards," fact sheet; text by John W. Valdemarsen; in *FAO Fisheries and Aquaculture Department* (Rome, May 2005). http://www.fao.org/fishery/topic/14832/en. Cited November 2, 2011.

3 **Bottom trawling is no better:** Les Watling and Elliott Norse, "Disturbance of the Seabed by Mobile Fishing Gear: A Comparison with Forest Clear-Cutting," *Conservation Biology* 12, no. 6 (December 1998). In work done more than a decade later, Watling used satellite data to confirm the destruction to the ocean floor by trawling. At the 2008 American Association for the Advancement of Science (AAAS) meeting in Boston, Watling said, "Ten years ago, Elliott Norse and I calculated that, each year, worldwide, bottom trawlers drag an area equivalent to twice the lower 48 states. Most of that trawling happens in deep waters, out of sight. But now we can more clearly envision what trawling impacts down there by looking at the sediment plumes that are shallow enough for us to see from satellites." See also "Dragnet: Bottom Trawling, the World's Most Severe and Extensive Seafloor Disturbance," 2008 AAAS Annual Meeting. http://mcbi.org/what/AAASsymposia.htm #Dragnet.

3 **1.5 billion hooks:** This statement is an extrapolation from a number given in the January 2007 WWF report "Tuna in Trouble: Major Problems for the World's Tuna Fisheries," which states that the world's tuna longline fisheries "deployed an estimated 1.2 billion hooks in 2000 alone." Given this, it seems

reasonable to assert that the total number of hooks deployed annually in longlining of all types of fish would easily exceed 1.5 billion.

3 **500 million metric tons of food per year without depletion:** Bureau of Commercial Fisheries, U.S. Department of the Interior, "Fisheries of the United States–1966," introduction by Donald L. McKernan, director of the Bureau of Commercial Fisheries (March 1967, C.F.S. 4400, vi). McKernan writes: "That the seas offer hope of providing more food to meet the world's growing need is indicated by various experts whose predictions of the sustainable annual harvest range as high as 500 million metric tons."

5 **99 percent of the weight of all finfish and bivalve mollusks:** These figures are based on calculations done by University of New Hampshire scientists participating in the Census of Marine Life project, and specifically one of its subprojects, the History of Marine Animal Populations (HMAP). My contact, Bill Leavenworth, a historian of Nature, accumulated evidence from old captains' logs, scientific publications, U.S. Fish Commission records, and other scientific and observational resources to assemble a picture of what has happened in the Gulf of Maine since roughly 1860. His data show that bluefin tuna and swordfish fisheries were *inshore* fisheries, carried out with small boats (under twenty tons) launched from shore and not straying beyond sight of land. There are illustrated newspaper images from the late 1800s of these shoreline fish traps being used in New England for mackerel along the shore and up rivers, and occasionally these traps would catch "horse mackerel," i.e., bluefin tuna. The fishery began to migrate offshore as demand for these fish increased. In an e-mail from April 21, 2009, Leavenworth writes, "The destruction of swordfish in the Gulf of Maine since 1860 has been nearly total; I understand that there are still a few tuna out there, but they are relatively scarce and small. What would they eat? The herring, mackerel, menhaden, shad, smelt and alewife populations are down to a tiny fraction of their 1880 sizes. I've been told by a young scientist that herring don't come into shore to spawn; I fished spawning herring off Seabrook [New Hampshire] in the fall of 1980, and they used to spawn in nearly every estuary from Machias [Maine] to Cape Ann [Massachusetts] in the 19th century." In another e-mail, from June 11, 2008, Leavenworth writes that "by 1960, the Northwest Atlantic populations of major species had already fallen 90% from their levels a century earlier." He writes this in response to a question about the 2003 Myers and Worm paper stating that 90 percent of the ocean's large pelagic species were gone based on analyses of "available data from the beginning of exploitation" (mostly starting in the late 1940s and early 1950s). In other words, Leavenworth asserts that the Myers and Worm report's benchmarks from around 1950 did not reflect an unfished state that mirrored the ocean's true abundance but instead reflected a starting point of only 10 percent of what had been there. Not being a scientist, I won't weigh in on these specific numbers, but I can reflect that while there has been significant debate in the scientific community about the accuracy and specificity (by locale) of the

Myers and Worm paper's claims, the scope of decline would seem fairly char-
acterized as being between 70 percent and 90 percent (or more), depending on
which fish is being discussed, and where in the world. Dozens of scientific
papers I've read cite figures within this range of 70 to 90 percent or more to
characterize the general decline of ocean species and habitat suffered in the past
150 to 300 years. Part of the argument is that declines in fish landings cannot
account for the entire picture of degradation, which includes habitat destruction, degraded water quality, species invasions, and other factors. Noteworthy
references are listed below.

Ransom A. Myers and Boris Worm, "Rapid Worldwide Depletion of Predatory Fish Communities," *Nature* 423 (2003): 280–83. This is the landmark
Myers and Worm paper that posited that as much as 90 percent of the stock
of the ocean's top predators had been depleted.

Jeremy B. C. Jackson, "Ecological Extinction and Evolution in the Brave
New Ocean," *Proceedings of the National Academy of Sciences of the United
States of America* 105 (2008): 11458–65.

Jeremy B. C. Jackson, "What Was Natural in the Coastal Oceans," *Proceedings of the National Academy of Sciences of the United States of America* 98,
no. 10 (2001): 5411–18.

Jeremy B. C. Jackson and Enric Sala, "Unnatural Oceans," *Scientia Marina*
65, no. 2 (2001): 273–81. This paper makes the case that most of our knowledge of marine ecosystems was attained long after intensive fishing began and
that the basic precepts underlying our understanding of how the oceans operate and what their true carrying capacity is for all life is poorly understood and
therefore needs to be questioned.

H. K. Lotze et al., "Depletion, Degradation, and Recovery Potential of
Estuaries and Coastal Seas," *Science* 312 (2006): 1806–9.

Callum Roberts, *The Unnatural History of the Sea* (Washington, DC: Island
Press, 2007). Roberts's book offers dozens of firsthand observational accounts
of what oceans looked like when they were first encountered by explorers to
Newfoundland, the Gulf of Maine, Chesapeake Bay, Palmyra Atoll, Alaska,
and many other locations. Roberts gives one account by Goldsmith in 1810,
in which he references schools of haddock that annually visit British coasts that
are "above 100 miles in length, and 300 in breadth. On the Yorkshire coast,
they keep close to the shore, and such is their numbers, that two or three fishermen will sometimes take each a ton of them in a day" (139).

Book 1: Discovery

In the Kingdom of Sapphire Waters: Cabo San Lucas, Mexico

15 **More striped marlin . . . thirty thousand per year:** The Billfish Foundation
Economic Impact Report. The Billfish Foundation study indicates that over

354,000 people went sportfishing in the Los Cabos area (Cabo San Lucas, San Jose del Cabo, and the East Cape) in 2007. They spent over $633,600,000 for lodging, charters, food, transportation, tackle, fuel, and more. These expenditures created and supported more than 24,000 jobs locally, $245 million in local and federal taxes, and more than $1.1 billion in overall economic impact. An additional 10,469 jobs were supported elsewhere through Los Cabos sportfishing tourism. From the report "The Economic Contributions of Anglers to the Los Cabos Economy," Southwick Associates Inc., Fernandina Beach, Florida; Nelson Resources Consulting Inc., Oakland Park, Florida; and FIRMUS Consulting, Mexico City; August 11, 2008. http://www.billfish.org/new /newsarticle.asp?ArticleID=107.

16 **$1 billion to the Los Cabos region:** Ibid.

16 **180,000 and growing fast:** The 2005 Mexican census indicated there were 165,000 people in Los Cabos. That number has certainly increased as of the writing of this chapter in 2009; 180,000 is a conservative rounding up to account for four years' growth. The number is likely closer to 200,000 permanent residents. http://en.wikipedia.org/wiki/Los_Cabos.

21 **to battle an angler for half a day or more:** On September 24–25, 2011, Richard Biehl of Traverse City, Michigan, fought a blue marlin for twenty-eight hours aboard the boat *Go Deep,* out of Cabo San Lucas. The exact weight of the marlin is uncertain but was very likely over one thousand pounds: "The marlin registered only 972 pounds because the hook of the electronic scale used to weigh the fish was not high enough for all of the fish to clear the ground, so a time-tested measurement formula—using length and girth—was used to determine [a weight of] 1,213 pounds. The marlin measured 137 inches long, or 11.4 feet, not counting its bill or tail. It was 75 inches, or 6.25 feet around." Peter Thomas, "Monster Blue Marlin Caught After 28-Hour Battle off Cabo San Lucas," GrindTV.com, September 27, 2011. http://www .grindtv.com/outdoor/blog/30401/monster+blue+marlin+caught+after+ 28-hour+battle+off+cabo+san+lucas.

22 **burst speeds close to seventy miles an hour:** Elasmo-research.org cites an instance of a crude speed trial of a sailfish done at Long Key Fish Camp, where the fish was hooked and sprinted over a distance of a hundred yards (as gauged by how much line was taken off the reel) in three seconds. The fish was bounding out of the water and was calculated to have attained a speed of 68 mph. http://elasmo-research.org/education/topics/r_haulin%27_bass.htm.

23 **The alliances and positions of the players change:** The sportfishing community in Mexico is not united in opposition to Shark Norma 029. Among the major figures who support 029 are "Chuy" Valdez, owner of Hotel Buenavista Beach and Resort, located on the East Cape, and Pedro Sors García, president of the National Federation of Sport Fishing (Federation Nacional de Pesca Deportiva). Their support of 029 is based on the idea that it is a start toward conservation and a "tool to stop the illegality with which billfish

are caught." It imposes restrictions on gear type and proximity of fishing to shore. The NFSF pushed CONAPESCA and SAGARPA (Secretaría de Agricultura, Ganadería, Desarrollo Rural, Pesca y Alimentación, or the Ministry of Agriculture, Livestock, Rural Development, Fisheries and Food), the Mexican government agencies involved in fishing, to name percentage limits for bycatch in specific species (10 percent for sailfish, 8 percent for all marlin, and 5 percent for dorado). According to the *Baja Road Trekker* blog, the NFSF is still pushing to make the sale of bycatch illegal. http://roadtrekker.blogspot .com/2008/06/shark-norma-nom-029-defended.html.

What doesn't make sense about this support of Shark Norma are the facts that, first, it contradicts the established law, Ley de Pesca, which created the conservation zones in the first place and made any catch or sale of these species illegal. Second, the issue of overfishing in the Cortez has always been an issue of lack of enforcement, not a lack of laws on paper. The Mexican government can put any percentage of allowable bycatch on paper and make it illegal to sell any of these species, and it can even dictate gear restrictions, but none of this makes any difference if there continues to be a lack of enforcement and accountability. The killing of these species will go on, and the sale of illegal fish out of the Cortez and Baja protected zones will continue unabated. Support for Shark Norma, even on the grounds that it is a good first step, only gives encouragement to those who have been flouting the protected-zone laws since they were established.

24 **an estimated 218,000 hooks:** Seawatch, "Shark Norma Fact Sheet," July 21, 2004 (http://www.seawatch.org/shark_norma/fact_sheet.pdf), and Seawatch press release, May 12, 2007 (http://seawatch.org/en/Resource-Library/174/shark-norma-029-continues-to-kill-protected-species).

24 **1.5 million hooks being fished commercially:** Billfish Foundation, "Mexico's New Shark and Ray Fishing Regulations Threaten Billfish & Other Ocean Resources," May 16, 2007. http://www.billfish.org/new/newsarticle.asp?ArticleID=60.

24 **equivalent of 250 sportfishing yachts:** "Low Shrimp Returns," Seawatch, "Shark Norma Fact Sheet," July 21, 2004. http://www.seawatch.org/shark _norma/fact_sheet.pdf.

24 **60 to 80 percent of a longliner's take around Baja:** P. Arenas et al., *Mexican National Report,* Second Meeting of the Interim Scientific Committee for Tuna and Tuna-like Species in the North Pacific Ocean, Honolulu, Hawaii, 1999; and R. Nelson et al., *A New Marine Resources Conservation Management Approach in Baja California Sur (BCS), Mexico: An Evolving Case Study,* North American Protected Areas Network: Symposium on Financing and Economic Benefits of Marine Protected Areas, Loreto, Baja California Sur, Mexico, 2005. These striped marlin bycatch rates seem unusually high. In a paper by Santana-Hernandez in 2001, the striped marlin bycatch rate in the Mexican Pacific was rated at 5.8 percent. The striped marlin bycatch rate according to

the May 16, 2007, Billfish Foundation newsletter was much higher, at between 70 and 80 percent.

Olaf Jensen comments: "Catch rates of different species in longline gear are, in general, highly variable depending on set depth, time of year, time of day, and location among other things. I would not be surprised if vessels targeting striped marlin could get 70–80% striped marlin in some locations such as Magdalena Bay and Baja California Sur. To call it bycatch in that situation would be kind of misleading. If you're allowed to sell it and it makes up 80% of the catch, then it's the de facto target. It's entirely possible that fleets targeting tuna would get bycatch rates of striped marlin that are fairly low, particularly if they're using deep sets. So, I suspect the explanation here is that the lower bycatch rate comes from the entire longline fleet (maybe including joint-venture vessels [Japanese] as well as Mexican flagged vessels), much of which does not target marlin and may not fish in areas of high marlin abundance. The higher bycatch rates sound like they come from a few boats that were targeting marlin in an area of very high marlin abundance." Olaf Jensen, e-mail message to author, October 5, 2009.

24 **150 to 200 tons of it every month:** Billfish Foundation, "Mexico's New Shark and Ray Fishing Regulations Threaten Billfish & Other Ocean Resources," May 16, 2007. http://www.billfish.org/new/newsarticle.asp?ArticleID=60.

25 **only seven tons of shrimp:** Seawatch, "Shark Norma Fact Sheet," July 21, 2004. http://www.seawatch.org/shark_norma/fact_sheet.pdf.

25 **increase in creatures lower in the food chain:** E. Sala et al., "Fishing Down Coastal Food Webs in the Gulf of California," *Fisheries,* March 2004, 19–25. Also, summary of this information can be found at http://www.seaweb.org/resources/briefings/fishdownweb.php.

25 **sea full of jellyfish:** Jeremy B. C. Jackson, "Ecological Extinction and Evolution in the Brave New Ocean," *Proceedings of the National Academy of Sciences of the United States of America* 105 (2008): 11458–65. "Synergistic effects of habitat destruction, overfishing, introduced species, warming, acidification, toxins, and massive runoff of nutrients are transforming once complex ecosystems like coral reefs and kelp forests into monotonous level bottoms, transforming clear and productive coastal seas into anoxic dead zones, and transforming complex food webs topped by big animals into simplified, microbially dominated ecosystems with boom and bust cycles of toxic dinoflagellate blooms, jellyfish, and disease." See also D. Pauly, V. Christensen, J. Dalsgaard, R. Froese, and F. Torres, "Fishing Down Marine Food Webs," *Science* 279 (1998): 860–63.

31 **Choy's Monster:** "Capt. Cornelius Choy and his daughter Gail acting as deckhand had taken six holiday makers out for a day's sport fishing. None were experienced anglers. After fighting the fish for some time and passing the rod around, Capt. Choy finally took the rod and brought the fish to the boat where

his daughter wired it. Naturally, it could not qualify for an IGFA world record, but it does stand to this day as the largest blue ever taken on rod and reel." "Photos of Huge Pacific Blue Marlin," http://www.bigmarinefish.com/photos _blue_marlin_pg6.html.

31 **a marlin caught near Tahiti in 1966:** George Reiger, "The First Thousand-Pounder," in Zane Grey, *Zane Grey, Outdoorsman: Zane Grey's Best Hunting and Fishing Tales Published in Commemoration of His Centennial Year,* ed. George Reiger (Englewood Cliffs, NJ: Prentice-Hall, 1972), 236.

31 **a fish estimated at 2,500 pounds:** Peter Goadby, *Big Fish and Blue Water: Gamefishing in the Pacific* (New York: Henry Holt & Co., 1972), 63.

31 **Zane Grey himself writes about the first thousand-pound marlin:** Zane Grey, *Zane Grey, Outdoorsman,* 248.

On the subject of giant fish, in Frank Gray Griswold's excellent book *Some Fish and Some Fishing,* published in 1921, he cites a 1914 excerpt from the French newspaper *Le Figaro* that reports that "a huge sailfish, rarely met with in the Atlantic, has been captured by fishermen off Concarneau and towed to that port. The fish measures eight metres long and four metres in circumference and weighs four tons. The fishermen are greatly disturbed over the presence in the vicinity of the fish's female companion, who followed her captured lord throughout the whole of the night he was being towed to port." Griswold asserts that the fish in question must have been what he calls a *Tetrapturus amplus,* a species name coined by the taxonomist Poey in 1860 to describe the blue marlin. (The accepted formulation is from Lacepède in 1802: *Makaira nigricans.*) The proportions described by Griswold are way off for a blue marlin, however. If the measurements can be taken as accurate, the creature was twenty-six feet long and thirteen feet around and weighed 8,820 pounds. Why it was called a "sailfish" is a mystery, but the proportions put the creature squarely in the ballpark of either an orca (killer whale) or a basking shark. The dorsal fins of both species at this size can be very large (a male orca's can be six feet tall), with the triangular shape of a sail. A photo from that date sent to me by Josyane Billochon, an archivist in Concarneau, France, confirms the animal was in fact a basking shark. Josyane Billochon, e-mail message to author, October 5, 2009.

35 **"pictures of my father-in-law catching totoaba":** The decline of totoaba is thought to be due to heavy commercial fishing, which peaked at two thousand metric tons in 1943 and had fallen to only fifty metric tons by 1975, at which point the Mexican government banned the fishery. Totoaba are still caught as bycatch in other finfish fisheries in the Sea of Cortez. The other major cause of the totoaba's decline is the diversion of the Colorado River by the United States. This has significantly altered the Colorado delta in the upper Sea of Cortez and changed the salinity of that region. Totoaba is listed on CITES (the Convention on International Trade in Endangered Species of Wild Fauna and Flora), the IUCN (International Union for Conservation of Nature) Red

List of Threatened Species, and the Endangered Species Act (ESA). "Totoaba,"
Wikipedia, http://en.wikipedia.org/wiki/Totoaba.

37 **"some by the sportfishing fleet acting as commercial boats":** Interestingly,
in his 2001 paper "A Case Against Longlining Inside the EEZ off California"
(http://www.seawatch.org/.../pdf/A%20case%20against%20longlining.pdf),
Seawatch founder Mike McGettigan provides an interview with Ricardo Agundez, the former captain of the *Adriana,* the same boat I fished on out of Cabo
San Lucas in May 2008. Agundez gives the following testimony (excerpted).

> Q: What percentage change have you seen in the numbers of the follow-
> ing pelagic fish (striped marlin, blue marlin, sailfish, blue sharks, mako
> sharks, thresher sharks, dorado, yellowtail) in the areas you fished in the
> last 15 years?
>
> A: For striped marlin, a drop of 30 percent; blue marlin a drop of 40
> percent; sailfish a 70 percent drop; sharks of all types a 90 percent drop.
>
> Q: Has the average size of the striped marlin caught dropped in the last
> 15 years?
>
> A: About 15 years ago weights were varied, a good sized fish would have
> been 160 to 180 pounds. Today a good-sized fish is between 100 and
> 140 pounds.
>
> Q: What about the average size of the sailfish caught?
>
> A: In the past 80 to 100 pounds, now the few that remain are from 40
> to 70 pounds.
>
> Q: Give as many examples as you can of how fishing used to be 15–20
> years ago versus what it is today? Try to quantify these examples as
> much as possible. We are most interested in the pelagics mentioned
> above.
>
> A: Before fishing was very successful and plentiful. Before there were no
> limits as to how many marlin could be killed and some captains killed
> 2 to 3 marlin per day. Before there was no commercial exploitation.
> Today, we should not only preserve certain species, but we should do
> something about the sportfishing boats that catch fish indiscriminately
> and then sell their catch. Many of these boats doing this belong to well-
> known and important companies. It is not right that some of us try to
> preserve marlin and other species, while others don't help us in the
> slightest, killing one or as many fish as they can, a day. It is really impor-
> tant that fishermen and boat owners help each other to preserve our
> natural resources and our jobs for the future. We should not make the
> same mistakes that have been made in other fishing ports.
>
> Q: Do you have to travel further today to get fish than you did 15 years
> ago?
>
> A: Before we only had to go out 2 or 3 miles. Today, we sometimes have
> to go as far as 35 miles out and sometimes we don't have any luck.

Surveys of fleet captains compiled by Seawatch with the help of David
Holts of the United States National Marine Fisheries Service (NMFS). For full
testimony from Agundez and other captains, go to http://www.seawatch.org
/bibliography/billfish.php#questions.

37 **"hundreds of metric tons per year of illegal dorado and marlin":** "In ocean
waters and estuaries the limit is a total of ten fish per day, with no more than
5 catches of a single specie, except of the species of Marlin, Sailfish and Swordfish and Shark, of which only one specimen of either is allowed, and which
counts as five toward the overall 10 fish limit, or Dorado, Roosterfish, Shad,
or Tarpon, of which only two samples of each specie are allowed, and which
count as five toward the overall 10 fish limit." Furthermore, the regulations
state, "It is prohibited to receive any financial gain from the product obtained
through sportfishing." "Mexican Sport Fishing Regulations," http://www.san
carlosmexico.com/fishregs.html.

37 **"commercial fleets . . . must be killing ten to twenty times as many":** Olaf
Jensen's paper on the effects of longline closure periods and recreational catch-
and-release shows that the best catch data for all commercial fishing (but *not*
including *ribereño* pangas) collected from the Inter-American Tropical Tuna
Commission (IATTC) put the commercial catch at an average of *ten times* the
amount caught in sportfishing from Cabo San Lucas. Jensen confirms that this
ratio is a *minimal* comparison, which means that the actual ratio is likely
higher than ten to one (Olaf Jensen, e-mail message to author, October 6,
2009).

It is critical to note that this comparison is based on longline information
gathered from Japanese fleets fishing off the Pacific coast of Mexico between
1964 and 1975. These were the peak years for longlining off Mexico, but they
were comparatively sparse years for sportfishing, because the tourism and
sportfishing industries were not nearly as developed in southern Baja and the
Sea of Cortez as they are now. Sosa-Nishizaki cites a report by Talbot and
Wares (1975) that found that U.S. citizens sportfishing in northwest Mexico
in 1969 spent $10 million. In Baja and the East Cape, sportfishing was a sig-
nificant industry at this time but a fraction of what it is today. The same report
cites information from SEPESCA (1991) that in 1989 the direct sportfishing
expenditures in all of Mexico produced $69 million, while tuna and shrimp
exports were $65.7 million and $357.8 million, respectively. By 1991, the
direct economic impact of sportfishing had risen to $79 million (Thompson
and Gomez, 1992). The most recent Billfish Foundation report calculates the
direct impact of sportfishing to the Los Cabos region to be over $633 million.

Because so little of the commercial catch is tracked sufficiently in Mexico,
it is difficult to know the exact proportionate impacts on fish populations over
the course of time by commercial and sportfishers in the areas being discussed.
But it is important to consider that a strong catch-and-release ethic now exists
in the Mexican sportfishing community, so despite a huge increase in the

number of fishing trips made in the past three decades, the adoption of circle hooks and the catch-and-release ethic have likely resulted in fewer fish being kept and killed, or dying after release, than when sportfishing first started in Mexico.

And while actual commercial fishing harvests are not tracked, the United Nations Food and Agriculture Organization (FAO) data for longline landings in the Eastern Tropical Pacific, from 1970 to 2001, show significant and steady declines for blue marlin, black marlin, and striped marlin. So despite Mexico's having closed off all of the Sea of Cortez and the first fifty miles from shore, these fish are still declining. The UN FAO data show that blue marlin catches declined from a high of more than nine thousand metric tons in the early 1990s to less than a thousand metric tons in 2001; black marlin catches declined from a high of just over 450 metric tons in the early 1970s to a low, in 2001, of a few dozen metric tons. Striped marlin went from a high of over eleven thousand metric tons in 1970 to around one hundred tons in 2001. These are declines on the order of ten to a hundred times. Sources:

O. P. Jensen et al., "Local Management of a 'Highly Migratory Species,'" *Progress in Oceanography,* 2010. doi:10.1016/j.pocean.2010.04.020.

O. Sosa-Nishizaki, "Historical Review of the Billfish Management in the Mexican Pacific," *Ciencias Marinas* 24, no. 1 (1998): 95–111.

G. B. Talbot and P. G. Wares, "Fishery for Pacific Billfish off Southern California and Mexico, 1903–1969," *Transactions of the American Fisheries Society* 104, no. 1 (1975): 1–12.

C. J. Thompson and S. I. Gomez, *Results of the Mexican Sportfish Economic Survey,* NOAA-TM-NMFS-SWFSC-173, 1992.

Note: For more information on the number of striped marlin landed in Cabo San Lucas by the sportfishing fleet, refer to the first note to p. 37 above.

43 **"they've never released the report to the general public":** In its mission statement, CIBNOR says that it aims "to contribute to the welfare of society through scientific research, technological innovation, and human resource development in sustainable management of natural resources." http://www.cibnor.org/cibnor/ienintro.php.

43 **"bycatch of sea turtles":** Several reports indicate that bycatch rates in the Sea of Cortez result in sea turtle mortality in the tens of thousands. A Seawatch document cites a *National Geographic* article stating that "Mexico's illegal turtle catch exceeds 35,000 per year." The Sea of Cortez is a much smaller area than the northwest Pacific, but even Mexico's Instituto Nacional de la Pesca (INP), in its National Report of Mexico 1999 (cited in the Seawatch document), estimates that ".25 to .50 turtles are caught per 1000 hooks," resulting in between forty-five and ninety turtles daily.

A report by Peckham et al., published in 2008 and looking at loggerhead mortality in the state of Baja California Sur, found that between 1,500 and

2,950 loggerhead turtles died annually due to bycatch in only two observed small-scale longline fleets. This is exclusive of all other sources of mortality (bycatch by other small-scale and industrial fleets, poaching, and natural mortality). The actual mortality of this species alone (not counting any other turtles) is likely to be much higher.

Seawatch, "The Effects of Allowing Longliners into the Sea of Cortez Would Be Catastrophic to Already Severely Depleted Dorado, Shark, Billfish, and Turtle Stocks." http://www.seawatch.org/newsroom/proposed _regulations_effects.pdf.

S. H. Peckham, D. Maldonado-Diaz, V. Koch, A. Mancini, A. Gaos, M. T. Tinker, and W. J. Nichols, "High Mortality of Loggerhead Turtles Due to Bycatch, Human Consumption and Strandings at Baja California Sur, Mexico, 2003 to 2007," *Endangered Species Research,* October 13, 2008. http:// www.int-res.com/articles/esr2008/5/n005p171.pdf.

43 **"60 percent of it goes to the States":** Scientist Russ Nelson of the Billfish Foundation confirmed that 60 percent is a reasonable estimate.

44 **"The current guy in charge of enforcement is Ramón Corral":** In September 2008, Mexican senators Luís Alberto Coppola Joffroy and Humberto Andrade Quezada, along with a number of other senators, sponsored a resolution that was introduced and passed by the Senate Natural Resources and Fisheries Committee (Comisión de Medio Ambiente, Recursos Naturales y Pesca). The resolution called for SAGARPA to revise Shark Norma immediately to do the following: ban the sale of any of the species originally protected by the Ley de Pesca; close spawning and nursery areas to protect shark stocks; initiate a data collection program to scientifically assess shark populations; and define permissible levels of fishing effort and precautionary limits for targeted shark species. Almost immediately, CONAPESCA chief Ramón Corral unilaterally issued a contradictory resolution permitting the retention and sale, by medium and large vessels, of certain percentages of the previously protected species (11 percent sailfish, 4 percent striped and blue marlin, 7 percent swordfish, and 4 percent dorado). Panga fishermen were authorized to land 15 percent sailfish and 10 percent dorado. This action created the first open market for these protected species in twenty-four years. Critics filed suit, claiming that Corral's action exceeded CONAPESCA's authority and directly contradicted the Mexican fisheries protection law. Billfish Foundation president Ellen Peel commented, "We find it amazing Corral—a single individual—can defy the Mexican Congress and the will of the people." "Mexico: Fierce Battle Rages Over Sportfishing Paradise," *Billfish: The Billfish Foundation's Sportfishing Conservation Magazine* 3 (2008): 10–11.

44 **"the fish mafia":** Victor M. González, "El Dorado, Secuestrado por la Mafia," Noticias CaboVision TV, November 22, 2011. http://noticias.cabovision.tv /editoriales/victor-manuel-gonzalez /7294-el-dorado-secuestrado-por-la-mafia .html.

51 **some level of pain can be felt:** An excellent book on the topic of pain in fish is Victoria Braithwaite's *Do Fish Feel Pain?* (New York: Oxford University Press, 2010).

51 **This was Hemingway's view:** In *Green Hills of Africa,* Hemingway's nonfiction account of hunting various game in East Africa, he writes, "I did not mind killing anything, any animal, if I killed it cleanly, they all had to die and my interference with the nightly and seasonal killing that went on all the time was very minute and I had no guilty feeling at all. We ate the meat and kept the hides and horns. But I felt rotten sick over this sable bull." The sable bull he refers to was not killed cleanly but was gut-shot, and he was not able to track it. When he realizes the bull is gut-shot, Hemingway writes, "I was thinking about the bull and wishing to God I had never hit him . . . Tonight he would die and the hyenas would eat him, or worse, they would get him before he died, hamstringing him or pulling his guts out when he was alive." Hemingway recognizes his role in the food chain and acknowledges that an essential part of what makes his hunting permissible when his survival does not depend on it are two things: the fact that the entire animal is used and that his impact overall is, as he says, "minute." But even within these conditions, he feels right about it only as long as the animal's pain and suffering are minimized as much as possible. Ernest Hemingway, *Green Hills of Africa* (New York: Charles Scribner's Sons, 1935), 271.

51 **twenty thousand fish left in the world:** In the case of the western Atlantic population of bluefin tuna, the existing adult breeders are thought to number in the vicinity of only forty thousand individuals.

55 **the Lacey Act:** Originally written in 1900, the Lacey Act began as an attempt to curb illegal commercial hunting that was threatening many game species in the United States. The law prohibited the transport of illegally captured animals across state lines and has been updated with amendments, most recently in 2008. U.S. Code: Title 16, Chapter 53 (Control of Illegally Taken Fish and Wildlife), § 3372 (Prohibited acts). From Cornell University Law School Legal Information Institute, http://www.law.cornell.edu/uscode/16/usc_sup _01_16_10_53.html.

55 **de facto informants of illegal activity:** Seizure of the *Salada I:* Billfish Foundation, "Longliner Busted! Angler Observations Help Bust Illegal Longline Fishing," July 2006. http://www.billfish.org/new/newsarticle.asp?Arti cleID=31.

  Seizure of the *Jesus Omar "El Concho":* Verónica S. González, "Capturan a tiburonero que violó NOM-029," *El Sudcaliforniano,* June 23, 2007. http:// www.oem.com.mx/elsudcaliforniano/notas/n322632.htm.

  Seizure of the *Tele:* Billfish Foundation, "Another Vessel Seized—Nom029 Fails Again," June 26, 2007. http://www.billfish.org/new/newsarticle.asp ?ArticleID=74.

Seizures at Loreto and of boats owned by Henry Collard: Billfish Foundation press release, "Mexican 'Fishing Mafia' Tagged for Three Illegal Catches: Conservation Efforts of the Billfish Foundation in Baja Region Beginning to Pay Off," September 12, 2008. http://www.billfishfoundation.org/new/News Article.asp?ArticleID=117.

57 **pillaging by hookah divers and *pistolero* (speargun) fishermen:** The Loreto Marine Park was established in 1996 and covers over 790 square miles in the Sea of Cortez around Loreto, including the islands of Coronado, Danzante, Carmen, Monserrat, and Santa Catalina. In 2005, the park was listed as a United Nations World Heritage site. Seawatch estimates that since 1997, 90 percent of the reef fish have been removed by hookah divers and *pistoleros*. Hookah divers use an air compressor and long hoses to reach depths of 140 feet, where they can remain for longer periods than if they were using scuba gear. During the day, hookah divers use clear monofilament gill nets, which are all but invisible to sea life, and at night they revert to spearguns and hunt the remaining fish wherever they hide. In 2007, Seawatch sponsored a federal regulation to ban hookah gear; it was passed later that year. Immediately, CONAPESCA in Baja undermined this regulation by issuing new permits that allowed the use of hookah gear for the retrieval of nets caught on the reef and also allowed for the retention of whatever was in the nets. In the two years after that time, Seawatch fought to make the regulation a permanent law. The effort was successful: On August 13, 2009, the CONAPESCA permits allowing hookah use were canceled. To watch the Seawatch video on the impact of hookah divers and *pistoleros,* go to http://www.youtube.com/watch?v=L-eWlzy5Pko.

Seawatch, "Mexico's First Citizen-Funded and Run Vigilance Program Starts." http://seawatch.org/en/Vigilance-Program/333/mexicos-first-citizen -funded-and-run-vigilance-program-starts-in-la-paz-bcs.

Seawatch, "To Some, Laws Just Don't Matter." http://seawatch.org/en/Hot -Issues/329/conapesca-the-wolf-guarding-the-henhouse.

58 **Scientists estimate that in the next ten to twenty years:** The idea that how we treat the ocean in the next decade may resonate for thousands of years to come is attributed to renowned oceanographer Dr. Sylvia Earle (see http:// philadelphiaathome.com/dct/54/id/15739/mid/1249/Renowned-Ocean ographer-Dr-Sylvia-Earle-discusses-Fate-of-Oceans.aspx). This assertion is supported by her book *The World Is Blue: How Our Fate and the Ocean's Are One* (Washington, DC: National Geographic Society, 2009).

The Harpooner's Last Stand: The Northeast Peak of Georges Bank

60 **thick oak hulls of colonial sailing ships:** In George Brown Goode's *Materials for a History of the Swordfishes* (Washington, DC: Government Printing Office, 1883), he presents numerous accounts of swordfish (and likely at least

one marlin) attacking ships. In some cases, the penetration through inch-thick copper sheathing and hardwood planking and timbers was greater than twelve inches. One specific account gives a sense of the power required to do this: "A more curious affair was brought to light in 1725 in overhauling His Majesty's ship 'Leopard,' from the coast of Africa. The sword of this marine spearsman had pierced the sheathing one inch, next it went through a three-inch plank, and beyond that three inches and a half into the firm timber. It was the opinion of the mechanics that it would have required nine strokes of a hammer weighing twenty-five pounds to drive an iron bolt of the same dimensions to the same depth in the hull. Yet the fish drove it at a single thrust" (48).

There is more recent proof of this on the Internet, pertaining to a blue marlin that ran about two feet of its bill through six inches of the hard rubber wall of a massive oil pipeline off the coast of Angola. See http://bikesafe.word press.com/2011/03/13/a-bad-day-for-this-blue-marlin.

64 **A hundred years ago . . . swordfish were abundant:** The first account of commercial Canadian harpoon swordfishery dates only to 1903 (see Fitzgerald, below). New Englanders had been harpooning on the continental shelf off of Nova Scotia (the Scotian Shelf) since about 1880, and earlier along the coast of New England.

65 **harpooned or netted within sight of land:** Goode, *Materials for a History of the Swordfishes,* 27–28.

65 **three hundred pounds or better:** The 1884 *Maine Mining and Industry Journal* cites the area of ocean ten miles off Woods Island, at the mouth of the Saco River, as being "the best swordfishing grounds on the New England coast."

65 **factors conspired to change that:** Gretchen Fitzgerald of the Ecology Action Centre, in Halifax, Nova Scotia, provides a succinct report on the ecology of swordfish off Canada and the history of Canadian swordfishing in her work *The Decline of the Cape Breton Swordfish Fishery: An Exploration of the Past and Recommendations for the Future of the Nova Scotia Fishery,* Marine Issues Committee Special Publication no. 6 (Halifax, NS: Ecology Action Centre, 2000). Drawing from interviews as well as historical, scientific, and fisheries data, Fitzgerald describes the decline of the swordfish fishery off of Canada's Maritime Provinces in clear detail.

65 **In the 1962–63 season, swordfish landings more than tripled:** Fitzgerald, *Decline,* 20.

65 **increases in effort and major improvements in technology and gear:** It is important to note that the overall Atlantic swordfish catch increased until its peak in the early 1980s.

66 **overfishing . . . has transformed the western North Atlantic coastal and continental-shelf ecosystems:** Boris Worm, Marcel Sandow, Andreas Oschlies, Heike K. Lotze, and Ransom Myers, "Global Patterns of Predator Diversity in the Open Oceans," *Science* 309 (2005): 1365–69.

Jeremy B. C. Jackson and E. Sala, "Unnatural Oceans," *Scientia Marina* 65, no. 2 (2001): 273–81.

Jeremy B. C. Jackson et al., "Historical Overfishing and the Recent Collapse of Coastal Ecosystems," *Science* 293 (2001): 629–38.

M. R. Heithaus et al., "Predicting Ecological Consequences of Marine Top Predator Declines," *Trends in Ecology and Evolution* 23, no 4 (2008): 202–10.

66 **"the persistent myth of oceans as wilderness":** Jeremy B. C. Jackson, "What Was Natural in the Coastal Oceans," *Proceedings of the National Academy of Sciences of the United States of America* 98, no. 10 (2001): 5411–18.

67 **"what happened in coast seas only a century ago":** Ibid. For green turtles and wildebeests, see page 5413. For cod, page 5414. For the Pleistocene, page 5416.

67 **By 1970 it was down to 88 pounds:** To support these figures, Fitzgerald cites S. N. Tibbo, L. R. Day, and W. F. Doucet, "The Swordfish (Xiphias Gladius L.), Its Life-History and Economic Importance in the Northwest Atlantic," *Bulletin of the Fisheries Research Board of Canada* 130 (1961); and P. C. F. Hurley and T. D. Iles, "A Review of the Canadian Swordfish Fishery," Canadian Atlantic Fisheries Science Advisory Committee (CAFAC) Research Document 80/81 (1980): 9.

81 **longline catches actually fell 60 percent:** Carl Safina, "Song for the Swordfish: The Last Hunt for Wild Fish," *Audubon,* May–June 1998, 58–69.

81 **Income . . . fell from $35.6 million to $17.6 million:** Ibid.

81 **number of U.S. longline boats began dropping:** Figures confirmed by Ken Hinman of the National Coalition for Marine Conservation (NCMC). There were many more licenses available, but some of these were not active during the periods in question.

81 **two of every three swordfish . . . never reached sexual maturity:** National Coalition for Marine Conservation (NCMC), "Ocean Roulette: Conserving Swordfish, Sharks and Other Threatened Pelagic Fish in Longline Infested Waters," February 1998. Ken Hinman, president of NCMC, wrote to me in an e-mail dated November 3, 2011, that "in the U.S. Atlantic swordfish fishery, in which 98 percent of the fish are taken by longline, two out of three fish caught are juveniles. The statement that two out of three fish caught are juveniles is based on the figures on page 53, Table 7, showing U.S. longline catch and discards 1992–96 (the last year available when the report was done). The source is ICCAT SCRS/9630. October 21, 1996. The '96 figures were deemed preliminary . . . The rate of discards over this period was over 30 percent. One study estimated that 76 percent of juvenile fish were dead upon release." (Jane Dicosimo and Steven A. Berkeley, "Potential Impacts of Minimum Sizes on the Swordfish Longline Fishery," South Atlantic Fishery Management Council, May 1989.)

81 **40 percent of the swordfish caught were discarded:** Ken Hinman, National Coalition for Marine Conservation president, e-mail message to author,

November 3, 2011. Hinman writes: "Here's what we say in *Ocean Roulette* (1998): 'The adult breeding population—swordfish grow to over 1,000 pounds—has decreased by two-thirds over the last ten years and is still shrinking at an alarming rate. The average fish landed in 1995 weighed just 90 pounds (whole weight), an immature fish two years shy of its first chance to reproduce. A minimum size limit intended to protect enough young fish to eventually rebuild the adult population merely results in 30–40% of the swordfish catch being discarded, with most of those fish—an estimated 40,000 in 1996—dead or dying when returned to the water.' . . . The discarded swordfish were almost entirely regulatory discards, i.e., fish under the legal size limit. Since the minimum size was 55 pounds (whole weight), and female swordfish mature at over 100 pounds, it was safe to say that one-third of the catch being immature fish is conservative."

81 **U.S. longliners threw forty thousand swordfish overboard:** Safina, "Song for the Swordfish."

81 **the millions of pounds of other species:** Ibid.

82 **seven rather than the predicted ten years:** The 2009 ICCAT North Atlantic swordfish stock assessment shows that there is a better than 50 percent likelihood that the estimated biomass of swordfish will produce a maximum sustainable yield (MSY). MSY tries to calculate the maximum sustainable amount of fish that can be taken from a stock while leaving the population at the point of its maximum possible growth rate. MSY has been criticized as a fisheries management benchmark because it looks at only one species rather than across multiple species in an ecosystem (for example, it doesn't include assessments of the forage fish and squid that swordfish consume). This broader "ecosystem approach" attempts to take into account many more variables that affect fish population health. In the case of North Atlantic swordfish, the recent 2009 ICCAT stock assessment takes into account only estimations of biomass and not age distribution across the population. In other words, the assessment provides no sense of whether the population is composed of a high percentage of older, large breeding females or whether it is dominated by juvenile fish. This makes an important difference in assessing the overall health of the stock. Hinman notes that the average weight of swordfish caught now is 33 kilograms (72 pounds), which is a small fish.

82 **the possibility of more access:** The real issue driving U.S. commercial fishers' desire to gain access to the closed areas is the fact that they have been unable to catch their ICCAT-allocated quota in swordfish for a number of years. Under ICCAT, uncaught quota is subject to redistribution to other countries, which will certainly fish under fewer restrictions and with more damaging gear than U.S. fishers. The answer should be to find ways to support U.S. commercial fishers in reaching their swordfish quota (assuming the overall quota is sustainable) and encouraging them to use sustainable gear techniques. However, solutions should not include opening the closed zones, which are essential

nurseries for young and juvenile swordfish to grow to breeding maturity. In a commentary issued on February 25, 2010, Billfish Foundation president Ellen Peel rightly identifies recreational fishers (legally fishing in the closed zones) as abusing the privilege of access by catching and illegally selling swordfish from the zone. Finally, she also identifies the need for real legal enforcement of the zones' regulations by the National Marine Fisheries Service (NMFS). See Ellen Peel, "It's Time for a Change in the Closed Zones," Billfish Foundation, http:// billfish.org/786-its-time-for-a-change-in-the-closed-zones.

83 **no meaningful observer coverage:** The figure is about 5 percent observer coverage.

83 **The second destructive practice . . . is what's called high-grading:** I have confirmed both shacking and high-grading in conversations with Canadian longline deckhands who wished to remain anonymous.

87 **Paul Newlin of the Center for Environmental Civics:** E-mail message to author, November 25, 2011.

87 **short-term gain at the expense of long-term stability:** See Paul Molyneaux, *The Doryman's Reflection: A Fisherman's Life* (New York: Thunder's Mouth Press, 2005) for more on the rise of industrial fishing, in this case in the Gulf of Maine. Also see "The *Warrior* in Malta: Greenpeace and the Battle in the Mediterranean," later in this book.

88 **new shipbuilding to continue to increase fleet power:** Ibid.

88 **poor fisheries management costs the world economy $50 billion annually:** In 2008, the World Bank and the United Nations Food and Agricultural Organization reported that the world economy loses $50 billion annually as a result of "poor fisheries management, inefficiencies, and overfishing," for a total of $2 trillion of "avoidable economic losses over the last three decades." The World Business Council for Sustainable Development (WBCSD), "Fisheries Losing $50 Billion a Year: World Bank," from *The Sunken Billions: The Economic Justification for Fisheries Reform* (Washington, DC: The International Bank for Reconstruction and Development / The World Bank, 2009). Accessed at Thomson Financial News Super Focus, October 9, 2008.

88 **The DFO, whose supposed mission:** http://www.dfo-mpo.gc.ca/us-nous /vision-eng.htm.

89 **A July 2009 study:** Boris Worm et al., "Rebuilding Global Fisheries," *Science* 325 (2009): 578–85.

92 **"Nature gave the word *glory* a meaning for me":** C. S. Lewis, *The Four Loves* (New York: Harcourt, Brace, Jovanovich, 1960), 37.

94 **there is only 0.003 percent of the light:** Kerstin Fritsches et al., "Warm Eyes Provide Superior Vision in Swordfishes," *Current Biology* 15, no. 1 (January 2005): 55–58.

94 **depths almost three times as great:** Odile Chancollona, Claire Pusineria, and Vincent Ridouxa, "Food and Feeding Ecology of Northeast Atlantic Swordfish (Xiphias gladius) off the Bay of Biscay," *ICES Journal of*

Marine Science: Journal du Conseil 63, no. 6 (2006): 1075–85. doi:10.1016 /j.icesjms. 2006.03.013. "The species forages near the surface at night (0–90 m) and as deep as 650 m, with a maximum depth recorded at 900 m, by day (Carey and Robison, 1981; Matsumoto et al., 2003; Takahashi et al., 2003)."

94 **propulsion efficiencies that exceed 500 percent:** The paper by Chinese propulsion dynamics researchers in the Department of Mechanical Engineering at the National Chung-Hsing University describes the broadbill swordfish as having a speed of 130 km per hour, or 78 mph. From the abstract: "The swordfish has evolved a light thin/high crescent tail fin for pushing a large amount of water backward with a small velocity difference. Together with a streamlined forward-enlarged thin/high body and forward-biased dorsal fin enclosing sizable muscles as the power source, the swordfish can thus achieve unimaginably high propulsion efficiency and an awesome maximum speed of 130 km/h as the speed champion at sea. This paper presents the innovative concepts of 'kidnapped airfoils' and 'circulating horsepower' using a vivid neat-digit model to illustrate the swordfish's superior swimming strategy. The body and tail work like two nimble deformable airfoils tightly linked to use their lift forces in a mutually beneficial manner. Moreover, they use sensitive rostrum/lateral-line sensors to detect upcoming/ambient water pressure and attain the best attack angle to capture the body lift power aided by the forward-biased dorsal fin to compensate for most of the water resistance power. This strategy can thus enhance the propulsion efficiency greatly to easily exceed an astonishing 500%. Meanwhile, this amazing synergy of force/beauty also solves the perplexity of dolphin's Gray paradox lasting for more than 70 years." Hsing-Juin Lee, Yow-Jeng Jong, Li-Min Chang, and Wen-Lin Wu, "Propulsion Strategy Analysis of High-Speed Swordfish," *Transactions of the Japan Society for Aeronautical and Space Sciences* 52 (2009): 11–20.

95 **lubricating the head to minimize drag:** J. Videler, "Extreme Drag Reducing Adaptations in the Swordfish *Xiphias gladius,*" *Comparative Biochemistry and Physiology—Part A: Molecular & Integrative Physiology* 146, no. 4, supplement 1 (2007): S140.

Book 2: Destruction

Introduction: Annihilation of a Fish

111 **a self-generated equivalent of over fifty horsepower:** C. S. Wardle et al., "The Muscle Twitch and the Maximum Swimming Speed of Giant Bluefin Tuna, Thunnus thynnus L.," *Journal of Fish Biology* 35, no. 1 (1989): 129–37.

111 **the overall balance of relationships throughout the food web:** M. R. Heithaus et al., "Predicting Ecological Consequences of Marine Top Predator Declines," *Trends in Ecology and Evolution* 23, no 4 (2008): 202–10.

B. Worm, E. B. Barbier, N. Beaumont, E. Duffy, C. Folke, B. S. Halpern, J. B C. Jackson, H. K. Lotze, F. Micheli, S. R. Palumbi, E. Sala, K. A. Seloke, J. J. Stachowicz, and R. Watson, "Response to Comments on 'Impacts of Biodiversity Loss on Ocean Ecosystem Services,'" *Science* 316 (2007): 1285. This paper, which presents a meta-analysis of published experimental data, historical time series, global catch trends, and studies of marine reserves and fisheries closures, reveals that biodiversity is closely related to productivity, stability, and the supply of ecosystem services.

111 **Much like wolves in the Rocky Mountains:** D. H. Chadwick, "Wolf Wars," *National Geographic,* March 2008, 34–55.

112 **"ruler of the Valhalla of fishermen":** Ernest Hemingway, "Tuna Fishing in Spain," *Toronto Star Weekly,* February 18, 1922.

112 **The largest ever caught on rod and reel:** International Game Fish Association Records Database. The world-record bluefin was 128.5 inches long, 99 inches around.

112 **true extinction of an oceanic species is difficult:** N. K. Dulvy et al., "Extinction Vulnerability in Marine Populations," *Fish and Fisheries* 4 (2003): 25–64. Also: Carl Safina, president of the Blue Ocean Institute, e-mail exchange with author, March 12, 2010.

112 **Japan consumes roughly 80 percent of the global catch:** Advanced Tuna Ranching Technologies (ATRT) compiled export and import data for the major tuna-consuming countries between 1998 and 2009 and determined that Japan consumes roughly 80 percent of the bluefin tuna harvested globally.

113 **catches two to three times the quota limit:** "The Plunder of Bluefin Tuna in the Mediterranean and East Atlantic in 2004 and 2005: Uncovering the Real Story," World Wildlife Fund for Nature, study conducted by Advanced Tuna Ranching Technologies (ATRT), May 2006.

On page 78 of the Report of the Standing Committee on Research and Statistics (SCRS) (Madrid, Spain, October 3–7, 2011), ICCAT's own science cites that between the mid-1990s and 2007, the likely legal and illegal harvests of bluefin tuna in the Mediterranean were on the order of 50,000 to 60,000 metric tons. (SCRS is the scientific committee of ICCAT.)

113 **$400 million annually—one-third the value of the entire catch:** The $400 million figure is supported by the International Consortium of Investigative Journalists (ICIJ) report "Looting the Seas: How Overfishing, Fraud, and Negligence Plundered the Majestic Bluefin Tuna," in the section by Marcos Garcia Rey titled "Diving into the Tuna Ranching Industry: Sea 'Farms' Become Centers for Bluefin Black Market," page 2. It says, "At its peak, from 1998 to 2007, the illegal trade comprised more than one out of every three bluefin caught, at a market value of about $400 million annually, ICIJ found."

114 **reduced the population of breeding adults to less than one-fifth:** "Where Have All the Tuna Gone? How Tuna Ranching and Pirate Fishing Are Wiping Out Bluefin Tuna in the Mediterranean Sea," Greenpeace International, 2006.

114 **estimated to have declined by more than 85 percent:** The Panel 2 Annex of
the 2009 ICCAT SCRS document "Extension of the 2009 SCRS Meeting to
Consider the Status of Atlantic Bluefin Tuna Populations with Respect to
CITES Biological Listing Criteria" (Doc. No. PA2-604) shows a slide titled
"Chances of Meeting or Exceeding the Appropriate Decline Criterion." In this
slide, SCRS does a probability projection showing that its estimate of spawning stock biomass decline for both western Atlantic and eastern Atlantic bluefin tuna is 85 percent or greater, as compared with its best estimates of
"maximum observed" spawning stock biomass (SSB). The SSB figure referred
to is "estimated . . . on the time-series of available information, which does not
reflect the total history of exploitation." In other words, SCRS's projections of
spawning stock biomass decline are in comparison with a picture of population
based on available fisheries data, *not compared with maximum spawning stock
projections going back in history.* Nevertheless, the SCRS projections indicate
that the 2009 western Atlantic bluefin spawning population has a 90 percent
probability of representing 15 percent or less of the maximum observed spawning stock biomass. The 2009 eastern Atlantic bluefin spawning population is
calculated as having a 96 percent probability of being 15 percent or less of the
maximum observed stock biomass. In a preceding slide, "What is the 'baseline'?," SCRS acknowledges that the "'Maximum observed' biomass is likely
an underestimate of the real maximum [i.e., historical maximum], [because it]
can suffer from 'shifting baseline' syndrome." In other words, as of 2009, both
stocks had lost 85 percent or more of their spawners compared with estimates
of the maximum observed spawning stock, which itself is an underestimate of
the real and likely historical maximum.

114 **The western stock . . . is in similar peril:** Extensive research has been done in
the past twenty years to understand the relationship between eastern Atlantic
and western Atlantic populations of bluefin tuna in terms of spawning areas,
locations, and times of year when the populations mix, and the effects of overfishing on both populations. Ingenious techniques have been used, including
satellite pop-up tags, DNA analysis, and measurement of stable isotopes in
otoliths (fish ear bones), which indicate the nursery location of the fish. It is
known that the populations do not interbreed. Findings as recent as 2010
(Barbara Block, page 15 of the Status Review Report of Atlantic Bluefin Tuna,
May 20, 2011) indicate that there may be distinct sub-populations constituting
eastern and western Atlantic stocks, breeding in different areas of each home
spawning region. The western stock takes longer to mature and gives rise to the
true giants of this species—fish attaining weights in excess of a thousand
pounds. The western stock is also felt to be on the order of one-tenth the size
of the eastern Atlantic stock. In terms of extinction risk, the Report of the
2008 Atlantic Bluefin Stock Assessment Session (Madrid, Spain, June 23–July
4, 2008), page 101, fig. 33, in the graph titled "Spawning Stock Abundance

(Ages 8+)," indicates a spawning adult population of about only forty thousand fish for the entire western Atlantic.

115 **fewer than half a dozen fish per day for the entire forty-ship fleet:** Martin Fackler, "Tuna Town in Japan Sees Falloff of Its Fish," *New York Times,* September 19, 2009.

Whirlwind: Tokyo and Oma, Japan; Port Lincoln, South Australia

116 **Four and a half million pounds:** Kathryn Graddy, "The Fulton Fish Market," *Journal of Economic Perspectives* 20, no. 2 (2006): 207–20.

122 **a 593-pound specimen that sold for $736,000:** Malcolm Foster, "Bluefin Tuna Auctioned in Tokyo for Record $736,000," *Christian Science Monitor,* January 5, 2012. http://www.csmonitor.com/Business/Latest-News-Wires /2012/0105/Bluefin-tuna-auctioned-in-Tokyo-for-record-736-000.

125 **the human eye is incapable of perceiving it:** Wardle et al., "The Muscle Twitch."

138 **despite warnings about unrestricted access:** Evelyn Wallace-Carter, *For They Were Fishers: The History of the Fishing Industry in South Australia* (Adelaide, SA: Amphitrite Publishing House, 1987), 291. "Another to express concern was Billy Haldane. He said: 'By 1963 the catch and effort statistics were showing that despite the increase in numbers of boats entering the fishery, there wasn't a corresponding increase in the total catch. It was obvious that the warning signs were flashing as to the future of the fishery.'"

   Also, on page 295: "The industry had now reached the bonanza years. In 1964, 1965 and 1966 record catches were made, reaching a peak in 1966, when the catch was 5,900 tons (almost 6,000 tons). The number of vessels had also increased to thirty-four."

138 **by the eighties the fishery had been pushed to its limits:** Ibid., 302: "A CSIRO survey in 1981 had shown that stocks of bluefin tuna were at a dangerously low level and international management of the fishery was necessary." CSIRO stands for the Commonwealth Scientific and Industrial Research Organisation, Australia's national science agency.

138 **nineteen thousand metric tons per year for the Australians alone:** Commission for the Conservation of Southern Bluefin Tuna (CCSBT) data set, "Catch by Ocean, Year, and Flag (Inclusive)." This shows a total of 19,198 metric tons harvested by the Australians in the Indian Ocean (which includes the South Australia Bight) in 1982. http://www.ccsbt.org/site/sbt_ data.php.

139 *fifty times* **more valuable than one destined for the cannery:** Wallace-Carter, *For They Were Fishers,* 50: "If carefully caught and kept below minus 60° centigrade, one tuna can bring . . . [more than] fifty times the price that is paid per kilogram for tuna that is to be canned."

139 **vessels cost hundreds of thousands to more than a million dollars:** Ibid., 302: "The Australian tuna fleet began expanding rapidly. In South Australia, eight vessels, worth more than eight million dollars, were being constructed to join the fleet in 1982. It was expected that they would add 5000 tonnes to the catch."

141 **between *110 and 165 million pounds* of pilchards:** These figures (5,000 metric tons of southern bluefin tuna ranched per year, 100 million pounds of pilchards, and the conversion ratio of 10–15:1) were confirmed by Peter Trott, Fisheries Program, World Wildlife Fund, Australia, in an e-mail to me on August 16, 2010. The baitfish poundage was from the 2001–2 season.

142 **a herpes virus in pilchards:** Daniel J. Gaughan, "Disease-Translocation Across Geographic Boundaries Must Be Recognized as a Risk Even in the Absence of Disease Identification: The Case with Australian *Sardinops*," *Reviews in Fish Biology and Fisheries* 11 (2002): 113–23. "[Pilchard herpes virus] was again present in dying *Sardinops* in 1998/99: there is no doubt that this virus was the pathogen responsible for both epizootics."

142 **endangered the entire ecosystem of the Spencer Gulf:** T. M. Ward, F. E. Hoedt, L. J. McLeay, W. F. Dimmlich, M. W. Kinloch, G. Jackson, R. McGarvey, P. J. Rogers, and K. Jones, "Effects of the 1995 and 1998 Mass Mortalities on the Spawning Biomass of Sardinops sagax in South Australia," *ICES Journal of Marine Sciences* 58, no. 4 (2001): 865–75. The abstract for this paper reads as follows: "This paper estimates and compares the effects of the mass mortalities of *Sardinops sagax* that occurred in South Australian waters in 1995 and 1998. After the 1995 event, the spawning biomass of *S. sagax* in South Australian waters fell by over 75% from approximately 165 000 tonnes to approximately 37 000 tonnes. No juvenile mortality was observed during 1995 and the population recovered quickly, with spawning biomass reaching 147 000 (70 000 to 234 000, 95%CI) tonnes in 1998. After the mass mortality event in October–November, spawning biomass fell by over 70% to 36 000 (19 000 to 67 000, 95%CI) tonnes; significant numbers of juveniles were also killed. The mortality of juveniles in 1998 and the recent increase in the abundance of *Engraulis australis* suggest that the population may recover more slowly from the 1998 mortality event than it did after 1995. The initiation of the two largest mono-specific mass mortalities of fish ever recorded in South Australian waters within a period of less than four years suggests that the timing and location of the events was non-random. Both events occurred since 1993–1994, when large-scale tuna farming began in South Australia, and less than 250 km from Port Lincoln, where large quantities of untreated imported frozen *S. sagax* are fed to caged tuna. The introduction of untreated imported frozen fish products into the marine environment may be one of the mechanisms that has facilitated the range shifts of pathogens that have been associated with the increased frequency of mass mortalities due to disease in the ocean."

142 **"two largest single-species mass mortalities of fish ever recorded":** Ibid., 874.

142 **their starting point off the Eyre Peninsula:** R. J. Whittington et al., "Herpesvirus That Caused Epizootic Mortality in 1995 and 1998 in Pilchard, Sardinops Sagax Neopilchardus (Steindachner), in Australia Is Now Endemic," *Journal of Fish Diseases* 31 (2008): 97–105. "Mathematical modelling suggested that in both 1995 and 1998–99 the virus originated from a point source, travelled without the need for vectors [meaning other sources like seabirds] in a host-density independent manner, and had an incubation time of several days, all of which fitted the observed pattern of disease spread and the pathogenesis of the lesions in gills (Whittington et al. 1997; Murray, O'Callaghan & Jones 2000, 2001a,b, 2003)."

142 **significant economic ramifications:** R. J. Whittington, J. B. Jones, and A. D. Hyatt, "Pilchard Herpesvirus in Australia 1995-1999," in P. Walker, R. Lester, and M.G. Bondad-Reantaso, eds., *Diseases in Asian Aquaculture V* (Manila: Asian Fisheries Society, 2005), 137–40. The amounts in Australian dollars were roughly $12 million in 1995 and $15 million in 1998, which, owing to changing exchange rates, both equaled about $9 million U.S. at those times.

142 **closed the pilchard fishery:** D. J. Gaughan, R. W. Mitchell, and S. J. Blight, "Impact of Mortality, Possibly Due to Herpesvirus, on Pilchard Sardinops Sagax Stocks Along the South Coast of Western Australia in 1998–99," *Marine & Freshwater Research* 51 (2000): 601–12.

142 **the same energy-transfer function**: Ibid.

142 **anticipated similar impacts:** Ibid.

142 **direct connection . . . has never been definitively established:** Daniel J. Gaughan, "Disease-Translocation Across Geographic Boundaries Must Be Recognized as a Risk Even in the Absence of Disease Identification: The Case with Australian *Sardinops,*" *Reviews in Fish Biology and Fisheries* 11 (2002): 113–23. "Following the studies arising from the 1995 and 1998/99 mortalities, doubts were raised as to whether PHV had been shown conclusively to be the fatal agent. This is not particularly surprising: fulfilling cause-and-effect requirements developed for veterinary and human medicine (Koch's postulates) can be impossible for aquatic species (Bakke and Harris, 1998) . . . Although it was clear that scientists thought there was a link between the 1995 epizootics and imported *Sardinops* (Harvell et al., 1999), the lack of a formally identified causative agent stalled, and eventually stopped, any effectual risk-management action."

143 **the most difficult one to reject:** Ibid. "The probability of such a mass mortality event starting randomly within any particular 250 km unit of coastline within this species' 7,700 km range in Australia is 0.032 (i.e., 250/7,700). Although not inherently significant, *this probability is low* and indicates that such events should be rare for any one region. The probability of a second mass

mortality starting randomly within the same 250 km stretch of coast is about 0.001 (i.e., 0.0322). This very low probability indicates that the focal origin, in central South Australia, of the two mass mortality events was not random, as has already been suggested by Jones (2000). The non-random origin suggests against the ballast water, sea bird and mutation hypotheses. Although Hyatt et al. (1997) invoked the need for a vector to explain the pattern of spread of the *Sardinops* mortality in 1995, subsequent modeling of the wave-like progression of the disease from a focal origin indicates that no vectors were involved in its spread around southern Australia (Murray et al., 2000). This finding also provides evidence against sea birds having brought the disease into Australia.

"Although the origin of the implicated PHV has not been formally determined, it appears more than coincidental that both outbreaks began in the same region (Figure 1) where mature *Sardinops* [pilchards] are abundant and where thousands of tonnes of imported, untreated (frozen whole) *Sardinops* are placed annually into the marine environment to feed caged southern bluefin tuna (*Thunnus maccoyii*), a practice which began in the early 1990s (Whittington et al., 1997; Jones, 2000; Gaughan et al., 2000; Ward et al., 2001). In 1995, the quantity of *Sardinops* imported was around 10,000–16,000 tonnes; this has gradually increased and more recently the amount imported for tuna feed was 40,000–50,000 tonnes, and possibly up to 70,000 tonnes."

143 **"almost a religious faith in technology":** Paul Molyneaux, *Swimming in Circles: Aquaculture and the End of Wild Oceans* (New York: Basic Books, 2007), 156.

145 **"a million metric tons of farmed salmon":** The average annual production of Norwegian salmon is in fact about 570,000 tons. http://norwegiansalmon.com.

147 **Every square mile of estuary lost:** Data from the U.S. Army Corps of Engineers on past hurricanes suggest that the loss of a one-mile strip of wetlands along the coast in the Barataria-Terrebonne Estuary System of the Mississippi Delta results in "an estimated $5,752,816 average annual increase in property damage. The estimated value of this protection per wetland acre is between $6,879 and $8,020 annually. Rex H. Caffey et al., "Portrait of an Estuary: Functions and Values of the Barataria-Terrebonne Estuary System," Louisiana State University Agricultural Center, Pub. 2802, 2000.

148 **population in 2006 would have been five times as large:** Gillian Bradford, "Bluefin Tuna Plundering Catches Up with Japan," Australian Broadcasting Corporation, October 16, 2006. http://www.abc.net.au/news/2006-10-16 /bluefin-tuna-plundering-catches-up-with-japan/1286956.

149 **"3 to 7 percent of the historical maximum":** Commission for the Conservation of Southern Bluefin Tuna (CCSBT) 2011 stock assessment. http://www .ccsbt.org/site/recent_assessment.php.

149 **"minimum safe level until at least 2020":** From Attachment 11 of the Report of the Sixteenth Meeting of the Scientific Committee for CCSBT (the

Commission for the Conservation of Southern Bluefin Tuna). Page 4: "The median constant catch projection under the current TAC [total allowable catch] (of 9449 t) for the base case show the interim rebuilding target of 0.2 SSB_0 being reached in 2024, and for the zero TAC case it is reached in 2020." (See ESC report figure 7, page 32). The stocks are projected to reach 20 percent SSB at a given year based on probabilities, so that, for example, there is a 70 percent probability that 20 percent SSB will be reached by 2030. http://www.ccsbt.org /site/recent_assessment.php.

156 **fifteen to twenty million eggs:** T. L. O. Davis, V. Lyne, and G. P. Jenkins, "Advection, Dispersion and Mortality of a Patch of Southern Bluefin Tuna Larvae *Thunnus maccoyii* in the East Indian Ocean," Marine Ecology Progress Series 73 (1991): 33–45. See page 43: "Kikawa (1964) estimated fecundity to be 15×10^6 eggs in a 158 cm (80 kg) fish." http://www.int-res.com/articles /meps/73/m073 p033.pdf.

S. Kikawa (1964), "Estimated Number of Eggs Spawned out of the Ovaries of an Indomaguro (*Thunnus maccoyii*)," Report of the Nankai Regional Fisheries Research Laboratory 20: 27–35.

156 **low-to-moderate-reproductivity species:** Notes offered in "A Guide to the ICCAT Scientific Committee's Advice on the Listing of Atlantic Bluefin Tuna Under CITES Appendix I," by Greenpeace, the Pew Environment Group, and WWF (October 2009), cites work by Silfvergrip, Cooke, Fromentin, et al., to support the assertion that Atlantic bluefin tuna are a low-to-moderate-reproductivity species (see below). Southern bluefin tuna: The IUCN Red List entry for southern bluefin tuna makes clear that very little is known about spawning behavior or reproductive success: "It is not known whether all mature fish spawn each year, every few years, or even only once in their lifetime." http://www.iucnredlist.org/apps/redlist/details/21858/0.

A. Silfvergrip, "Supplementary Information to the Draft Proposal to CoP15 to Include Bluefin Tuna Thunnus thynnus on Appendix I of CITES as Proposed by Monaco," September 18, 2009.

SCRS/2009/197. A note on the evaluation of Atlantic bluefin tuna (Thunnus thynnus) with respect to the biological criteria for CITES Appendix I.

SCRS/2009/193. Estimating the productivity of Atlantic bluefin tuna from validated scientific data.

157 **between 45,000 and 49,000 metric tons:** Peter Trott of the Fisheries Program, World Wildlife Fund, Australia, e-mail message to author, August 8, 2010: "Regarding 'how many adult SBT remain' in the wild . . . this is a very difficult question to answer due to many variances. Basically we do know that SBT reach maturity around 8-12 years of age and live up to around 40 years and that there is currently around 45,000 tonnes of spawning stock (i.e., adult SBT) in the water [this figure is amended to 45,400 tonnes as of the latest assessment]. But to convert this to actual numbers is quite difficult since the weight per adult fish can range from as little as approximately 50 kg up to 200+ kg, so the upper range

indicates that there could be as many as 1 million adult SBT in the world's oceans (sounds like a lot but this is extremely small considering that both juvenile and adult fish are taken by the fishery) or at the lower end there could be less than 500,000 adults remaining. Currently the fishery will be allowed to take over 11,000 tonnes of SBT. [This has since been lowered to 9449 tonnes as of July 2011.] Furthermore, I was checking up on the modeled projections for recovery of SBT under certain catches. Remembering that the management target for SBT is to rebuild the stock to 20 percent Spawning Stock Biomass—the only way to potentially and realistically reach this target, as identified by these independent scientific models, is to stop fishing altogether, and even if fishing mortality was to stop altogether it would still take until after the year 2025 to reach the 20 percent target. [This estimate has been changed to the year 2020, with the caveat by the Scientific Committee that "constant catch projections make no allowance for future conditions such as poor recruitments, and hence the ESC strongly recommended the adoption of an adaptive MP (management plan) to properly deal with such circumstances."] It is important to note that *none* of the scientific models that included some level of commercial take reached the desired 20 percent target [with 70 percent probability] before 2035." The reason for this at the time of Trott's e-mail to me was that the TAC (total allowable catch) was high enough that the 20 percent spawning stock biomass would not be reached before 2035 under any scenario that allowed a commercial take. It is also important to recognize that, because of Japan's twenty-year period of overfishing, the level of robustness of these calculations is reduced.

In an e-mail from November 8, 2011, Peter Trott added that since the 2010 e-mails there have been changes in the "expected and modeled rebuilding timeframes under the current TAC (9449 t) [such that] the interim rebuilding target of Spawning Stock Biomass now has a 70% probability of being reached by 2030, and for the zero TAC case it is reached by 2020." He notes these figures do not account for changes in recruitment to the breeding stock from the juveniles that may be hindered by unforeseen factors like climate change, illegal fishing, or a poor recruitment year. Furthermore, there remain unreported discards in the fishery, the total 2010 catch excludes any unreported catch (the actual catch was therefore higher), and the Australian government has listed southern bluefin tuna as a conservation-dependent species.

158 **one in several million:** T. L. O. Davis et al., "Advection, Dispersion and Mortality." http://www.int-res.com/articles/meps/73/m073p033.pdf.

The *Warrior* in Malta: Greenpeace and the Battle in the Mediterranean

162 **a resource that supported the local cultures:** Jean Desse and Nathalie Desset-Berset, "Stratégies de pêche au 8e millénaire: Les poissons de Cap Andreas Kastros (Chypre)," in A. Le Brun, *Fouilles Récentes à Khirokitia 3* (Paris: Éditions Recherche sur les Civilisations, 1994): 335–60.

162 **the eastern stock . . . continuing to be heavily exploited:** Report of the 2008 Atlantic Bluefin Tuna Stock Assessment Session (Madrid: ICCAT, 2008), 72–73.

162 **21,000 metric tons:** "Where Have All the Tuna Gone? How Tuna Ranching and Pirate Fishing Are Wiping Out Bluefin Tuna in the Mediterranean Sea," Greenpeace International, 2006, page 13.

162 **between 45,000 and 50,000 metric tons per year:** Ibid.

162 **population of spawning adults was down by more than 80 percent:** Assumpta Gual, "The Bluefin Tuna in the Eastern Atlantic and Mediterranean: Chronicle of a Death Foretold," Greenpeace International, 1999; and ICCAT 2008 Bluefin Tuna Stock Assessment, fig. 34, page 102.

163 **fishing at the rate of 50,000 to 60,000 metric tons per year:** In the Report of the Standing Committee on Research and Statistics (SCRS) (Madrid, Spain, October 3–7, 2011), ICCAT's own scientists state (page 78) that between the mid-1990s and 2007, the likely legal and illegal harvests of bluefin tuna in the Mediterranean were on the order of 50,000 to 60,000 metric tons. (SCRS is the scientific committee of ICCAT.)

163 **throwing off ICCAT stock assessments:** Advanced Tuna Ranching Technologies, "Requiem for a Bluefin Tuna: An International Trade Analysis 1998/2008 (Uncovering the Relentless Overfishing of a Collapsed Fish Stock)," 2009, slide 10.

163 **ranching capacity of more than 60,000 metric tons of tuna per year:** Ibid., slide 4.

166 **"capacity of nine thousand metric tons":** "The Plunder of Bluefin Tuna in the Mediterranean and East Atlantic in 2004 and 2005: Uncovering the Real Story," World Wildlife Fund for Nature study, conducted by Advanced Tuna Ranching Technologies (ATRT), S.L., May 2006, page 10.

166 **"closer to eleven thousand metric tons":** Conti's estimation of the Maltese ranching facility's capacity is verified by the report "Looting the Seas: How Overfishing, Fraud, and Negligence Plundered the Majestic Bluefin Tuna," ICIJ, 2010. See part 2 under the section "The Maltese Bluefin."

166 **entire western Atlantic quota for bluefin is roughly 1,900 metric tons:** Report of the Standing Committee on Research and Statistics (SCRS) (Madrid, Spain, October 3–7, 2011), 85.

166 **the ICCAT science committee's recommended quota:** Ibid., 2.

176 **while blaming others for doing so:** ATRT, "Requiem for a Bluefin," slide 13.

176 **no more than 12,000 metric tons to avoid collapse of the stock:** Coalition Pour Des Accords de Pêche Equitables (CAPE) 2010 Annex: Regional Examples, page 6, section B. "ICCAT: The Mediterranean Tuna Fishery: Overcapacity, Poor Data and Subsidies Driving Overfishing," B.1. Overview. http://www.cape-cffa.org/IMG/pdf/Final_Annexes_Overcapacity.pdf.

179 **warships of Alexander the Great:** This anecdote is attributed to the Roman naturalist Pliny the Elder in his work *Naturalis Historiae*.

194 **overseeing the sustainable management of EU fisheries:** Ivan Camilleri, "Commissioner Borg Rebuts Bias Claims in Bluefin Tuna Debate," *Times of Malta,* September 8, 2009. Borg claimed that the decision was scientifically justified.

194 **88 percent of EU fisheries were considered to be overfished:** "Bluefin Tuna Is a Litmus Test of the EU's Ability to Reform the Much-Maligned Common Fisheries Policy. And It Cannot Afford to Fail," EuropeanVoice.com, September 24, 2009. http://www.europeanvoice.com/article/imported/an-approach -that-must-be-cast-aside/65944.aspx.

194 **annual revenues of approximately $346 million:** Intrafish news release, June 22, 2009. http://www.intrafish.no/global /news/article249878.ece.

195 **enforcement . . . is unlikely to happen at all:** John Hocevar, Greenpeace, e-mail message to author, June 28, 2009.

195 **a risk we are prepared to take:** John Hocevar, "Massimo Cappitta Is a Thug," Greenpeace Campaign Blog, June 24, 2009. http://members.greenpeace.org /blog/greenpeaceusa_blog/2009/06/24/massimo_cappitta_is_a_thug_1.

197 **builds momentum for the effort:** John Hocevar, Greenpeace, e-mail message to author, July 6, 2009.

198 **"our children and the generations to come":** World Wildlife Fund press release, "Future of Bluefin Tuna Hangs in the Balance," August 28, 2009. http://www.wwf.org.uk/news_feed.cfm?uNewsID=3269.

199 **"link between international trade and overexploitation of the species":** Stanley Pignal, "EU Considers Bluefin Tuna Protection," London *Financial Times,* August 21, 2009.

199 **Maltese bluefin industry . . . is worth $131 million a year:** Martin Hickman, "Political Infighting Threatens Survival of the Bluefin Tuna," *Independent,* September 5, 2009.

199 **the UK's *Guardian* published an article:** David Adam, "Measures to Protect Mediterranean Tuna Are Failing, Report Warns," *Guardian,* September 17, 2009. http://www.guardian.co.uk/environment/2009/sep/17/bluefin -tuna-fishing.

200 **cover-up of 210 metric tons of bluefin:** "Algerian Officials, Ship Owners Charged with Illegal Fishing," Lebanon *Daily Star,* October 17, 2009.

200 **estimated population at roughly five million fish:** Doreen Leggett, "Rare Tuna? Fishermen Protest Proposed CITES Listing for Bluefin Tuna," *Cape Codder,* December 16, 2009. http://www.wickedlocal.com/yarmouth/news /business/x2010182909/Rare-tuna-Fishermen-protest-proposed-CITES -listing-for-bluefin-tuna.

201 **a huge incentive for poaching:** International Centre for Trade and Sustainable Development (ICTSD), "Bluefin Tuna Poachers Find Opportunity in Libyan Crisis: Reports," *Bridges Trade and Biological News Resources Digest* 11, no. 20 (November 14, 2011). http://ictsd.org/i/news/biores/118292/#respond.

ICTSD Reporting, "Tuna Fished 'Illegally' During Libya Conflict," BBC News, November 7, 2011.

201 **output from the tuna industry is 70 to 80 percent higher:** ICTSD, "Bluefin Tuna Poachers Find Opportunity in Libyan Crisis."

201 **as opposed to the industry's figures of 100 percent or more increase:** "WWF Reveals Huge Overcapacity Still in Place in Mediterranean Bluefin Tuna Fishery," WWF News, November 10, 2011.

201 **exceeded the official quota by 141 percent:** Pew Environment Group, *Mind the Gap: An Analysis of the Mediterranean Bluefin Tuna Trade.* http://www .pewenvironment.org/news-room/video-library/mind-the-gap-85899365419.

202 **annual cost of $400 million per year:** This estimate is supported by Advanced Tuna Ranching Technologies (ATRT) analyses and my interview with ATRT's Roberto Mielgo Bregazzi, March 3, 2010. The $400 million figure is also supported by the ICIJ report "Looting the Seas," in the section titled "Diving into the Tuna Ranching Industry: Sea 'Farms' Become Centers for Bluefin Black Market," page 2: "At its peak, from 1998 to 2007, the illegal trade comprised more than one out of every three bluefin caught, at a market value of about $400 million annually, ICIJ found."

202 **some $16.4 billion between 1998 and 2008:** ATRT, "Requiem for a Bluefin." The U.S. dollar figures are calculated from figures initially presented in euros and converted according to a euro-to-dollar conversion rate of 1:1.3, based on currency conversion rates in March 2010.

202 **global trade in shark fins . . . :** Ibid. Sources cited:
Shark fins: S. Clarke et al., "Social, Economic, and Regulatory Drivers of the Shark Fin Trade," *Marine Resource Economics* 22, no. 3 (2007): 305–27.
Whale meat: World Wildlife Fund TRAFFIC.
Elephant ivory: Aminta Raffalovich, "'White Gold': The Ivory Trade Ban" for EEP 131. http://are.berkeley.edu/ . . . /The%20Ivory%20Trade% 20BanAmintaR.pdf.

202 **"an international tuna cartel":** ATRT, "Requiem for a Bluefin," slide 13.

202 **"international black market in East Atlantic bluefin tuna":** "Looting the Seas," ICIJ, 2010. http://www.publicintegrity.org/treesaver/tuna/index.html.

202 **allegations of Mafia involvement in the trade:** "International €4 Million Bluefin Tuna Trafficking Ring Busted," *AGI/La Nuova Sardegna,* Italy, July 26, 2011.

202 **Sicilian funeral flowers:** "Sleeping with the Fishes: High Time to Save the Mediterranean Bluefin," *Economist,* October 20, 2008. http://www.econo mist.com/node/12448356.

Book 3: The Primal Wild

Granders in the Coral Sea: Lizard Island, Great Barrier Reef, Australia

208 **fewer than 150 are likely to tip the scales at over half a ton:** This figure is an estimate based on discussions with various scientists and anglers located in the "grander hotspots" around the world, including Cairns, Australia, the

Canary Islands, and Hawaii. Dr. Julian Pepperell, of Pepperell Research & Consulting, in Queensland, Australia, supported these ballpark figures in e-mails on November 30, 2011. The number of granders caught and released every year between Cairns and Lizard Island is, according to Pepperell, "certainly less than 50. (This is based on the numbers of fish of that size captured, and tagged and released, between 1966 and 2006, averaging about 20 per year)." Pepperell calculates that off Hawaii, in the rest of the Pacific, and in the Atlantic, there are likely fewer than thirty thousand-pound-or-greater fish caught per year on rod and reel. The figure of 150 granders is a rounded-up number intended to account for untagged or unreported fish and other unusual varieties of fish uncommonly reaching the weight of half a ton, but it is arbitrary in that there is no definitive way to ascertain this. The figure of 150 is meant to indicate that this is likely an upper range (versus, say, five hundred granders or five thousand granders). The figure of 150 does not account for granders of any kind (swordfish, bluefin tuna, marlin, etc.) caught by commercial vessels, nor does it include rod-and-reel catches of swordfish (there are no known reports over a thousand pounds in recent years), nor of great whites, tiger sharks, or makos.

216 **"the sportive brutality of the sea":** From the closing lines of *A Canticle for Leibowitz,* by Walter M. Miller Jr. (Philadephia: J. B. Lippincott, 1959). The book is a post-apocalyptic vision of the world in which human technology leads to the cyclical destruction and rebirth of civilization.

The Last Voyage of *Primetime*: Two Hundred Miles off the Coast of New Zealand

236 **"more ancient than the mountains":** H. P. Lovecraft, "The White Ship," *The United Amateur* 19, no. 2 (1919): 30–33.

269 **final leg of the voyage:** At the time I made the trip with John Gregory, he had every intention of selling the boat and closing down his charter operation. For a number of positive reasons, he eventually reversed this decision, and he continues the operation, albeit on a small scale, as of the publication of this book.

Epilogue

272 **"the beast that eats its future":** Tim Flannery is the author of *The Future Eaters: An Ecological History of the Australasian Lands and People* (Sydney: Reed Books, 1994).

273 **"the myth of oceans as wilderness":** Jeremy B. C. Jackson, "What Was Natural in the Coastal Oceans," *Proceedings of the National Academy of Sciences of the United States of America* 98, no. 10 (2001): 5411–18.

INDEX

Grateful acknowledgment is made for permission to reprint the following copyrighted works:

Quote by Roberto Mielgo Bregazzi from *Requiem for a Bluefin: An International Trade Analysis (1998–2009)* by Advanced Tuna Ranching Technologies, S.L. By permission of Roberto Mielgo Bregazzi.

Excerpt from "All the Hemispheres" from *The Subject Tonight Is Love: 60 Wild and Sweet Poems of Hafiz* by Daniel Ladinsky (Penguin Books). Copyright © Daniel Ladinsky, 1996, 2003. Used by permission of Daniel Ladinsky.

Excerpt from "Death All Day" from *The Inland Ground* by Richard Rhodes. Reprinted with permission of the University Press of Kansas.

Excerpt from "The Earth Falls Down" from *The Awful Rowing Toward God* by Anne Sexton. Copyright © 1975 by Loring Conant, Jr., Executor of the Estate; renewed 2003 by Linda G. Sexton. Reprinted by permission of Houghton Mifflin Harcourt Publishing Company and SLL / Sterling Lord Literistic, Inc.

Excerpt from "Tracks in the Wilderness" from *The Klamath Knot: Explorations of Myth and Evolution* by David Rains Wallace. Copyright © 1983 by David Rains Wallace. Reprinted by permission of University of California Press.

Excerpts from correspondence and blogs by the following individuals: John Hocevar, Olaf Jensen, Bill Leavenworth, Michel Marchandise, Paul Newlin, Julian Pepperell, Carl Safina, and Peter Trott. Used by permission.

Image credits

Insert page 1 (top and bottom): Courtesy of Matt Rigney; 2: Pisces Sportfishing & Yachting; 3: Photo copyright © Brandon Cole; 4: Al Barnes (www.albarnes.com); 5 (top and bottom), 6 (inset), 8 (bottom), 9 (top), 11 (inset), 13: Photos by Matt Rigney; 6–7: Paul Murray; 8 (top): Courtesy of Michael T. Adams; 9 (bottom): Cleanseas Tuna Ltd.; 10–11, 12: Photo copyright © Giulio di Sturco; 14: Copyright © Michael Domeier; 15: Copyright © Mike Harris; 16: Photo courtesy of Colin Hooper